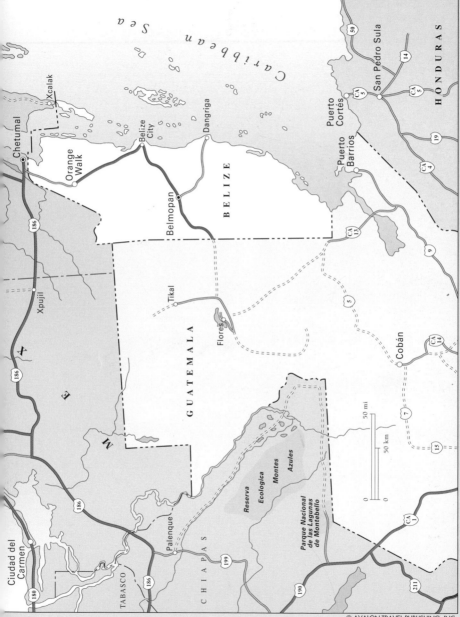

© AVALON TRAVEL PUBLISHING, INC.

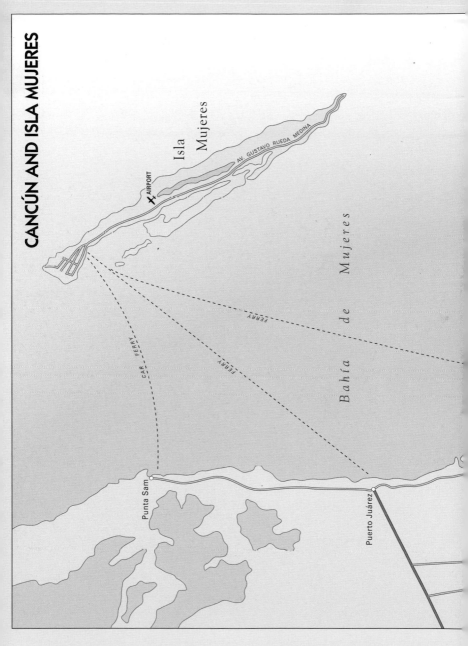

CANCÚN AND ISLA MUJERES

Isla
Mujeres

AV. GUSTAVO RUEDA MEDINA

AIRPORT

Bahía   de   Mujeres

CAR FERRY

FERRY

FERRY

Punta Sam

Puerto Juárez

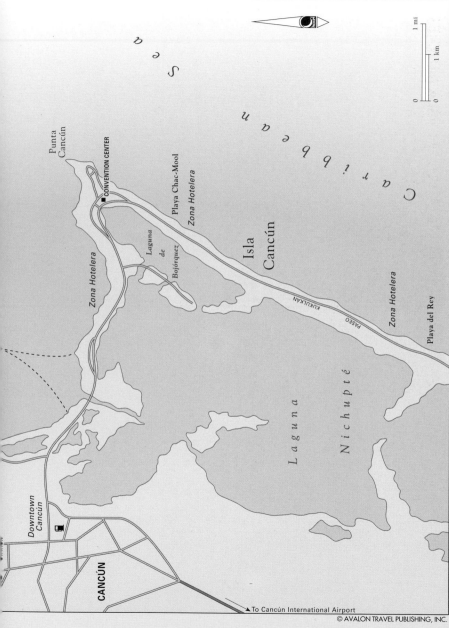

Mar Caribbean Sea

Punta Cancún

CONVENTION CENTER

Zona Hotelera

Laguna de Bojórquez

Playa Chac-Mool

Zona Hotelera

Isla Cancún

PASEO KUKULKÁN

Zona Hotelera

Playa del Rey

Laguna Nichupté

Downtown Cancún

CANCÚN

To Cancún International Airport

1 mi
1 km

© AVALON TRAVEL PUBLISHING, INC.

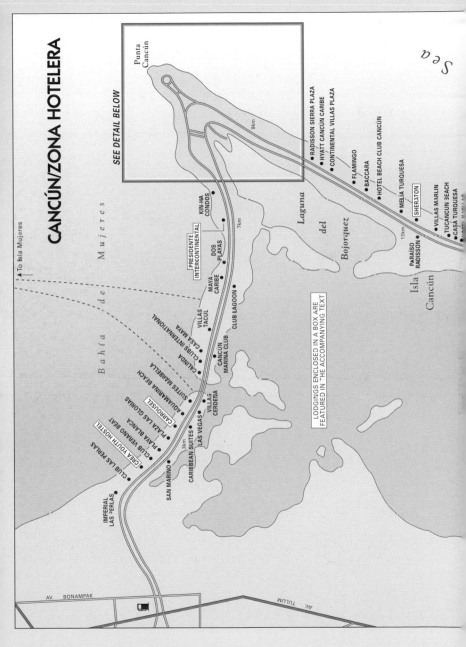

CANCÚN/ZONA HOTELERA

To Isla Mujeres

Bahía de Mujeres

SEE DETAIL BELOW

Punta Cancún

Sea

9km

Laguna del Bojorquez

Isla Cancún

7km

12km

LODGINGS ENCLOSED IN A BOX ARE FEATURED IN THE ACCOMPANYING TEXT

- RADISSON SIERRA PLAZA
- HYATT CANCUN CARIBE
- CONTINENTAL VILLAS PLAZA
- FLAMINGO
- BACCARA
- HOTEL BEACH CLUB CANCÚN
- MELIA TURQUESA
- SHERATON
- VILLAS MARLIN
- TUCANCUN BEACH
- CASA TURQUESA
- PARAISO RADISSON

KIN-HA CONDOS

PRESIDENTE INTERCONTINENTAL

DOS PLAYAS

MAYA CARIBE

VILLAS TACUL

CLUB LAGOON

CASA MAYA

CLUBS INTERNATIONAL

CAI INDA

CANCUN MARINA CLUB

SUITES MIRABELLA

VILLAS CERDEÑA

AQUAMARINA BEACH

CARROUSEL

PLAYA LAS GLORIAS

PLAYA BLANCA

LAS VEGAS

CARIBBEAN SUITES

CLUB VERANO BEAT

3km

CREA YOUTH HOSTEL

SAN MARINO

CLUB LAS PERLAS

IMPERIAL LAS PERLAS

AV. BONAMPAK

AV. TULUM

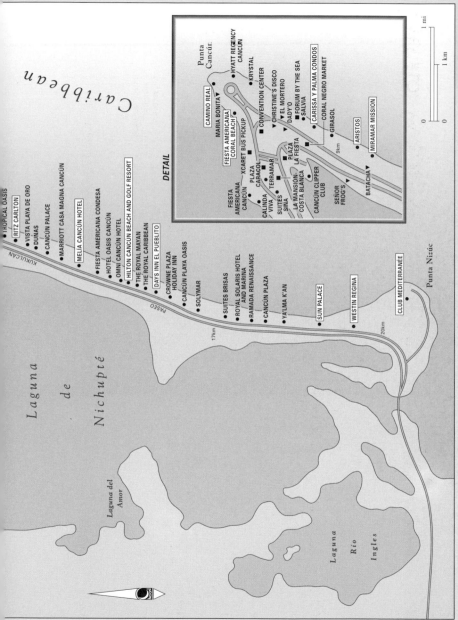

Caribbean

Laguna de Nichupté

Laguna del Amor

Laguna Río Ingles

KUKULCAN

PASEO

17km

20km

Punta Nizúc

TROPICAL OASIS
RITZ CARLTON
VISTA PLAYA DE ORO
DUÑAS
CANCÚN PALACE
MARRIOTT CASA MAGNA CANCÚN
MELIA CANCÚN HOTEL
FIESTA AMERICANA CONDESA
HOTEL OASIS CANCÚN
OMNI CANCÚN HOTEL
HILTON CANCÚN BEACH AND GOLF RESORT
THE ROYAL MAYAN
THE ROYAL CARIBBEAN
DAYS INN EL PUEBLITO
CROWNE PLAZA HOLIDAY INN
CANCÚN PLAYA OASIS
SOLYMAR
SUITES BRISAS
ROYAL SOLARIS HOTEL AND MARINA
RAMADA RENAISSANCE
CANCÚN PLAZA
YALMA K'AN
SUN PALACE
WESTIN REGINA
CLUB MEDITERRANÉE

DETAIL

Punta Cancún

CAMINO REAL
MARIA BONITA
FIESTA AMERICANA CORAL BEACH
XCARET BUS PICKUP
FIESTA AMERICANA CANCÚN
PLAZA CARACOL
CALINDA VIVA
TERRAMAR
SUITES SINA
LA MANSION-COSTA BLANCA
PLAZA LA FIESTA
CANCÚN CLIPPER CLUB
SEÑOR FROG'S
BATACHA
HYATT REGENCY CANCÚN
KRYSTAL
CONVENTION CENTER
CHRISTINE'S DISCO
EL MORTERO
DADY'O
FORUM BY THE SEA
SALVIA
CARISSA Y PALMA CONDOS
CORAL NEGRO MARKET
GIRASOL
ARISTOS
MIRAMAR MISSION
9km

1 mi
1 km
0

© AVALON TRAVEL PUBLISHING, INC.

CANCÚN

MEXICO'S CARIBBEAN COAST

SIXTH EDITION

CHICKI MALLAN

AND

PHOTOGRAPHS BY OZ MALLAN

AVALON
TRAVEL

MOON HANDBOOKS: CANCÚN
SIXTH EDITION
Chicki Mallan

Published by
Avalon Travel Publishing
5855 Beaudry St.
Emeryville, CA 94608, USA

Printing History
1st edition—1990
6th edition—October 2001
5 4 3 2 1

Please send all comments,
corrections, additions,
amendments, and critiques to:

**MOON HANDBOOKS:
CANCÚN
AVALON TRAVEL PUBLISHING
5855 BEAUDRY ST.
EMERYVILLE, CA 94608, USA
email: info@travelmatters.com
www.travelmatters.com**

Text and photographs © 2001 by Chicki Mallan.
All rights reserved.
Illustrations and maps © 2001 by Avalon Travel Publishing.
All rights reserved.
Some photos and illustrations are used by permission
and are the property of the original copyright owners.

ISBN: 1-56691-328-4
ISSN: 1534-0503

Editor: Grace Fujimoto
Series Manager: Erin Van Rheenen
Copy Editor: Chris Hayhurst
Map Editor: Naomi Dancis
Graphics Coordinator: Erika Howsare
Production: Alvaro Villanueva
Cartography: Mike Morgenfeld, Kat Kalamaras, Chris Folks
Proofreader: Gina Wilson Birtcil
Index: Vera Gross

Front cover photo: Ruins at Tulum, © Oz Mallan

Distributed in the United States and Canada by Publishers Group West

Printed in China through Colorcraft Ltd., Hong Kong

to my friends in Mexico

CONTENTS

ABBREVIATIONS

a/c—air-conditioning
C—Celsius
d—double occupancy

km—kilometer
s—single occupancy
s/n—*sin numero* (without a
street number)

t—triple occupancy
tel.—telephone

ACCOMMODATIONS PRICE KEY

Under US$50
US$50–100
US$100–150
US$150–200
US$200 and up
All-inclusive Resorts

ACKNOWLEDGMENTS

The Caribbean Sea seduces all who view it—it sure did Oz and me. Somehow the tranquil water influences everyone in some way, especially those who are privileged to live there permanently. When returning to the sunny, white-sand environment, spending weeks or months talking and trying to memorize all the new things that continue to pop up along the elegant coastline is ultimate pleasure. Thank you to all the folks who go out of their way to help us "get it right" in: Cancún, Cozumel, Playa del Carmen, Tulum, Isla Mujeres, Chetumal, the entire Riviera Maya and all the small cities in between.

MAPS

MAP SYMBOLS

═══	Primary Road	○	City/Town	⛳	Golf Course
═══	Secondary Road	★	Point of Interest	⛽	Gas Station
=========	Unpaved Road	•	Accommodation	✈ ✈	Airport/Airstrip
---------	Trail/Footpath	▼	Restaurant/Bar	▲	Archaeological Site
....	Ferry	▪	Other Location	▒	Reef

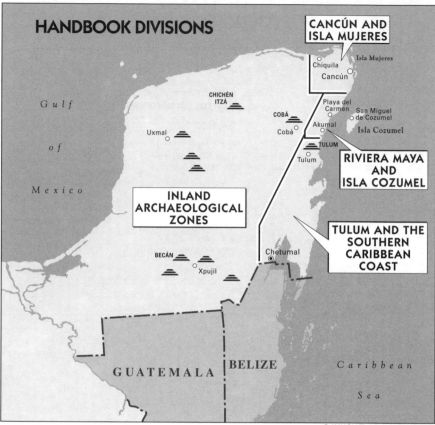

HANDBOOK DIVISIONS

CANCÚN AND
ISLA MUJERES

Isla Mujeres

Chiquila
Cancún

CHICHÉN
ITZÁ

Playa del
Carmen
San Miguel
de Cozumel

COBÁ

Uxmal

Akumal
Isla Cozumel

Cobá

Gulf

TULUM

o f

Tulum

RIVIERA MAYA
AND
ISLA COZUMEL

Mexico

INLAND
ARCHAEOLOGICAL
ZONES

Chetumal

TULUM AND THE
SOUTHERN
CARIBBEAN
COAST

BECÁN

Xpujil

GUATEMALA   BELIZE

Caribbean

Sea

© AVALON TRAVEL PUBLISHING, INC.

KEEPING CURRENT

W e strive to keep our book as up to date as possible and would appreciate your help. Prices go up and down and it's virtually impossible to keep up with them; the prices and price categories in this book are not guaranteed and are intended as a guide only. But if you find a hot new resort or attraction, or if we have neglected to include an important bit of information, please let us know. Our mapmakers take extraordinary care to be accurate, but if you find an error, let us know that as well.

We're especially interested in hearing from female travelers, RVers, outdoor enthusiasts, expatriates, and local residents. And we'd also welcome comments from the Mexican tourist industry, including hotel owners and individuals who specialize in accommodating visitors to their country.

Address your letters to:

Moon Handbooks: Cancún
Avalon Travel Publishing
5855 Beaudry Street
Emeryville, CA 94608, U.S.A
email: info@travelmatters.com

KATHY ESCOVEDO SANDERS

INTRODUCTION

In the end it's the visitor who decides whether a tourist area will survive—either the sightseer likes it, tells friends, and they all come back, or not. As the statistics show, visitors love this part of Mexico's Yucatán Peninsula called Cancún. They keep coming and coming, and the narrow 17-mile-long sliver of sand that is Cancún keeps building and building. As a result a whole new area has opened up with all the same glorious attributes: aqua sea, white sand, and impressive places to stay and eat and play. Development is wildly running south down the coast like a rabbit with a fox on its tail.

Some of us think that's a sad thing, but it's reality. Now Cancún finds itself in friendly competition with many upscale hotels on spacious Quintana Roo beaches to the south, where there's more than just sand and sea. Here, visitors take beach breaks to check out the other side of Highway 307, where natural treasures—including small Maya structures, caves with watery cenote entrances or yawning mouths of stone and vines, and the ancient history of the Maya—have long been veiled by a thick growth of trees that parallels the coast all the way to

the Rio Hondo River. Today the growth is being cleared away and opened to the world.

For years the smart people kept small hideaway resorts along this stretch of coast as their own secret "desert island" getaways. But today the coast is no longer discussed in whispers. Bigger and grander hotels have set out roots and are shouting invitations to the world. Welcome to Cancún and the Riviera Maya!

The southern coast has been called many things—Tulum Corridor, Playa Coast, Sunshine Coast, and others—but the newest, and probably the name that will survive, is Riviera Maya. No matter what you call it, Mexico's Caribbean coast has become Mexico's sizzling coast, attracting travelers from all over the world.

Travelers who have enjoyed Cancún for years are now discovering new and wonderful luxuries like all-inclusive party palaces, family-style condos, fishing camps, diving resorts, clothing-optional beaches, yoga retreats, low-key but comfortable thatch huts, birding enclaves, and hammock cabañas. Some are small and intimate, built for two; others are giant hotels with enough rooms to accommodate a thousand.

Who knows what we'll find along this Quintana Roo coast next year? What we can be certain of, the diverse variety of people that pick and choose a resort along here all have one thing in common: they love the Caribbean-crystalline water the color of imperial jade.

One of the perks of well-known destinations is good food. Restaurants, where the chef can be from Paris, Rome, Mexico City, or a small Maya village in this Yucatán Peninsula, are amazing. Many of these dining rooms stand alone and are popping up like mushrooms along the once-isolated corridor.

Adventurers, too, are finding new places to explore. Many cenotes are now opened to swimmers and divers. New natural parks with rivers and lagoons and wildlife have now been named and mapped. These places have always been there, but with no roads, no facilities, and no signs they remained incognito. Now kayakers, canoers, divers, and spelunkers share the hidden waterways of the ancient Maya. A few Maya villages, like Pac Chen, for example, have become destinations for small groups of tourists with a guide. While in these villages visitors can meet the Maya people, visit them in their huts, and have lunch next to a lovely lagoon. The promoters' idea is to give the villagers' economy a shot in the arm, while introducing their culture to outsiders. Our hope is that it's the visitors who will come away deeply impressed and changed; that the locals will carry on with their old ways and rituals; that we outsiders will not rush the intrusion of MTV into thatch huts; and the beach, the sea, and all the precious life within will continue to thrive.

INTRODUCTION TO CANCÚN

One of the top vacation destinations in the world, Cancún basks under year-round warm sun. This crowded Mexican resort offers pleasure seekers water sports galore, as well as vigorous entertainment that goes on till the wee hours. Add excellent accommodations, gourmet restaurants, and outstanding shopping, and you've got the ultimate escape—whether from the nine-to-five grind or from the chilly winters of the north.

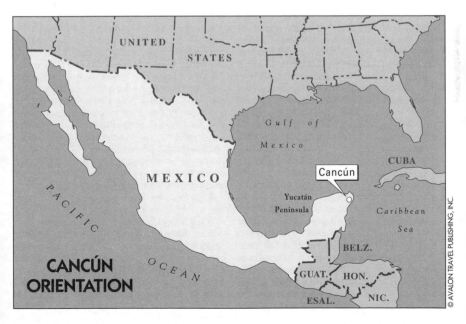

CANCÚN ORIENTATION

© AVALON TRAVEL PUBLISHING, INC.

LAND AND CLIMATE

Cancún is on the east coast of Mexico's Yucatán Peninsula in the state of Quintana Roo, which is bordered by the Mexican states of Yucatán to the northwest and Campeche to the west, and the countries of Belize and Guatemala to the south. Quintana Roo occupies 50,350 square kilometers and has a population of over 800,000. Mostly flat, this long-isolated state is covered with tropical forest and boasts the most beautiful white-sand beaches on the Peninsula. Several islands lie offshore and a colorful 250-kilometer-long coral reef runs parallel to the coast, providing a world-class attraction with its abundant under-sea life. Chetumal, capital of Quintana Roo, borders Belize.

Geologically, this flat shelf of limestone and coral composition is like a stone sponge; rain is absorbed into the ground and delivered to natural stone-lined sinks and underground rivers. The abundant limestone provided the early Maya with sturdy material to create the mammoth structures that survived hundreds of years to become one of the region's chief attractions. The soft rock was readily cut with hand-hewn implements but created a problem in the Maya's search for water; thanks to the predominantly porous rock, there are few surface rivers and lakes in Quintana Roo. Only in the extreme south does a sizeable river exist—the Río Hondo cuts a natural boundary between Belize and Quintana Roo, at the city of Chetumal. Four shallow lakes at Cobá are scattered between ancient ruins, and many small lagoons are hidden in the jungle.

Cenotes

The early inhabitants found their water mostly in cenotes ("say-NO-tay"), natural wells. Limestone and coral create eerie shorelines, caves, and, fortunately, waterholes. When flying over the Peninsula you see occasional circular ground patterns caused by the hidden movement of underground rivers and lakes. The water level rises and falls with the cycle of rain and drought. The constant ebb and flow erodes the underside of these limestone containers, creating steep-walled caverns; the surface crust eventually wears so thin that it caves in, exposing the water below. Around these water sources Maya villages grew. Some

of the wells are shallow, seven meters below the jungle floor; some are treacherously deep, with the surface of the water as much as 90 meters below. In times of drought, the Maya fetched water by carving steps into slick limestone walls or by hanging long ladders into abysmal hollows that lead to underground lakes.

John Stephens's book, *Incidents of Travel in Central America, Chiapas, and Yucatán,* covers his 1841 expedition with Frederick Catherwood. Catherwood's realistic art reproduces accurately how the Indians in the northern part of the Peninsula survived from year to year with little or no rainfall by burrowing deep into the earth to retrieve water. The two American explorers observed long lines of naked Indian men carrying calabash containers of the precious liquid from deep holes.

The Peninsula Coast

The Quintana Roo coast is composed of many lagoons, sandbars, and mangrove swamps, and is edged with coral reefs; several islands lie off shore—Cozumel, Isla Mujeres, Isla Holbox, and Contoy. The fifth-largest reef in the world, the Belize Reef, extends from the tip of Isla Mujeres 250 kilometers south to the Bay of Honduras. Many varieties of coral—including rare black coral found at great depths—grow in the hills and valleys of the often-deep reef that protects Quintana Roo. Diving for coral is prohibited in many places along the reef, and where permitted it makes for a dangerous, but lucrative, occupation. Since tourists are willing to buy it, the local divers continue to retrieve it from the crags and crevices of underwater canyons. In addition to attracting profit-seekers, the coral ridges of the reef draw thousands of sport divers from all over the world each year.

Climate

The weather in Quintana Roo falls into a wet season (May–October) and a dry season (November–April). Though most travelers prefer the milder conditions of the dry season, you can enjoy the area any time of year. Travelers to the area in the dry season can expect hot days, cooling showers, occasional brief storms called *nortes,* and plenty of tourists. Travel in the wet season can be more difficult, with regular rains and hot, muggy air. May and June are infamous in the Yucatán for heat and humidity both on the sweaty side of 90 (°F/percent).

Hurricane season runs July–November with most activity occurring September–October. However, with the appearance of La Niña, previously predictable patterns often change. Tropical storms are common this time of year and sometimes disrupt travel plans. Definitely leave the area quickly if a hurricane is on the way.

FLORA AND FAUNA

Quintana Roo's forests are home to mangroves, bamboo, and swamp cypresses. Ferns, vines, and flowers creep from tree to tree and create a dense growth. On topmost limbs, orchids and air ferns reach for the sun. The southern part of the Yucatán Peninsula, with its classic tropical rainforest, hosts tall mahoganies, *campeche, zapote,* and *kapok,* also covered with wild jungle vines.

Many exotic animals found nowhere else in Mexico inhabit the state's flatlands and thick jungles. With patience it's possible to observe animals not normally seen in the wild. If you're serious about this venture, bring a small folding stool (unless you prefer to sit in a tree), a pair of binoculars, a camera, and plenty of bug repellent, and then quietly wait.

FLORA
Palms

A wide variety of palm trees and their relatives grow on the Peninsula—tall, short, fruited, and even oil-producing varieties. Though they're all somewhat similar, various palms have distinct characteristics.

Royal palms are tall with smooth trunks. Queen palms are often used for landscaping and bear a sweet fruit. Thatch palms are called *chit* by the Indians, who use the fronds extensively for roof thatch.

The coconut palm serves the Yucatecan well; one of the most useful trees in the world, it produces oil, food, drink, and shelter. The tree matures in 6–7 years and then for 5–7 years bears coconuts, which are valued by locals as a nutritious food source and cash crop. Presently, this source of income has all but disappeared on much of the Quintana Roo coast due to "yellowing" disease, which has attacked palm trees from Florida to Central America. These tall trees have been replaced in many areas by a shorter and more disease-resistant palm.

Henequen is a cousin to the palm tree; from its fiber comes twine, rope, matting, and other products. New uses are sought constantly since this plant is abundant in the area.

From Fruit to Flowers

Quintana Roo grows delicious sweet and sour oranges, limes, and grapefruit. Avocado is abundant, and the papaya tree is practically a weed. The mamey tree grows tall (15–20 meters) and full, providing not only welcome shade but also an avocado-shaped fruit, brown on the outside with a vivid, salmon-pink flesh that makes a sweet snack (the flavor similar to a sweet yam's). Another unusual fruit tree is the guaya, a member of the litchi nut family. This rangy evergreen thrives on sea air and is commonly seen along the coast and throughout the Yucatán Peninsula. Its small, green, leathery pods grow in clumps like grapes and contain a sweet, yellowish, jellylike flesh—tasty! The calabash tree, a friend to the Maya for many years, provides gourds used for containers.

The tall ceiba is a very special tree to those close to the Maya religion. Considered the tree of life, even today locals leave it undisturbed, even if it sprouts in the middle of a fertile *milpa* (cornfield).

BOB RACE

royal palm

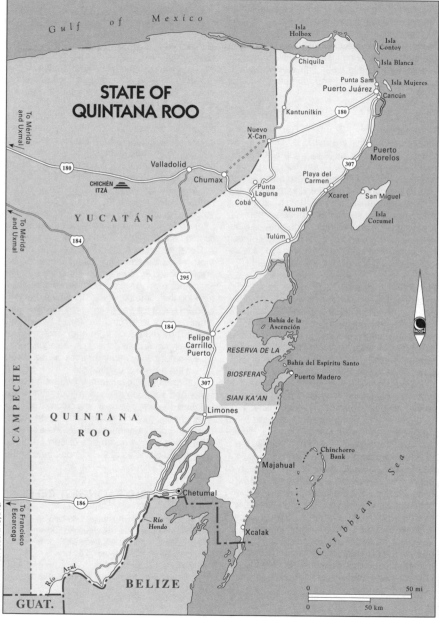

Gulf of Mexico

STATE OF
QUINTANA ROO

To Mérida
and Uxmal

To Mérida
and Uxmal

Isla
Holbox

Isla
Contoy

Chiquila

Isla Blanca

Punta Sam
Puerto Juárez

Isla Mujeres

Cancún

Kantunilkin

180

Nuevo
X-Can

Puerto
Morelos

180

Valladolid

307

Chumax

CHICHÉN
ITZÁ

Punta
Laguna

Playa del
Carmen

Cobá

Xcaret

San Miguel

Y U C A T Á N

184

Akumal

Isla
Cozumel

Tulúm

295

Bahía de la
Ascención

184

RESERVA DE LA

Felipe
Carrillo
Puerto

Bahía del Espíritu Santo

BIOSFERA

Puerto Madero

307

SIAN KA'AN

Limones

C A M P E C H E

Chinchorro
Bank

Q U I N T A N A
R O O

Majahual

Caribbean Sea

186

Chetumal

To Francisco
Escárcega

Río
Hondo

Xcalak

Río
Azul

B E L I Z E

GUAT.

0   50 mi

0   50 km

© AVALON TRAVEL PUBLISHING, INC.

When visiting in the summer, you can't miss the beautiful *framboyanes* (royal poinciana). As its name implies, when in bloom it is the most flamboyant tree around, with wide-spreading branches covered in clusters of brilliant orange-red flowers. These trees line sidewalks and plazas and when clustered together present a dazzling show.

Orchids

In remote areas of Quintana Roo one of the more exotic blooms, the orchid, is often found on the highest limbs of tall trees. Of the 71 species reported on the Yucatán Peninsula, 20 percent are terrestrial and 80 percent are epiphytic, attached to host trees and deriving moisture and nutrients from the air and rain. Both types grow in many sizes and shapes: tiny buttons spanning the length of a long branch, large-petaled blossoms with ruffled edges, or intense, tiger-striped miniatures. The lovely flowers come in a wide variety of colors, some subtle, some brilliant.

Nature's Hothouse

In spring, flowering trees are a beautiful sight—and sound: hundreds of singing birds gather in the treetops throughout the mating season. While wandering through jungle landscapes, you'll see, thriving in the wild, a gamut of plants that we so carefully nurture and coax to survive on windowsills at home. Here in its natural environment, the croton exhibits wild colors, the pothos grows 30-centimeter leaves, and the philodendron splits every leaf in gargantuan glory.

White and red ginger are among the more exotic herbs that grow on the Peninsula. Plumeria (called "frangipani" in the South Pacific) has a wonderful fragrance and appears in many colors. Hibiscus and bougainvillea bloom in an array of bright hues. A walk through the jungle will introduce you to many delicate strangers in the world of tropical flowers. But you'll find old friends, too, such as the common morning glory creeping and climbing for miles over bushes and trees. Viny coils thicken daily. Keeping jungle growth away from the roads, utility poles, and wires is an endless job for local authorities, because warm, humid air and ample rainfall encourage a lush green wonderland.

CORAL REEFS

The spectacular coral reefs that grace the Yucatán's east coast are made up of millions of tiny carnivorous organisms called polyps. Coral grows in innumerable shapes: delicate lace, trees with reaching branches, pleated mushrooms, stovepipes, petaled flowers, fans, domes, heads of cabbage, and stalks of broccoli. The polyps can be less than a centimeter long or as big as 15 centimeters in diameter. Related to the jellyfish and sea anemone, polyps need sunlight and clear saltwater no colder than 20°C to survive. Coral polyps have cylinder-shaped bodies. One end is attached to a hard surface (the bottom of the ocean, the rim of a submerged volcano, or the reef itself) and the other, the mouth, is circled with tiny tentacles that capture its minute prey with a deadly sting.

Coral reefs are formed when polyps attach themselves to each other. Stony coral, for example, makes the connection with a flat sheet of tissue between the middle of both bodies. They develop their limestone skeletons by extracting calcium out of the seawater and depositing calcium carbonate around the lower half of the body. They reproduce from buds or eggs. Occasionally small buds appear on the adult polyp; when mature, they separate from the adult and add to the growth of existing colonies. Eggs, on the other hand, grow into tiny forms that swim away and settle on the ocean floor. When developed, the egg begins a new colony.

As these small creatures continue to reproduce and die, their sturdy skeletons accumulate. Over eons, broken bits of coral, animal waste, and granules of soil all contribute to the

THE WORLD'S LONGEST REEFS

Great Barrier Reef, Australia: 1,600 km
S.W. Barrier Reef, New Caledonia: 600 km
N.E. Barrier Reef, New Caledonia: 540 km
Great Sea Reef, Fiji Islands: 260 km
Belize Reef: 250 km
S. Louisiade Archipelago Reef, Papua New Guinea: 200 km

strong foundation for a reef, which slowly rises toward the surface. To grow, a reef must have a base no more than 25 meters below the water's surface, and in a healthy environment it can grow 4–5 centimeters a year. One small piece of coral represents millions of polyps and many years of construction.

Reefs are divided into three types: atoll, fringing, and barrier. An atoll can be formed around the crater of a submerged volcano. The polyps begin building their colonies on the round edge of the crater, forming a circular coral island with a lagoon in the center. Thousands of atolls occupy tropical waters of the world. A fringing reef is coral living on a shallow shelf that extends outward from shore into the sea. A barrier reef runs parallel to the coast. Water separates it from the land, and it can be a series of reefs with channels of water in between. This is the case with some of the largest barrier reefs in the Pacific and Indian Oceans.

The Yucatán Peninsula's Belize Reef (the most common of several names) extends from the tip of Isla Mujeres to Sapodilla Caye in the Gulf of Honduras. This reef is 280 kilometers long, fifth longest in the world. The beauty of the reef attracts divers and snorkelers from distant parts of the world to investigate its unspoiled marinelife.

Conservation

The Mexican government has strict laws gov-

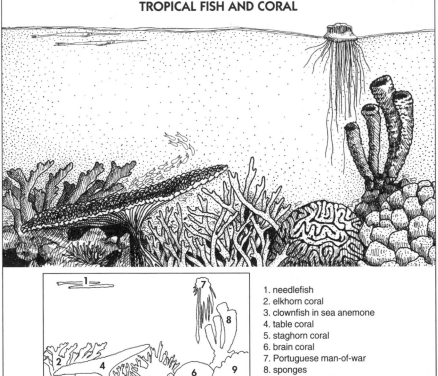

TROPICAL FISH AND CORAL

1. needlefish
2. elkhorn coral
3. clownfish in sea anemone
4. table coral
5. staghorn coral
6. brain coral
7. Portuguese man-of-war
8. sponges
9. lobed star coral

DIANA LASICH HARPER

erning the reef, to which most divers are more than willing to comply in order to preserve this natural treasure and its inhabitants. It takes hundreds of years to form large colonies, so please don't break off pieces of coral for souvenirs. After a very short time out of water the polyps lose their color and you have only a piece of chalky white coral—just like the pieces you see while beachcombing. Stiff fines await those who remove anything from the reef, and spearfishing along the reef is strictly prohibited.

FISH

The fish and other sealife of the Quintana Roo coast are world-famous among divers and snorkelers. The barrier reef that runs the length of the Peninsula from Isla Mujeres to Belize is home to myriad fish species, including parrot fish, candy bass, moray eels, spotted scorpionfish, turquoise angelfish, fairy basslets, flame fish, and gargantuan manta rays. Several species of shark thrive in the waters off Quintana Roo, though they're not considered a major threat to swimmers and divers.

Sport fish, including sailfish, marlin, and bluefin tuna, inhabit the outer Caribbean waters. Check with a hotel or tourist office to arrange a fishing trip. Hard-fighting bonefish and pompano can be found in the area's lagoons. Catching and releasing these fish is becoming a popular sport in the Caribbean.

In the shark caves off Isla Mujeres, sharks "sleep" on the cave floor due to low water salinity. Though some brave divers boast of petting the sluggish predators, most choose not to disturb them.

The clear waters of the cenotes, or giant wells, of the Yucatán are home to several species of blind fish, which live out their existence in darkness.

The Meaning of Color

Most people interested in a reef already know they're in for a brilliant display of colored fish. In the fish world, color isn't only for exterior decoration. Fish change hues for a number of reasons, including anger, protection, and sexual attraction. This is still a little-known science. For example, because of the many colors grouper

appear in, marine biologists are uncertain how many species (or moods) there are. A male damselfish clearly imparts his aggression—and his desire for love—by turning vivid blue. Some fish have as many as 12 different recognizable color patterns, and they can change within seconds.

These color changes, along with other body signals, combine to make communication simple between species. Scientists have discovered that a layer of color-bearing cells lies just beneath a fish's transparent scales. These cells contain orange, yellow, black, or red pigments: some fish combine their colors to make yellow or green. A crystalline tissue adds white, silver, or iridescence. Color changes when the pigmented cells are revealed, combined, or masked.

Fish communicate in many other surprising ways, including electrical impulses and flashing bioluminescence (cold light). If fish communication intrigues you, read Robert Burgess's book, *Secret Languages of the Sea* (Dodd, Mead and Company).

CARIBBEAN FISH

angelfish
barracuda
barred cardinal
big eye
blue chromis
bluestriped grunt
butterfly indigo hamlet
French grunt
grouper
hogfish
porkfish
queen angelfish
sand tilefish
sergeant major
spotted drum
stoplight parrot fish
toadfish
triggerfish
trumpetfish
trunkfish

REPTILES

Although reptiles thrive in Quintana Roo's warm, sunny environment, humans are their worst enemy. In the past some species were greatly reduced in number because they were hunted for their unusual skin. Though this activity is against the law in most countries today, a few black marketeers still take their toll on the species.

Caymans

The cayman is part of the crocodilian order. Its habits and appearance are similar to those of crocodiles; the main difference is its underskin. The cayman's skin is reinforced with bony plates on the belly, making it useless for the leather market. (Alligators and crocodiles, with smooth belly skin and sides, have been hunted almost to extinction in some parts of the world.)

Of the five species of cayman, several frequent the brackish inlet waters near the estuaries on the north edge of the Yucatán Peninsula along the Río Lagartos (loosely translated to mean "River of Lizards"). They have broad snouts and often look as though they sport a pair of spectacles. A large cayman can be 2.5 meters long and very dark gray-green with eyelids that look swollen and wrinkled. Some species have eyelids that look like a pair of blunt horns. They are quicker than alligators and have longer, sharper teeth. Their disposition is vicious and treacherous; don't be fooled by the old myth that on land they're cumbersome and slow. When cornered they move swiftly and are known for their viciousness toward people. The best advice you can heed is to give the cayman a wide berth when you spot one.

Iguanas

This group of American lizards—family Iguanidae—includes various large plant-eaters seen frequently in Quintana Roo. The iguana grows to one meter long and has a blunt head and long, flat tail. Bands of black and gray circle its body and a serrated column reaches down the middle of its back almost to the tail. The young iguana is bright emerald green.

The lizard's forelimbs hold the front half of its body up off the ground while its two back limbs are kept relaxed and splayed alongside its hindquarters. However, when the iguana is frightened, its hind legs do everything they're supposed to, and the iguana crashes quickly (though clumsily) into the brush searching for its burrow and safety. This reptile is not aggressive, but if cornered it will bite and use its tail in self-defense.

The iguana mostly enjoys basking in the bright sunshine along the Caribbean. Though they are herbivores, the young also eat insects and larvae. Certain varieties in some areas of the Peninsula are almost hunted out—for example, the spiny-tailed iguana in the central valley of Chiapas. In isolated parts of Quintana

iguana

OZ MALLAN

Roo it is not unusual to see locals along dirt paths carrying sturdy specimens by the tail to put in the cookpot.

From centuries past, recorded references attest to the iguana's medicinal value, which partly explains the active trade of live iguana in the marketplaces of some parts of the Peninsula. Iguana stew is believed to cure or relieve human ailments such as impotence. Another reason for their popularity at the market is their delicate white flesh, which tastes a lot like a very firm chicken but is much more expensive.

Other Lizards

You'll see a great variety of other lizards as well, from the skinny two-inch miniature gecko to the chameleonlike black anole that changes colors to match its environment, either when danger is imminent or as subterfuge to fool the insects that it preys on. At mating time, the male anole's bright-red throat fan is puffed out to make sure that all female lizards will see it.

Some lizards are brightly striped in various shades of green and yellow; others are earth colors that blend with the gray and beige limestone that dots the landscape. Skinny as wisps of thread running on hind legs, or chunky and waddling with armorlike skin, the range is endless and fascinating!

Coral Snakes

In North and South America are several species of coral snakes, which are close relatives of cobras. Many false coral snakes with similar coloring are also around, but they're harmless. The coral snakes found from the southern part of the Yucatán Peninsula to Panama grow much larger (1–1.5 meters) than the ones in the southern United States. The body is slender, with no pronounced distinction between head and neck.

The two North American coral snakes have prominent rings around their bodies in the same sequence of black, yellow or white, and red. Coral snakes are nocturnal and spend the day in mossy clumps under rocks or logs. They don't look for trouble and seldom strike, but will bite if stepped on; their short fangs, however, can be stopped by shoes or clothing. Even though some Mexicans call this the "20-minute snake"—meaning if you are bitten and don't get antivenin within 20 minutes, you die—it's actually more like a 24-hour period. According to Mexico's Instituto Nacional de Higiene, an average of 135 snakebite deaths per year (mostly children) are reported for the country, but the number is declining as more villages receive antivenin.

Chances of the average tourist being bitten by a coral (or any other) snake are slim. However, if you plan on extensive jungle exploration, check with your doctor before you leave home. Antivenin is available in Mexico, and it's wise to be prepared for an allergic reaction to the antivenin by bringing antihistamine and epinephrine. The most important thing to remember if bitten: *Don't panic and don't run.* Physical exertion and panic cause the venom to travel through your body much faster. Lie down and stay calm; have someone carry you to a doctor.

Tropical Rattlesnakes

The tropical rattlesnake, called *cascabel* in Mexico and Mesoamerica, is the deadliest and most treacherous species of rattler. It differs slightly from other species by having vividly contrasting neck bands. Contrary to popular myth, this serpent doesn't always rattle a warning of its impending strike. It grows 2–2.5 meters long and is found mainly in higher, drier areas of the tropics.

Sea Turtles

At one time many species of giant turtles inhabited the coastal regions of Quintana Roo, laying their eggs in the warm Caribbean sands. Though many hatchlings didn't survive birds, crabs, and sharks, thousands of turtles managed to return each year to their birthplace. The Sea Turtle Rescue Organization claims that in 1947, during one day, over 40,000 nesting Kemp's ridley sea turtles were counted. In 1984 fewer than 500 Kemp's ridleys nested during the entire season.

In spite of concentrated efforts by the Mexican government, the number of turtles is still decreasing. They were a valuable source of food for the Maya Indians for centuries. But only in recent years has the wholesale theft of turtle eggs, coupled with the senseless slaughter of the hawksbill for its beautiful shell, begun to deplete these species. Refrigeration and freezer holds enable large fishing boats to capture thousands of turtles at one time and smuggle meat by the ton into various countries, to be canned as soup or frozen for the unwary consumer. Processors often claim the turtle meat in their product is from the legal freshwater variety.

Another problem is the belief that turtle eggs cure impotence. Despite huge fines for anyone possessing turtle eggs, every summer nesting grounds along the Yucatán Peninsula are raided. There is no hunting season for these threatened creatures, and the meat is illegal on menus throughout the state, though some restaurants ignore the law and verbally offer turtle meat. The eggs are kept much more secretively.

Ecological organizations are trying hard to save the dwindling turtle population. Turtle eggs are kept in captivity; when the hatchlings break through their shells, they are brought to a beach and allowed to rush toward the sea, hopefully imprinting a sense of belonging there so that they will later return to the spot. After a while at the beach, the hatchlings are scooped up and placed in tanks to grow larger before being released into the open sea. All of these efforts are in the experimental stage; the results will not be known for years. The government is enforcing tough penalties for people who take turtle eggs or capture, kill, sell, or imprison endangered animals.

Pronatura is a grassroots Yucatecan organization valiantly working against the tide, trying to save sea turtles from extinction. They also maintain a deer reproduction center, engage in coastal and reef management planning, study toucan habitat and jaguar populations, and manage general conservation funds. For more information or to make a donation, write Pronatura, Calle 1d #254a, entre 36 y 38, Col. Campestre, Mérida, Yucatán 97120, Mexico; tel./fax 99/44-2290. Specify your interest. Donations made out to "Friends of Pronatura" are tax deductible in the United States.

MAMMALS

Nine-banded Armadillos

This strange creature looks like a miniature prehistoric monster. The size of a small dog, its most unusual feature is the tough coat of plate armor that encases it. Even the tail has its own armor! Flexibility comes from nine bands (or external "joints") that circle the midsection. Living on a diet of insects, the armadillo's extremely keen sense of smell can locate grubs 15 centimeters underground. Its front paws are sharp, enabling it to dig easily into the earth and build underground burrows. After digging the hole, the animal carries down as much as a bushel of grass to make its nest. Here it bears and rears its young and sleeps during the day. Unlike some armadillos that roll up into a tight ball when threatened, this species will race for the burrow, stiffly arch its back, and wedge in so that it cannot be pulled out. The tip of the Yucatán Peninsula is a favored habitat due to its scant rainfall and warm temperatures; too much rain floods the burrow and can drown young armadillos.

Giant Anteaters

This extraordinary cousin of the armadillo measures two meters from the tip of its tubular snout to the end of its bushy tail. Its body is colored shades of brown-gray; the hindquarters become darker in tone, while a contrasting wedge-shaped pattern of black outlined with white decorates the throat and shoulders. This creature walks on the knuckles of its paws, keeping the foreclaws razor sharp. Its claws allow it to rip open the leathery mud walls of termite or white ant nests, the contents of which are a main food source. After opening the nest, the anteater begins flicking its tongue. Ants don't have a chance; the long, viscous tongue quickly transfers them to a toothless, elongated mouth.

armadillo

DIANA LASICH HARPER

MANATEE BREEDING PROGRAM

The state of Florida, under the auspices of the Miami Seaquarium and Dr. Jesse White, has begun a captive breeding program hoping to learn more about the habits of the manatee and to try to increase the declining numbers. Several manatees have been born in captivity; they along with others that have recuperated from injury or illness will be or have been released into Florida's Crystal River, where boat traffic is restricted. They are tagged and closely observed.

Florida maintains a 24-hour hotline where people report manatees in need of help for any reason. Rescues can include removing an adult male from a cramped storm drain or rushing to the seaquarium newborns that somehow managed to get separated from their mothers and have washed ashore. These newborns are readily accepted by surrogate-mother manatees and are offered nourishment (by way of a thumb-sized teat under the front flipper) and lots of TLC. Medical aid is given to mammals that have been slashed by the propellers of cruising boats. The manatee has a playful curiosity and investigates anything found in its underwater environment, many times sustaining grave damage.

a close-up of the truncated snout and prehensile lips of the manatee, which surprisingly is a distant relative of the elephant

While particularly dangerous to ants, its long claws are capable of injuring humans, making the anteater a deadly beast when threatened.

Tapirs

South American tapirs are found from the southern part of Mexico to southern Brazil. A stout-bodied animal, its tail and legs are short, its eyes are small, and its ears are round. The nose and upper lip extend into a short but very mobile proboscis. Totally herbivorous, tapirs usually live near streams or rivers in the forest. They bathe daily and also use the water as an escape when hunted either by humans or by their prime predator, the jaguar. Shy and unaggressive, these nocturnal animals have a definite home range, wearing a path between the jungle and their feeding area. If attacked, the tapir lowers its head and blindly crashes off through the forest; they've been known to collide with trees and knock themselves out in their chaotic attempt to flee!

Peccaries

Next to deer, peccaries are the most widely hunted game on the Yucatán Peninsula. Other names for this piglike creature are musk hog and javelina. Some compare peccaries to the wild pigs found in Europe, though in fact they're part of an entirely different family.

Two species found on the Peninsula are the collared and the white-lipped peccaries. The feisty collared peccary stands 50 centimeters at the shoulder and can be one meter long, weighing as much as 30 kilograms. It is black and white with a narrow, semicircular collar of white hair on the shoulders. In Spanish *javelina* means "spear," descriptive of the two spearlike tusks that protrude from its mouth. This more familiar peccary is found in the desert, woodlands, and rainforests, and travels in groups of 5–15. Also with tusks, the white-lipped peccary is reddish brown to black and has an area of white around its mouth. This larger animal, which can grow to 105 centimeters long, is found deep in tropical rainforests and lives in herds of 100-plus.

Cats

Seven species of cats are found in North America, four tropically distributed. The jaguar has a heavy chest and sturdy, muscled forelegs. It has small, rounded ears and its tail is relatively short. Colors range from tan on top and white on the underside to pure black. The male can weigh 65–115 kilograms; females range from 45–85 kilograms. Largest of the cats on the Peninsula, the jaguar is about the same size as a leopard. Other cats found in Quintana Roo are the ocelot and puma. In tropical forests of the past the large cats were the only predators capable of controlling the populations of hoofed game such as deer, peccaries, and tapirs. If hunting is poor and times are tough, the jaguar (el tigre) will go into rivers and scoop up fish with its large paws. The river is also one of the jaguar's favorite spots for hunting the large tapir when it comes to drink.

Manatees

Probably the most unusual mammal, the manatee is an elephantine creature of immense proportions with gentle manners and the curiosity of a kitten. Though today seldom seen, this enormous animal, often referred to as the sea cow, at one time roamed the shallow inlets, bays, and estuaries of the Caribbean in large numbers. The manatee is said to be the basis for seamen's myths of mermaids. In South America this particular mammal is revered by certain Indian tribes. The manatee image is frequently seen in the art of the ancient Maya, who hunted it for its flesh. In modern times, the population has been reduced by the encroachment of large numbers of people in the manatees' habitats along the riverways and shorelines. Ever-growing numbers of motorboats inflict often-deadly gashes on the nosy creatures.

At birth the manatee weighs 30–35 kilograms; it can grow up to four meters long and weigh over a ton. Gray with a pinkish cast and shaped like an Idaho potato, it has a spatulate tail, two forelimbs with toenails, pebbled coarse skin, tiny sunken eyes, numerous fine-bristled hairs scattered sparsely over its body, and a permanent Mona Lisa smile. The head of the mammal seems small for its gargantuan body, and its preproboscidean lineage includes dugongs (in Australia), hyrax, and elephants. The manatee's truncated snout and prehensile lips help push food into its mouth. The only aquatic mammal that exists on vegetation, the manatee grazes on bottom-growing grasses and other aquatic plantlife. It ingests as much as 225 kilograms per day, cleaning rivers of oxygen-choking growth. It is unique among mammals in that it constantly grows new teeth—to replace worn ones, which fall out regularly. Posing no threat to any other living thing, it has been hunted for its oil, skin, and flesh, which is said to be tasty.

The manatee thrives in shallow, warm water; in Quintana Roo the mammal has been reported in shallow bays between Playa del Carmen and Punta Allen, but very infrequently. One spring evening, in a small bay in Belize near the Chetumal border, we watched as a curious manatee spent about an hour lazily swimming the cove, lifting its truncated snout, and often its entire head, out of the water about every four minutes. The few of us standing on a small dock in the bay were thrilled to see the shy animal.

In neighboring Guatemala, the government is sponsoring a manatee reserve in Lago de Izabal. In the United States the mammal is found mostly in the inshore and estuarine areas of Florida. It is protected under the Federal U.S. Marine Mammal Protection Act of 1972, the Endangered Species Act of 1973, and the Florida Manatee Sanctuary Act of 1978. It is estimated that its total population numbers about 2,000.

BIRDS

Since a major part of Quintana Roo is still undeveloped and covered with trees and brush, it isn't surprising to find exotic, rarely seen birds all across the landscape. The Mexican government is beginning to realize the great value in this (almost) undiscovered treasure trove of nature and is making initial efforts to protect nesting grounds. The birds of the Yucatán, which attract scientists and laypeople alike, have until recent years been free from pesticides, smog, and human beings' encroachment. If you're a serious birdwatcher, you probably know all about Quintana Roo. Undoubtedly, however, change is coming as more people intrude into the rangeland of the birds, exploring these still undeveloped tracts on the Peninsula. Hopefully, stringent regulations will take hold before many of these lovely birds are chased away or destroyed.

Cobá, with its marshy-rimmed lakes, nearby cornfields, and relatively tall, humid forest, is worth a couple of days to the ornithologist. One of the more impressive birds to look for is the keel-billed toucan, often seen perched high on a bare limb in the early hours of the morning. Others include chachalacas (held in reverence by the Maya), screeching parrots, and occasionally the ocellated turkey. For an excellent bird book that deals with the Yucatán Peninsula, check out *100 Common Birds of the Yucatán Peninsula,* written by Barbara MacKinnon. A well-known birdwatcher, Barbara has lived in the Cancún area for many years and is donating all the profits from her book to the Sian Ka'an Reserve. Available for US$30 through Amigos de Sian Ka'an, Apdo. Postal 770, Cancún, Quintana Roo 77500, Mexico.

Sooty Terns

In Cancún, on a coral island just offshore from the Camino Real Hotel, lives a breeding colony of sooty terns. The sooty tern is one of several seabirds that lack waterproof feathers. It is the only one that will not venture to land on a passing ship or drifting debris. Feeding on tiny fish and squid that swim near the ocean surface, the bird hovers close to the water, snatching unsuspecting prey. They nest April–September, but if they're frightened, the parent birds panic, leaving the eggs exposed to the hot tropical sun or knocking the young into the sea where they drown immediately. For good reason, the Camino Real Hotel is being urged to warn guests to stay away from the rocky island.

Flamingos

The far north end of the Peninsula at Río Lagartos plays host to thousands of long-necked, long-legged flamingos during the nesting season (June–August). They begin arriving around the end of May, when the rains begin. This homecoming is a breathtaking sight: a profusion of pink/salmon colors clustered together on the white sand, or sailing across a blue sky, long, curved necks straight in flight, the flapping movement exposing contrasting black and pink on the undersides of their wings. The flamingo population on the Yucatán Peninsula is estimated at 30,000. This wildlife refuge, called **El Cuyo,** protects the largest colony of nesting American flamingos in the world.

Many of these flamingos winter in Celestún, a small fishing village on the northwest coast a few kilometers north of the Campeche-Yucatán state border. Celestún lies between the Gulf of Mexico and a long tidal estuary known as La Cienega. Since the disruption of Hurricane Gilbert, a flock of flamingos has found a new feeding ground near Chicxulub. If you're visiting Mérida and want to see flamingos during the winter season, it's a shorter drive to Celestún or Chicxulub (about one hour) than to Río Lagartos (about three hours). Don't forget your camera and color film!

Estuary Havens

Estuaries play host to hundreds of bird species. A boat ride into one of them will give you an opportunity to see a variety of ducks; this is a wintering spot for many North American flocks. Among others, you'll see the blue-winged teal, northern shoveler, and lesser scaup. You'll also see a variety of wading birds feeding in the shallow waters, including numerous types of heron, snowy egret, and, in the summer, white ibis. Seven species of birds are endemic to the Yucatán Peninsula: ocellated turkey, Yucatán whippoorwill, Yucatán flycatcher, orange oriole, black catbird, yellow-lored parrot, and the quetzal.

quetzals

BOB RACE

Quetzals

Though the ancient Maya made abundant use of the dazzling quetzal feathers for ceremonial costumes and headdresses, they hunted other

---

DIFFERENTIATING MOTHS AND BUTTERFLIES

1. Butterflies fly during the day; moths fly at dusk or at night.

2. Butterflies rest with their wings folded straight up over their bodies; most moths rest with their wings spread flat.

3. All butterflies have bare knobs at the end of both antennae (feelers); moths' antennae are either plumy or hairlike and end in a point.

4. Butterflies have slender bodies; moths are plump. Both insects are of the order Lepidoptera. So, lepidopterists, you are in butterfly heaven in the jungle areas of the Quintana Roo. To see them up close go to Xcaret Flyway in the Ecoarchaeological Park.

---

fowl in much larger quantities for food; nonetheless, the quetzal is the only known bird from the pre-Cortesian era that is almost extinct. These birds live only in the very high cloud forests where they thrive on the constant moisture. Today they are still found (though rarely) in the cloud forest of Chiapas and in Guatemala, where the government has established a quetzal sanctuary not too far from the city of Cobán. The beautifully designed reserve is open to hikers, with several kilometers of good trails leading up into the cloud forest. For the birder this could be a worthwhile detour to search out the gorgeous quetzal. The tourist office in Cobán, INGUAT, hands out an informative leaflet with a map and description of the quetzal sanctuary.

INSECTS AND ARACHNIDS

Pesky air-breathing invertebrates are unavoidable in any tropical locale. Some are annoying (mosquitoes and gnats), some are dangerous (black widows, bird spiders, and scorpions), and others can cause pain when they bite (red ants), but many are beautiful (butterflies and moths), and *all* are fascinating studies in evolved socialization and specialization. Note: Cockroaches

also live in the jungle, so don't be surprised if you run into one.

Butterflies and Moths

The Yucatán has an abundance of beautiful moths and butterflies. Of the 90,000 types of butterflies in the world, a large percentage is seen in Quintana Roo. You'll see, among others, the magnificent blue morpho, orange-barred sulphur, copperhead, cloudless sulphur, malachite, admiral, calico, ruddy dagger-wing, tropical buckeye, and emperor. The famous monarch is also a visitor during its annual migration from the Florida Peninsula. It usually makes a stopover on Quintana Roo's east coast, including Cancún and Cozumel, on its way south to the Central American mountains and Mexican highlands where it spends the winter. Trying to photograph a live butterfly is a testy business. Just when you have it in your crosshairs, the comely critter flutters off to another spot! If butterflies fascinate you, be sure to check out the butterfly pavilion at Xcaret.

SIAN KA'AN

With the growing number of visitors to Quintana Roo and the continual development of its natural wonders, there's a real danger of decimating the wildlife and destroying the ancient culture of its people. In 1981 authorities and scientists collaborated on a plan to stem that threat. The plan, which takes into account land titles, logging, hunting, agriculture, cattle ranching, and tourist development—and which local people feel comfortable with—culminated in the October 1986 establishment of the **Reserva de la Biosfera Sian Ka'an,** part of UNESCO's World Network of Biosphere Reserves.

Ongoing environmental efforts address several important issues, among them deforestation, which is becoming commonplace in Quintana Roo as the growing population clears more land for farms and ranches. Even in traditional fishing villages, growth is affecting the environment. In Punta Allen, to supplement their income fishermen were turning to the ancient method of slash-and-burn agriculture that for centuries had worked fine for the small groups of people inhabiting the Quintana Roo region. But with the

WHAT IS A BIOSPHERE RESERVE?

The biosphere is the thin mantle of the earth in which we live. It consists of parts of the lithosphere, hydrosphere, and atmosphere. The biosphere maintains our life and that of all organisms. We need to protect it and keep it livable.

The program Man and Biosphere was created by UNESCO in 1971, and it deals with the interaction of man with his environment. The program contains various projects, among which the concept of biosphere reserve has gained popularity and has become very important worldwide.

The idea of a biosphere reserve is new in conservation. It promotes the protection of different natural ecosystems of the world, and at the same time allows the presence of human activities through the rational use and development of natural resources on an ecological basis.

A biosphere reserve has a nucleus that is for conservation and limited scientific investigation only. A buffer zone surrounds this nucleus in which people may live and use the resources on a regulated, ecological basis. Conservation in a biosphere reserve is the challenge of good use rather than prohibiting use. This concept sets it apart from the national parks in which people are only observers. Biosphere reserves are especially appropriate in Mexico where conservation and economic development are equally important.

—from the bulletin of the
Amigos de Sian Ka'an

---

continued systematic destruction of the forest to create new growing fields, the entire rainforest along the Caribbean could be destroyed in just a few years.

The people need an alternative means to support their families. Many of the people are fishermen. Many more are being trained as guides and learning about the flora and fauna of their reserve, and they're learning English along the way.

Among other problems receiving attention is the plight of the palm tree. The palm is an important part of the cultural and practical lifestyle of the indigenous people of Quintana Roo. The Maya have for years used two particular types of palm, *Thrinax radiata* and *Coccothrinax readdi,* as thatch for the roofs of their houses, and in the past 10 years fishermen have been cutting *Thrinax* to construct lobster traps. This palm is growing increasingly rare in the reserve today. Amigos de Sian Ka'an, with the World Wildlife Fund, is studying the palms' growth patterns and rates, anticipating a management plan that will encourage future growth. Other projects on the table include limiting commercial fishing, relocating an entire fishing village to an area that will better support the families, halting tourist development where it would endanger the ecology, and studying the lobster industry and its future. A number of other worthwhile projects are waiting in line. Like most ambitious endeavors, these take a lot of money. If you're interested in helping out, join the booster club. Your donation will help a worthy cause, and you'll get a newsletter with fascinating facts about the area and its people as well as updates on current projects. For more detailed information write to: Amigos de Sian Ka'an, Apdo. Postal 770, Cancún, Quintana Roo 77500, Mexico.

Ecology Publications

For birders or any visitor intrigued with wildlife and interested in helping the ecological preservation of the Yucatán Peninsula, a fairly new book, *100 Common Birds of the Yucatán Peninsula* by Barbara MacKinnon, is available through the Amigos de Sian Ka'an.

HISTORY OF THE YUCATÁN PENINSULA

ANCIENTS

Earliest Humans

People and animals from Asia crossed the Bering land bridge into North America in the Pleistocene Epoch about 50,000 years ago, when sea levels were much lower. The epic human trek south continued until only 3,000 years ago, when anthropologists say people first reached Tierra del Fuego, at the tip of South America.

As early as 10,000 B.C., Ice Age humans hunted woolly mammoth and other large animals roaming the cool, moist landscape of Central Mexico. Between 7000 and 2000 B.C., society evolved from hunters and gatherers to farmers. After about 6000 B.C., corn, squash, and beans were independently cultivated in widely separated areas of Mexico. The remains of clay figurines from the preclassic period, presumed to be fertility symbols, marked the rise of religion in Mesoamerica, beginning around 2000 B.C.

Around 1000 B.C. the Olmec Indian culture, believed to be the region's earliest, began to spread throughout Mesoamerica. Large-scale ceremonial centers grew along Gulf coastlands, and much of Mesoamerica was influenced by these Indians' religion of worshiping jaguarlike gods. Also at this time, the New World's first calendar and a beginning system of writing were developed.

Classic Period

The classic period, beginning about A.D. 300, is now hailed by many as the peak of cultural development among the Maya Indians and other cultures throughout Mexico. Until A.D. 900, phenomenal progress was made in the development of artistic, architectural, and astronomical skills. Impressive buildings were constructed during this period, and codices (folded bark books) were written and filled with hieroglyphic symbols that detailed complicated mathematical calculations of days, months, and years. Only the priests and the privileged held this knowledge, and continued to learn and develop it until, for an unknown reason, the growth halted suddenly.

Postclassic

After A.D. 900, the Toltec influence took hold, marking the end of the most artistic era and the birth of a new militaristic society built around a blend of ceremonialism, civic and social organization, and conquest.

THE COLONIAL ERA

Hernán Cortés

Following Columbus's arrival in the New World, other adventurers traveling the same seas soon found the Yucatán Peninsula. In 1519, 34-year-old Hernán Cortés sailed from Cuba against the wishes of the Spanish governor. With 11 ships, 120 sailors, and 550 soldiers he set out to search for slaves, a lucrative business with or without the government's blessing. His search began on the Yucatán coast and would eventually encompass most of Mexico. However, he hadn't counted on the ferocious resistance and cunning of the Maya Indians. The fighting was destined to continue for many years—a time of

Hernán Cortés

bloodshed and death for many of his men. (This "war" didn't really end on the Peninsula until the Chan Santa Cruz Indians finally signed a peace treaty with the Mexican federal government in 1935, over 400 years later.) By the time Cortés died in 1547 (while exiled in Spain), the Spanish military and Franciscan friars were well entrenched in the Yucatán Peninsula.

Diego de Landa

The Franciscan priests were shocked by Mayan religious customs such as body mutilation and human sacrifice, which they believed to be influences of the devil. The Franciscans believed it their holy duty to eliminate the Maya religion and convert the Indians.

Diego de Landa arrived in Mexico in 1549 as a 25-year-old friar and was instrumental in the destruction of many thousands of Maya idols on the Yucatán Peninsula. He oversaw the burning of 27 codices filled with characters and symbols that he could not understand, but which he believed contained only superstitions and the devil's lies. Since then, only four codices have been found and studied, and only parts of them have been completely deciphered. While Landa was directly responsible for destroying the history of these ancient people, his reputation is partly redeemed by his writing the most complete and detailed account of Maya life in his book *Relaciones de las Cosas de Yucatán*. Landa's book describes daily living in great detail, including the growth and preparation of food, the structure of society, the priesthood, and the sciences. Although he was aware of the sophisticated "count of ages," he didn't understand it. Fortunately, he left a one-line formula which, used as a mathematical and chronological key by later researchers, opened up the science of Maya calculations and their great knowledge of astronomy. Without his book we would know very little about the prehispanic Maya.

Landa was called back to Spain in 1563 after colonial civil and religious leaders accused him of "despotic mismanagement." He spent a year in prison, and while his fate was being decided, he wrote the book as a defense against the charges. During his absence, his replacement, Bishop Toral, acted with great compassion toward the Indians. Landa was ultimately cleared and was allowed to return to the New World in 1573, where he became a bishop and resumed his previous methods of proselytizing. He lived in the Yucatán until his death in 1579.

Franciscan Power

Bishop Toral was cut from a different cloth. A humanitarian, he was appalled by the unjust treatment of Indians. Though Toral, after Landa's imprisonment, tried to impose sweeping changes, he was unable to make inroads into the power held by the Franciscans in the Yucatán. Defeated, he retired to Mexico. However, shortly before his death in 1571, his reforms were implemented with the "Royal Cedula," which prohibited friars from shaving the heads of Indians against their will, flogging them, or keeping prison cells in monasteries. It also called for the immediate release of all Indian prisoners.

Catholicism

Over the years, the majority of Indians were baptized into the Catholic faith. Most priests did their best to educate the people, teach them to read and write, and protect them from the growing number of Spanish settlers who used them as slaves. The Indians, then and now, practice Catholicism in their own manner, combining their ancient beliefs, handed down through centuries, with Christian doctrine. These mystic yet Christian ceremonies are performed in baptism, courtship, marriage, illness, farming, house building, and fiestas.

Further Subjugation

While all of Mexico dealt with the problems of economic colonialism, the Yucatán Peninsula had an additional one: harassment by vicious pirates who made life on the Gulf coast unstable. Around 1600, when silver production began to wane, Spain's economic power faltered. In the following years, haciendas (self-supporting estates or small feudal systems) began to thrive, overrunning communal villages jointly owned by the Maya. But later, between 1700 and 1810 as Mexico endured the backlash of several government upheavals in Europe, Spanish settlers on the Peninsula began exploiting the native Maya in earnest. The passive Indians were ground down, their lands taken away, and their numbers greatly reduced by the white man's epidemics and mistreatment.

Caste War

The Spaniards grabbed the Maya land and planted it with tobacco and sugarcane year after year until the soil had worn out. Added to the other abuses, it was inevitable that the Indians' rage would eventually explode in a furious attack. This bloody uprising in the 1840s was called the Caste War. Though the Maya were farmers, not soldiers, this savage war saw them taking revenge on every white man, woman, and child by means of rape and murder. European survivors made their way to the last Spanish strongholds of Mérida and Campeche. The governments of the two cities appealed for help to Spain, France, and the United States. No one answered the call, and it was soon apparent that the remaining two cities would be wiped out. But fate would not have it that way; just as the governor of Mérida was about to begin evacuating the city, the Maya picked up their primitive weapons and headed for their homes.

Attuned to the signals of the land, the Maya knew that the appearance of the flying ant was the first sign of rain and signaled the time to plant corn. When, on the brink of destroying the enemy, the winged ant made an unusually early appearance, the Indians turned their backs on certain victory and returned to their villages to plant corn.

This was just the breather the Spanish settlers needed. Help came from Cuba and Mexico City, as well as 1,000 U.S. mercenary troops. Vengeance was merciless. Most Maya were killed indiscriminately. Some were taken prisoner and sold to Cuba as slaves; others left their villages and hid in the jungles, in some cases for decades. Between 1846 and 1850, the population of the Yucatán Peninsula was reduced from 500,000 to 300,000. Quintana Roo along the Caribbean coast was considered a dangerous no-man's-land for almost another hundred years.

Growing Maya Power

Many Maya Indians escaped slaughter during the Caste War by fleeing to the isolated territory known today as Quintana Roo. The Maya revived the "talking cross," a pre-Cortesian oracle representing gods of the four cardinal directions. This was a religious/political marriage.

Three determined survivors of the Caste War— a priest, a master spy, and a ventriloquist—all wise leaders, knew their people's desperate need for divine leadership. As a result of the words from the "talking cross," shattered Indians came together in large numbers and began to organize. Studies indicate that the Maya knew full well that a human voice was responsible for the "talking," but they believed it was inspired by God. The community guarded the cross's location, and the advice it gave continued to strengthen the Maya.

They called themselves Chan Santa Cruz (meaning "People of the Holy Cross"). As their confidence developed, so did the growth and power of their communities. Living in dense forests very close to the border with British Honduras (now Belize), they found they had something their neighbors wanted: timber. The Chan Santa Cruz Maya began selling timber to the British and were given arms in return. These weapons gave the Maya even more power. From 1855 to 1857, internal strife weakened the relations between Campeche and Mérida. While the Spaniards were dealing with the problem on the Gulf coast, the Maya took advantage of the vulnerability of Fort Bacalar and in 1857 took it over, gaining control of the entire Caribbean coast from Cabo Catouche in the far north to the border of British Honduras in the south. In three years they destroyed all of the Spanish settlements while slaughtering or capturing thousands of whites.

The Indians of the coastal community of Chan Santa Cruz, also known as Cruzobs, for years had murdered their captives. But starting in 1858 they took lessons from the colonials and began to keep whites for slave labor in the fields and forest; women were put to work doing household chores and some became concubines. For the next 40 years, the Chan Santa Cruz Indians kept the east coast of the Yucatán for themselves; a shaky truce with the Mexican government endured. The Indians were financially independent (they didn't need money—they bartered for everything), self-governing, and, with no roads in, totally isolated from technological advancements beginning to take place in other parts of the Peninsula. They were not at war as long as everyone left them alone.

The Last Stand

Only when Pres. Porfirio Díaz took power in 1877 did the Mexican federal government begin to think seriously about the Yucatán Peninsula. Over the years, Quintana Roo's isolation and the strength of the Maya in their treacherous jungle had foiled repeated efforts by Mexican soldiers to capture the Indians. The army's expeditions were infrequent, but it rankled Díaz that a handful of Indians had been able to keep the Mexican federal army at bay for so long. Finally, an assault in 1901, under the command of Gral. Ignacio Bravo, broke the government's losing streak. The general captured a village, laid railroad tracks, and built a walled fort. Supplies arriving by rail kept the fort stocked, but the Indian army held the fort under siege for an entire year. When reinforcements arrived from the capital, the upstarts were finally put down. Thus began another cycle of brutal Mexican occupation until 1915. The scattered Indians didn't give up. They persisted with guerilla raids from the rainforest until the Mexicans, finally defeated once again, pulled out and returned Quintana Roo to the Maya.

Trivia note: In Quintana Roo, it is said the word *guerrilla* comes from the first Spaniard to marry a Maya, Guerrero.

Between 1917 and 1920, hundreds of thousands of Indians died from influenza and smallpox epidemics introduced by the Spanish. An Indian leader, General May, took stock of his troops and saw clearly that the old soldiers were fading. They had put up a long, tough battle to hold onto their land and culture. The year 1920 marked the end of their independent reign in Quintana Roo's jungle. Foreign gummakers initiated the chicle boom, bringing *chicleros* to work the trees. It was then that General May demanded (and received) a negotiated settlement. In 1935 the Chan Santa Cruz Indians signed a peace treaty with the Mexican Federales.

MODERN TIMES

Meanwhile, in the northern part of the Peninsula, international demand for the henequen plant brought prosperity to Mérida, capital of the state

---

RECENT MAYA HISTORY

1847: The beginning of the Caste War.

1849: The Caste War goes against the Maya and they retreat, getting lost in the thick jungles of Quintana Roo.

1850: The "Talking Cross" appears at the cenote and delivers commands for reviving the war against the whites.

1850–58: The Maya warriors have their ups and downs, but life goes on for the Indians as they manage to hold off their adversaries.

1858: The Maya capture the fortress of Bacalar (just outside of Chetumal) and begin building a ceremonial city complete with church, palaces, barracks, and schools. This is the beginning of their total independence from the rest of Mexico.

1863: The British at Belize recognize the Indian state and engage in arms trade with them.

1863–1893: The Maya lose great numbers of people due to epidemics and internal conflicts.

1893: Mexico and Britain wrangle a peace treaty; the Indians no longer have their important source of arms.

1901: Under General Ignacio Bravo, the Mexican federal army takes over the stronghold city of Chan Santa Cruz and renames it Felipe Carrillo Puerto.

1901–15: While the Mexicans occupy the Maya city with brutality, the Maya in the jungle continue to raid and harass the Mexicans, virtually isolating them from the rest of Mexico.

1915: The Mexicans give up and return Quintana Roo to the Maya.

1917–20: Influenza and smallpox epidemics decimate the Indians.

1920–29: Chicle boom. General May, the Indian leader, accepts a peace treaty with Mexico, distressing the more militant Indians.

1929: These militant traditional Maya disclaim May's "sell-out" and revive the cult of the "Talking Cross" at X-Cacal Guardia.

of Yucatán. Twine and rope made from the sword-shaped leaves of this variety of agave plant were in demand all over the world. Soon after the henequen boom began in 1875, Mérida had become the jewel of the Peninsula. Spanish haciendas staffed by Indian slaves cultivated the easily grown plant, and for miles the outlying areas were planted with the henequen, which required little rainfall and thrived in the Peninsula's thin, rocky soil. Beautiful mansions were built by entrepreneurs who led the gracious life, sending their children to school in Europe and cruising with their wives to New Orleans in search of new luxuries and entertainment. Port towns were developed on the Gulf coast, and a two-kilometer-long wharf named Progreso was built to accommodate the large ships that came for sisal (hemp from the henequen plant).

The only thing that didn't change was the lifestyle of the *peones.* The Indian peasants' life was still devoid of human rights. They labored long, hard hours, living in constant debt to the company store, where their meager peso wage was spent before it was received. The Indians were caught up in a cycle of bondage that endured for many years in Mérida. One story holds than it was during this time that the lovely *huipil* (Indian dress) was mandated to be worn by all Indians and mestizos (those of mixed blood) on the Peninsula. There would then be no problem distinguishing Indians from pure-blooded Spaniards.

Hacienda Wealth

The outside world was becoming aware of the Peninsula, its newly found economic activity, and its rich *patrones.* In 1908 an American journalist, John Kenneth Turner, stirred things up when he documented the difficult lives of the Indian plantation workers, and the accompanying opulence enjoyed by the owners. From this time forward, reform was inevitable. In 1915 wealthy hacienda owners were compelled to pay an enormous tax to President Venustiano Carranza. This tax was forcibly extracted under the watchful eye of General Alvarado and 7,000 armed soldiers, who needed the money to put down revolutionaries Emiliano Zapata and Pancho Villa in the northern regions of Mexico. Millions of pesos changed hands. But still none made it to the Maya.

The next thorn in the side of the Maya hacienda owners was upstart Felipe Carrillo Puerto, the first socialist governor of Mérida. Under his tutelage the Indians set up a labor union, educational center, and political club that amounted to leagues of resistance. These leagues gave the *peones* the first secular hope ever held out to them. Through them, workers wielded a power that wealthy Yucatecans were forced to acknowledge. Carrillo pushed on, making agrarian reforms at every turn. He decreed that abandoned haciendas were up for appropriation by the government. He was so successful that his opponents began to worry seriously about the

Hacienda Yaxcopoil dates back to the turn of the 20th century.

OZ MALLAN

power he was amassing. With the number of his followers growing, conservatives saw only one way to stop him. In 1923 Felipe Carrillo Puerto was assassinated.

The Revolution

The fight against wealthy landowners and the power elite did not die with Carrillo. In the south, Emiliano Zapata was demanding land reform; shortly thereafter, the revolution put an end to the elitist control of wealth in the country. The constitution of 1917 had made some inroads. It was instrumental in dividing up the large haciendas, giving the country back to the people (*some* of the people), and making sweeping political changes. The education of all children was mandated and many new schools were built. Power of the church was curtailed and church land redistributed.

In this war of ideals, however, Indian villages were broken up along with the large haciendas, and turmoil continued. Again it was the rich against the poor; a whole new class of rich had been created—those who had the new power. In 1936, President Lázaro Cárdenas declared Quintana Roo a territory of the Mexican government. It wasn't until later years that some of the Indians received favorable treatment, when Cárdenas gave half the usable land in Quintana Roo to the poor. In 1974, with the promise of tourism, the territory was admitted to the Federation of States of Mexico. It was only now that the history of Cancún would commence.

Mexican Unity

Between 1934 and 1940, the Mexican government nationalized most foreign companies, which were taking more out of the country than they were putting in. Mexico suffered through a series of economic setbacks but gained unity and national self-confidence. Like a child learning to walk, the country took many falls. But progress continued; the people of the country saw more jobs, fairer wages, and more products on the market. The progress lasted until the 1970s, when inflation began to rise. By 1976 it was totally out of hand. Mexico was pricing itself out of the market, both for tourists and capital investors. Eventually, a change in the monetary policy let the peso float, finding its own value against the dollar. The policy brought back tourists and investors.

The condition of the peso is a boon for visitors, but a burden for the people. The belief is that enough tourism will create more jobs so that the economic condition will ultimately remedy itself. Smart Mexican businesspeople began developing the natural beauty of the Caribbean coast, and indeed visitors are coming from all over the world.

GOVERNMENT AND ECONOMY

GOVERNMENT

Theoretically, Mexico enjoys a constitutional democracy modeled after that of the United States. A president, a two-house congress, and a judiciary branch see to the business of running the country. Theoretically, Mexico's elections are/were free. Realistically, for more than 70 years the country was controlled by one party, the PRI (Partido Revolución Institutional, or Institutional Revolution Party). Political dissent—represented primarily by PAN (Partido Acción Nacional, or National Action Party) and PMS (Partido Mexicano Socialista)—has never had much voice. The president, who serves only a single six-year term, hand-picked the next PRI candidate who was historically guaranteed the office through use of the state-controlled media and dubious election procedures. In 2000, Vicente Fox from the PAN party was elected and already the people are seeing changes. Fox is a successful businessman, but Mexico is used to "buying" power. It may take a while for the people to accept this free-market type government. It's obvious that the PRI has lost a lot of its power, and that many people are willing to oppose them. However, the representatives in the two houses of congress are still heavily PRI.

In addition to Mexico's 32 states, the country has the *Distrito Federal,* or Federal District in Mexico City, which encompasses the government center. The states are allowed a small measure of autonomy, but the reach of the federal government is long. City mayors, called *presidentes municipales,* appoint federal *delegatos* to represent the national government at the municipal level.

Fraud and corruption have been ugly mainstays of Mexican government from its beginning. In the 1988 presidential election, PRI candidate Carlos Salinas Gortari officially garnered 51 percent of the vote, a figure many critics believe was invented by the PRI after polls closed. (A suspicious "breakdown" in the election computer delayed the results for several days.) Kind of like U.S. elections in 2000!

But Salinas's term will likely be remembered as a time of historic reforms, such as expanding the number of Senate seats to allow more for the opposition, limiting campaign spending, and changing the rules of the body that oversees Mexican elections. But even Salinas ended up with blood on his hands, and did he know about the shady dealings involving his brother? He continues to live in exile.

The only certainty in Mexico's tumultuous political arena is that, after decades of a government static in its ways, things are changing fast. The U.S. Congress's passage of NAFTA in 1993 sealed a free-trade deal between Mexico, the United States, and Canada that will likely change Mexico's economic landscape forever—the political ramifications of which are still unclear. The March 1994 election-year shooting of PRI presidential candidate Luis Donaldo Colosio in Tijuana was Mexico's first major political assassination since 1928. Soon after, Colosio's campaign manager, technocrat Ernesto Zedillo, was nominated to fill the candidacy. Mexico's political future is anyone's guess. President Fox gained friends in Southern California when he agreed to furnish electricity during a ravaging shortage after California lifted government regulations.

ECONOMY

Mexico's chief industries are tourism, oil, and mining. Mexican oil is produced by Pemex, the national corporation, and most is shipped at OPEC prices to the United States (its number-one customer), Canada, Israel, France, and Japan. Rich in natural gas, the country sends the United States 10 percent of its total output. Two-thirds of Mexico's export revenue comes from fossil fuels.

The Yucatán

The leading industry on the Yucatán Peninsula is the oil business. Along the Gulf coast from Campeche south into the state of Tabasco, the oil industry is booming. Yucatán cities are beginning to show signs of good financial health due to tourism.

Yucatecan fisheries are abundant along the Gulf coast. At one time fishing was not much more than a ma-and-pa business here, but today fleets of large-purse seiners with their adjacent processing plants can be seen on the Gulf of Mexico just south of the city of Campeche and on Isla del Carmen. With the renewed interest in preserving fishing grounds for the future, the industry could continue to thrive for many years.

Tourism is developing into a top contributor to the economy. Going with a good thing, the government has set up a national trust to finance a program of developing beautiful areas of the country to attract visitors. Cancún is the most successful thus far. The Cancún international airport receives millions of passengers each year who come to vacation in Cancún and nearby Maya Riviera.

Cancún

Until the 1970s, Quintana Roo's economy amounted to very little. For a few years the chicle boom brought a flurry of activity up and down the state. At that time chicle, used to make chewing gum, was shipped from the harbor of Isla Cozumel. Native and hardwood trees have always been in demand; coconuts and fishing were the only other natural resources that added to the economy—but neither on a large scale. With the development of an offshore sandbar—Cancún—into a multimillion-dollar resort, tourism is now its number-one moneymaker. Cancún is one of Mexico's most modern and popular resorts. Construction is continuing south along the coast. Other naturally attractive sites south are home to modern hotels, while still more are earmarked for future development. Growth includes a marina, an 18-hole golf course, and talk of another international airport. With several small landing strips already built, new roads give access to previously unknown beaches and often-unseen Maya structures. Many more roads are needed to open the frontier of magnificent Quintana Roo.

Agriculture

The land in the northernmost part of the Yucatán was described by Diego de Landa, an early Spanish priest, as "a country with the least earth ever seen, since all of it is one living rock." Surprisingly, the thin layer of soil is enough to support agriculture. This monotonous landscape is dotted with a multitude of sword-shaped plants called henequen. At the turn of the century, Spanish settlers on the Peninsula made vast fortunes growing and selling henequen, which was used for rope-making. However, it was the Maya who showed the Spanish its many valuable uses, especially for building their houses. When traveling in the area surrounding Cancún, notice the *palapa* huts. Without nails or tools, houses are tied together with handmade henequen twine. Wherever *palapa*-style structures are built today by the Indians, the same nail-free method is used.

With careful nurturing of the soil, the early Indians managed to support a large population of people on the land. The northern tip of the Peninsula can be dry and arid. While rainfall is spotty and unreliable, the land is surprisingly fertile and each year produces corn and other vegetables on small farms. On the northwest edge where trade winds bring more rain, the land is slightly

greener. As you travel south, the desert gradually becomes green and you find yourself in a jungle plain fringed by the turquoise Caribbean and the Río Hondo. In southern Quintana Roo large farms of citrus fruits are seen along the coast.

Along this coast remnants of large coconut plantations, now broken up into small tracts and humble *ranchitos,* are being developed by farmers with modest government assistance. At one time it was commonplace to see copra lining the roadside, drying in the sun. The number of coconut trees afflicted with "yellowing disease" in the Yucatán has greatly decreased the output of copra in the state. The disease and several hurricanes combined to turn what was once a mixture of thick, lush coconut trees and rich, verdant jungle into what looked like a war zone, with dead limbs and topless trees. But only temporarily. Fortunately, the jungle rejuvenates quickly, and within a few years nature covered the dead with new growth. As for the coconut trees, new strains are being planted that are resistant to this dreadful disease.

Different parts of the Peninsula produce different crops. In most areas you'll find juicy oranges for sale everywhere; in the marketplace and at roadside stands, vendors often remove the green peel, leaving the sweet fruit ready to eat. The earliest chocolate drink was developed by the Indians in Mexico and presented to the Spanish. Today chocolate manufactured in Mexico is shipped all over the world. Bananas of

teacher and students

OZ MALLAN

many kinds, from finger-size to 15-inch red plantains, are grown in thick groves close to the Gulf coast. Tabasco bananas are recognized worldwide as among the finest.

Many of the crops now produced by American farmers were introduced by the Maya and Aztecs, including corn, sweet potatoes, tomatoes, peppers, squash, pumpkin, and avocados. Many other products favored by Americans are native to the Yucatán Peninsula: papaya, cotton, tobacco, rubber, and turkey.

PEOPLE

Today, an estimated 75–80 percent of the entire population of Mexico is mestizo (mixed blood, mostly Indian and Spanish), with 10–15 percent pure Indian. For comparison, as recently as 1870, pure-blooded Indians made up over 50 percent of the population. While no statistics are available, it's believed most of the country's pure Indians live on the Peninsula (and the state of Chiapas).

Language
The farther you go from a city, the less Spanish and more Mayan, or a dialect of Mayan, you'll hear. The government estimates that of the 10 million Mexican Indians in the country, about 25 percent speak only an Indian dialect. Of the original 125 native languages, 70 are still spoken, 20 of which are classified as Maya languages, including Tzeltal, Tzotzil, Chol, and Yucatec Mayan. Mexican education was made compulsory in 1917, though like most laws this one didn't reach the Yucatán Peninsula till quite recently. Despite efforts to integrate the Indian into Mexican society, many remain content with the status quo. Schools throughout the Peninsula use Spanish-language books, even though many children speak only a Mayan dialect. This is all changing. As more outsiders arrive and more development (especially roads) continues, the small and once-isolated villages are coming in contact with the modern world. In some of the smaller, more rural, schools, bilingual teachers are recruited to help children make the transition from Mayan to Spanish.

Higher Education
Though education is free, many rural parents need their children to help with work on the *ranchito*. That and the cost of books still prevent many Yucatecan children from getting a higher education. For years, Peninsula students wanting an education had to travel to the university at Mérida. Now, the number of students going on to college grows with each generation, and universities are slowly being built. College is available in Campeche and Tabasco, and another one has been built in Mérida.

Housing and Family
The major difference in today's rural housing is the growth of the *ranchito,* typically one hut on a family farm that raises corn, sometimes a few pigs and turkeys, and maybe even a few head of cattle. While far from posh, the Indians' homes have become slightly more comfortable than their ancestors', commonly furnished with a table and chairs, a lamp, and maybe a metal bathtub, but still, the Yucatán hammock sleeps the whole family.

Abundance of wood explains the difference in rural housing between the north and south ends of the Quintana Roo Caribbean coastline. In the north, where wood is less abundant, structures are commonly made with walls of stucco or slender saplings set close together. Small houses in the south are built mostly of milled board, with either thatch or tin roofs. Many huts have electric lighting and TV antennae and some even have refrigerators.

Until recently families usually had many children. A man validated his masculinity and gained respect by having a large family. The labor around the family plot was doled out to children as they came along.

The Maya
Maya men and women average 1.62 meters (five feet, six inches) and 1.5 meters (four feet, 11 inches) tall respectively. Generally muscular bodied, they have straight black hair, round heads, broad faces with pronounced cheekbones, aquiline noses, almond-shaped

dark eyes, and eyelids with the epicanthic or Mongolian fold.

Bishop Diego de Landa writes in his *Relaciones* that when the Spanish arrived, the Maya still practiced the ancient method of flattening a newborn's head with a wooden press. By pressing the infant's forehead, the fronto-nasal portion of the face was pushed forward, as can be seen in carvings and other human depictions from the pre-Cortesian period. The Maya considered this a beautiful trait. They also dangled a bead in front of babies' eyes to encourage cross-eyedness, another Maya beauty mark. Dental mutilation was practiced by filing the teeth to give them different shapes or by inlaying carvings with pyrite, jade, or turquoise. Tattooing and scarification were accomplished by lightly cutting a design into the skin and purposely infecting it, creating a scar of beauty. Adult noblemen often wore a phony nosepiece to give the illusion of an even longer nose sweeping back into the long, flat forehead.

ANCIENT CULTURE OF THE YUCATÁN PENINSULA

EARLY MAYA

The origins of the Maya world lie in the Pacific coastal plains of Chiapas and Guatemala. From here, Maya culture slowly moved north and west to encompass all of Guatemala, the Yucatán Peninsula, most of the states of Chiapas and Tabasco, and the western parts of Honduras and El Salvador. The earliest traces of human presence found in this area are obsidian spear points and stone tools dating back to 9000 B.C. The Loltún caves in the Yucatán contain a cache of extinct mammal bones, including mammoth and an early horse, which were probably dragged there by a roving band of hunters. As the region dried out and large game disappeared over the next millennia, tools of a more settled way of life appeared, like grinding stones for preparing seeds and plant fibers. The first sedentary villages began to appear after 2000 B.C. With them came the hallmarks of a more developed culture: primitive agriculture and ceramics.

Proto-Maya

Archaeologists believe that the earliest people we can call Maya, or proto-Maya, lived on the Pacific coast of Chiapas and Guatemala. These tribes lived in villages that may have held over 1,000 inhabitants and made beautiful painted and incised ceramic jars for food storage. After 1000 B.C. this way of life spread north to the highlands site of Kaminaljuyú (now part of Guatemala City) and, over the next millennium, to the rest of the Maya world. Meanwhile, in what are now the Mexican states of Veracruz and Tabasco to the northwest, another culture, the Olmecs, was developing what is now considered Mesoamerica's first civilization. Its influence was felt throughout Mexico and Central America. Archaeologists believe that before the Olmecs disappeared around 300 B.C. they contributed two crucial cultural advances to the Maya, the long-count calendar and the hieroglyphic writing system, though some researchers think the latter may have actually originated in the Zapotec culture of Oaxaca.

Izapa and Petén

During the late preclassic era (after 300 B.C.), that same Pacific coastal plain saw the rise of a Maya culture at a place called Izapa near Tapachula, Chiapas. The Izapans worshiped gods that are obviously precursors of the classic Maya pantheon and commemorated religious and historical events in bas-relief carvings that emphasized costume and finery. All that was missing were long-count dates and hieroglyphs. Those appeared as the Izapan style spread north into the Guatemalan highlands. This was the heyday of Kaminaljuyú, which grew to enormous size, with over 120 temple-mounds and numerous stelae. The earliest calendar inscription that researchers are able to read comes from a monument found at El Baúl to the southwest of Kaminaljuyú; it has been translated as A.D. 36. The Izapan style's northernmost reach was Yucatán's Loltún caves, where an Izapan warrior-relief is carved out of the rock at the cave entrance.

In the Petén jungle region just north of the highlands, the dominant culture was the Chicanel, whose hallmarks are elaborate temple-pyramids lined with enormous stucco god-masks (as in Kohunlich). The recently excavated Petén sites of Nakbé and El Mirador are the most spectacular Chicanel cities yet found. El Mirador contains a 70-meter-tall temple-pyramid complex that may be the most massive structure in Mesoamerica. Despite the obvious prosperity of this region, there is almost no evidence of long-count dates or writing systems in either the Petén jungle or the Yucatán Peninsula just to the north.

The great efflorescence of the southern Maya world stops at the end of the late preclassic (A.D. 250). Kaminaljuyú and other cities were abandoned, and researchers believe that the area was invaded by Teotihuacano warriors extending the reach of their Valley of Mexico–based empire. On the Yucatán Peninsula, there is evidence of Teotihuacano occupation at the Río Bec site of Becán and at Acanceh near Mérida. You can see Teotihuacano-style costumes and gods in carvings at the great Petén city of Tikal and at Copán in Honduras. By A.D. 600, the Teotihuacano empire had collapsed, and the stage was set for the classic Maya era.

CLASSIC AND POSTCLASSIC MAYA

Maya Heartland

The heartland of the classic Maya (A.D. 600–800) runs from Copán in Western Honduras through the Petén region to Tikal, and ends at Palenque in Chiapas. The development of these city-states, which also included Yaxchilán and Bonampak, almost always followed the same pattern. Early in this era, a new and vigorous breed of rulers founded across the region a series of dynasties bent on deifying themselves and their ancestors. All the arts and sciences of the Maya world, from architecture to astronomy, were focused on this goal. The long-count calendar and the hieroglyphic writing system were the most crucial tools in this effort, as the rulers needed to re-count the stories of their dynasty and of their own glorious careers. During the classic era, painting, sculpture, and carving reached their climax; objects like Lord Pacal's sarcophagus lid from Palenque are now recognized as among the finest pieces of world art.

Royal monuments stood at the center of large and bustling cities. Cobá and Dzibilchaltún each probably hosted 50,000 inhabitants, and there was vigorous intercity trade. In the northern area, the largest classic-era cities, including the Río Bec sites and Cobá, are more obscure to travelers due to their relatively poor state of preservation. Each classic city-state reached its apogee at a different time—the southern cities generally peaked first—but by A.D. 800 nearly all of them had collapsed and were left in a state of near-abandonment.

The classic Maya decline is one of the great enigmas of Mesoamerican archaeology. There are a myriad of theories—disease, invasion, etc.—but many researchers now believe the collapse was caused by starvation brought on by overpopulation and destruction of the environment. With the abandonment of the cities, the classic Maya's cultural advances disappeared as well. The last long-count date was recorded in 909, and many religious customs and beliefs were never seen again.

Northern Yucatán

However, Maya culture was far from dead; the new heartland was the northern end of the Yucatán Peninsula. Much archaeological work remains to be done in this area, and there are a number of controversies now raging as to who settled it where and when. For a brief period between A.D. 800 and 925, it was the Puuc region's turn to prosper. The art of architecture reached its climax in city-states like Uxmal, where the Nun-

HISTORICAL PERIOD CLASSIFICATIONS

PERIOD	BEGINNING DATE
ARCHAIC	2000 B.C.
EARLY PRECLASSIC	800 B.C.
MIDDLE PRECLASSIC	300 B.C.
LATE PRECLASSIC	A.D. 250
EARLY CLASSIC	A.D. 600
LATE CLASSIC	A.D. 900
EARLY POSTCLASSIC	A.D. 1200
LATE POSTCLASSIC	A.D. 1530

nery Quadrangle and the Governor's Palace are considered among the finest Maya buildings. After the Puuc region was abandoned, almost certainly due to a foreign invasion, the center of Maya power moved east to Chichén Itzá. The debate rages as to who built (or rebuilt) Chichén, but the possibilities have narrowed to two tribes: Putún Maya warrior-traders or Toltecs escaping political strife in their Central Mexican homeland. Everyone agrees that there is Mexican influence at Chichén; the question is, was it carried by the Putún or by an invading Toltec army?

During the early postclassic era (A.D. 925–1200), Chichén was the great power of northern Yucatán. Competing city-states either bowed before its warriors or, like the Puuc cities and Cobá, were destroyed. After Chichén's fall in 1224—probably due to an invasion—a heretofore lowly tribe calling themselves the Itzá became the late postclassic (1200–1530) masters of Yucatecan power politics. The Itzá's ruling Cocom lineage was finally toppled in the mid-15th century.

Northern Yucatán dissolved into an unruly group of jealous city-states ready to go to war with each other at a moment's notice. By the time of the Spanish conquest, culture was once again being imported from outside the Maya world. Putún Maya seafaring traders brought new styles of art and religious beliefs back from their trips to Central Mexico. Their influence may be seen in the Mixtec-style frescoes at Tulum on the Quintana Roo coast.

Mayapán

Kukulcán II of Chichén Itzá founded Mayapán between A.D. 1263 and 1283. After his death and the abandonment of Chichén, an aggressive Itzá lineage named the Cocom seized power and used Mayapán as a base to subjugate northern Yucatán. They succeeded through wars using Tabascan mercenaries and intermarrying with other powerful lineages. Foreign lineage heads were forced to live in Mayapán, where they could easily be controlled. At its height, the city covered 6.5 square kilometers within a defensive wall that contained over 15,000 inhabitants. Architecturally, Mayapán leaves much to be desired; the city plan was haphazard, and its greatest monument was a sloppy, smaller copy of Chichén's Pyramid of Kukulcán.

The Cocom ruled for 250 years until A.D. 1441–1461, when an upstart Uxmal-based lineage named the Xiu rebelled and slaughtered the Cocom. Mayapán was abandoned and Yucatán's city-states weakened themselves in a series of bloody intramural wars that left them hopelessly divided when it came time to face the conquistadors.

RELIGION AND SOCIETY

The Earth

The Maya saw the world as a flat layered square. At the four corners (each representing a cardinal direction) stood four bearded gods called Becabs who held up the skies. In the underworld, four gods called Pahuatuns steadied the earth. The layered skies and underworld were divided by a determined number of steps up and down. Each god and direction was associated with a color: black for west, white for north, yellow for south, and, most important, red for east. In the center of the earth stood the Tree of Life, "La Ceiba." Its powerful roots reached the underworld, and its lofty foliage swept the heavens, connecting the two. The ceiba tree was associated with the color blue-green *(yax)* along with all important things—water, jade, and new corn.

The Indians were terrified of the underworld and what it represented: odious rivers of rotting flesh and blood and evil gods such as Jaguar, god of the night, whose spotty hide was symbolized by the starry sky. Only the priests could communicate with and control the gods. For this reason, the populace was content to pay tribute to and care for all the needs of the priests.

Ceremonies

Ceremony appears to have been a vital part of the daily lives of the Maya. Important rituals took place on specific dates of their accurate calendar; everyone took part. These activities were performed in the plazas, on the platforms, and around the broad grounds of the temple-cities. Sweat baths apparently were incorporated into the religion. Some rituals were secret and only priests took part within the inner sanctums of the temple. Other ceremonies included fasts, periods of abstinence, purification, dancing, prayers, and simple sacrifices of food, animals, or possessions (jewelry, beads, and ceramics) amid clouds of smoky incense.

The later Maya took part in self-mutilation. Carvings found at several sites depict an Indian pulling a string of thorns through a hole in his tongue or penis. The most brutal ceremonies involved human sacrifice. Sacrificial victims were thrown into a sacred well; if they didn't drown within a certain length of time (often overnight), they were rescued and then expected to relate the conversation of the spirits who lived in the bottom of the well. Other methods of sacrifice were spearing, beheading, or removing the heart of the victim with a knife and offering it, still beating, to the spirits.

Although old myths and stories say young female virgins were most often sacrificed in the sacred cenotes, anthropological dredging and diving in the muddy water in various Peninsula ruins has turned up evidence suggesting most of the victims were young children, both male and female.

Time

The priests of the classic period represented time as a parade of gods who were really numbers moving through Maya eternity in careful mathematical order. They were shown carrying heavy loads with tumplines around their heads. The combination of the gods and their burdens reflected the exact number of days gone by since the beginning of the Maya calendar count. Each god has particular characteristics; number nine, an attractive young man with the spots of a serpent on his chin, sits leaning forward, jade necklace dangling on one knee, right hand reaching up to adjust his tumpline. His load is the screech owl of the *baktun* (the 144,000-day period). Together, the two represent nine times 144,000, or 1,296,000 days—the number of days elapsed since the beginning of the Maya day count and the day the glyph was carved, maybe 1,275 years ago. Archaeologists call this a long-count date. Simpler methods also were used, including combinations of dots and bars (ones and fives, respectively, with special signs for zero). Most Mayanists agree that the date of the beginning of the long count was August 10, 3114 B.C.

Maya computation of time

Status

If the Maya's sophisticated calendar sounds complicated, so will the complex, stratified society that made up the Maya civilization. Their society of many classes was headed by the elite, who controlled matters of warfare, religion, government, and commerce. Also in this group were architects who designed the magnificent temples and pyramids. Skilled masons belonged to a class that included servants of royalty. Priests directed the people in the many rites and festivals demanded by a pantheon of gods.

Farmers were instrumental in maintaining the social order. They battled a hostile environment, constantly fighting the jungle and frequent droughts. Creativity enabled them to win out most of the time. They slashed fields from rainforest, constructed raised plots in swampy depressions, and built irrigation canals. In some areas farmers terraced the land to conserve soil and water. The results of working by hand and using stone and wood tools were sufficient to feed a growing population. All aspects of Maya life were permeated by the society's religion.

Housing

Thanks to remaining stone carvings, we know that the ancient Maya lived in houses almost identical to the *palapa* huts that many Yucatán residents still live in today. These huts were built with tall, thin sapling trees placed close together to form the walls, then topped with a *palapa* roof. This type of house provided air circulation through the walls, and the thick *palapa* roof allowed the rain to run off easily, keeping the inside snug and dry. In the early years there were no real doors, and furnishings were sparse. Then, as now, families slept in hammocks, the coolest way to sleep. For the rare times when it turned cold, tiny fires were built on the floor below the hammocks to keep the family warm. Most of the cooking was done either outdoors or in another hut. Often a small group of people—extended family—built their huts together on one plot and lived an almost communal lifestyle. If one member of the group brought home a deer, everyone shared in this trophy. Though changing, this is still commonplace throughout the rural areas of the Peninsula.

Maya "Basketball"

Ball courts were prevalent in the ceremonial centers located throughout the Yucatán Peninsula. Though today's Maya are peaceful, at one time bloody games were part of the ancient culture, as may be seen from the remaining artwork (for example the panel in Chichén Itzá's Temple of the Bearded Man). The carvings graphically show that the losing (or as a few far-out researchers have suggested, the winning) team was awarded a bloody death. The players were heavily padded with cotton padding stuffed with salt, and the object of the game was to hit a hard rubber ball into a cement ring attached to a wall eight meters off the ground. Legend says the game went on for hours and the winners (or losers) were awarded clothes and jewelry from the spectators.

THE ARTS

Pottery

The Maya were outstanding potters. Some of the earliest Maya pottery, found at Izapan, dates to 36 B.C. Evidence of artistic advancement is apparent in the variety of new forms, techniques, and artistic motifs that developed during the classic period. Growth has been traced from simple monochrome ceramics of early periods to bichrome and later to rich polychrome. Polychrome drawings on pottery work have been found with recognizable color still visible. Three-legged plates with a basal edge and small conical supports, as well as covered and uncovered vessels, were prevalent. A jar with a screw-on lid was found recently in Río Azul, a Maya site in an isolated corner of Guatemala.

Figurines, especially those found in graves on the island of Jaina, were faithful reproductions of the people and their times. Many decorated pottery vessels used for everyday purposes tell us something about these people who enjoyed beauty even in mundane objects. Decorative motifs ranged from simple geometric designs to highly stylized natural figures to simple true-to-life reproductions. We have learned much from Maya artists' realistic representations of body alterations, garments, and adornments typical of their time. All social classes are represented: common men and women, nobility, priests, musicians, craftspeople, merchants, warriors, ball players, even animals. Many of these clay figurines were used as flutes, whistles, ocarinas, rattles, or incense holders. Noteworthy is the quantity of female figurines that represent the fertility goddess Ix Chel.

Sculpture

The Maya used their great talent for sculpture almost exclusively to decorate temples and sanctuaries. They employed a number of techniques, which varied depending on the area and the natural resources available. They excelled in freestanding stone carving, such as the stelae and altars. In areas such as Palenque, where stone wasn't as available, stucco art is outstanding. The Indians added rubber to the plaster-and-water mixture, creating an extremely durable surface that would polish to a fine luster. In Palenque you'll see marvelous examples of stucco bas-reliefs adorning pyramids, pillars, stairways, walls, friezes, masks, and heads. Sculpting was done not only in stone but also in pre-

cious materials such as gold and silver. Some of the Maya's finest work was done in jade, a substance they held in great reverence.

Painting

Paints were of mineral and vegetable origin in hues of red, yellow, brown, blue, green, black, and white. Mural painting was highly refined by the Maya. Murals found in several ancient sites depict everyday life, ceremonies, and battle scenes in brilliant colors. Bright color was also applied to the walls of carved stone structures, pyramids, and stelae. Today all color has disappeared from the outside of these buildings along with most of the finishing plaster that was used as a smooth coating over large building stones. When Cortés's men first viewed the coast of Tulum, it must have been quite a sight to behold: brilliantly colored buildings in the midst of lush green jungle overlooking a clear turquoise sea.

SCIENCE

Maya inscriptions relate to calculations of time, mathematics, and the gods. Astronomy was also a highly developed science. The Maya shared their calendar system and concept of zero with other Mesoamerican groups, but they went on to perfect and develop their sophisticated calendar, more exact to a ten-thousandth of a day than the Gregorian calendar in use today.

Hieroglyphics

The hieroglyphics the Maya used in scientific calculations and descriptions are seen everywhere on the Yucatán Peninsula—in carved temple panels, on pyramid steps, and in stelae commonly installed in front of the great structures, carrying pertinent data about the buildings and people of that era. The most important examples of the system are the three codices that survived the coming of the conquistadors. In the codices, symbols were put carefully on pounded fig bark with brushes and various dyes developed from plants and trees. As with all fine Maya art, it was the upper class and priests who learned, developed, and became highly skilled in hieroglyphics. Science and artwork ceased suddenly with the end of the classic period, around

OZ MALLAN

serpent head from Chichén Itzá

A.D. 900. Theories over the years have ranged from outer space intervention, to famine, to outside conquerors, to the one that many scientists are studying: overpopulation. The Yucatán's population had grown so much, and the countryside was becoming so urbanized that there was not enough land to grow food and to continue to support and care for the nobles and priests of their society, as well as themselves. Too much cement and not enough green space. Does that sound familiar?

EARLY AGRICULTURE

Enriching the Soil

Scientists believe Maya priests studied celestial movements. A prime function performed in the elaborate temples, which were built to strict astronomical guidelines, may have been charting the changing seasons and deciding when to begin the planting cycle. Farmers used the slash-and-burn method of agriculture, and still do today. Before the rains began in the spring, Indians cut the trees on a section of land, leaving stumps about half a meter above ground. Downed trees were spread evenly across the landscape in order to burn uniformly; residual ash was left to nourish the soil. At the proper time, holes were made with a pointed stick, and precious maize kernels were dropped into the earth, one by one. At each corner (the cardinal points) of the cornfield, offerings of *pozole* (maize stew) were left to encourage the gods to give forth great rains. With abundant moisture, crops were bountiful and rich enough to provide food even into the following year.

The Maya knew the value of allowing the land to lay fallow after two seasons of growth, and each family's *milpa* (cornfield) was moved from place to place around the villages scattered through the jungle. Often, squash and tomatoes were planted in the shade of towering corn stalks to make double use of the land. Today, you see windmills across the countryside (many stamped "Chicago, Inc."); with the coming of electricity to the outlying areas, pumps are being used to bring water from underground rivers and lakes to irrigate crops. Outside of irrigation methods, the Maya follow the same ancient pattern of farming their ancestors did.

Maize

Corn was the heart of Maya nutrition, eaten at each meal. From it the Indians made tortillas, stew, and beverages—some of them alcoholic.

CORN: A MAYA MAINSTAY

Corn was much more than food to the ancient Maya. The crop was apparently intertwined in Maya legend with the notion of the beginning of life. It's depicted in many of the remaining ancient Maya carvings and drawings; a fresco at the ruins of Tulum, for example, shows human feet as corn.

The crop was so significant to the Maya that everything else would stop when the signs implied it was time to plant the fields. In ancient times, it was Maya priests who calculated—by means of astronomical observation—the perfect time to fire the fields before the rains. While some Maya farmers still refer to the calendar keeper of their village for the proper planting date, today most base their planting date on observation of natural phenomena, such as the swarming of flying ants or the rhythm and frequency of croaking frogs—a Maya version of a Farmer's Almanac.

Corn is not the critical staple it was before the days of stores and supermarkets, but many poor villages still rely for their survival on what the people raise in their small *milpas,* or cornfields. The *milpas* are planted in a centuries-old method. The process begins with a plea to the Chacs—the Maya rain gods. Performed at the end of each April, the ceremony arouses the Chacs from their seasonal sleep. Bowls of corn porridge are left at the four corners of a family's *milpa* for the age-old deities, who are still treated with great respect. To anger the Chacs could bring a drought, and without the yearly rains the corn crop fails. With the Chacs satisfied, the farmers then cut trees and grasses and leave them in the field to dry before setting them aflame. The fire is allowed to burn until all is reduced to ash. A stick is used to poke holes in the ash-covered earth, and seeds are then dropped into the holes one by one.

Corn cultivation was such a vital part of Maya life that it is represented in drawings and carvings along with other social and religious symbols. In their combination of beans and corn, the Maya enjoyed all the protein they needed. They did not raise livestock until Spanish times.

Corn tortillas are still a main staple of the Mexican people. Native women in small towns can be seen early in the morning carrying bowls of corn kernels on their heads to the grinding mill where the corn becomes tortilla dough. This was done by hand for centuries, and still is in some isolated villages, but in most there is a mill. With the advent of electricity on the Peninsula, it's become much quicker to pay a peso or two to grind dough automatically. Others pay a few more pesos (price is controlled by the government) and buy their tortillas by the kilo hot off the griddle. In many upscale restaurants in Cancún and other Caribbean resorts, you will find only flour tortillas. When I asked why it was changing I was told that the flour tortillas are easy to obtain, are cheaper because they are made completely with machines from already processed flour, have a longer shelf life, and are easier to transport. Eat your local corn tortillas so they won't disappear!

ENTER THE SPANIARDS

When the conquistadors arrived in 1517, the Maya of northern Yucatán were too divided to put up a successful long-term resistance. Nevertheless, they fought fiercely, and Francisco de Montejo was not able to establish his capital, Mérida, until 1542. Sporadic revolts by Yucatecan Maya have continued over the centuries, with the last ending only in the early 1900s. In the late 19th century, the Chiapan Maya fought several pitched battles with the Mexican army. The Guatemalan Maya city-states were conquered by the brutal Pedro de Alvarado, ending almost all resistance by 1541. However, one tribe managed to evade the conquistadors and settled deep in the jungle on an island in the middle of Lake Petén. Their traditional Maya city-state, called Tayasol, thrived until 1697, when a Spanish army finally penetrated that remote zone.

KATHY ESCOVEDO SANDERS

ON THE ROAD
RECREATION AND ENTERTAINMENT

SNORKELING AND SCUBA DIVING

Not everyone who travels to Quintana Roo is a diver or even a snorkeler—at first. One peek through the "looking glass"—a diving mask—changes everything. The Caribbean is one of the most notoriously seductive bodies of water in the world. Turquoise blue and crystal clear with perfect tepid temperature, the coastal waters, protected by offshore reefs, are ideal for a languid float during hot, humid days.

Snorkeling

You'll find that the sea is where you'll want to spend a good part of your trip. So even if you never considered underwater sports in the past, you'll probably be eager to learn. First-timers should have little trouble learning to snorkel. Once you master breathing through a tube, it's simply a matter of relaxing and floating. Time disappears once you are introduced to a world of fish in rainbow colors of garish yellow, electric blue, crimson, and a hundred shades of purple.

The longer you look, the more you'll discover: underwater caverns, tall pillars of coral, giant tubular sponges, shy fish hiding on the sandy bottom, and delicate wisps of fine grass.

Scuba Diving

For the diver, there's even more adventure. Reefs, caves, and the rugged coastline harbor the unknown. Ships wrecked hundreds of years ago hide undiscovered secrets. Swimming among the curious and brazen fish puts you into another world. This is raw excitement!

Expect to see an astounding array of corals. Even close to shore, these amazing little animals create exotic displays of shape and form, dense or delicate depending on species, depth, light, and current. Most need light to survive; in deeper, low-light areas, some species of coral take the form of a large plate, thereby performing the duties of a solar collector. The sponge, another curious underwater creature, comes in all sizes, shapes, and colors, from common brown to vivid red.

Choosing a Dive Company

Diving lessons are offered at nearly all the dive shops in the state. Before you make a commitment, ask about the instructor and check his accident record, then talk to the harbormaster or, if you're in a small village, ask at the local cantina. Most of these divers (many are American) are conscientious, but a few are not, and the locals know whom to trust.

Bringing your own equipment to Mexico might save you a little money, depending on the length of your trip and means of transportation. But if you plan on staying just a couple of weeks and want to join a group on board a dive boat by the day, it's generally not much more to rent, which will save you the hassle.

Choose your boat carefully. Look it over first. Nowadays most of the dive shops offer first-class boats and equipment. Ask the usual questions; most of the divemasters speak English. Does it have a platform for getting in and out of the water? How many tanks of air may be used per trip? How many dives? Exactly where are you going? How fast does the boat go and how long will it take to get there?

Detailed information is available for divers and snorkelers who wish to know about the dive sites they plan to visit. Online you'll find all kinds of information on dive shops, reefs, depths, and especially currents. Wherever diving is good, you'll almost always find a dive shop. There are a few high-adventure dives where diving with an experienced guide is recommended.

Underwater Hazards and First Aid

A word here about some of the less inviting members of marine society. Anemones and sea urchins are everywhere. Some can be dangerous if touched or stepped on. The long-spined, black sea urchin can inflict great pain and its poison can cause an uncomfortable infection. Don't think that you're safe in a wetsuit, booties, and gloves. The spines easily slip through the rubber. In certain areas, such as around the island of Cozumel, the urchin is encountered at all depths and is very abundant close to shore where you'll probably be wading in and out; keep your eyes open. If diving at night, use your flashlight. If you should run into one of the spines, remove it quickly and carefully, disinfect the wound, and apply antibiotic cream. If you have

snorkeling in Xelha Lagoon

difficulty removing the spine, or if it breaks, see a doctor—pronto!

Cuts from coral, even if just a scratch, will often cause an infection. Antibiotic cream or powder will usually take care of it. If you get a deep cut, or if minute bits of coral are left in the wound, a serious and long-lasting infection can ensue. See a doctor.

Wise divers watch out for the color red, as many submarine hazards bear that hue. If you scrape against red coral, or "fire coral," you'll feel a burning sensation that lasts anywhere from a few minutes to five days. On some, it causes an allergic reaction and will raise large red welts. Cortisone cream will reduce inflammation and discomfort.

Fire worms (also known as bristle worms), if touched, will deposit tiny, cactuslike bristles in the skin. They can cause the same reaction as fire coral. *Carefully* scraping the skin with the edge of a sharp knife (as you would to remove a bee stinger) might remove the bristles. Any leftover bristles will ultimately work their way out, but will

EMERGENCY ASSISTANCE FOR DIVERS

C heck with your divemaster about emergency procedures before your boat goes out to sea. Also check with your medical insurance company; generally they will pay for emergency decompression and air-evacuation services.

Cozumel Decompression Chamber: tel. 987/2-2387

Divers Alert Network (DAN): tel. 919/684-8111 or 684-4326 (24 hours); non-emergency, 919/684-2949; members call 800/446-2671

Life Flight: tel. 800/392-4357 from Mexico; 713/704-3590 in Houston, TX; 800/231-4357 elsewhere in the United States.

be very uncomfortable in the meantime. Cortisone cream helps relieve this inflammation, too.

Several species of sponges have fine, sharp spicules (hard, minute, pointed calcareous or siliceous bodies that support the tissue) that you should not touch with a bare hand. The attractive red fire sponge can cause great pain; a mild solution of vinegar or ammonia (or urine if there's nothing else) will help. The burning lasts a couple of days, and cortisone cream soothes. But don't be fooled by dull-colored sponges. Many have the same sharp spicules, and touching them with a bare hand is risky at best.

Some divers feel the need to touch the fish they swim with. A few beginners want an underwater picture taken of them feeding the fish— bad news! When you offer fish a tasty morsel from your hand, you could start an underwater riot. Fish are always hungry and always ready for a free meal. Some of those denizens of the deep may not be so big, but in the frenzy to be first in line, their very efficient teeth have been known to miss the target. Another way to save your hands from unexpected danger is to keep them out of cracks and crevices, where moray eels live. A moray will usually leave you alone if you do likewise, but their many needle-sharp teeth can cause a painful wound that's apt to get infected.

A few seagoing critters resent being stepped on, and they can retaliate. The scorpion fish, hardly recognizable with its natural camouflage, lies hidden most of the time on a reef shelf or the bottom of the sea. If you should step on or touch it you can expect a painful, dangerous sting. If this happens, see a doctor immediately.

Another sinister fellow is the ray. There are several varieties in the Caribbean, including the yellow and southern stingrays. If you leave them alone they're generally peaceful, but if you step on them they will zap you with a tail that carries a poisonous sting, which can lead to anaphylactic shock in some people. Symptoms include respiratory difficulties, fainting, and severe itching. Go quickly to the doctor and tell him what caused the sting. Jellyfish can inflict a miserable sting. In particular try to avoid the long streamers of the Portuguese man-of-war, but know that some of the smaller jellyfish are just as hazardous.

Whatever you do, don't let these what-ifs discourage you from an underwater adventure. Thousands of people dive in the Caribbean every day of the year and only a small number of accidents occur.

Note: Please don't touch the coral; doing so is a death sentence to the polyps!

OTHER OUTDOOR ACTIVITIES

Water-skiing, Parasailing, Windsurfing

With so many fine beaches, bays, and coves along the Caribbean, all water sports are available. Because so many beaches are protected by the reef that runs parallel to Quintana Roo's east coast, calm **swimming beaches** are easy to find. Also, many hotels have pools. Water-skiing is not that common, but it is available if you search. Parasailing is popular and windsurfing lessons and rental boards are available at most resort areas, including Cozumel, Cancún, and up and down the Riviera Maya.

Fishing

A fishing license is required for all anglers 16 years or older. Good for three days, one month, or a year, licenses are available for a small fee at most fresh- and saltwater fishing areas. Ask in the small cafés at the more isolated beaches. Check with the closest Mexican consulate about where you can get a permit for your sportfishing craft; you can also get current information there on fishing seasons and regulations which vary from area to area. Fishing gear may be brought into Mexico without customs tax; however, the customs officials at the border crossing from Brownsville, Texas, into Mexico are notorious for expecting to have their palms greased before allowing the RVer or boater to cross the border. If you find yourself in this position, start with dollar bills (bring lots of them with you); several people need to be soothed before you can cross. If you choose not to pay the bribe, they can keep you hanging around for hours, even days, before they will allow you to cross. Sadly, it's a no-win situation. For more fishing information write to: General de Pesca, Av. Alvaro Obregón 269, Mexico 7, D.F.

Spearfishing is allowed in some areas along the coast, but not on the reef. The spear must be totally unmechanized and used freehand or with a rubber band only (no spear guns). If you plan on spearfishing, a Mexican fishing license is required. You can obtain one from sportfishing operations and bait and tackle shops in Cancún and Cozumel. If you're visiting a remote fishing lodge, ask if they supply licenses. For further information write to Oficina de Pesca, 2550 Fifth Ave., Suite 101, San Diego, CA 92103-6622; tel. 619/233-6956.

Bird-watching and Flora Fancying

Bird-watching is wonderful throughout the Yucatán. From north to south the variety of birds is broad and changes with the geography and the weather. Bring binoculars and wear boots and lightweight trousers if you plan on watching in jungle areas.

Studying tropical flora is also a popular activity. For this you most certainly will be in the backcountry—don't forget bug repellent, and be prepared for an occasional rain shower, even in the dry season. For most orchids and bromeliads, look up in the trees, but remember, the jungle also has ground orchids. And please, don't take anything away with you except pictures.

Photography

There's a world of beauty to photograph here, what with the sea, the people, and the natural landscape of the Peninsula. If you plan on **videotaping,** check with your local Mexican tourist office for information on what you can bring into the country. Most archaeological zones prohibit tripods. For the photographer who wants to film *everything,* small planes are available for charter in the larger cities and resorts. In Cancún, for instance, you can take pictures from a plane that tours for about 15 minutes over Cancún and the surrounding coast. Per-person price is US$45–55. (For further information see "Photography" under "Services and Information".)

Golf and Tennis

Golf courses are sprouting up all along the coast. You can play in Cancún, Riviera Maya, and Puerto Aventuras, and a new course is going in on Isla Cozumel. Tennis courts are scattered about Quintana Roo; the large hotels at Cancún, Akumal, Cozumel, and Puerto Aventuras have them. Bring your own racket.

FIESTAS

Mexico knows how to throw a party! Everyone who visits Quintana Roo should take advantage of any holidays falling during their stay. Workers are given a day off on legal holidays. See the special topic "Holidays and Fiestas" for dates of the biggest fiestas.

As well as the public festivities listed, a birthday, baptism, saint's day, wedding, departure, return, good crop, and many more reasons than we'd ever think of are good excuses to celebrate with a fiesta. One of the simplest but most charming celebrations is Mother's Day in Playa del Carmen, Mérida, and many other colonial cities. Children both young and old serenade mothers (often with a live band) with beautiful music outside their windows on the evening of the holiday. This is getting harder to see in the busy tourist towns. But if you're invited to a fiesta, join in and have fun.

Village Festivities

Half the fun of any fiesta is watching preparations, which generally take all day and involve everyone. Fireworks displays are set up by *especialistas* who wrap and tie bamboo poles together with packets of paper-wrapped explosives. At some point this often-tall *castillo* (structure holding the fireworks) will be tilted up and set

HOLIDAYS AND FIESTAS

Jan. 1: **New Year's Day.** Legal holiday.

Jan. 6: **Día de los Reyes Magos.** Day of the Three Kings. On this day Christmas gifts are exchanged.

Feb. 2: **Candelaria.** Candlemas. Many villages celebrate with candlelight processions.

Feb. 5: **Flag Day.** Legal holiday.

Feb./March: **Carnaval.** The week before Ash Wednesday, the beginning of Lent. Some of the best-planned festivals of the year are held this week. In Mérida, Isla Mujeres, Cozumel, Campeche: Easter parades with colorful floats, costume balls, and sporting events. Chetumal: a parade with floats, music, and folk dances from all over Mesoamerica.

March 21: **Birthday of Benito Juárez** (1806). Legal holiday.

Vernal Equinox. Chichén Itzá: A phenomenon of light and shadow displays the pattern of a serpent slithering down the steps of the Pyramid of Kukulcán.

May 1: **Labor Day.** Legal holiday.

May 3: **Day of the Holy Cross.** Dance of the Pig's Head performed during fiestas at Celestún, Felipe Carrillo Puerto, and Hopelchén.

May 5: **Battle of Puebla,** also known as **Cinco de Mayo.** In remembrance of the 1862 defeat of the French. Legal holiday.

May 12–18: **Chankah Veracruz** (near Felipe Carrillo Puerto). Honors the Virgin of the Immaculate Conception. Maya music, bullfights, and religious procession.

May 15: **San Isidro Labrador.** Festivals held at Panaba (near Valladolid) and Calkini (southwest of Mérida).

May 20–30: **Becal.** Jipi Fiesta in honor of the plant *jipijapa,* used in making Panama hats, the big moneymaker for most of the population.

June 29: **Day of San Pedro.** All towns with the name of San Pedro. Fiestas held in Sanah-cat and Cacalchen (near Mérida), Tekom, and Panaba (near Valladolid).

Early July: **Ticul** (near Uxmal). Weeklong fiesta celebrating the establishment of Ticul. Music, athletic events, dancing, and fireworks.

Sept. 15: **Independence Day.** Legal holiday.

Sept. 27–Oct. 14: **El Señor de las Ampollas** in Mérida. Religious holiday. Big fiesta with fireworks, religious services, music, and dancing.

Oct. 4: **Feast Day of San Francisco de Asisi.** Usually a weeklong fiesta precedes this day in Uman, Hocaba, Conkal, and Telchac Pueblo (each near Mérida).

Oct. 12: **Columbus Day.** Legal holiday.

Oct. 18–28: **Izamal.** Fiesta honoring El Cristo de Sitilpech. A procession carries an image of Christ from Sitilpech to the church in Izamal. Religious services, fireworks, music, and dancing. Biggest celebration on the 25th.

Oct. 31: **Eve of All Souls' Day.** Celebrated throughout the Yucatán. Flowers and candles placed on graves, the beginning of an eight-day observance.

Nov. 1–2: **All Souls' Day and Day of the Dead.** Graveside and church ceremonies. A partylike atmosphere in all the cemeteries. Food and drink vendors do a lively business, as do candy makers with their sugar skulls and skeletons. A symbolic family meal is eaten at the gravesite.

Nov. 8: **Conclusion of El Día de Muerte.** Day of the Dead.

Nov. 20. **Día de la Revolución.** Revolution Day of 1910. Legal holiday.

Dec. 8: **Feast of the Immaculate Conception.** Fiestas at Izamal, Celestún (including a boat procession), and Champotón (boat procession carrying a statue of Mary, water-skiing show, other aquatic events, dancing, fair).

Dec. 12: **Our Lady of Guadalupe.**

Dec. 25: **Christmas.** Legal holiday.

---

off with a spray of light and sound followed by appreciative cheers of delight.

Village fiestas are a wonderful time of dancing, music, noise, colorful costumes, good food, and usually lots of drinking. A public fiesta is generally held in the central plaza surrounded by temporary stalls where you can get Mexican fast food: tamales (both sweet and meat), *buñuelos* (sweet rolls), tacos, *refrescos* (soft drinks), *churros* (fried

dough dusted with sugar), *carne asada* (barbecued meat), and plenty of beer chilling in any convenient ice-filled container.

A Marriage of Cultures

Many festivals in Mexico honor religious feast days. You'll see a unique combination of religious fervor and ancient beliefs mixed with plain old good times. In the church plaza, dances passed down from family to family since before Cortés introduced Christianity to the New World continue for hours. Dancers dress in symbolic costumes of bright colors, feathers, and bells, reminding local onlookers about their Maya past. Inside the church is a constant stream of the candle-carrying devout, some traveling long distances on their knees to the church, repaying a promise made to a deity months before in thanks for a personal favor, a healing, or a job found.

Some villages offer a corrida (bullfight) as part of the festivities. Even a small town will have a simple bullring; in the backcountry these rings are frequently built of bamboo. In Maya fashion, no nails are used—only henequen twine to hold together a two-tiered bullring! The country corrida has a special charm. If celebrating a religious holiday, a procession carrying the image of the honored deity might lead off the proceedings. The bull has it good here; there are no bloodletting ceremonies and the animal is allowed to live. Only a tight rope around its middle provokes sufficient anger for the fight. Local young men perform in the arena with as much heart and grace as professionals in Mexico City. And though the clothes are not satin and velvet, they are simple cotton heavily embroidered with beautiful flowers and designs. The crowd shows its admiration with shouts, cheers, and, of course, *música!*—even if the band is composed only of a drum and a trumpet. In the end, someone unties the bull—*very carefully!* It's good fun for everyone, even those who don't understand the art of the corrida. Even now you might run across a tiny town celebrating with a pig's-head dance, a very old Maya celebration.

Religious Feast Days

Christmas and Easter are wonderful holidays. The *posada* (procession) of Christmas begins nine days before the holiday, when families and friends take part in processions that portray Mary and Joseph and their search for lodging before the birth of Christ. The streets are alive with people, bright lights, and colorful nativity scenes. Families provide swinging piñatas (pottery covered with papier-mâché in the shape of a popular animal or perky character and filled with candy and small surprises); children and adults alike enjoy watching the blindfolded small

fry swing away with a heavy board or baseball bat while an adult moves and sways the piñata with a rope, making the fun last, giving everyone a chance. Eventually, someone gets lucky and smashes the piñata with a hard blow (it takes strength to break it), and kids skitter around the floor retrieving the loot. Piñatas are common, not only for Christmas and Easter but also for birthdays and other special occasions in the Mexican home.

Another common sight, even around tourist communities, are groups of teenagers carrying torches and running a kilometer at a time with a pickup truck filled with teenagers following slowly behind. At the end of a kilometer, another teen replaces the runner. The dedicated run ends at a church to celebrate a festival honoring the Blessed Mother.

The Fiesta and Visitors—Practicalities

A few practical things to remember about fiesta times. Cities will probably be crowded. If you know in advance that you'll be in town, make hotel and car reservations as soon as possible. Easter and Christmas at any of the beach hotels will be crowded, and you may need to make reservations as far as six months in advance. And expect rates to really go up for Christmas holiday. Respect the privacy of people; the Indians have definite feelings and religious beliefs about having their pictures taken, so ask first and abide by their wishes.

BULLFIGHTING

The bullfight is not for everyone. Many foreigners feel it amounts to inhumane treatment of a helpless animal. The bullfight is a blood sport; if you can't tolerate this sort of thing, you'd probably be happier not attending. Bullfighting is big business in Mexico, Spain, Portugal, and South America. The *corrida de toros* (running of the bulls) is made up of a troupe of (now) well-paid men all playing an important part in the drama. The only ring in Quintana Roo is in Cancún, and the corrida is every Wednesday during the season. The afternoon starts off promptly at 4 P.M. with music and a colorful parade of solemn pomp with matadors, picadors on horseback, and banderilleros.

ACCOMMODATIONS AND FOOD

Quintana Roo offers a wide variety of accommodations. There's a myriad of hotels to choose from in cities, villages, beach resorts, and offshore islands, in many price ranges. If you like the idea of light housekeeping and preparing your own food, condos are available in many locales. If your lifestyle is suited to outdoor living, beach camping is limited but available along the Caribbean, and the number of small bungalows for tourists is growing beyond imagination. And there's still plenty of open white beach that somebody somewhere wants to cover with hotels.

CAMPING

Note: We have had readers ask us why we don't include more campsites in *Moon Handbooks: Cancún.* The reason is there are not anywhere near as many trailer or campsites in Quintana Roo as there are in many other parts of Mexico.

If you are traveling in your own vehicle, you must obtain a vehicle permit when entering the country. Camping with a vehicle allows you to become a "luxury camper," bringing all the equipment you'll need (and more). A van or small camper truck will fit on almost any road you'll run into. Many of today's large RVs will not do well on the small limestone roads that cut off from highway 307, which is the main highway from Cancún to Chetumal and the Belize border. With an RV you can "street camp" in the city. Parking lots of large hotels (check with the manager) or side streets near downtown activities are generally safe and offer easy access to entertainment.

Vehicle Supplies

A few reminders and some common-sense planning make a difference when traveling and camping with a vehicle. There are many swampy areas near the Caribbean coast, so check for marshy ground before pulling off the road. When beach camping, park above the high-tide line. Many beaches that at one time allowed beach camping are now filled with hotels, and campers are out of luck. Remember that gas stations are not as frequently found on the Peninsula as in most parts of Mexico. If you plan on traveling for any length of time, especially in out-of-the-way places, carry extra gas and fill up whenever the opportunity arises. Along with your food supply, always carry enough water for both the car and passengers. Be practical and come prepared with a few necessities (see our checklist).

Sleeping Outdoors

Sleeping under a jeweled sky in a warm clime can be either a wonderful or an excruciating experience. Two factors that will make or break it are the heat and the mosquito population in the immediate vicinity. Some campers sleep in tents

Some beach huts offer little more than sapling walls, thatch roof, and hammock hooks; this one goes further with hanging beds and mosquito netting.

to get away from biting critters, which helps but is no guarantee; also, heat hangs heavily inside a closed tent. Sleeping bags cushion the ground but tend to be much too warm. If you have a bag that zips across the bottom, it's cooling to let your feet hang out (well marinated in bug repellent or wearing a pair of socks. An air mattress or foam pad softens the ground (bring along a patch kit). Mexican campers often just roll up in a lightweight blanket, covering all skin, head to toe, to defy possible bug attacks. Your best bet is to sleep in a hammock with good netting.

For a very small fee, many rural resorts provide *palapa* hammock-huts that usually include water (for washing only); these places are great if you want to meet other backpackers. Though they are fast giving way to bungalow construction, a few hammock-huts are still found in the southern part of the Riviera Maya.

HOTELS

Prices
Accommodation prices in this book are subject to change at any moment after the book is printed. But these prices should at least give you an idea of general range of the hotel. We give you the price of a standard room for high season, generally from January to April 15. The holiday season is the highest of the year, and the prices are for a period of about two weeks. We do *not* give those prices. We try to give you telephone numbers and email addresses so that you can get the most accurate price at the time you are going. So use the prices in the spirit they were given, and don't pretend they are carved in stone. Remember to add 12 percent tax to most hotel prices. Some of the hotels include the tax, but most don't, so ask. Many hotels include breakfast, but not all.

All-inclusive Resorts
These resorts are growing rapidly in Cancún, Cozumel, and all along the coast of the Riviera Maya. People don't have to leave the premises for the entire stay, and sadly many don't. The prices generally include all food, drinks (alcohol, but some include only Mexican brands), most nonmechanized activities, parties, theme nights, parties, parties, and ways to get you in-

volved in more parties. It's just what many tourists want so that's great. There are a few all-inclusive places that are more upscale, and some offer nature activities. Look around and you'll find something to suit you.

Reservations
Traveling during the peak season (December 15–April 15) requires a little planning if you wish to stay at the popular cities. Make reservations well in advance, especially at the beach. Many hotels can be contacted through a toll-free 800 number, travel agency, or auto club. A few of the well-known American chains are represented in the larger resorts (Cancún, Cozumel, and along the Riviera Maya, and their international desks can make reservations for you. Many now have email addresses. If you're traveling May–June or September–October, rooms are generally available and usually cheaper in price. Searching the net can also be a shortcut, but don't depend on what you find there without

---

YOUTH HOSTELS

CREA Cancún
200 Paseo Kukulcán, Km 3, Zona Hotelera
Cancún, Quintana Roo, Mexico

CREA Playa del Carmen
Take the road that goes behind the Pemex station; look for the sign.

CREA Campeche
Av. Agustín Melgar s/n, Col. Buenavista
Campeche, Campeche, Mexico

CREA Chetumal
Alvaro Obregón y General Anaya s/n
Chetumal, Quintana Roo, Mexico

Poc Na Isla Mujeres
Av. Matamoros 91
Isla Mujeres, Quintana Roo, Mexico

For more information contact:
CREA, Agencia Nacional de Juvenil, Glorieta Metro Insurgentes, Local CC-11, Col. Juárez, C.P. 06600 Mexico, D.F., tel. 5/25-2548 or 5/25-2974

double checking with an email, fax message, or a telephone call. The sites are often not updated for many months or years.

Please note, when prepaying, make sure you travel with your paid receipts and any other paperwork. Also, ask for the sales manager's name. We have heard a lot of sad stories from people whose reservations apparently were never received. In such situations it either takes a long time to get things straight or you don't get a room (that doesn't happen too frequently). Either way it's a hassle.

Under US$50

This is almost an impossible task. Travelers looking to spend nights cheaply may be able to find a *few* overnight accommodations in Isla Mujeres, Playa del Carmen, Tulum, and Xcalak, but they won't be much.

US$50–100

In this range you will find some pretty nice rooms. Again, they won't be upscale, but generally they are clean (always check for cleanliness) and closer to the hotel zone. The nicer downtown places are around this price.

US$100–150

If you're lucky you'll find fine hotels at this price by using packages purchased before you leave home. Generally you must stay for a certain length of time, and there are other requirements.

US$150–200

Even in Cancún you can find some nice hotels in this price range. In addition to rooms, the hotels will have private beaches, at least one nice dining room, car rentals, and—usually—a travel agent to help you plan your activities.

US$200 and up

If you're willing to pay more than US$200 you shouldn't have any trouble finding a very nice room. Still, the really plush places go for US$300 or more.

Condos and Villas

Cancún has hundreds of condos lining the beach and many more under construction. Isla Mujeres, Cozumel, Playa del Carmen, and Akumal have a few condominiums, and others are sprouting up along the southern coastal beaches as well. If you're vacationing with family or a group, condo living can be a real money-saver while still providing the fine services of a luxury hotel. Fully equipped kitchens make cooking a snap. In many cases the price includes daily maid service. Some condos (like the Condumel on Isla Cozumel) welcome you with a refrigerator stocked with food basics; you pay only for the foods and beverages that you use each day. Details are given in the appropriate travel sections.

Time Shares

Time-share mania is putting down roots. One of the biggest complaints from travelers to Cancún, Puerto Aventuras, and Cozumel in the last couple of years concerns the salespeople who pester visitors to buy condos and time-share accommodations. Their come-on is an offer for a free breakfast and often a free day's rental of a motorbike, or some other freebies. After the

cooking ribs at the market

breakfast or lunch, they give a sales presentation, a tour of the facilities, and then each guest gets a hard pitch from a very experienced salesperson. These people have learned American sales methods down to the nitty-gritty. If you succumb to the offer of free breakfast and aren't interested in buying, better practice saying *"No."*

FOOD

Taste as many different dishes as possible! You'll be introduced to spices that add a new dimension to your diet. Naturally, you won't be wild about everything—it takes a while to become accustomed to squid served in its own black ink, for instance! A hamburger might not taste like one from your favorite fast-food place back home. It should also not come as a shock to find that your favorite down-home Tex-Mex enchiladas and tacos are nothing like those you order in U.S. Mexican restaurants.

Seafood

You won't travel far before realizing that one of Quintana Roo's specialties is fresh fish. All along the Caribbean you'll have opportunities to indulge in piscine delicacies: lobster, shrimp, red snapper, sea bass, halibut, barracuda, and lots more. Even the tiniest café will prepare sweet fresh fish à la Veracruz, using ripe tomatoes, green peppers, and onions. Or if you prefer, ask for the fish *con ajo,* sautéed in garlic and butter—scrumptious! Most menus offer an oppor-

CORN TORTILLAS

The staple of the Mexican diet, tortillas, are still made by hand in many homes, but a large percentage of people buy them for a reasonable price, saving themselves hours of work on the *metate* (grinder) and the *tomal* (griddle). In any public market, the tortilla shop is always the busiest place. Folks line up to buy two, four, or six kilograms of tortillas every day. One traveler tells of spending 20 minutes in fascinated concentration observing the whole operation: 50-pound plastic sacks of shucked corn kernels stacked in a corner of the stall, the machinery that grinds it, the pale yellow dough, the unsophisticated conveyor belt that carries the dough across the live-flame cooking surface, the patrons who patiently line up for the fresh results, and the baker who hands the traveler several tortillas hot off the fire along with a friendly smile that says thanks for being interested.

In most restaurants in Mexico today, however, you will find flour tortillas are taking over in most dishes. This most Mexican of Mexican staples is fading out in the commercial and tourist centers of the country. According to one restaurateur, it is much simpler and more economical to buy commercial flour tortillas. They have a longer shelf life and are cheaper but, alas, they're not nearly as good as the old maize tortillas now found mostly in small villages and in the tiny cafés that still buy them at the marketplace.

OZ MALLAN

tortilla maker at work

MEXICAN WINE

It would seem the most natural thing in the world for Mexico to produce good wines, considering the Spanish conquistadors came from a land with a long history of growing rich and flavorful grapes and were experts in the field of fermentation. Pre-Hispanics didn't have wine as the Spanish knew it, but did make fermented beverages from such things as corn. It was not long before vine cuttings were brought to the New World and colonists were tending vineyards. By 1524 wine was so successful that Mexican wines were soon competing with Spanish wines. Pressure from vintners at home forced King Felipe II to outlaw its production in Mexico. However, over the years church use continued and no doubt many gallons of the forbidden drink found their way to private cellars. But for all practical purposes and development, the industry was stopped before it had the opportunity to make itself known around the world.

Not until 1930 under Pres. Lázaro Cárdenas did Mexican winemaking begin to make a name for itself. Experts from around the world are beginning to recognize the industry in general and several of the wines are considered world-class. Over 125,000 acres of vineyards are under cultivation in the states of Baja California Norte, Aguascalientes, Querétaro, and Zacatecas; the vineyards of Baja produce almost 80 percent of the country's wines. Some of the well-known wineries from this area are **Domecq**, **L.A. Cetto**, and **Santo Tomas**.

The wineries **Cavas de San Juan** and **Casa Martell** are found in Querétaro, some 2,000 miles south of Baja. This was due to the suggestion of a University of California professor of enology who came to the conclusion that the area's 6,100-foot elevation compensated for its location outside the celebrated "wine belt." Zacatecas is the location of the relatively new and promising **Unión Vinícola Zacateca**, while **La Esplendida** and **Valle Redondo** are from Aguascalientes.

According to Walter Stender of ACA Imports, some Mexican wines are now being imported to the United States. Note: Mexican wines don't age well and you need not be impressed by dates. In other words, the whites are ready when released and the reds need age no more than 18 months.

If you want champagne, remember to ask for *vino espumoso* or "bubbly wine." A label that reads *methode champenoise* means that the French system for producing sparkling wine was used. Mexico signed an agreement with the French government not to label its sparkling wines "champagne."

Of course, there are many imported wines from all over the world available in the fine restaurants of Cancún—many from California—but while in Mexico be adventurous and try the Mexican wine. A personal favorite is L.A. Cetto's white.

tunity to order *al gusto* (cooked to your pleasure). Try the unusual conch *(kaahnk),* which has been a staple in the diet of the Maya along the Caribbean coast for centuries. It's often used in ceviche. Some consider this dish raw; actually, the conch or fish is marinated in a lime dressing with onions, peppers, and a host of spices—very tasty! Often conch is pounded, dipped in egg and cracker crumbs, and sautéed quickly (like abalone steak in California), with a squirt of fresh lime. (If it's cooked too long it becomes tough and rubbery.)

If you happen to be on a boat trip during which the crew prepares a meal of fresh fish on the beach, more than likely you'll be served *tik 'n' chik* cooked over an open fire. The whole fish (catch of the day) is placed on a wire rack and seasoned with onions, peppers, and *achiote,* a fragrant red spice grown on the Yucatán Peninsula since the time of the early Maya. Bishop Diego de Landa identified *achiote* in his *Relaciones,* written in the 1500s.

Wild Game

The Mayas are hunters, and if you explore the countryside very much, you'll commonly see men and boys on bicycles, motor scooters, or horses with rifles slung over their shoulders and full game bags tied behind them. Game found in the jungle varies. Deer used to be a popular prey, but it's becoming extinct along the coast. Deer is discouraged in restaurants, but still pops up now and then. If you're offered *venado,* just say no.

Restaurants

Some restaurants add a service charge to the bill. If so, the check will say *incluido propina.* It's still gracious to leave a few coins for the waiter. If the tip isn't added to the bill, leaving 10–15 percent is customary. Remember, in Mexico it's considered an insult if a waiter submits a bill before it's requested; when you're ready to pay, say, *"La cuenta, por favor"* ("The bill, please"). In many cases, the waiters don't make even the pittance that is daily wage because they get tips. Don't be stingy.

Strolling musicians are common in Mexican cafés. If you enjoy the music, several dollars is a considerate gift. In certain cities, cafés that cater to Mexicans will commonly serve free snacks in the afternoon with a beer or cocktail. The Café Prosperidad (Calle 56 #456A) in downtown Mérida is very generous with its *antojitos* (snacks). The place is always packed with locals ordering the *comida corrida,* complete with live entertainment and waitresses wearing a long version of the *huipil.* Here you'll get the real essence of the city, and you may be the only gringo present. Remember, we didn't say the café is spotless!

Yucatán has its own version of junk food. You'll find hole-in-the-wall stands selling *tortas* (sandwiches), tacos, tamales, or *licuados* (fruit drinks), as well as corner vendors selling mangos on a stick, slices of pineapple, peeled oranges, candies of all kinds (including tall pink fluffs of cotton candy), and barbecued meat. The public markets have foods of every description, usually very cheap. In other words, there's a huge variety to choose from, so have fun.

A ploy used by many seasoned adventurers when they're tired of eating cold food from their backpacks: In a village where there isn't a café of any kind, go to the local cantina (or grocery store, church, or city hall) and ask if there's a woman in town who (for a fee) would be willing to include you at her dinner table. Almost always you'll find someone, usually at a fair price (determine price when you make your deal). With any luck you'll find a woman renowned not only for her *tortillas por manos* but also for the tastiest *poc chuc* this side of Ticul. You gain a lot more than food in this arrangement; the culture swap is priceless.

Food Safety

When preparing your own food in the backcountry, a few possible sources of bacteria are fresh fruit and vegetables, especially those with thin skins that don't get peeled, like lettuce or tomatoes. When washing these foods in local water (and they should definitely be washed thoroughly before consuming), add either bleach or iodine (8–10 drops per quart) to the water. Soaking vegetables together in a container or plastic Ziploc bag for about 20 minutes is easy. If at the beach and short of water, substitute seawater (for everything but drinking). Remember not to rinse the bleached food with contaminated water. Just pat dry, and if it has a distasteful lingering flavor, add a squirt of lime juice (tastes great and is very healthy). Nature has packaged some foods hygienically—a banana, for instance, has its own protective seal so is considered safe (luckily, since they're so abundant on the Peninsula). Foods that are cooked and eaten immediately are also considered safe.

TRANSPORTATION

For centuries, getting to the Yucatán Peninsula required a major sea voyage to one of the few ports on the Gulf of Mexico, followed by harrowing and uncertain land treks limited to mule trains and narrow paths through the tangled jungle. Today the Peninsula is accessible from anywhere in the solar system! Arrive via modern airports, a network of new (good) highways, a reasonably frequent train system (very limited), or an excellent bus service that reaches large cities as well as an incredible number of small villages in remote areas.

BY CAR

Renting a car in Mexico is usually a simple matter but can cost much more than in the United States—and is always subject to Murphy's Law. If you know exactly when you want the car and where, it's helpful to make reservations in the United States in advance. It used to be that if you waited until you arrived in Mexico, you paid a high going rate, typically about $60 per day for a small car. Most offices gave little or no weekly discount. Not any more. Today there are so many car-rental agencies that you have room to bargain.

Car Rental

If it's just before closing time, and if someone has cancelled a reservation, and if it's off-season on the Peninsula, it's possible to get a car for a good rate. However, that's a lot of ifs to count on when you want and need a car as soon as you arrive. Also, it's often difficult to get a car without reservations; you may have to wait around for one to be returned.

Hertz, Avis, and Budget franchise representatives can be found in many parts of Mexico. (Avis, Hertz, and Budget all list 800 numbers in the Yellow Pages; ask for the international desk). If you make your arrangements before you leave home, always ask for current specials or the best deal, usually a weekly arrangement. Even if you only plan to use the car for four or five days, use your calculator; it might still be a better deal, especially with unlimited mileage thrown in. If you belong to AAA or other auto clubs, the car-rental agency might give you a 10–20 percent discount (be sure you bring your membership card), but not in conjunction with another special deal. The Volkswagen Beetle is generally the best buy and does well on the narrow roads along the coast.

Another advantage to making advance reservations is the verification receipt. Hang onto it; when you arrive at the airport and show your verification receipt (be sure you get it back), a car will almost always be waiting for you. Once in a while you'll even get an upgrade for the same fee if your reserved car is not available. On the other side of the coin, be sure that you go over the car carefully before you take it far. Drive it around the block and check the following:

- Make sure there's a spare tire and working jack.
- All doors lock and unlock, including trunk.
- The seats move forward, have no sprung backs, etc.
- All windows lock, unlock, and roll up and down properly.
- The proper legal papers are in the car, with address and phone numbers of associate car-rental agencies in cities you plan to visit (in

case of an unexpected car problem).
- Horn, emergency brake, and foot brakes work properly.
- Clutch, gearshift, and all gears (including reverse) work properly.
- Get directions to the nearest gas station; the gas tank may be empty. If it's full it's wise to return it full, since you'll be charged top dollar per liter of gas. Ask to have any damage, even a small dent, missing doorknob, etc., noted on your contract, if it hasn't been already.
- Note the hour you picked up the car and try to return it before that time; a few minutes over will cost you another full day's rental fee.

When you pick up your rental car, the company makes an imprint of your credit card on a blank bill and keeps a copy attached to the papers you give the agent when you return the car. Keep in mind that the car agency has a limit on how much you can charge on one credit card at one time. If you go over the limit, be prepared to pay the balance in cash or with another credit card. If you pick up a car in one city and return it to another, there's a hefty drop-off fee (per kilometer). Most agents will figure out in advance exactly how much it will be so that there aren't any surprises when you return the car.

In 99 percent of cases, all will go smoothly. However, if you run into a problem or are overcharged, don't panic—charge everything and save all your paperwork; when you return home, make copies of everything and call the company; chances are very good that you'll get a refund.

Insurance

It's dangerous to skip insurance. In most cases in Mexico, when there's an accident the police take action first and ask questions later. With an insurance policy, most of the problems are eased over. Rental agencies also offer medical insurance for US$4 per day. Your private medical insurance should cover this (check). Also, ask your credit-card provider exactly what insurance they provide when you rent a car.

Documents

An international driver's license is not required to drive or rent a car in Mexico. However, if you feel safer with it, get one from an auto club. At AAA in California you will need two passport

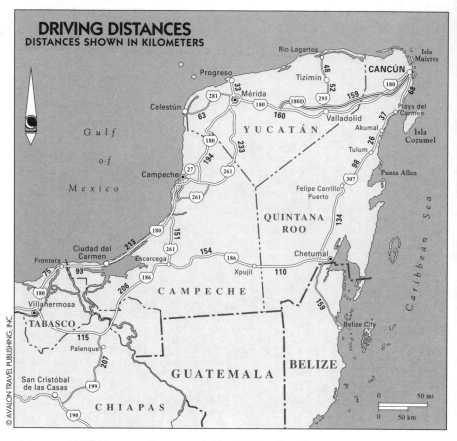

DRIVING DISTANCES
DISTANCES SHOWN IN KILOMETERS

Gulf

o f

Mexico

Rio Lagartos

Isla
Mujeres

Progreso

Tizimín

CANCÚN

48

Celestún

281

33

Mérida

52

159

180

180

180D

295

68

Playa del
Carmen

Celestún

63

160

Valladolid

37

YUCATÁN

Akumal

Isla
Cozumel

180

194

233

Tulum

26

Campeche

27

261

98

Punta Allen

261

307

Felipe Carrillo
Puerto

QUINTANA
ROO

134

180

151

261

Ciudad del
Carmen

Escarcega

154

186

Chetumal

Frontera

75

93

Xpujil

110

186

206

CAMPECHE

180

Villahermosa

159

Caribbean Sea

TABASCO

115

Belize City

Palenque

207

San Cristóbal
de las Casas

199

GUATEMALA

BELIZE

190

CHIAPAS

0   50 mi

0   50 km

© AVALON TRAVEL PUBLISHING, INC.

pictures and US$15, along with a current driver's license from your home state. The international license is another good form of identification if you should have an accident or other driving problems.

When you cross the border from the United States into Mexico, your car insurance is no longer valid. You can buy insurance from AAA or an auto club before you leave home. Numerous insurance agencies at most border cities sell Mexican insurance: Sanborn's is one of the largest. Ask Sanborn's for their excellent free road maps of the areas you plan to visit. For more information write: Sanborn's Mexican Insurance Service, P.O. Box 1210, McAllen, TX 78501; tel. 512/682-3401.

In the last 15 years highway construction has been priority work on the Peninsula. A growing number of well-engineered roads—many of them expensive toll roads—provide access to cities and towns. However, before taking your car into the country, consider the manufacturer and the condition of the car. Will parts be available in the event of a breakdown? Volkswagen, Renault, Ford, General Motors, and Chrysler have Mexican branches and parts should be available. If you drive an expensive foreign sports car or a large luxury model, you might be better off making other arrangements. Repairs might be unavailable and you could be stranded in an unlikely place for days waiting for a part. It's always wise to make sure you and the mechanic understand the cost of repairs before he begins—just like at home! **Note:** Selling your car in Mexico is illegal.

Driving Tips
In Mexico, it's recommended that you don't drive outside the cities at night unless it's a necessity. The highways have no streetlights—it's hard to see a black cow on a black road in the black night. Also, pedestrians have no other place to walk; shoulders are nonexistent on the roads. Public phones are few and far between, and gas stations close when the sun goes down. If you should have a problem while driving during daylight hours on a *main* road, stay with your car. The Green Angels, a government-sponsored tow truck service, cruise the roads several times a day on the lookout for drivers in trouble. They carry gas and small parts and are prepared to fix tires. Each car is equipped with a CB radio and the driver is trained to give first aid, or will call a doctor. If you foolishly travel an isolated road after dark and break down, your best bet is to lock yourself in and stick it out for the night; go for help in the morning. The Mexican people are friendly, especially when they see someone in trouble, but sometimes you'll get more help than you want.

Toll Roads vs. Free Roads
Toll roads are springing up all over Mexico. The fees are high and generally the highways are in great shape. In almost all cases, you can still use the old roads to get to your destination (which is what the budget-minded locals use). On the free roads expect *topes*—big traffic bumps all along the highways. In some cases there's a sign to warn you; in others it will be a big surprise, and the underside of the car can be damaged if you're traveling too fast. These roads can be very slow. Look for the signs that say *libre* (free); the toll road is the *cuota*. If you can't find the old road, ask a local.

BY PLANE

Today, planes fly to two international airports in Quintana Roo: Cancún and Cozumel. Jets arrive daily, with connections from most countries in the world. In Quintana Roo there are several small landing strips for private planes and small commuter airlines. More area airports are in the planning stages.

BY BUS

Bus service to and around Quintana Roo is very efficient. Fares will fit the most meager budget, scheduling is frequent, and even the smallest village is accessible from most cities in the northern section of the Peninsula. When NAFTA matures, transportation across the borders between Mexico and destinations in the States may become less complicated.

Class Choice
You have a choice of Plus, super-deluxe, deluxe, and first-, second-, and third-class buses. Third-class passengers can bring their animals (and often do); second- and third-class buses are usually older models, with no toilets or air-conditioning. Third-class bus tickets are cheap (as little as a Mexican taco at Taco Bell in the United States). First-class and above buses have assigned seats. Any bus with the word "Plus" attached is one of the really upscale buses that have airline seats, cold drinks, and TVs. They're fast (usually no stops) and quite comfortable. The price is much higher, but still not prohibitive. Deluxe buses are comfortable, have fewer seats, and are often triple the price, but are still very affordable compared to U.S. prices. Make reservations in advance. Your ticket will read *asiento* (seat) with a number. Some first-class buses sell food and drinks onboard. If you're traveling a long distance, buy at least first class; the difference in comfort is worth the small added expense. Second- and third-class buses stop for anyone who flags them, and at every small village along the way. First class operates almost exclusively between terminals. This cuts a lot of time off a long journey.

Luggage
If it fits in the overhead rack, almost anything can be carried on. The usual allowance is 25 kilograms, but unless you're ridiculously overloaded, no one ever objects to what you bring

AIRLINES SERVING THE YUCATÁN PENINSULA

American: tel. 800/433-7300; flies from Dallas/Fort Worth to Cancún.

Aeromexico: tel. 800/237-6639; flies from Los Angeles and Houston to Cancún and Mérida.

Continental: tel. 800/231-0856; flies from Houston to Cancún and Cozumel; connecting flights (via Houston) from Los Angeles, San Francisco, and Denver.

Mexicana: tel. 800/531-7921; flies from Newark, Los Angeles, San Francisco, San Jose, Denver, San Antonio, and Chicago to Cancún and Cozumel.

aboard. If a driver should refuse your load, you can usually come to an amicable (monetary) agreement. Larger luggage is carried in the cargo hold under the bus where breakables have a short life span. Purses and cameras are best kept between your feet on the floor, rather than in the overhead rack—just in case. Luggage should always be labeled, inside and out, with your name, address, and telephone number.

Seat Comfort
If you can, choose the shady side of the bus during the day: Going south sit on the left side, and going north sit on the right. At night sit on the right, which eliminates the glare of oncoming headlights. The middle of the bus is the best place to be. Steer clear of seats near the bathroom, usually the last few rows. They can be smelly and the aisle traffic and constant door activity can keep you awake. Bring a book and just relax.

BY CRUISE SHIP

One of the fastest-growing industries in tourism is ocean cruising. What was once reserved for the idle rich is becoming commonplace for the ordinary vacationer. Cruising is no longer a means of getting from point A across an ocean to point B; cruise ships are for fun! And the more luxuri-

ous the better—though for obvious financial reasons some ships cater to fun-seekers rather than luxury-seekers. Daily prices can start as low as US$150 per person and climb to as much as US$700 per person.

More and more cruise ships are being built yearly, and some of the new ships can carry as many as 5,000 people. Each year a few more glamorous ships anchor offshore at Cozumel and Playa del Carmen, and if rumors are to be believed, soon we'll see them at Calica (next to Xcaret) and Majahual (on the Xcalak Peninsula).

Special-interest groups are finding a ship the perfect gathering place. For groups ranging from Smithsonian Associates' naturalists and archaeologists to theater guilds, appropriate speakers and plans are coordinated with the ship's personnel.

The Money Factor
Shop carefully if price is the most important factor; prices are competitive. A variety of ships offer mass-market Las Vegas–type cruises aimed at younger passengers interested in short three- to five-day trips. Upscale luxury boats reminiscent of first-class on the "Queens"—*Mary* and *Elizabeth*—cruise for two weeks or longer and cost the most. These are the ones with large cabins, restaurants where one orders from a complete menu, and passengers who are pampered outrageously, with a price tag to match. For the adventurer, small, casual ships capable of traveling narrow river passages into often virgin territory where nature and people have not been exposed to the diluting effects of tourism— for a while, at least—run a gamut of prices from moderate to exorbitant.

Ways to Cut Costs
Go standby. Once you put your name on the list, you'll have no choice of cabin location or size, and airfare is usually not included. Passengers are notified two weeks prior to departure. **Last-minute travel clubs** and **discount agencies** include cruises available at the last minute in their inventories. These clubs charge a yearly membership fee, around US$50; for that, the member receives a newsletter with phone numbers, a list of trips, and other pertinent information that provides access to upcoming values. Those who are willing to pack up at a moment's notice

cruising to Cozumel

(two weeks) can save 10–50 percent.

By the same token, some cruise lines will give a substantial discount to folks who book and buy passage six months to a year in advance. **Cunard, Princess, Holland America,** and **Royal Cruise Line** are all willing to give a 10–50 percent discount. Often, ships offer specials for various reasons; study the travel sections of newspapers and get to know your travel agent. Let him or her know what you would like, and ask him or her to call you if and when the price is right.

Sharing a quad room generally gives you a good discount. If you don't have any roomies to bring along, some lines will sell you a same-sex quad for a set price.

Ask for **senior citizen discounts;** though not many lines give them, there are a few.

To Quintana Roo

Several passenger ships make stops at Quintana Roo's islands and ports. Many sail out of Miami, stopping at Key West before continuing to the Caribbean and Mexico's Playa del Carmen and Isla Cozumel. Many lines will take you one-way and drop you off at Cancún, Cozumel, or Playa del Carmen. Check with Princess Lines, Chandris, and Carnival Cruises; your travel agent can give you the names of others that stop along the Yucatán coast. New cruise ships are continually adding the Mexican Caribbean to their ports of call.

Cruise passengers have the opportunity to make shore excursions from the Caribbean coast ports to Chichén Itzá, Tulum, Cobá, and Xelha, or they can just lie around the white beach, enjoy the turquoise sea, or shop at the many *tiendas* for typical souvenirs.

Some cruise ships to the Quintana Roo coast specialize in diving and might carry a dive doctor, a small decompression chamber for treating the bends, and air compressors for filling tanks. Divers can either bring their own equipment or rent on board. Certification courses in scuba diving are offered, as are a multitude of watersports equipment and events. Dress is casual on these ships and fine entertainment can be had on board at the disco, pool, bars, or cinema. Fitness centers, shops, and film processing make ship life convenient and pleasant.

GROUP TRAVEL

Travel agents offer many choices of escorted tours. You pay a little extra, but all arrangements and reservations are made for you to tour by plane, train, ship, or RV caravan. Special-interest tours with a guest expert are another possibility. For instance, archaeology buffs can usually find a group through a university that includes a knowledgeable professor to guide them through chosen Maya ruins. Evenings are spent together reviewing the day's investigation and discussing the next day's itinerary.

Archaeology laypeople will find many opportunities, including trips offered through Earthwatch (P.O. Box 403, Watertown, MA 02172); volunteers can work on a dig under the supervision of professionals. Destinations change regularly. *Transitions Abroad* (18 Hulst Rd., Box 344, Amherst, MA 01004) is a magazine that offers information about study and teaching opportunities around the world. Travel agencies, student publications, and professional organizations can give you more information. Or call **Yucatán Reservations Central**, tel. 800/555-8842.

NOTES FOR THE PHYSICALLY CHALLENGED

Mexico hasn't caught up with many parts of the world that have made life a little easier for the physically challenged. Sidewalks are narrow and often hazardous due to myriad holes and cracks. Streets in the older cities are often cobblestone. Curbs are exceptionally steep and require more than one pushing person to maneuver a wheelchair. And most of the small resorts along the Quintana Roo coast are sand resorts—even some of the dining rooms have sand floors. Fortunately, Cancún and Cozumel both have paved streets, but Isla Mujeres still has lots of sand on its streets and it's hard to roll a wheelchair.

Toilets are not designed for anyone but the physically agile. Few hotels have large doors to the stalls or offer ramps for wheelchairs, and many—the old colonial buildings, especially—don't have elevators. The more upscale the hotel, the more preparation for the challenged. Always ask in advance, as there is seldom more than one handicapped room. Caveat emptor!

WHAT TO TAKE

Whatever time of year you travel to Mexico's Caribbean coast, you can expect warm weather, which means you can pack less in your suitcase. Most airlines allow you to check two suitcases, and you can bring another carry-on bag that fits either under your seat or in the overhead rack; this is great if you're planning a one-destination trip to a self-contained resort hotel and want a change of clothes each day. But if you plan on moving around a lot, keep it light.

Experienced travelers pack a small collapsible pocketbook into their carry-on, which then gives them only one thing to carry while en route. And be sure to include a few overnight necessities in your carry-on in the event your luggage doesn't arrive when you do. Valuables and medications are safest stowed under the seat in front of you rather than in the overhead rack, whether you're on a plane, train, or bus.

Clothing
How you dress depends on where you are. In today's Mexico, *almost* any clothing is acceptable, but look to see what the people of the area are wearing and follow their dress codes. A swimsuit is a must, and if you're not staying at one of the larger hotels, bring a beach towel. Beach attire is best worn at the beach; it isn't appropriate in urban areas, especially churches. Note: Though you may come upon it here and there, nude sunbathing in Mexico is almost always inappropriate and unsafe—and *always* illegal.

If traveling during November, December, or January, bring along a light jacket since it can cool off in the evening. The rest of the year you'll probably carry the jacket in your suitcase. For women, a wraparound skirt is a useful item that can quickly cover up shorts when traveling through villages and cities (many small-village residents gawk at women wearing shorts; whatever you do, don't enter a church wearing them). The wraparound skirt also makes a good shawl for cool evenings. Cotton underwear stays cool in the tropics, but nylon is less bulky and dries overnight, cutting down on the number needed. Be sure that you bring broken-in, comfortable walking shoes; blisters can wreck a vacation.

Necessities

If you wear glasses and are planning an extended trip in Mexico, it's a good idea to bring an extra pair or carry the lens prescription. The same goes for medications (make sure the prescription is written in general terms), though many Mexican pharmacies sell prescription drugs over the counter.

Avid readers in any language besides Spanish should bring a supply of books; English-language reading materials are for sale in limited quantities, mostly in big hotel gift shops and only a few bookstores. Both small and large hotels have book-trading shelves. Ask at the desk to see their collection. Most travelers are delighted to trade books.

A Note on Toilets

Nowadays in almost all of Quintana Roo, at least in all the tourist areas, toilets are very civilized and there are many. But if you're off in the jungle, the toilets are non-existent, or consist of a hole in the floor. Whether you're in that situation or trekking the jungle, a couple of items make it easier. For women, **Le Funelle** is a scooplike paper funnel with a wide mouth and easy-to-hold handle that enables women to stand up to urinate in comfort and safety. Made of biodegradable paper, it can be tossed down the toilet when you get to one. Each Le Funnelle is packaged with a couple of tissues in an envelope about the size of a playing card, and comes with instructions. A pack of four costs US$2.85; a 20-pack costs US$8.99.

This and some other really clever toilet articles and traveling items can be seen in a great little catalog called **Magellan's, Essentials for the Traveler.** Take a look at the anti-bacterial wipes (pre-moistened towelettes with germ killers). A disinfectant spray also serves as a good room deodorizer. To receive your own catalog, call 800/962-4943.

The smaller the town, the more difficulty you'll have in finding a toilet. You can always go into a restaurant, buy a cold drink, and use the facilities. If there are no restaurants in the village, you must either stop at the local *tienda* or cantina and ask, *"¿Dónde está el baño?"* ("Where is the bathroom?"), or take a walk into the countryside. There was a time not too many years ago when you could not find facilities at any of the archaeological sites; however, in all of the mid- to large-size sites today, you will find a restroom.

Note: When you see a wastebasket in the stall with toilet paper in it, do not flush paper down the toilet; instead, drop the used paper into the wastebasket. Often, the toilet will overflow if you put paper in it.

Backpackers

If you plan on hitchhiking or using public transportation, don't use a large external-frame pack; it won't fit in most small cars or public lockers. Smaller packs with zippered compartments that will accommodate mini-padlocks are most practical. A strong bike cable and lock secures the pack to a bed or a bus or train rack. None of the above will deter the real criminal, but it might make it difficult enough to discourage anyone else.

Experienced backpackers travel light with a pack, an additional canvas bag, a small water purifier and mosquito-proof tent, a hammock, and mosquito netting.

Campers

For the purist who vows to cook every meal, here's a list for a handy carried kitchen:

- single-burner stove, two fuel cylinders (fuel not allowed on commercial airlines)
- one large, sharp, machete-type knife; one small, sturdy, sharp knife
- pair of pliers—good hot pot grabber
- plastic pot scrubber
- can opener (with bottle hook)
- hot pad, two if there's room
- two pots that nest, one Silverstone skillet
- wire holder to barbecue fish or meat over open fire
- small sharpening stone
- soap and laundry detergent
- plate, cup, fork, and spoon, plastic or metal
- two large metal cooking spoons
- one long-handled wooden spoon
- one egg spatula
- three fast-drying dish towels (not terrycloth)
- plastic Ziploc bags, large trash bags
- paper towels or napkins
- two or three plastic containers with tight-fitting lids, nested
- coffee drinkers who don't like instant will want a coffee pot
- several short candles and matches
- flashlight (batteries are usually easy to find)

KEEPING THE INSECTS AWAY

Of the many insect repellents around, some are better than others. Read the labels and ask questions. Some formulas were designed to spray the outdoors, some a room, others your clothes—none of these are for the skin. Some repellents are harmful to plants and animals, some can dissolve watch crystals, and others can damage plastic eyeglass lenses. This can be a particular problem if labels are written in a foreign language that you cannot read. It's best to bring your repellent from home.

Many of the most efficient repellents contain diethyl-toluamide (DEET). Test it out before you leave home; the more concentrated solutions can cause an allergic reaction in some people, and for children a milder mix is recommended. Avoid use on skin with sores and abrasions.

When using repellents, remember:
- If redness and itching begin, wash off with soap and water.
- Apply repellent by pouring into the palms of your hands, then rubbing together and applying evenly to the skin. If you're sweating, reapply every two hours. Use caution if perspiration mixed with repellent runs down your forehead and into your eyes. An absorbent headband helps.
- If you swim, reapply after coming out of the water.
- It's helpful to dip your socks, spray them heavily, or (as suggested by the World Health Organization) dip strips of cotton cloth, two or three inches wide, and wrap around your lower legs. One strip is effective for several weeks. Mosquitoes hover close to the ground in many areas.
- Apply liberally around the edges of your sleeves, pants cuffs, or shorts cuffs.

Sleeping in an air-conditioned room with tight-fitting windows is one good way to avoid nighttime buzzing attacks; in other situations use a mosquito net over the bed. It helps if the netting has been dipped in repellent, and make sure it's large enough to tuck well under the mattress. A rectangular shape is more efficient than the usual conical, giving you more room to sit up so you'll avoid contact with the critters that might bite through the net.

An Alternative

Long Road Travel Supplies, 111 Avenida Dr., Berkeley, CA 94708, USA, tel. 800/359-6040 or 510/540-4763, fax 510/540-0652, has come up with the **Indoor Travel Tent.** This lightweight and portable net housing is made of ultrafine mesh netting and fits right on top of the bed. A nylon floor and lightweight poles provide you with a roomy rectangular shape and freestanding protection from both flying and crawling insects that can make sleeping impossible. It's convenient with a zipper door, folding flap for extra foot room, and inside pocket for keeping valuables close at hand. Packed in its own carrying bag, it weighs just 2.3 pounds (for single bed) and costs US$79; the double weighs 2.8 pounds and costs US$99. Ask about the budget-priced Indoor Tent II, with a drawstring door; single size is US$49 and weighs 1.25 pounds.

DOCUMENTS

U.S. and Canadian citizens can obtain a free tourist card with proof of citizenship (birth certificate, passport, voter's registration, or notarized affidavit) good for 180 days. It can be obtained at any Mexican consulate or tourist office, at all border entry points, or from airport ticket offices for those traveling by plane. Hang onto your tourist card for the entire trip. You won't need it after you go through customs until it's time to leave the country. Then you must give it back. If you're visiting Mexico for 72 hours or less, you don't need a tourist card. Ask at the Mexican consulate about extensions for longer periods. If you're a naturalized citizen, carry your naturalization papers or passport. Citizens of the United States or Canada are not required to obtain certificates of vaccination to enter Mexico; other nationals should check with a local Mexican consulate. Those under 18 without a parent or legal guardian must present a notarized letter from the parents or guardian granting permission to travel alone in Mexico. If a single parent is traveling with a minor, he or she should carry a notarized letter from the other parent granting permission. This is important going in both directions.

Passports

If you have a passport, bring it along even though it's not required (tuck your tourist card inside); it's the simplest ID when cashing traveler's checks, registering at hotels, and going through immigration. If you're visiting an area that has a current health problem and you have a health card with current information, keep that with the passport also. Keep all documents in a waterproof plastic case and in a safe place. Contact the **Centers for Disease Control** for the most recent information about isolated areas that might be on the list for immunization. If traveling to such places, you'll need proof of vaccination to get back into the United States, and perhaps other countries as well.

Driving Procedures

If you're driving, the tourist card serves as a vehicle permit when completed and validated at the border point of entry. Vehicle title or registration and a driver's license are required. If you should happen to reach a remote border crossing at night, you may find it unstaffed. *Do not*

cross the border with your car until you have obtained the proper papers; if you do, it will cause problems when you exit the country. Mexican vehicle insurance is available at most border towns 24 hours a day.

Pets

If you're traveling with a pet, a veterinarian's certificate verifying good health and a rabies inoculation within the last six months is required. This certificate can be validated by any Mexican consulate for a small fee.

Purchases

When departing by land, air, or sea, you must declare at the point of reentry into your own country all items acquired in Mexico. To facilitate this procedure, it is wise to register any foreign-made possessions with customs officials before entering Mexico and to retain the receipts for purchases made while there. Limitations on the value of imported, duty-free goods vary from country to country and should be checked before traveling. U.S. citizens are allowed to carry through customs US$600 worth of purchases per person duty free and up to US$1,000 at a 10 percent tax. However, about 2,700 items, mostly those handcrafted or manufactured in Mexico, are exempt from this limit. Consular offices or embassies in Mexico City can supply additional information on exempt items. Plants and certain foods are not allowed into the United States and Mexico. Authentic archaeological finds, colonial art, and other original artifacts cannot be exported from Mexico. And, of course, trying to bring marijuana or any other narcotic into or out of Mexico or the United States is foolhardy. Jail is one place in Mexico you definitely want to avoid.

HEALTH AND SAFETY

TURISTA

Some travelers to Mexico worry about getting sick the moment they cross the border. But with a few simple precautions, it's not a foregone conclusion that you'll come down with something in Mexico. The most common illness to strike visitors is turista, Montezuma's revenge,

the trots, travelers illness, or, in plain Latin—diarrhea. No fun, it can cause uncomfortable cramping, fever, dehydration, and the need to stay close to a toilet for the duration. It's caused by, among other things, various strains of bacteria in food or water.

Statistics show that most tourists get sick on the third day of their visit. Interested doctors note that this traveler's illness is common in every country. They say that in addition to bacteria, a change in diet is equally to blame and suggest that the visitor slip slowly into the eating habits of Mexico. In other words, don't blast your tummy with the *habanera* or *jalapeño* pepper right off the bat. Work into the fried food, drinks, local specialties, and new spices gradually; take your time changing over to foods that you may never eat while at home, including the large quantities of wonderful tropical fruits that you'll want to eat every morning. Turista can also be blamed on alcohol mixed with longer-than-usual periods of time in the tropical sun.

The Water

Water is probably the worst culprit. Carry bottled water at all times. Many parts of the Yucatán Peninsula (such as Cancún and the newer developments along the Caribbean coast) have modern sewage systems, but small villages and isolated areas still have little or none—all waste is redeposited in the earth and can contaminate the natural water supply. While in these places you should take special precautions.

In the backcountry water should be boiled or purified with chemicals, whether the source is the tap or a crystal-clear cenote. That goes for brushing your teeth as well. If you have nothing else, a bottle of beer will make a safe (though maybe not sane) mouth rinse. If using ice, ask where it was made and if it's pure. Think about the water you're swimming in; some small local pools are better avoided.

The easiest way to purify the water is with purification tablets; Hidroclonozone and Halazone are two, but many brands are available at drugstores in all countries—in Mexico ask at the *farmacia*. Another common method is to carry a small plastic bottle of liquid bleach (use 8–10 drops per quart of water) or iodine (called *yodo;* five–seven drops per quart). Whichever you use, let the water stand for 20 minutes to improve the flavor. If you're not prepared with any of the above, boiling the water for 20–30 minutes will purify it. Even though it takes a heck of a lot of fuel that you'll probably be carrying on your back, don't get lazy in this department. You can get very sick drinking contaminated water and you can't tell by looking at it—unless you travel with a microscope!

When camping on the beach where fresh water is scarce, use seawater to wash dishes and even yourself. If you have access to a sporting goods or marine store, ask for Sea Saver soap. Otherwise, use Castille soap. It only takes a small squirt of the soap to do a good job. (A rub of soap on the backsides of pots and pans before setting them over an open fire makes for easy cleaning after cooking.)

In the larger cities, purified water is generally provided in bottles in each room. Large hotels often maintain their own purification plants on the premises. In Cozumel, for example, the Sol Caribe Hotel has a modern purification plant behind glass walls for all to see, and they're proud to show it off and explain how it works. If the tap water is pure, a sign over the spigot will specify this. If you're not sure about the water, ask the desk clerk; he'll let you know the status (they prefer healthy guests who will return).

Other Sources of Bacteria

Handling money can be a source of germs. Wash your hands frequently, don't put your fingers in your mouth, and carry individual foil packets of disinfectant cleansers, like Wash Up (handy and refreshing in the tropic heat) or liquid disinfectants that just rub dry. Hepatitis is another bug that can be contracted easily if you're around it.

When in backcountry cafés, remember that fruits and vegetables, especially those with thin, edible skins (like tomatoes), are a possible source of bacteria. If you like to eat food purchased from street vendors (and some should not be missed), use common sense. If you see the food being cooked (killing all the grubby little bacteria) before your eyes, have at it. If it's hanging there already cooked and nibbled on by small flying creatures, pass it by. It may have been there all day, and what was once a nice sterile morsel could easily have gone bad in the heat or been contaminated by flies.

Treatment

Remember, it's not just the visiting gringo who gets sick because of bacteria. Many Mexicans die each year from the same germs, and the Mexican government is working hard to remedy their sanitation problems. Tremendous improvements have taken place that ultimately will be accomplished all over Mexico, but it's a slow process. In the meantime, many careful visitors come and go each year with nary a touch of turista.

If after all your precautions you still come down with traveler's illness, many medications are available for relief. Most can be bought over the counter in Mexico, but in the United States you'll need a prescription from your doctor. Lomotil and Imodium A-D are common and certainly turn off the faucet after a few hours of dosing; however, each has the side effect of becoming a plug. It does not cure the problem, only the symptoms; if you quit taking it too soon your symptoms reappear and you're back to square one. In its favor, Lomotil probably works faster than any of the other drugs, and if you're about to embark on a 12-hour bus ride across the Yucatán Peninsula you might consider Lomotil a lifesaver. A few other over-the-counter remedies are Kaopectate in the United States and Imodium and Donamycin in Mexico. Be sure to read and follow the directions. If you're concerned, check with your doctor before leaving home. Also ask him or her about some new formulas called Septra and Bactrim. While traveling, we count on a combination of Imodium (which stops the symptoms fairly quickly) and Septra or Bactrim, which supposedly kills the bug. Don't forget the common Pepto-Bismol. Some swear by it; be aware that it can turn the tongue a dark brownish color—nothing to be alarmed about. Septra and Bactrim must be bought in the United States with a prescription under a different name; check with your doctor.

For those who prefer natural remedies, lime juice and garlic are both considered good when taken as preventatives. They need to be taken in large quantities. Douse everything with the readily available lime juice (it's delicious on salads and fresh fruit and in drinks). You'll have to figure out your own ways of using garlic (some believers carry garlic capsules, available in most U.S. health-food stores). Mexicans imbibe fresh coconut juice (don't eat the oily flesh, it makes your problem worse!). Plain boiled white rice and chamomile tea *(té de manzanillo)* also soothe the stomach. While letting the ailment run its course, stay away from spicy and oily foods and fresh fruits. Don't be surprised if you have chills, nausea, vomiting, stomach cramps, and a fever. This could go on for about three days. If the problem persists, see a doctor.

SUNBURN

Sunburn can spoil a vacation quicker than anything else, so approach the sun cautiously. Expose yourself for short periods the first few days, and wear a hat and sunglasses. Use sunscreen and apply it to all exposed areas of the body (don't forget feet, hands, nose, backs of your knees, and forehead—especially if you have a receding hairline). Remember that after each time you go into the water for a swim, sunscreen lotion must be reapplied. Even after a few days of desensitizing your skin, wear a T-shirt in the water when snorkeling to protect your exposed back. And thoroughly douse the back of your neck with sunscreen lotion. The higher the number on the sunscreen bottle, the more protection it offers. Some users are allergic, so try a small patch test before leaving home. If you have a reaction, investigate the new "natural" sunscreens that use mica. Ask at your pharmacy.

If, despite precautions, you still get a painful sunburn, do not return to the sun. Cover up with clothes if it's impossible to find protective deep shade (like in the depths of a dark, thick forest). Keep in mind that even in partial shade (such as under a beach umbrella), the reflection of the sun off the sand or water will burn your skin. Reburning the skin can result in painful blisters that easily become infected. Soothing suntan lotions, coconut oil, vinegar, cool tea, and preparations like Solarcaine will help relieve the pain. Drink plenty of liquids (especially water) and take tepid showers. A few days out of the sun is the best medicine.

HEALING

Most small cities in Quintana Roo have a resident doctor. He or she may or may not speak English, but will usually make a house call. When staying in a hotel, get a doctor quickly by asking the hotel manager; in the larger resorts, an English-speaking doctor is on call 24 hours a day. If you need to ask someone to get you a doctor, say, *"¡Necesito doctor, por favor!"* Emergency clinics are found in all but the smallest villages, and a taxi driver can be your quick-

pool games at the Hyatt Regency, Cancún

OZ MALLAN

est way to get there when you're a stranger in town. In small rural villages, if you have a serious problem and no doctor is around, you can usually find a *curandero*. These healers deal with the old natural methods (and maybe just a few chants thrown in for good measure), and can be helpful in a desperate situation away from modern technology.

Self Help
The smart traveler carries a first-aid kit of some kind. If backpacking, carry at least the following:
• adhesive tape
• alcohol
• antibiotic ointment
• aspirin
• baking soda
• Band-Aids
• cornstarch
• gauze
• hydrogen peroxide
• insect repellent
• iodine
• Lomotil
• pain pills
• sewing needle
• sunscreen
• water-purification tablets

Many of these products are available in Mexico, but certain items, like aspirin and Band-Aids, are sold individually in small shops and are much cheaper in your hometown. Even if you're not out in the wilderness, you should carry at least a few Band-Aids, aspirin, and an antibiotic ointment or powder or both. Travelers should be aware that in the tropics, with its heavy humidity, a simple scrape can become infected more easily than in a dry climate. So keep cuts and scratches as clean and dry as possible.

Another great addition to your first-aid kit is David Werner's book, *Where There Is No Doctor.* Also published in Spanish, it can be ordered from the Hesperian Foundation, P.O. Box 1692, Palo Alto, CA 94302. David Werner drew on his experience living in Mexico's backcountry when creating this informative book.

Shots
Check on your tetanus shot before you leave home, especially if you're backpacking in isolated regions. A gamma globulin shot may also be necessary; ask your physician.

SIMPLE FIRST-AID GUIDE

Acute Allergic Reaction: This, the most serious complication of insect bites, can be fatal. Common symptoms are hives, rash, pallor, nausea, tightness in chest or throat, and trouble speaking or breathing. Be alert for symptoms. If they appear, get prompt medical help. If you know you have allergies, like to shell fish, don't eat them, but always carry a bottle of Benadryl with you just in case. Start CPR if needed and continue until medical help is available.

Animal Bites: Bites, especially on the face and neck, need immediate medical attention. If possible, catch and hold the animal for observation, taking care not to be bitten. Wash the wound with soap and water (hold under running water for two–three minutes unless the bleeding is heavy). Do not use iodine or other antiseptics. Bandage. This also applies to bites by human beings. In the case of human bites the danger of infection is high.

Bee Stings: Apply cold compresses quickly. If possible, remove the stinger by gentle scraping with a clean fingernail and continue cold applications till the pain is gone. Be alert for symptoms of acute allergic reaction or infection requiring medical aid.

Bleeding: For severe bleeding apply direct pressure to the wound with a bandage or the heel of the hand. Do not remove cloths when blood-soaked; just add others on top and continue pressure till bleeding stops. Elevate the bleeding part above heart level. If bleeding continues, apply a pressure bandage to arterial points. Do not put on a tourniquet unless advised by a physician. Do not use iodine or other disinfectants. Get medical aid.

Blister on Heel: It is better not to open a blister if you can rest the foot. If you can't, wash the foot with soap and water. Make a small hole at the base of the blister with a needle sterilized in 70 percent alcohol or in a match flame. Drain the fluid and cover with a strip bandage or moleskin. If a blister breaks on its own, wash with soap and water, bandage, and be alert for signs of infection (redness, festering) that call for medical attention.

Burns: For minor burns (redness, swelling, pain), apply cold water or immerse the burned part in cold water immediately. Use burn medication if necessary. For deeper burns (blisters develop), immerse in cold water (not ice water) or apply cold compresses for one to two hours. Blot dry and protect with a sterile bandage. Do not use antiseptic, ointment, or home remedies. Consult a doctor. For deep burns (skin layers destroyed, skin may be charred), cover with sterile cloth; be alert for breathing difficulties and treat for shock if necessary. Do not remove clothing stuck to the burn. Do not apply ice. Do not use burn remedies. Get medical help quickly.

Cuts: For small cuts, wash with clean water and soap. Hold the wound under running water. Bandage. Use hydrogen peroxide or another antiseptic. For large wounds, see Bleeding. If a finger or toe has been cut off, treat the severed end to control bleeding. Put the severed part in clean cloth for the doctor (it may be possible to reattach it by surgery). Treat for shock if necessary. Get medical help at once.

Diving Accident: There may be injury to the cervical spine (such as a broken neck). Call for medical help. (See "Drowning.")

Drowning: Clear the airway and start CPR even before trying to get water out of the lungs. Continue CPR until medical help arrives. In case of vomiting, turn the victim's head to one side to prevent inhalation of vomitus.

Food Poisoning: Symptoms appear a varying number of hours after eating and are generally like those of the flu—headache, diarrhea, vomiting, abdominal cramps, fever, a general sick feeling. See a doctor. A rare form, botulism, has a high fatality rate. Symptoms are double vision, inability to swallow, difficulty speaking, and respiratory paralysis. Get to an emergency facility at once.

Fractures: Do not move the victim unless absolutely necessary. Suspected victims of back, neck, or hip injuries should not be moved at all. Suspected breaks of arms or legs should be splinted to avoid further damage before the victim is moved, if moving is necessary.

Heat Exhaustion: Symptoms are cool and moist skin, profuse sweating, headache, fatigue, and drowsiness with essentially normal body temperature. Remove the victim to cool surroundings, raise feet and legs, loosen clothing, and apply cool cloths. Give sips of salt water—one teaspoon of salt to a glass of water—for rehydration. If the victim vomits, stop fluids and take the victim to an emergency facility as soon as possible.

Heatstroke: Rush the victim to a hospital. Heatstroke can be fatal. The victim may be unconscious or severely confused. The skin feels hot and is red and dry, with no perspiration. Body temperature is high. Pulse is rapid. Remove the victim to a cool area, sponge with cool water or rubbing alcohol; use fans or air-conditioning and wrap the victim in wet sheets, but do not over-chill. Massage arms and legs to increase circulation. Do not give large amounts of liquids. Do not give liquids if the victim is unconscious.

Insect Bites: Be alert for an acute allergic reaction that requires quick medical aid. Otherwise, apply cold compresses and soothing lotions. If the bites are scratched and infection starts (fever, swelling, redness), see a doctor.

Jellyfish Stings: Symptom is acute pain and may include local paralysis. Immerse the affected area in ice water from for 5–10 minutes or apply aromatic spirits of ammonia to remove venom from the skin. Be alert for symptoms of acute allergic reaction and/or shock. If this happens, get the victim to a hospital as soon as possible.

Motion Sickness: Get a prescription from your doctor if boat travel is anticipated and this illness is a problem. Many over-the-counter remedies are sold in the United States—Bonine and Dramamine are two. If you prefer not to take chemicals or if you get drowsy, the new Sea Band is a cloth band that you place around the pressure point of the wrist. For more information write: Sea Band, 1645 Palm Beach Lake Blvd., Suite 220, W. Palm Beach, FL 33401 U.S.A. Also available by prescription from your doctor is medication administered in adhesive patches behind the ear.

Muscle Cramps: Usually a result of unaccustomed exertion, "working" the muscle or kneading it with the hand usually relieves the cramp. If in water, head for shore (you can swim even with a muscle cramp), or knead the muscle with your hand. Call for help if needed. Do not panic.

Mushroom Poisoning: Even a small ingestion may be serious. Induce vomiting immediately if there is any question of mushroom poisoning. Symptoms—vomiting, diarrhea, difficult breathing—may begin in one to two hours or up to 24 hours. Convulsions and delirium may develop. Go to a doctor or emergency facility at once.

Nosebleed: Press the bleeding nostril closed, or pinch the nostrils together, or pack them with sterile cotton or gauze. Apply a cold cloth or ice to the nose and face. The victim should sit up, leaning forward, or lie down with head and shoulders raised. If bleeding does not stop in 10 minutes, get medical help.

Obstructed Airway: Find out if the victim can talk by asking, "Can you talk?" If he or she can talk, encourage the victim to cough the obstruction out. If he or she can't speak, a trained person must apply the Heimlich maneuver. If you are alone and choking, try to forcefully cough the object out. Or press your fist into your upper abdomen with a quick upward thrust, or lean forward and quickly press your upper abdomen over any firm object with a rounded edge (back of chair, edge of sink, porch railing). Keep trying until the object comes out.

Plant Poisoning: Many plants are poisonous if eaten or chewed. If the leaves of the diffenbachia (common in the Yucatán jungle) are chewed, one of the first symptoms is swelling of the throat. Induce vomiting immediately. Take the victim to an emergency facility for treatment.

Poison Ivy, Oak, or Sumac: After contact, wash the affected area with an alkali laundry soap, lathering well. Have a poison-ivy remedy available in case itching and blisters develop.

Puncture Wounds: Usually caused by stepping on a tack or a nail, these often do not bleed, so try to squeeze out some blood. Wash thoroughly with soap and water and apply a sterile bandage. Check with a doctor about tetanus. If pain, heat, throbbing, or redness develops, get medical attention at once.

Rabies: Bites from bats, raccoons, rats, or other wild animals are the most common threat of rabies today. Try to capture the animal, avoiding getting bitten, so it can be observed; do not kill the animal unless necessary and try not to injure the head so the brain can be examined. If the animal can't be found, see a doctor, who may decide to use antirabies immunization. In any case, flush the bite with water and apply a dry dressing; keep the victim quiet and see a doctor as soon as possible.

Scrapes: Sponge with soap and water; dry. Apply antibiotic ointment or powder and cover with a nonstick dressing (or tape on a piece of cellophane). When healing starts, stop the ointment and use an antiseptic powder to help a scab form. Ask a doctor about tetanus.

Shock: Can be a side effect in any kind of injury. Get immediate medical help. Symptoms may be pallor, clammy skin, shallow breathing, fast pulse, weakness, or thirst. Loosen clothing, cover the victim with blanket but do not apply other heat, and place the victim on his or her back with the feet raised. If necessary, start CPR. Do not give water or other fluids.

Snakebite or Lizard Bite: If the reptile is not poisonous, tooth marks usually appear in an even row (an exception, the poisonous Gila monster, shows even tooth marks). Wash the bite with soap and water and apply a sterile bandage. See a doctor. If the snake is poisonous, puncture marks (1–6) can usually be seen. Kill the snake for identification if possible, taking care not to be bitten. Keep the victim quiet and immobilize the bitten arm or leg, keeping it on a lower level than the heart. If possible, phone ahead to check that antivenin is available and get medical treatment as soon as possible. Do not give alcohol in any form. If treatment must be delayed and a snakebite kit is available, use as directed.

Spider Bites: The black widow bite may produce only a light reaction at the place of the bite, but severe pain, a general sick feeling, sweating, abdominal cramps, and breathing and speaking difficulty may develop. The more dangerous brown recluse spider's venom produces a severe reaction at the bite, generally in two–eight hours, plus chills, fever, joint pain, nausea, and vomiting. Apply a cold compress to the bite in either case. Get medical aid quickly.

Sprain: Treat as a fracture until the injured part has been X-rayed. Raise the sprained ankle or other joint and apply cold compresses or immerse in cold water. If the swelling is pronounced, try not to use the injured part until it has been X-rayed. Get prompt medical help.

Sunburn: For skin that is moderately red and slightly swollen, apply wet dressings of gauze dipped in a solution of one tablespoon baking soda and one tablespoon cornstarch to two quarts of cool water. Or take a cool bath with a cup of baking soda to a tub of water. Sunburn remedies are helpful in relieving pain. See a doctor if the burn is severe.

Sunstroke: This is a severe emergency. See "Heatstroke." The skin is hot and dry; body temperature is high. The victim may be delirious or unconscious. Get medical help immediately.

Ticks: Cover ticks with mineral oil or kerosene to exclude air from them, and they will usually drop off or can be lifted off with tweezers in 30 minutes. To avoid infection, be sure to remove the whole tick. Wash the area with soap and water. Check with a doctor or health department to see if deadly ticks are in the area.

Wasp Sting: Apply cold compresses to the sting and watch for an acute allergic reaction. If such symptoms develop, get the victim to a medical facility immediately.

HAZARDS

Security
It's smart to keep passports, traveler's checks, money, and important papers on your person or in a safe-deposit box at all times. (It's always a good idea to keep a separate list of document numbers in your luggage and leave a copy with a friend back home. This expedites replacement in case of loss.) The do-it-yourselfer can sew inside pockets into clothes; buy extra-long pants that can be turned up and sewn three-fourths of the way around, the last section closed with a piece of Velcro. Separate shoulder-holster pockets, money belts, and pockets around the neck inside clothing—all made of cotton—are available commercially. If you're going to be backpacking and sloshing in jungle streams, etc., put everything in Ziploc bags before placing them in pockets. Waterproof plastic tubes will hold a limited number of items around your neck while you swim.

Before You Leave Home
Probably the best way to save money is to make sure you don't lose anything along the way. Be practical; leave expensive jewelry at home. Take five minutes to go through your wallet before leaving and remove all credit cards you won't be using and put a good part of your money in traveler's checks. Make two copies of your passport-picture page and any credit cards you carry. Leave one copy of each with someone at home you can reach in case of emergency. After you get your visitor's card, also make a copy of that for your wallet if possible. Keep these copies where you'll have them in the event your wallet and cards are stolen—in another piece of luggage. If your cards should get pinched, the

copies will expedite replacement wherever you are in the world. Keep the original visitor's card with your passport in a hotel safe when sightseeing or swimming.

The Hotel Safe

Even the smallest hotels have safe-deposit boxes or some other security system for their guests. Many of the more upscale hotels have in-room safes now, which is very convenient. Use it for your airline tickets and passports as well as other valuables. Don't leave anything valuable lying around your room. Why create a tempting situation? Most hotel employees are honest (honestly!); working in a hotel is a good job, and for the most part that's far more important to the employee than stealing. However (you knew a *however* was coming, didn't you?), you might be the unlucky person to draw the unscrupulous thief, maid, or bellboy.

A hotel robbery is less common than, say, a setup on the street (a jostle, attention diverted by one person while the other grabs your purse or cuts the strap of a carry bag). Take precautions, act sensibly, be aware of what is going on around you at all times; don't flash large wads of cash, and don't give your room number to strangers. If you're invited to go anywhere with a stranger, suggest meeting him or her there; let someone know where you are going, even if it's the desk clerk.

Pickpockets

Don't forget pickpockets! They love fairs and all celebrations where there are lots of people. It's really easy to jostle people in crowds (that includes buses), so make sure you've got your money where a quick hand can't get to it, like a money belt, or a holster worn over your shoulder under your clothing. Many types are available; check the trendy travel stores and catalogs. It's a good idea to put everything in a plastic bag before you stash it in your belt or holster; sweat makes ink run.

Legal Help

If after all precautions you still have a problem, contact the 24-hour national hotline of the office of **La Procuradoría de Protección al Turista** (Attorney General for the Protection of Tourists). Each state has an office. The following number is located in Mexico City (tell the English-speaking operator you have an emergency and she will direct your call): tel. 5/250-0293, 250-0151, or 250-0589.

In the event you should be arrested, contact the nearest American Consul's office. If nothing else, they will visit you and advise you of your rights. Whatever you do, don't get caught with illegal substances; there's little that anyone can do given the current U.S. pressures to stop drug trafficking.

Insurance

Most homeowner's policies cover loss of property while on vacation; check it out before you leave home. *Do* make a police report if you're robbed. It's a long bureaucratic chore, but sometimes your property is recovered as a result. It also helps to have the report in hand when you deal with your insurance back home.

Lastly (yes, this is a repeat), always make a copy of the front pages of your passport with pictures and all the vital information, numbers, etc. This is critical in the event you lose your passport. Leave one set behind with a friend, put one set in a separate piece of luggage, and place one in your purse. When you go to your American consul or ambassador, this will expedite the passport replacement process.

Women Travelers

A solo female traveler is considered very approachable by scammers and con artists. The "May I join you?" scam is typical in tourist areas. A seemingly harmless man may ask if he can join you; he orders a drink (or more), and you foot the bill. If you really would like some company, make sure to specify *"Cuentas separadas por favor"* ("Separate checks please") to your waiter.

Hitchhiking

Neither men nor women are advised to hitchhike. When walking at night, find other travelers or trustworthy companions. Let your hotel staff know your plans; they can often provide you with a reliable list of taxi drivers and look out for your well-being.

SERVICES AND INFORMATION

PHOTOGRAPHY

Bring a camera to the Yucatán Peninsula! Nature and the Maya combine to provide unforgettable panoramas, well worth taking home with you on film to savor again at your leisure. Many people bring simple cameras that point and shoot and are easy to carry. For boat trips and snorkeling the new "disposable" waterproof cameras are great. Others prefer 35-mm cameras, which offer higher-quality pictures, are easier than ever to use, and are available in any price range. They come equipped with built-in light meters, automatic exposure, self-focus, and self-advance—with little more to do than aim and click. Or, bring along several disposable cameras. If you just want snap shots, they're about as easy as they get.

Film
Two reasons to bring film with you: It's cheaper and more readily available in the United States. Two reasons not to bring lots of film: space may be a problem and heat can affect film quality, both before and after exposure. If you're traveling for more than two weeks and will be in a car or bus a good part of the time, carry film in an insulated case. You can buy a soft-sided insulated bag in most camera shops or order one out of a professional photography magazine. For the average vacation, if your film is kept in your room, there should be no problem. Many varieties of Kodak film are found in camera shops and hotel gift shops on the Yucatán Peninsula. In the smaller towns along the Caribbean coast you may not be able to find slide film.

X-ray Protection
If you carry film with you when traveling by plane, take precautions. Each time film is passed through the security X-ray machine, a little damage is done. It's cumulative, and perhaps one time won't make much difference, but most photographers won't take the chance. Request hand inspection. With today's tight security at airports, some guards insist on passing your film and camera through the X-ray machine. If your film is packed in your checked luggage, it's wise to keep it in protective lead-lined bags, available at camera shops in two sizes; the larger size holds up to 22 rolls of 35-mm film, the smaller holds eight rolls. If you use fast film, ASA 400 or higher, buy the double lead-lined bag designed to protect more sensitive film. Carry an extra lead-lined bag for your film-loaded camera if you want to drop it into a piece of carry-on luggage. (These bags also protect medications from X-ray damage.)

If you decide to request hand examination (rarely if ever refused at a Mexican airport), make it simple for the security guard. Have the film out of boxes and canisters placed together in one clear plastic bag that you can hand him for quick examination both coming and going. He'll also want to look at the camera; load it with film *after* crossing the border.

Film Processing
For processing film, the traveler has several options. Most people take their film home and have it processed at a familiar lab. Again, if the trip is lengthy and you are shooting lots of photos, it's impractical to carry used rolls around for more than a couple of weeks. Larger cities have one-hour photo labs, but they only handle color prints; color slides must be processed at a lab in Mexico City, which usually takes a week or two. If you'll be passing through the same city on another leg of your trip, the lab is a good cool place to store your slides while you travel. Just tell the lab technician when you think you'll be picking them up. Kodak mailers are another option but most photographers won't let their film out of sight until they reach their own favorite lab.

Camera Protection
Take a few precautions with your camera while traveling. At the beach remember that a combination of wind and sand can really gum up the works and scratch the lens. On 35-mm cameras keep a clear skylight filter on the lens instead of a lens cap so the camera can hang around your neck or in a fanny pack always at the ready

for that spectacular shot that comes when least expected. If something is going to get scratched, better a $15 filter than a $300 lens.

It also helps to carry as little equipment as possible. If you want more than candids and you carry a 35-mm camera, basic equipment can be simple. Padded camera cases are good and come in all sizes. A canvas bag is lighter and less conspicuous than a heavy photo bag, but doesn't have the extra protection the padding provides. At army/military surplus stores you can find small military bags and webbed belts with eyelet holes from which to hang canteen pouches and clip holders for extra equipment. It helps to have your hands free while climbing pyramids or on long hikes.

Safety Tips

Keep your camera dry; carrying a couple of big Ziploc bags affords instant protection. Don't *store* cameras in plastic bags for any length of time because the moisture that builds up in the bag can damage a camera as much as leaving it in the rain.

It's always wise to keep cameras out of sight in a car or when camping out. Put your name and address on the camera. Chances are if it gets left behind or stolen it won't matter whether your name is there or not, and don't expect to see it again; however, miracles do happen. (You *can* put a rider on most homeowner's insurance policies for a nominal sum that will cover the

cost if a camera is lost or stolen.) It's a nuisance to carry cameras every second when traveling for a long period. During an evening out, you can leave your cameras and equipment (out of sight) in the hotel room—unless it makes you crazy all evening worrying about it! Some hotel safes are large enough to accommodate your equipment.

Cameras can be a help and a hindrance when trying to get to know the people. Traveling in the backcountry, you'll run into folks frightened of having their pictures taken. Keep your camera put away until the right moment. The main thing to remember is to ask permission first and then, if someone doesn't want his/her picture taken, accept the refusal with a gracious smile and move on.

Camera Fees

There is an additional charge of US$8–10 to use a video camera at most archaeological sites. There is talk of a similar charge for still cameras as well, though we had no problems using a camera, without tripod, on our last visit. To be sure, check with your nearest Mexican tourist office before you leave home.

MONEY

New Pesos

After the collapse of the stock market in 1994, the

street snacks

OZ MALLAN

peso plunged in value. Mexicans in all walks of life suffered as U.S. residents would if without warning US$1 was suddenly worth US$.50. Their buying power was stifled, and every individual and business with debt was pushed deeper into the hole. Things have since leveled off somewhat; however, when the peso drops, the dollar becomes more valuable in Mexico. So, sadly, what is a hardship on Mexicans becomes a boon to the traveler. Don't expect bargains in upscale hotels. Their prices are geared to the foreign traveler, and those prices have risen to make up some of the difference. It's in the smaller towns and businesses that you'll notice "cheap." The exchange rate can go up or down in today's volatile financial climate in Mexico; most of the prices are quoted in U.S. dollars in this book, since that seems to be fairly stable. And when you tip, remember that these service people make a minuscule salary, so do tip as you would in the United States.

Cashing personal checks in Mexico is not easy; however, it is possible to withdraw money against your credit card in some banks and instant teller machines. Wearing a money belt is always a good idea while traveling—in any country.

Exchange

Usually your best rate of exchange is at the bank, but small shops frequently give a good rate if you're making a purchase. Hotels are notorious for giving the poorest exchange. Check to see what kind of fee, if any, is charged. You can learn the current exchange rate daily in all banks and most hotels. Try not to run out of money over the weekend because the new rate often is not posted until noon on Monday; you will get the previous Friday's rate of exchange even if the weekend newspaper may be announcing an overwhelming difference in your favor.

Note: According to many foreign travelers in Mexico, it's easier to exchange U.S. dollars for pesos than many other currencies (perhaps with the exception of Canadian dollars). So, foreign travelers might want to come prepared with either U.S. dollars or U.S. traveler's checks. Also, try to spend all your coinage before leaving the country, since most banks or money changers will not buy peso coins with U.S. dollars.

Always go with pesos in hand to the small rural

TIPPING

Tipping is of course up to the individual, but for a guideline in Quintana Roo the following seems to be average:

Porters: About US$1 per bag. If you're staying at a hotel with no elevator and three flights of stairs and you have lots of luggage, you may wish to be more generous.

Hotel Maids: If staying more than one night, US$1–2 per day left at the end of your stay.

Waiters/Waitresses: If not already included on the bill, 15–20 percent is average for good service.

Tour Guides: Tour guides should receive about US$15 per person for a half-day trip and US$10–20 per person for longer trips, if they do a good job, of course! Also customary is US$5 per person for the driver.

Informal Site Guides: When visiting a ruin, cave, or lighthouse you will usually be shown the way by a young boy—US$1 is customary.

Gas Station Attendants: Usually tipped about US$.50 for pumping gas, cleaning the windshield, checking the oil and water, and providing other standard services.

Tipping **taxi drivers** is not customary.

Note: For the most part, American coins are useless in Mexico since moneychangers, whether banks or stores, will not accept them. So tip in pesos please.

---

areas of Mexico. And even more convenient, take them in small denominations. In most cases it's a real hassle to cash dollars or traveler's checks.

Credit Cards

Major credit cards are accepted at all of the larger hotels, upscale restaurants in big cities, travel agencies, and many shops throughout Cancún. But don't take it for granted; ask. The smaller businesses do not accept them. In some cases you will be asked to pay a fee on top of the charged amount. In Mexico, universally, gas stations *do not* accept credit cards.

Hours for Banks and Businesses

Banks are open Monday–Friday 9 A.M.–1:30 P.M. Business offices are open 8 A.M.–5 P.M. (or 8 A.M.–6 P.M.) and close for an hour or more in the early afternoon. Government offices are usually open until 3 P.M. Stores in cities are generally open 10 A.M.–7 P.M., sometimes closing 1–4 P.M., although that's pretty much out of style. Government offices, banks, and stores are closed on national holidays.

Moneda

The "$" sign in Mexico means pesos. Shops that accept dollars will often price items with the abbreviation "Dlls." If you see a price that says "m.n.," that indicates pesos, *moneda national.* Most large airports have money-exchange counters, but the hours generally depend on the flight schedules.

Traveler's Checks

Traveler's checks are the easiest way to carry money. However, certain moneychangers will pay more for cash and some banks charge a fee, so always ask before making a transaction. If you're in a really small town, don't expect the shops or vendors to cash a traveler's check; gas stations deal *only* in pesos—so far. Be prepared. If you need to change money after bank hours, look for a sign that says Casa de Cambio.

The favored credit cards in Mexico are Bancomer (Visa) and Carnet (MasterCard)—way down the list is American Express; in fact, most businesses refuse Amex as well as Diners Club. Look for ATMs in banks. Before leaving home, ask your bank teller if your particular card is authorized for use in Mexico, and, if so, at which branches.

Admission Fees

Admissions to the archaeological sites have taken large leaps in the past few years. INAH (Instituto Nacional de Antropología e Historia) is the arm of the government that directs the museums and archaeological sites of the country. The increase in fees certainly goes hand in hand with the improvements made on the sites. All the larger sites now have modern visitor's centers with restrooms, gift shops, snack shops, museums, and auditori-

ums. Most of the smaller sites will eventually have restrooms. INAH also sets the fees. There are still one or two sites in *way* out-of-the-way places that have not added restrooms or visitor's amenities and don't charge at all. Admission to all sites and museums is free on Sunday.

Remember that your video camera might cost more than you do to get into the archaeological grounds, about US$10.

Admission fees do not include the services of a guide; having an English-speaking guide is really worthwhile, but be sure to establish your fee (for your entire group), how long the guide will be with you, and where he will take you, before saying yes. A good starting point for negotiations for up to six people is US$25–30. If he was *really* good, a tip is fair. By yourself, expect to pay at least US$20 in the larger sites (much cheaper by the dozen) for a half day.

As at the sites, admission to state and national parks is free on Sunday. Fees range from US$.75–5.

Taxes

Note: A 12 percent IVA tax is added to room rates, restaurant and bar tabs, and gift purchases. When checking in or making reservations at a hotel, ask if tax has already been added. And once again, don't forget that when you leave the country or travel from Mexican city to Mexican city, you must pay an **airport departure tax.** National departures, US$6; international departures, US$12.

Watching Your Pesos

No matter where you travel in the world, it's wise to guard your money. A money belt worn under

---

YUCATÁN PENINSULA POSTAL CODES

Cancún: 77500
Campeche: 24000
Chetumal: 77000
Cozumel: 77600
Isla Mujeres: 77400
Playa del Carmen: 77710
Mérida: 97000
San Cristóbal: .29200

YUCATÁN PENINSULA TELEPHONE AREA CODES

Campeche: 981
Cancún: 98
Chetumal: 983
Chiapa de Corzo: 968
Chichén Itzá: 985
Cozumel: 987
Felipe Carrillo Puerto: 983
Isla Mujeres: 987
Izamal: 995
Mérida: 99
Palenque: 934
Piste: 985
Playa del Carmen: 987
Puerto Celestun: 991
San Cristóbal: 967
Ticul: 997
Tuxtla: 961
Uxmal: 99
Valladolid: 985
Villahermosa: 93

the clothes is probably the most unobtrusive. They come in a variety of styles, from a shoulder holster to a flat pocket worn around the neck, or even an honest-to-goodness leather belt with a fine flat zipper opening on the inside, where you can insert a few folded bills for an emergency. Using hotel safe facilities is also very practical. In most cases visitors encounter no problems, but take precautions—it only takes one pickpocket to ruin a good vacation.

Bargaining

This is one way a visitor really gets to know the people. Although the influx of many outsiders who don't appreciate the delicate art of bargaining has deteriorated this traditional verbal exchange, it's still a way of life among Mexicans, and it can still build a bridge between the gringo and the Yucatecan. Some Americans accustomed to shopping with plastic money either find bargaining distasteful or go overboard and insult the merchant by offering far too little. It would not be insulting to begin the bargaining at 50 percent below the asking price; expect to earn about a 20 percent discount (and new respect) after a lively, often jovial, repartee be-

tween buyer and seller. Bargaining is only done in the public markets and some of the artisans' markets.

COMMUNICATIONS AND MEDIA

Shipping

Mailing and shipping from Mexico is easy within certain limitations. Packages of less than US$25 in value can be sent to the United States. The package must be marked "Unsolicited Gift—Under $25" and addressed to someone other than the traveler. Only one package per day may be sent to the same addressee. Major stores will handle shipping arrangements on larger items and duty must be paid; this is in addition to the US$400 carried in person across the border.

Even the smallest town in Quintana Roo has a post office. If you can't find it by looking, ask—it may be located in someone's front parlor. Airmail postage is recommended for the best delivery. Post offices will hold travelers' mail for one week if it is marked *a/c Lista de Correos* ("care of General Delivery"). Hotels will extend the same service for mail marked "tourist mail, hold for arrival."

Telephone

One of the newest additions to the Yucatán Peninsula as well as other parts of Mexico is a scattering of Direct Dial USA telephone booths. These can be very costly. Look for phones labeled **Ladatel.** Many of these phones use telephone cards available at small markets and pharmacies. The cards are sold in 10-, 20-, 30-, and 50-peso amounts; when you use the card a digital screen shows how much money your call is costing and deducts it from the value of the card. It comes in very handy when calling ahead to confirm hotel rooms or making other arrangements, and it's certainly better than carrying peso coins. The card is quick and efficient. In small towns, expect the same old rules. Hotels (if they have phones) add enormous service charges to direct calls—always ask what it will be first. Calling collect is cheaper, and going to a *larga distancia* office is the most economical. Remember that although the Ladatel phones are really convenient, they are costly if you talk for any length of time, collect or not. Many think the "user-friendly" quality is worth the price.

Note: Probably the cheapest way to communicate with folks in any country is by email, as cyber cafés are everywhere. The fee is usually by 15-minute periods, and it's much cheaper than the telephone.

Radio and Television
AM and FM radio stations, in Spanish, are scattered throughout the Peninsula. Television is becoming more common as well. In the major cities, hotel rooms have TV entertainment. The large resort hotels all around Mexico have one or more cable stations from the United States, on which you can expect to see all the major baseball and football games, news, and latest movies.

STANDARDS AND MEASUREMENTS

Time
Quintana Roo and the rest of the Yucatán Peninsula are in the U.S. Central Standard Time Zone. All the states of the Yucatán observe daylight saving time April–October.

Electricity
Electric current has been standardized throughout Mexico, using the same 60-cycle, 110-volt AC current common in the United States. Small travel appliances can be used everywhere; if you have a problem, it will be because there's no electricity at all. In some areas electricity is supplied by small generators and is turned off at 10 P.M. Those hotels usually will offer you gas lanterns after the lights go out. Some areas use solar and wind for electric lights only. If the sun is behind clouds for a couple of days, or the wind dies, lights can be really dim.

Measurements
Mexico uses the metric system of weights and measures. Distances are measured in kilometers, weights are measured in grams and kilograms, gasoline is sold by the liter, and temperatures are given on the Celsius scale. A chart at the back of this book will help visitors accustomed to the Anglo-American system of measurement make the appropriate conversions.

USEFUL TELEPHONE NUMBERS

Assistance
Emergencies: 06
Directory assistance (within Mexico): 01
Long-distance operator: 02
International operator (English): 09

Long-Distance Dialing
Mexico long-distance: 91 (92 for person-to-person) + area code + number
International long-distance: 98 (99 for person-to-person) + area code + number
U.S. long-distance: 95 (96 for person-to-person) + area code + number

Long-Distance via U.S. Services:
AT&T: 001-95-800-462-4240
MCI: 001-95-800-674-7000
Sprint: 001-95-800-877-8000

OTHER VISITOR SERVICES

Studying in Mexico
In addition to fulfilling the requirements for a tourist card, students must present documents to a Mexican consulate demonstrating that they have been accepted at an educational institution and that they are financially solvent. A number of courses and workshops lasting two–eight weeks are offered throughout Mexico in addition to full-time study programs. Many adults as well as younger folks take part in language programs in which the student lives with a Spanish-speaking family for a period of two–four weeks and attends language classes daily. This total immersion into the language, even for a short time, is quite successful and popular as a cultural experience.

Write to the National Registration Center for Study Abroad (NRCSA), 823 N. Second St., Milwaukee, WI 53203 USA. Request their "Directory of Educational Programs," which describes programs in a number of Mexican cities.

Churches and Clubs
Mexico is predominantly a Catholic country.

However, you'll find a few churches of other denominations in the larger cities, and evangelical churches are becoming common. Local telephone books and hotel clerks have these listings. Many international organizations like the Lions, Rotary, Shriners, and foreign social groups have branches on the Yucatán Peninsula that welcome visitors.

U.S. Embassies and Consulates

If an American citizen finds herself with a problem of any kind, the nearest consul will provide advice or help. Travel advisories with up-to-the-minute information about traveling in remote areas of Mexico are available.

KATHY ESCOVEDO SANDERS

CANCÚN AND ISLA MUJERES

CANCÚN

Cancún has experienced more than three decades of successful world-class-resort fame. Everyone knows the old story—in 1967 a data-crunching computer selected a small, swampy finger of land covered with sparkling white sand in an isolated part of the aqua Mexican Caribbean as Mexico's most promising tourist town. Cancún resort was born. Lying on an island shaped like the number seven and connected by bridges with the mainland, the city was designed from the ground up. The resort sprang into being with new infrastructure, modern electrical plants, purified tap water, paved tree-lined avenues, and slick looking hotels, some resembling Maya temples. When the first hotel opened its doors in 1972, visitors came and they keep coming with just a few hiccups for a hurricane or two. Even the weather doesn't stop them for long. After Hurricane Gilbert, around-the-clock reconstruction of roads, beaches, and hundreds of windows made Cancún good

as new, and in some cases even better—in just a few months. What used to be a winter-only destination is now a year-round attraction.

For some, the name Cancún conjures images of sugar-fine sand, a palette-blue sea, and flashing dollar signs. Absolutely! The beaches *are* stunning and the water *is* enticing, but it can be costly to enjoy Cancún—especially if you just "drop in" at one of the fabulous resorts in the hotel zone. However, with careful shopping for package deals from your travel agent, in the travel pages of your local newspaper, or on Mexican websites, you'll find something to fit your pocketbook before you leave home.

Curiously, even high prices haven't slowed down the visitors. Today not only Americans and Canadians come to Cancún; the hotels *are* filled with visitors from all over the globe, and one of the many cruise ships calling on Cancún travels back and forth from Italy.

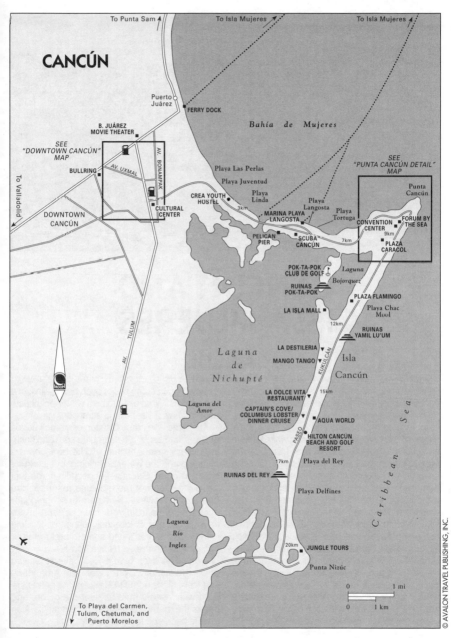

CANCÚN

To Punta Sam
To Isla Mujeres
To Isla Mujeres

Puerto Juárez

FERRY DOCK

Bahía de Mujeres

B. JUÁREZ MOVIE THEATER

SEE "DOWNTOWN CANCÚN" MAP

AV. UXMAL

AV. BONAMPAK

BULLRING

CULTURAL CENTER

DOWNTOWN CANCÚN

To Valladolid

Playa Las Perlas
Playa Juventud

CREA YOUTH HOSTEL

Playa Linda

3km

Playa Langosta

MARINA PLAYA LANGOSTA

Playa Tortuga

SEE "PUNTA CANCÚN DETAIL" MAP

Punta Cancún

CONVENTION CENTER

FORUM BY THE SEA

PELICAN PIER

SCUBA CANCÚN

7km

9km

PLAZA CARACOL

POK-TA-POK CLUB DE GOLF

Laguna Bojorquez

RUINAS POK-TA-POK

PLAZA FLAMINGO

LA ISLA MALL

Playa Chac Mool

AV. TULUM

12km

RUINAS YAMIL LU'UM

Laguna de Nichupté

LA DESTILERIA

MANGO TANGO

KUKULCAN

Isla Cancún

Laguna del Amor

LA DOLCE VITA RESTAURANT

15km

CAPTAIN'S COVE/ COLUMBUS LOBSTER DINNER CRUISE

AQUA WORLD

PASEO

HILTON CANCÚN BEACH AND GOLF RESORT

17km

Playa del Rey

RUINAS DEL REY

Playa Delfines

Caribbean Sea

Laguna Río Ingles

20km

JUNGLE TOURS

Punta Nizúc

To Playa del Carmen, Tulum, Chetumal, and Puerto Morelos

0   1 mi
0   1 km

A TALE OF TWO CITIES? DEFINITELY NOT

When the first visitors began coming to Cancún, all but one or two hotels were built along the ocean side of the one-time island. Downtown Cancún was a very separate area and plenty of empty space sprawled between downtown, along the Nichupté Lagoon, and the hotel zone. Over time the city and hotel zone have reached toward each other, and now they practically touch. Lots of businesses and new hotels have popped up in both downtown and the hotel zone, increasing the traffic all along the way. Paseo Kukulcán (also called Av., and Blvd.) is the only main boulevard to the hotel zone and has remained an attractive plant-lined roadway that runs past the Pok Ta Pok golf course. Maya stone reproductions are situated here and there under tall trees and amidst green grass with a pedestrian walkway meandering toward the hotel zone. The walkway continues to grow as the fine path meanders past sections of hotels and businesses and moves on toward the airport.

LAY OF THE LAND

From the air it's apparent that the Cancún hotel zone really was an island at one time. The two connecting bridges denote the beginning and the end of a long-legged "7". It's easy to not even notice the bridges when you cross, since they're only a few meters long.

Most visitors arrive via the Cancún airport, gather their luggage, grab transport, and head to their hotel. If you're staying in the hotel zone (the majority of travelers do) make your way via taxi, *collectivo,* and bus. As you pass over the bridge (near the bottom of the seven's long leg), you can see **Punta Nizuc** in the distance across a small lagoon paralleling the sea. This is near a popular park called **Parque Nizuc,** (admission: adults US$27, kids 3–11 US$21). The park offers water slides, a beach club, and dolphins (US$100 to swim with them; US$54 to touch them and talk to them). Kids, especially, will find there's a lot to do here.

Continuing on up the leg of the seven you'll pass the **Nichupte Lagune,** many hotels, golf courses, restaurants, and marinas filled with boats, ships, and people. At **Punta Cancún** the seven makes its turn. The road widens and traffic is like New York's 42nd Street. This is the center of Cancún activity—where the action is. You'll find lively discos, salsa, rock, jazz, labyrinth shops, extravagant malls, nightclubs, and a wonderful selection of fine and fast-food restaurants. Take your choice.

Playa Linda Embarcadero is just about at Kilometer 4, at the second bridge to the mainland. Various cruise ships, including the **Isla Mujeres Shuttle, El Galeon del Capitan Hook, Party Pirate Cruise,** and others, depart from this dock. Some ships cruise just to serve dinner; others go to Isla Mujeres and serve food and drinks and include music, dancing, continental breakfast, and offer snorkeling and shark tours.

There's lots to see and lots to do on the "magnificent seven." Taxis and buses travel up and down Paseo Kukulcan all day and night. Buses are the cheapest way to travel on Kukulcan (about US$.50 to go anywhere). Taxis are different—they can cost from US$4 for a quick ride to US$20 for a trip to the airport. You'll find taxi fares prominently posted at hotel entrances, but it's still always wise to ask the driver what a trip will cost before you get in. Most people know that getting the taxis parked in front of the hotels always cost a couple of dollars more than the ones zooming by that you (might be able to) flag down. Some people avoid taxis and buses altogether and rent cars (we always did, but now only for traveling out of the immediate area). Whether traveling by taxi or bus, do a little homework, know the address and name of the place you are going to, and write it down in case you have a language problem. Tell the bus driver where you want to go when you board—they're very good about letting you know when to get off. A new option for getting from place to place is the water taxi, also known as the **Agua Bus.**

SIGHTS

Archaeological Zones

Cancún's archaeological zones are minor compared to the big sites spread throughout the Yucatán Peninsula. But structures uncovered on this narrow strip of land have contributed important information to our knowledge about the people who lived here hundreds of years ago. Remnants of two sites, **Ruinas del Rey** on the south end of the island (at the Hilton Cancún Beach and Golf Resort), and **Yamil Lu'um** next to the Sheraton Hotel, are both worth a look.

To view Ruinas del Rey, head for the golf course on the lagoon side of the resort. The remains of the postclassic structure consist of a few platforms, two plazas, and a small pyramid. It is said that when the ruins were originally excavated, a skeleton believed to be that of a king was uncovered ("del Rey" means "of the King"). It's open 8 A.M.–5 P.M. and there's a small entrance fee.

Yamil Lu'um is on Cancún's highest point. The two small temples (15 meters high) were probably used as watchtowers and lighthouses along this navigational route. Between 400 and 700 years old, they were first noted in 1841 by two intrepid American explorers, John L. Stephens and Frederick Catherwood (who didn't stay long—the mosquitoes drove them on).

enjoying the sun and the sea, Cancún

OZ MALLAN

Laguna de Nichupté

This large lagoon, ringed by Paseo Kukulcán, is fed by a combination of freshwater from underground springs and saltwater that enters from two openings from the sea. There are many channels winding in and out of the mangroves, which act as nurseries for fish fry and many other creatures. Where the water is still and swampy, mangroves provide hiding places for young crocodiles. Bird life is plentiful, with a treasure trove of more than 200 cataloged species including herons, egrets, ospreys, parrots, and parakeets; the sooty tern returns here to nest each year. Guided jungle tours around the lagoon allow visitors to see the belly of the lagoon and its wildlife by boat or wave runner type vehicles.

Along the north end of the large lagoon marinas bustle with activity and the trim greens of the Pok-Ta-Pok golf course extend out over the water. Colorfully styled cruise boats are seen at sunset enjoying romantic dinner trips.

BEACHES

All of Cancún is scenic. But the most scenic beaches are on the seaward side of the island, a 21-kilometer stretch along Paseo Kukulcán. Walking along the coast is a five-star activity, and it's free (all beaches in Mexico are public). The panorama is capricious—the color of the sea changes subtly throughout the day from dawn's pale aqua to deep turquoise at noon, cerulean blue under the blazing afternoon sun to a pink-splashed gold during the elegant sunset. It's amazing what has transpired on this almost-flat sandbar since the hotel industry took over.

Hotel Beaches

The hotel-zone hotels all have beaches; some provide their guests with a variety of facilities, including *palapa* sun shelters, volleyball courts, aerobics classes, bars, restaurants, showers, restrooms, towels, and lifeguards. Note, however, that everyone is free to use the 18-meter (60-foot) strip of sand along the sea on any part of Cancún; signs indicating this are posted by SECTUR, the Ministry of Tourism. However, not many hoteliers are happy when unregistered tourists wander onto "their" beaches, especially if it means cutting through their hotel.

Swimming

The calmest and most protected ocean beaches face Bahía de Mujeres on the north end of the island. The lagoon is also usually calm, but it's not nearly as clear as the sea.

The water on the ocean side of Cancún can be hazardous. Many beaches do *not* have lifeguards. None of the Cancún beaches are suitable for surfing, but from Punta Cancún to Punta Nizúc the surf can occasionally be as high as three feet, and at certain times you'll encounter an undertow. The warning flags are now red (at your own risk) and black (don't swim!). When in doubt, don't swim. Each year a few people drown off the beaches of Cancún because of a lack of respect for the power of this beautiful sea.

You can walk out to sea 14 meters in shallow water before it begins to drop off. **Playa Delfines** at the south end of the hotel zone is a favorite of locals, since this stretch of sand is free of hotels—thus far. Sunsets viewed from the low rise over the beach here are particularly fine. Beachgoers will find a good sand beach at the Forum by the Sea Mall. A broad boardwalk with tables and chairs overlooks the activities on the sand and is a great place to eat and drink while you watch the fun.

Getting to the Beach

Transportation is often provided from downtown hotels to their private beach club. The Cancún hotel zone really is one big beach or, more accurately, a series of breathtaking beaches laid end to end. And it is true that most people come to Cancún *for* the beach. So it makes sense that the tourist industry has made it easy to reach any beach by bus. The regular route begins in downtown Cancún and makes a circuit the length of Paseo Kukulcán and back. The buses are modern, comfortable, and inexpensive. Remember that the locals use these buses to get to and from work, so expect them to be crowded during the commute hours. Fare is about five pesos anywhere, and buses run 24 hours a day. Bus stops are numerous and marked with blue signs that read "Parada." Most drivers will also stop for a waving arm almost anywhere (if there's room). Bear in mind that because of the immense increase in traffic, and many new businesses/bus stops, it can take 45 minutes to an hour to travel on the bus from downtown Cancún

to the end of the hotel zone. If you're in a hurry, take a taxi; if you feel leisurely, take the Agua Bus (water taxi). Some predict the Agua Bus will make it first.

WATER SPORTS

Snorkeling

Cancún's sandy sea floor doesn't hold the cool caves, coral outcroppings, and rocky crevices that attract abundant sea life; expert snorkelers will want to head for one of the several nearby reefs. In the immediate vicinity the most popular are Chital, Cuevones, Manchones Reefs, and Punta Nizuc (see "Scuba Diving," below). These reefs are composed of a variety of uniquely shaped and textured coral and are home to large populations of reef fish, including blue chromis and barracuda. Dive boats make scuba trips to these reefs and will usually take snorkelers along (room permitting).

For beginners (including children), Cancún is a great place to learn the mechanics of snorkeling. Though not as full of sea life as the reefs, the many areas of calm water around the hotel zone are by no means barren; you'll see plenty of sun-loving fish such as tanned beauties and burnt-back beach nappers. Intermediates can head to Punta Nizúc, where coral outcrops attract large numbers of fish. Parque Nacional El Garrafón, across from Cancún on Isla Mujeres, is another good spot for beginners and intermediates. Tour boats with snorkeling equipment go there daily from Cancún. Snorkeling equipment is also available for rent at all the marinas and some of the hotels.

Scuba Diving

For the experienced scuba diver, Cancún proper would be a distant second choice to Cozumel, but as dive spots go, none of the Caribbean is dull.

At **Punta Nizúc** (next to Club Med), divers and snorkelers can explore the starting point of the Belize Barrier Reef, which runs parallel to the Quintana Roo coast some 250 kilometers (150 miles) south to the Gulf of Honduras. It's the world's fifth-longest reef. Unfortunately, all the boat activity around Punta Nizúc has had a heavy impact and most of the coral here is dead.

Tropical fish still swarm to the area, however. The little fake island that was in place there has been removed for ecological reasons.

One of the most popular local reefs, despite its shallow depths, is **Chital,** a short distance north of the Hotel Presidente Intercontinental. The reef is made up of two sections, both about 20 meters wide. Expect a one-knot current and clear visibility up to 33 meters.

At **Cuevones Reef,** about three kilometers north of Punta Cancún, the body of the reef is comprised of elkhorn, rock, and brain corals. Several small caves *(cuevones)* at a depth of about 10 meters attract large schools of reef fish, groupers, amberjack, and the ever-lurking predatory barracudas. Visibility to 45 meters.

Manchones Reef is a shallow reef closer to Isla Mujeres (three kilometers south) than to Cancún (eight kilometers northeast). Its 10-meter depth, 60-meter visibility, lack of current, and abundant sea life make it an ideal dive site for beginners.

Cancún has a good selection of dive shops that provide equipment rentals and instruction; check with the marinas for recommendations. Before a diver can rent equipment, it's necessary to show a certified diver's card. Resort courses (for one dive, usually no more than 30 feet deep, accompanied by the divemaster) and certification classes are offered. For information, call **Mundo Marina** (PADI), tel. 988/3-0554; **Neptune** (NAUI), tel. 988/3-0722; **Aqua Tours,** tel. 988/3-0400, fax 988/3-0403; or **Scuba Cancún,** (NAUI and PADI), tel. 988/3-1011.

Sailing and Windsurfing

Hobie Cat and Sunfish rentals are available at a few hotels and most of the marinas. These small boats will give you a good fast ride if the wind is up. Negotiate for the fee—sometimes you can get a good daily rate, better than the hourly rate posted.

In a brisk breeze, sailboards (a.k.a. windsurfing) provide exhilarating rides, skimming across the waves at mind-blowing speeds. Usually six hours of lessons will give you a good start. Sailboards are available for rent at many of the hotels and marinas.

Parasailing

Parasailing is popular at the busy beaches. The rider, strapped into a colorful parachute and safety vest, is pulled high over the sand and surf by a speedboat; after about 10 minutes of "flying" he or she is gently deposited back on land with the help of two catchers. Once in a while the rider is inadvertently "landed" unexpectedly in the water—usually to the guffaws of the beach crowd. Most hotels post signs stating they are not responsible for parasailing accidents and injuries that occur by their beaches. Accidents do happen; watch a few passengers take the trip before you go up, and check your harness for wear and tear.

Jungle Tours

Wave runners travel in caravans behind a guide that knows Nipchute Lagoon. Groups travel in and around the many channels on the lagoon and see tropical birds that call the thick mangroves home. You can arrange a boat and guide at your hotel, or at one of many water-sports centers.

Options include travel in a caravan of wave runners led by a guide in and around the man-

Cancún parasailing

grove-lined channels, actives wheeling their way through the water, or small self-driven speed-boats with room for two people. All options include a guide boat. Such tours are becoming one of the most popular activities on Cancún.

Other Water Sports

Water-skiing is so-so popular in Cancún. Most skiers prefer Laguna Nichupté, although some can be seen on calm days in Bahía de Mujeres north of the island. Equipment and instruction are available from the marinas.

Kayaking is becoming popular in the Caribbean, and many hotels now offer kayaks to their guests free of charge.

At the Marinas

For something novel, check out the **Cancún Marina Club** on Kukulcán (Kilometer 5.5). There you can go for an underwater ride on a gadget called a **BOB** (Breathing Observation Bubble). I haven't tried it, but I've watched the commotion at the dock when a few brave people rode this scooter-like vehicle under the water with their heads in a clear bubble, breathing and observing sea life (US$75 per ride, 9 A.M., 11:30 A.M., and 2 P.M.). Let me know what it's like! At this price you wonder how much business they get—and how long it will last. But it does look like fun.

Aqua Tours marina, Paseo Kukulcán (Kilometer 6.25, by Fat Tuesday's), tel. 988/3-0400 or 3-1860, fax 988/3-0403, offers scuba diving, snorkeling, jungle tours, sportfishing, water-skiing, Isla Mujeres cruises, a floating casino cruise, and a lobster dinner cruise. **Royal Yacht Club,** Paseo Kukulcán (Kilometer 16.5, by the Captain's Cove restaurant and Royal Mayan Hotel), tel. 988/5-0391 or 5-2930, offers a variety of water sports and tours, canoe rentals, and showers and lockers.

Pelican Pier, Paseo Kukulcán (Kilometer 5.5), tel. 988/3-0315, offers sportfishing trips as well as spectacular flights over Cancún in an ultralight plane. They also have a Cessna for air-taxi service. **Mundo Marina,** Paseo Kukulcán (Kilometer 5.5), tel. 988/3-0554, offers snorkeling, diving, sportfishing, and cruises. **Marina Playa Langosta,** Paseo Kukulcán at Playa Langosta, tel. 988/3-2802, arranges sportfishing trips and cruises.

FISHING

Anglers come to Cancún for some of the world's finest sportfishing. Charters are available and easily arranged if you reserve a day or two in advance; call the marinas or check with your hotel. Sportfishing trips including gear for up to six passengers run about US$320 per trip for four hours, US$520 for eight hours. These fees are highly variable. On full-day trips you can cap off the afternoon with a fish barbecue on the beach (ask the captain in advance). One of the most exciting game fishes, the sailfish, runs from March–mid-July. Bonito and dorado run May–early July, wahoo and kingfish May–September. Barracuda, red snapper, bluefin, grouper, and mackerel are plentiful year-round.

Another trip currently popular among anglers is a fly-fishing excursion south of Cancún for permit, bonefish, and tarpon (catch and release is very popular). Ask at your hotel.

LAND-BASED SPORTS

Golf and Tennis

The **Pok Ta Pok Club de Golf,** Paseo Kukulcán (Kilometer 7.5), tel. 988/3-1277 or 2-1230, fax 988/3-3358, has tennis courts and a well-kept 18-hole golf course designed by Robert Trent Jones. The golf club is a great sports center, with a pro shop, swimming pool, marina, restaurant, bar, and even its own small restored Maya ruin near the 12th hole, discovered when the course was built. Temporary club membership allows you to play golf or tennis at the club; arrangements can be made through your hotel. Greens fees are about US$100; after 4 P.M. the rate drops to US$60. An additional US$30 is charged for golf-cart rental; clubs rent for US$18. The nearby **Holiday Inn Express Hotel** is within walking distance of the course.

Another fine golf course is at **Hilton Cancún Beach and Golf Resort,** right at the water's edge. The par-72 course is surrounded by small Maya ruins in a beautifully landscaped environment. Greens fees are US$106 (US$65 after 3 P.M.) and include a cart. Club rental costs US$25. More golf courses are found along the Caribbean coast's Riviera Maya going south.

Many of the hotels on the island have tennis courts. Some are lit for night play, and some are open to nonguests for a fee.

Horseback Riding
Rancho Loma Bonita, south of Cancún near Puerto Morelos, tel. 988/4-0907, provides horses for rides along the sea or into the jungle in a wide variety of locations. Transportation to and from the ranch, drinks, lunch, and a guide are included in the rates. Make arrangements through your hotel tour desk or call the ranch directly.

Rancho Grande
Another center offering exotic horseback tours is Rancho Grande, tel. 988/7-5423. It's also located south of Cancún. A bus leaves for the ranch from **OK Maguey** restaurant at Plaza Kukulcán Mall at 8 A.M. and 1:30 P.M. Tour prices start at US$62. Call for reservations.

Spectator Sports
Bullfighting has long been a popular pageant for Latin countries. Cancún's bullring is on Av. Bonampak at Sayil, tel. 988/4-5465 or 4-8372. Bullfights are held every Wednesday at 3:30 P.M. and are preceded by a Mexican fiesta with folkloric dance performances at 2:30 P.M. Tickets are available through tour desks or at the bullring (US$33). Ask for the shady side! (*Sombra.*) After the bullfights, and every afternoon, the myriad small cafés with entrances on the outside of the bullring are filled with locals enjoying *típico* food, tequila, *cerveza,* and good camaraderie.

ACCOMMODATIONS

At last count, Cancún held more than 24,000 rooms. Budget hotels are few. At the other end of the spectrum, the luxury accommodations of Cancún's hotel zone are among the most modern hostelries on Mexico's Caribbean coast.

Rates are lowest in late spring and early fall; some hotels raise their rates in August when Mexicans and Europeans typically take long vacations. Rates rise 20–50 percent around Thanksgiving and again at Christmas, with some hotels actually doubling their rates for the week between Christmas and New Year's Day. Package deals provide the best prices year-round.

As one hotel representative told us, "Nobody books a room at rack rates in Cancún anymore." Packages vary and may include reduced airfare, reduced rates for stays of three or more nights, reduced car-rental rates, and perks such as welcome cocktails, free meals, and free use of sports/fitness facilities. Have your travel agent check all these options, and keep an eye out for package deals advertised in newspapers and magazines. You can get amazing bargains when occupancy is low, even in the high season. Keep in mind that most prices you'll be quoted do not include the 12 percent room tax. All-inclusive resorts are very popular in Cancún and south along Riviera Maya. For many it's the most economical way to travel—if you're happy to stay in one place most of the time. It's kind of a grounded cruise ship ambience.

Zona Hotelera
Almost every hotel in the hotel zone falls into a premium price category. Many are quite elegant and offer one or more swimming pools; good beaches and beach activities; an assortment of restaurants, some of which are quite outstanding; gardens; bars and nightlife; travel, tour, and car-rental agencies; and laundry and room service.

US$50–100: The **Carrousel,** tel. 988/3-0513, fax 988/3-2312, is simple but comfy and on the beach. It's also affordable (under US$100).

US$100–150: The **Aristos,** U.S. tel. 800/527-4786, Mexico tel. 988/3-0011, fax 988/3-0078, is popular with families and Mexican tourists (US$125). Closer to the major malls, discos, and restaurants are **Calinda Viva,** tel. 988/3-0800, fax 988/3-2087, which is on a nice beach near Plaza Caracol; and **Miramar Mission Park Plaza,** tel. 988/3-1755, fax 988/3-1136, which is popular with tour groups.

Sheraton Cancún Resort and Towers, Blvd. Kukulcan, U.S. tel. 800/325-3535, includes butler service, great views of the ocean, private balconies, and a daily continental breakfast (oceanfront US$142, lagoon view US$130).

US$150–200: One of the all-time favorites is the durable **Camino Real Cancún,** U.S. tel. 800/722-6466, Mexico tel. 988/3-0100, fax 988/3-2965. You have plenty of space at this place, which is spread out on lovely grounds on the tip of the island. The rooms (US$166) have beautiful views with private balconies and cable TV.

Other amenities include beaches, a pool, and a small artificial "lagoon" inhabited by colorful fish. Guests in the hotel's "Tower" section are treated to complimentary continental breakfast, afternoon tea, snacks, and morning wake-up service—a hot cup of coffee served by a butler at your requested time. Take your pick of several restaurants, bars, and coffee shops, but the Maria Bonita restaurant, across the road, is superb. In the main building, live music is played during the cocktail hour and in the evening.

US$200 and up: Hilton Cancún Beach and Golf Resort, U.S. tel. 800/445-8667, tel. 988/1-8000, fax 988/5-2437, is a self-contained resort spread luxuriously on 250 acres near the lagoon. It features lounging areas, lots of grass, many pools, several great restaurants, and an 18-hole golf course built around an ancient Maya ruin. A shuttle takes you back and forth to the golf club. The rooms (US$275) are nicely appointed with air-conditioning, fans, lovely tile bathrooms, balconies, and glorious views. Ask about package prices, which are good value here.

Westin Regina Resort, U.S. tel. 800/228-3000, has all the luxury amenities as well as good food and good service. It's definitely upscale (US$305 with deluxe ocean view, US$285 with lagoon view).

Cancún Melia, U.S. tel. 800/336-3542, sits on a small bluff overlooking a broad beach. The hotel is conveniently located along Paseo Kukulcán. Walkways meander across the grounds to a beachside restaurant, swimming pools, beach *palapas,* and beach activities. The immense lobby is afloat in marble, and the staff is friendly when they aren't swamped at the front desk. Restaurants on the premises offer both colorful buffets and varied ethnic food. Rooms are US$319.

One of the largest hotels in Cancún, **Fiesta Americana Coral Beach,** U.S. tel. 800/343-7821, Mexico tel. 988/3-2900, fax 988/3-3076, features a spectacular atrium lobby covered by a stained-glass dome. A string quartet often plays in the lobby each afternoon—a nice change from the typical happy-hour scene. The 602 spacious suites (US$313) all have ocean-view balconies; master suites have hot tubs. A swimming pool flows the length of the property, past several sunning areas separated by waterfalls, a bridge, and palms. The hotel's Coral Reef restaurant is

Cancún coastline

superb. Ask about their all-inclusive program.

The **Ritz Carlton,** U.S. tel. 800/241-3333, tel. 988/5-0808, fax 988/5-1045, is Cancún's most extravagant hotel, a fact you'll note as soon as the white-gloved doorman ushers you into the crystal-chandelier-filled lobby. The lushly opulent rooms (US$369) are filled with luxury amenities, while the health club offers steam rooms, saunas, and massage. The private Club Lounge overlooks an atrium, providing a soothing yet formal setting for afternoon tea, and the Club Grill has become a favorite hideaway for locals (the food is excellent and the desserts are as extravagant as the decor). The Ritz is the ultimate for those seeking unparalleled service and elegance.

Downtown Hotels

The biggest drawback to staying downtown is the absence of beach. But blue sea and white sand are easily accessible, as buses run every 15 minutes and some hotels provide free transportation for their guests. Sometimes crowded, these hotels are good bargains. Yucatecan ambience pervades. Each accommodation listed below has a bar, one or more restaurants, and rooms with private bath, hot water, and phone. Some also have swimming pools.

Under US$50: Hotel Cotty, Uxmal 44 (between Tulum and Yaxchilán), tel. 988/4-0550, email: hotelcotty@prodigy.net.mx, is an oldie but goodie conveniently close to the bus station. All 38 rooms (US$37) now offer air-conditioning, cable TV, and private bathrooms.

Cancún Handall, Tulum at Cobá, tel. 988/4-1122, fax 988/4-9280, is popular with tour groups; ask about promotional rates. The 50 rooms (under US$100) include air-conditioning and small TVs, and there's a pool on the premises.

The rooms at **Hotel Rivemar,** Av. Tulum 49, tel. 988/4-1999, have private baths, tile floors, and air-conditioning, and cost under US$100. The hotel is clean and in a great location.

US$50–100: Howard Johnson Cancún, Av. Uxmal 26, U.S. tel. 800/446-4656, Mexico tel. 988/4-3218, fax 988/4-4335, is on a quiet block of Uxmal near Av. Nader. The four-story hotel has 48 standard rooms (US$68); 12 suites with kitchens and air-conditioning; a lobby bar, a swimming pool, a Jacuzzi, and a small roof garden; and offers free transportation to the beach. A small dining room in the lobby serves continental breakfast for about US$3.

Antillano, Claveles at Tulum, tel. 988/4-1532, fax 988/4-1878, sits right in the middle of the action. Its quieter rooms (under US$100) face the inner courtyard. **Hotel Hacienda,** Av. Sunyaxchen 39, tel. 988/4-3672, is a pleasant, low-key hotel with 40 air-conditioned rooms (under US$100), a swimming pool, pool bar, beach transportation, a café, parking, and a travel agency on the premises.

Mex Hotel Centro, Av. Yaxchilán 31, U.S. tel. 800/221-6509, Mexico tel. 988/4-3478 or 84-3888, fax 988/4-1309, has been around a long time and gets better every year. It's conveniently located in the middle of the city, with scores of cafés and shops within walking distance. Rooms (US$85) are smallish, but come with air-conditioning and TV. Other amenities include a pool, restaurant, coffee shop, and a free shuttle that takes guests to the beach (beach towels are provided). Terra-cotta pottery, tile floors, and

colorful textiles give the hotel a pleasant Mexican flavor.

Also getting high marks is the **Parador,** Av. Tulum 26, tel. 988/4-1043, fax 988/4-9712, in the center of downtown next to Pop, a favorite budget café. Each of the 66 air-conditioned rooms (US$55–89) has a private bath. Purified drinking water is available in the hall, and a pool and grassy area make sun worshippers happy.

The fine little **Best Western Plaza Caribe,** Av. Tulum 13, tel. 988/4-1377, fax 988/4-6352 has been around a long time and has comfortable rooms (US$55–85) and a pool.

US$100–150: The most expensive downtown hotel (and one of the nicest) is the **Holiday Inn Centro,** Av. Nader 1, U.S. tel. 800/HOLIDAY, Mexico tel. 988/7-4455, fax 988/4-8376. It offers all the amenities of the beachside hotels and provides free transportation to the sand. The pretty peach-and-white four-story building sits at the end of Av. Nader, far from just about everything. The 100 rooms (US$140) face an inner courtyard and large swimming pool. Banquet and meeting facilities are available.

All-inclusive Resorts

The all-inclusives that are springing up include meals and activities in their rates and can be economical in the long run. Prices have huge per-person variations; some will take only weeklong reservations, others will book for as few as three nights. The following all-inclusive options are just the tip of the iceberg.

Club Med, U.S. tel. 800/258-2633, Mexico tel. 988/5-2300, fax 988/5-2290, is quite a distance from downtown Cancún, but taxis are always lined up at the gate (fare to town runs about US$9 each way). All Club Med guests must pay a US$30 initiation fee; if you stay more than five nights you must pay an additional US$50 membership fee. Daily room rates start at $142 per person for a standard room, $156 per person for an ocean view. Good weekly rates are also offered, of course.

Another all-inclusive is the **Sun Palace,** in the hotel zone at Paseo Kukulcán (Kilometer 20), U.S. tel. 800/346-8225, Mexico tel. 988/5-1555, fax 988/5-2040. It offers 150 suites (US$184), three restaurants, great views, and three pools. **Beach Palace,** also in the hotel zone, U.S. tel. 800/346-8225, Mexico tel. 988/3-

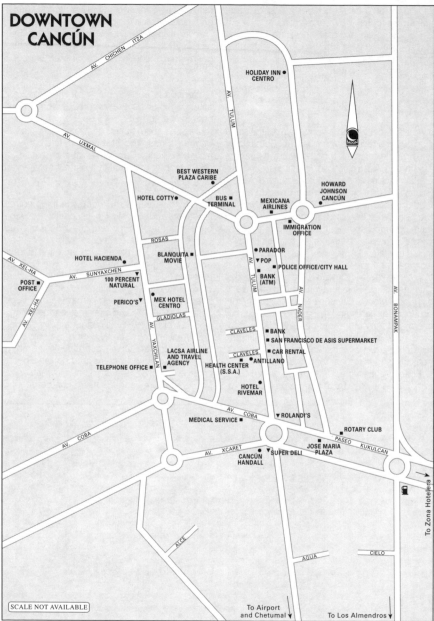

DOWNTOWN CANCÚN

AV. CHICHEN ITZA

AV. UXMAL

HOLIDAY INN CENTRO ●

AV. TULUM

MoonN

BEST WESTERN PLAZA CARIBE ■

HOWARD JOHNSON CANCÚN ■

HOTEL COTTY ●

BUS TERMINAL ■

MEXICANA AIRLINES ■

IMMIGRATION OFFICE ■

ROSAS

● PARADOR

AV. XEL-HA

HOTEL HACIENDA ●

BLANQUITA ■ MOVIE

▼ POP

● POLICE OFFICE/CITY HALL

AV. SUNYAXCHEN

AV. XEL-HA

POST OFFICE ■

100 PERCENT NATURAL ▼

AV. TULUM

BANK (ATM) ■

PERICO'S ▼

MEX HOTEL CENTRO ■

AV. NADER

GLADIOLAS

CLAVELES

■ BANK

■ SAN FRANCISCO DE ASIS SUPERMARKET

YAKCHILAN

CLAVELES

■ CAR RENTAL

LACSA AIRLINE AND TRAVEL AGENCY ■

● ANTILLANO

TELEPHONE OFFICE ■

HEALTH CENTER (S.S.A.) ■

AV. BONAMPAK

HOTEL RIVEMAR ●

AV. COBA

▼ ROLANDI'S

MEDICAL SERVICE ■

● ROTARY CLUB

AV. COBA

JOSE MARIA PLAZA ■

PASEO KUKULCAN

AV. XCARET

CANCÚN HANDALL

▼ SUPER DELI

To Zona Hotelera ►

ALCE

AGUA

CIELO

SCALE NOT AVAILABLE

To Airport and Chetumal ▼

To Los Almendros ▼

1177, fax 988/5-0439, includes a kids' club and has rooms for US$157 per person.

Palace hotels are really growing along the Riviera Maya coast and include spectacular beach locations. Call 800/346-8225 for reservations and information.

FOOD

It would take a year to sample each of the more than 400 fine restaurants in Cancún. Both budget and upscale cafés are found downtown near Av. Tulum and Av. Yaxchilán. You'll also find numerous choices along the hotel zone on Kukulcán Boulevard, especially at **Punta Cancún** and in modern malls like **La Isla Mall** and **Forum by the Sea.** While the ethnic demographics of food have changed slightly, the epicurean explorer can still find an excellent variety of diverse foods, including Italian, American, Cajun, Caribbean, Continental, French, Oriental, vegetarian, and Yucatecan cuisine. Cancún is the gourmet hub of Quintana Roo. Have a favorite? All you have to do is look! Most of Cancún's upscale restaurants accept credit cards and dining continues on until late in the evening. Most of the better restaurants have live music—mariachi, romantic guitar, or piano. Dress is casual, although some do not allow shorts or bare feet for dinner.

For seafood lovers, Cancún is a dream come true. Fish is always fresh and is cooked in a variety of styles, whether merely sautéed in butter and garlic or, as is the case with the exotic *tik 'n' chik* style, spiced with brick-colored *achiote*. Surprisingly, lobster can be as expensive here as it is anywhere else in the world. Most seafood restaurants in Cancún offer a few meat choices for the carnivore.

Cancún is a great place for big breakfast eaters. Buffets are everywhere. Elaborate hotel buffets average US$8–15 per person. Smaller (but just as good) buffets in mall restaurants like **Mama Romas, The Station** or in fine cafés on the water like the **Captain's Cove** start at US$3 per person. Most breakfast buffets are served until 11–11:30 A.M. Call it buffet, call it brunch—it's great!

Mexico is one of the world's leading coffee producers and almost all of its cafés serve good brewed coffee, the more upscale offer brewed decaf. Trendy coffee shops are also becoming more common and offer huge varieties of local and imported coffee beans. On some Cancún menus you'll notice a traditional favorite, *café de olla* (Mexican-style coffee cooked and sweetened with raw sugar and cinnamon in a large pottery jug, and served in a small earthen mug).

Below are a few of the restaurants we've tried and enjoyed consistently, some over a period of years, others only recently. Remember: Restaurants tend to come and go, and chefs change and prices move with new owners, new peso valuations, and the whims of the people.

Cancún resort

OZ MALLAN

But despite all of this, if you can't find good food that fits your budget, look a little harder. You're bound to find that perfect meal.

Mexican Cuisine

There's a great selection of Mexican restaurants from which to choose. One of our favorites, **La Destileria** (Kukulcán, Kilometer 12.65), tel. 988/5-1087, is a triple treat. The food is excellent, the tequila selection (more than 150 different kinds) is mind boggling, and it's a museum with a view of the lagoon. Wander around and take it all in. From colorful serigraphs discover the history of tequila, how it's made, and how agave is grown. See murals that depict life in old tequila haciendas, and dine in the shadow of immense copper stills once used to produce the universal drink of Mexico. It's a given: the contemporary Mexican food is delicious. With an appetizer, try the tequila sampler. This set of three kinds introduces the neophyte to a variety of diverse tequilas. Guaranteed, you will come away with a new opinion of tequila—not just Margaritas any more! A fine smooth tequila goes for as little as US$2 a shot, or as high as US$50. There's good live mariachi music and everything is open 2 P.M.–midnight. Dinner, appetizers, and drinks can add up to a hefty outlay here, but it's worth the expense.

Across from the Camino Real, the **Maria Bonita,** restaurant, tel. 988/3-0100, is a dazzler offering great Mexican food in a colorful setting with live music. Complete with miles of tile, it's reminiscent of an upscale Mexican home. The food is good, but the ambience is the star attraction here. Reservations are suggested.

Another fine choice, **La Casa Margarita,** is located in **La Isla Mall.** Resembling a small village, it offers live music and an unusual margarita made with tequila and *tuna* (the cactus variety). Personally I prefer their "classic" margarita. Nibble on their delectable Oaxacan specialty, *tlayuda* (it might resemble a pizza, but it's wonderfully Mexican). Waiters wear costumes from different regions of Mexico and are great dancers. This place is good fun and moderately priced.

El Café, in front of a commercial building on Av. Nader, has a vast breakfast menu, including platters of fresh papaya, pineapple, and bananas; baskets of homemade pastries and breads; fresh orange-papaya juice; and bargain-priced *molletes* (rolls split and covered with beans and melted cheese). The *chilaquiles* are the best we've had in Cancún, and *pozole* is prepared daily. A blossoming *framboyán* tree shades the outdoor patio beside the sidewalk. It's a casual place and obviously a big hit with local office workers and *políticos.*

Perico's, at Av. Yaxchilán 71 downtown, tel. 988/4-3152, continues to draw crowds that relish tasty food and a good time. It's worth a visit just for the decor: The bar seats are saddles, and a fanciful mural depicting Mexican heroes and Hollywood movie stars covers the wall. The emphasis is on fun, with amiable waiters dressed as bandits liberally pouring tequila. The food is dependably good; look for generous portions of barbecued ribs and chicken and huge Mexican combination plates. Be sure to tour the whole restaurant, including the restrooms.

El Mexicano, at La Mansion/Costa Blanca, tel. 988/3-2220, offers a tasty Mexican buffet and folkloric ballet with mariachi music daily; open noon–midnight. No shorts please.

El Mortero, at the Krystal Cancún Hotel, Kukulcán Blvd., Kilometer 9.5, tel. 988/3-1133, is an authentic replica of a lovely 18th-century hacienda, complete with a fountain on the patio. Both the architecture and the food are reminiscent of colonial Mexico. Open 6–10 P.M. The first time we had dinner here a dimutive man, one of the cooks came into the patio and sang his heart out. He was wonderful with the latin romantic balads, but the best part, he must have been at least 75 years old.

OK Maguey, at Kukulcán Plaza, tel. 988/5-0503, is a great cantina with an authentic Mexican *cocina* grill and mariachi music.

Italian

The longtime favorite among Italian-food lovers is **La Dolce Vita,** tel. 988/5-0150, now in the hotel zone with a view of the lagoon, across from the Marriott Hotel Kukulan at Kilometer 14.6. From *zuppa* to antipasto to *tutta* pasta to *pesce e frutta del mare* to the hazelnuts in your dessert, the food is scrumptious. If you like fish, try *boquinete Dolce Vita,* which consists of white snapper stuffed with shrimp and mushrooms and baked in golden puff pastry (shaped like a fish, of course)—*delizioso!* The coffee is fresh brewed and rich (even the decaf). A meal with wine averages about US$20–30 per person.

The atmosphere is casual but elegant. Open for lunch and dinner; reservations suggested.

Rolandi's, Av. Cobá 12, tel. 988/4-4047, might be more familiar to old-timers as Pizzeria Rolandi. No matter the name, the pizzas are still great, with thin, crisp crusts covered with an eclectic selection of toppings. And if you're not in the mood for a pizza, the handmade pastas, calzones, and a great garlicky antipasto round out the menu. Just be sure to save room for the coconut ice cream topped with Kahlúa. The atmosphere is casual and TV monitors show videos and sports events. Open for lunch and dinner, 1 P.M.–midnight, with moderate prices.

Casa Rolandi, Plaza Caracol, Kukulcán Blvd. (Kilometer 9), tel. 988/3-1817, offers shades of the Mediterranean with great *mangia* flavors. Ask about your favorite Italian dish, the pizza is always good, and don't forget to check the good wine menu.

Fantinos, at the Ritz Carlton Hotel, tel. 988/1-0808, is still another fine Italian restaurant that takes your breath away when you walk in the room—and that's before you taste the food. They advertise the largest *grappa* selection in Mexico. But also check out the cheese cart, the veal cheeks, and the *ossobuco.* It's a little costy, but it's good. Open Mon.–Sat. 7–11 P.M.

Other Italian options include: **Cenacolo,** Plaza Kukulcán, tel. 988/5-3603, offering outdoor seating; and **Savios,** Plaza Caracol, tel. 988/3-2085,

offering good food in a lovely setting. And, of course, there are countless pizza places.

Caribbean

From the Maya Caribbean, **Los Almendros Restaurant,** at the intersection of Sayil and Bonampak across from the bullring, gives the true Maya flavor of those people that first inhabited the Yucatán Peninsula. It's a favorite of locals and is conveniently close to the bullring. Aficionados spend their Wednesday afternoons here after the bullfight. Try the *tipico pok chuk* (exotic spices and grilled meat) or the *relleno negro* (a black picante sauce made with blackened chiles, and/or black *achiote* seeds, and often served over turkey, *pavo*).

Downtown, **La Habichuela,** Margaritas 25, tel. 988/4-3158, really takes pride in its Caribbean flavor. The idyllic, candlelit setting is perfect for romantics. Lush plants fill the courtyard and dining room, and carvings of Maya gods and rulers sit in niches and on platforms in the dining areas. Try the shrimp in a sauce of *huitlacoche* (a black, mushroomlike fungus grown on corn), or go all out with the house specialty, *cocobichuela* (shrimp and lobster in a luscious curry sauce and served in a coconut shell). Open for lunch and dinner, 1 P.M.–midnight; reservations suggested.

The **Plantation House,** Kukulcán (Kilometer 10.5), tel. 988/3-1455, recalls the days of European arrival in the Caribbean. It offers excellent European specialties blended with the spices of the tropics. If you're having a birthday party or other celebration, ask about the charming 10-person kiosk and their elegant imperial table. Both the food and the ambience are beautiful. Enjoy the end of the day in a peaceful setting overlooking the lagoon and the mangroves. The dinner house includes live music, and children over 12 are welcome. Open 5 P.M.–1 A.M.

Iguana Wana, in Plaza Caracol, tel. 988/3-0829, has something for everyone on its enormous menu, with such unusual finds as the well known Caribbean *fave,* conch fritters, vegetarian fajitas, fried bananas, and chicken with *chipotle* sauce. There's also frozen yogurt and a dazzling pastry tray.

Seafood

Ever popular **Lorenzillos,** Kukulcán Blvd. at Kilometer 10.5, tel. 988/3-3073, allows diners

---

CAFÉ DE OLLA

Served at most Mexican Folklorico Fiestas at various hotels.

Recipe:
1 small earthen pot
3 tbsp. dark roasted coarse-ground coffee
1 cinnamon stick
3 cloves
dark brown sugar to taste
1 liter of water

Bring water to boiling in pot, add coffee, cinnamon, and sugar. Bring to boil again, strain, and serve. Optional: Add tequila to taste. Especially good brewed over an open fire!

to choose their own live lobsters or soft-shell crabs. You'll appreciate the pleasant atmosphere and the salsa background music. Open noon–11 P.M.

The Seafood Market, at the Hyatt Regency, tel. 988/3-0966, displays shrimp, lobster, and fresh fish on ice and allows diners to select their dinner. Reservations suggested.

La Fisheria at the Plaza Caracol in the Hotel Zone, tel. 988/3-1395, serves a great Spanish paella in a light airy atmosphere with tranquil live music. Open daily 11 A.M.–11:30 P.M.

Faros, adjoining Mango Tango in the hotel zone, Kukulcán (Kilometer 14.2), tel. 988/5-1107, is open noon–11 P.M. Try the seafood grill—it includes a little bit of all the best: shrimp, lobster, fish filet, mussels, and squid. The seafood fettuccini is a favorite of pasta lovers.

At the **Captain's Cove,** Kukulcán (Kilometer 16.5), tel. 988/5-0016, it's possible to watch the sunset under a *palapa* roof by the sea. You'll enjoy a good happy hour (4–7 P.M.) and great seafood and teriyaki chicken. A great bargain breakfast buffet (US$3) is offered 7–11:30 A.M. Open daily 7 A.M.–11 P.M.

The **Shrimp Bucket,** Kukulcán Blvd. (Kilometer 5.5), is one of those "fun places" where zany waiters serve shrimp by the bucket—literally. Try their exotic drink, the "flying shrimp."

The **Crab House,** Kukulcán Blvd. (Kilometer 14.5), tel. 988/5-0730, should satisfy every seafood palate. The menu offers every variety of crab, plus live lobster, oysters, conch, octopus, and specialties like Aurora salmon. The bar is on the first floor and dining is on the second. Both floors offer great views.

Other Ethnic

Blue Bayou, at the Hyatt Cancún Caribe, tel. 988/3-0044, ext. 54, offers live jazz, a Cajun menu, great blackened fish, and butter-tender beef fillet. A romantic multilevel dining room with cool hanging greenery sets a tropical mood. Open daily from 6:30 P.M.–1 A.M., reservations are recommended.

Authentic Japanese and Thai food is served at **Mikado** in the Marriott Hotel. Enjoy the *tepanyaki,* and the showman who prepares it, as well as a tasty sushi bar. A varied menu includes steaks and seafood. Open daily 5:30–11 P.M.

An evening at **Bogarts,** next to the Kryustal

Cancún Hotel, Kukulcán Blvd. (Kilometer 5), tel. 988/3-1133, is an evening in Casablanca. Well, almost. It *is* glamorous and takes you back to Humphrey Bogart's popular movie. You'll find food with a hint of the Moroccan desert and Mediterranean Sea. Rest your feet on a soft cushion and take in the billowing silk overhead, and with a little imagination you'll be transported to a luxurious desert oasis.

Steak Houses

With **The Outback Steakhouse Cancún,** tel. 988/3-3350, the Aussies have arrived, at least in theme and *tucker* (food). Stop by for a *nosh-up* (good meal) and a *top drop* (good beer). And who can resist a fried blooming onion! This really is a *bonzer* place!

Ruth Chris Kukulcán Plaza, tel. 988/5-3301, is worth a stop if you like steak. The chef caters to big appetites here with a 40-ounce porterhouse. Ask about the flavorful blackened tuna steak. Open daily 1:30–11:30 P.M.

Dinner Cruises

The **Columbus Lobster Dinner Cruise** leaves the Royal Mayan Marina dock (hotel zone) daily at 4 and 7:30 P.M. The *Columbus,* tel. 988/3-3268 or 8/3-3271, is a 62-foot motor-sailing vessel that cruises for three hours at sunset or under the starry sky while guests enjoy an open bar and dine on delicious broiled lobster or steak. Dress is casual, but reservations are necessary.

On the **Pirate's Night Adventure,** tel. 988/3-3268 or 83-3283, diners ride the *Crucero Tropical Cruiser* to Treasure Island (actually a beach on Isla Mujeres facing Cancún). Once onshore, passengers enjoy a buffet dinner including drinks while watching a floor show with lively games and lots of audience participation. The ship departs nightly (except Sunday) from the Playa Langosta Pier at 6 P.M. and returns at 11 P.M.

The **Cancún Queen** is the only paddleboat on the lagoon (so far). Its dinner cruise offers gourmet steak and lobster, as well as an open bar, live music, dancing, and games. Board on Paseo Kukulcán, opposite the Melia Cancún Hotel; tel. 988/5-2288. Reservations are suggested.

Vegetarian Food

100 percent Natural has three locations: Plaza Kukulcán, The Forum by the Sea Mall, and Plaza

Terramar. Each serves fresh vegetarian dishes, crispy salads with a good selection of veggies, healthy shakes, and tasty wheat bread and cookies—you can really be creative here! Open daily 8 A.M.–midnight.

Fast Food
It's impossible to ignore the proliferation of U.S.-based restaurants and fast-food chains throughout Cancún, among them **McDonald's, Burger King, Wendy's, Subway, Kentucky Fried Chicken, Dunkin Donuts, Baskin Robbins, Dominos,** and **Mrs. Field's Cookies.** Add to that Mexico's own chains like **VIPs** and **T.G.I. Friday's,** one of the first franchises in Cancún (even the locals have come to love their burgers).

For the Kids
You may have seen the **Rainforest Café** in the States. Maybe the American Disneylands grit their collective teeth, but it puts in action some great life-size, animated jungle animals (elephants, monkeys, jaguars, etc.). Both the young and the young at heart get a bang out of lunching and listening to the elephant when he trumpets and lifts his long trunk while flapping those lifelike ears. The food is good, too. Kids love the clever menu.

Bakeries and Coffeehouses
Indulge yourself in fine Mexican and French pastries and crusty *bolillos* at **La Francesca Panadería** on Av. Uxmal at Av. Nader. A smaller bakery, **Los Globos,** on Tulipanes just west of Av. Tulum, offers a great selection of breakfast pastries and breads. **Coffee House International,** at Plaza Parilla, Punta Cancún, lures passersby with the heady aroma of exotic coffees. Take your choice of flavors.

Grocery Stores and Delis
The *mercado municipal* is six blocks north of the bus station on Av. Tulum. Find the tortilla makers, the *carne asada* man, the fresh juice squeezers, and piles of rolls and fresh fruit and vegetables. Old favorite **San Francisco de Asis Super Market** on Tulum now has a new location in the hotel zone. These are modern, well-stocked markets designed for one-stop shopping. **Comercial Mexicana,** Av. Uxmal at the traffic circle, is an enormous grocery and department store.

Super Gourmet and Deli is the current favorite with imported cheeses, cookies, crackers, and even frozen Sara Lee pastries and Haagen Dazs ice cream, plus a good bakery and deli section. Locations include the Forum Mall, Plaza Kukulcán, and Plaza La Isla. Prices are outrageously high, but it must not matter since they're always bustling. More **Haagen Dazs Ice Cream** shops are popping up all over the hotel zone.

Downtown and a Little out of Town
At **Pop,** Av. Tulum 26 (next to the Parador Hotel), tel. 988/4-1991, you can enjoy a straightforward, reasonable, no-nonsense, American-style breakfast, lunch, or dinner. Open daily 8 A.M.–11 P.M.

If you're looking for an authentic regional fish café, check out **Flamingos,** near Punta Sam, and **Mandinga's,** right next to the Puerto Juárez ferry pier. Both serve fresh-caught fish *tik 'n' chik*–style or grilled with garlic and butter. These two huge *palapa* restaurants are favored by locals who settle in for afternoon-long lunches of huge platters of fish, plenty of ice-cold beer, and good camaraderie. Don't ever try to rush a Mexican through lunch.

NIGHTLIFE

Cancún has a marvelous choice of nighttime entertainment. It's easy to dance the night away at a number of inviting places. Most of the hotels on the island have discos in motion until the early morning hours. Some cantinas offer live bands ranging from jazz to popular marimba to reggae, and several hotels offer Mexican "fiestas" weekly, including *típico* dinners, traditional dances, and colorful costumes.

Traditional Dance
The casual **Mexican Fiesta** at the Hyatt Regency, tel. 988/3-0966, has been running nightly for years, packing in guests for a lavish buffet and folkloric dance performances. **Ballet Folklórico de México** performs nightly at 7 P.M. during a Mexican buffet at the Continental Villas Plaza Hotel, tel. 988/5-1444.

For a full night of fine dining, dancing, and entertainment visit **El Mexicano,** La Mansión-Costa Blanca Mall, in the hotel zone, tel. 988/3-2220. Caribbean and Mexican shows accompany gourmet Mexican dishes, many flambéed tableside. The setting is elegant, and though tour groups tend to congregate here, even solo diners receive impeccable service.

Nightclubs and Discos

Cancún has some of Mexico's most upscale and modern clubs and discos. Many don't even open their doors until 10 or 11 P.M. and don't get wild till after midnight. Dress codes are enforced; most of the classy discos do not allow tank tops, sandals, or other casual wear. Men can usually get by with a nice T-shirt or polo shirt and dressy shorts (some discos don't allow shorts) or long pants. Women tend to wear sundresses. Expect cover charges of US$5 or more and high drink prices. You can tell by the decibel level which places cater to the youngest crowds.

Christine's Disco, next to Hotel Krystal, tel. 988/3-1133, is dressy and features a superb sound-and-light show. **Dady'O,** Paseo Kukulcán (Kilometer 9.5), tel. 988/3-3333, is known for its bikini contests and boisterous young crowd. The super-extravagant **Up and Down,** in front of the Oasis Cancún, offers a restaurant with mellow music upstairs and a full-scale disco downstairs.

Dance on the tables? You never know where you'll find dancers at **Coco Bongos.** Alternatively, hit the floor with rock 'n' roll oldies at the striking new **Hard Rock Café.** Both of these lively spots are located in the extravagant **Forum By the Sea.** Finally, if you want to go somewhere exquisite, try **Max'xo.** It's in front of Plaza La Isla Shopping Center in the Playa Linda Area.

La Boom, on Paseo Kukulcán (Kilometer 3.5), is a long-time-favorite club for the young crowd. A US$20 cover charge pays for all you can drink (as long as you're over 18).

Latin Music

Batacha, by the Miramar Mission Hotel, is casual and attracts couples of all ages who love the Salsa Latin beat. **Cat's Reggae Bar,** downtown on Av. Yaxchilán, is another good spot for Caribbean music. **Xtabentum D'Angelica,** downtown at Tulipanes 18 and Tulum Av., offers live jazz, Latin American, and Flamenco music.

Other Bars and Fun Spots

Classy spots for music and conversation are: the **Lobby Bar** and **Reflejos,** both at the Hyatt

Fiesta night at the Hyatt Regency Hotel

Regency, tel. 988/3-0966; **Tropical Oasis Piano Bar,** at the Hotel and Villas Tropical Oasis; the **Oasis Bar** at the Hyatt Cancún Caribe Villas and Resort, tel. 988/3-0044, offering live jazz and dancing; and the **Club Grill** at the Ritz Carlton Hotel, tel. 988/5-0808, an elegant restaurant with a cozy lounge where well-dressed couples dance to romantic music.

For zany fun with wild and comedic waiters as well as exceptionally good food, head to either **Carlos 'n Charlie's** or **Señor Frog's,** both on Paseo Kukulcán. Similar in ambience and decor, but with a more authentically Mexican flair, is **Perico's** on Av. Yaxchilán downtown.

For a serene, romantic spot to begin or end an evening, watch Cancún's sensational sunset or glittering stars in one of many mellow dockside bars and restaurants. Many serve snacks and exotic drinks and offer live music and dancing 9 P.M.–1:30 A.M.

Remember: This is a party town, and at last count about 100 businesses fit the description of fun, drink, and dance. Look for names like

Bum Bum Disco, Merengue, Mango Tango, Alebrije—half the fun is making your own discoveries.

Cinema

The majority of films shown in Cancún are American-made and in English (some with Spanish subtitles). Expect the bill to change every three or four days. **Cines Cancún,** Av. Xcaret 112, tel. 988/4-1646, and **Cine Royal,** Av. Tulum, present Mexican films. Check out the large new cinemas in **La Isla Plaza** and the **Forum by the Sea Mall.** Also, a little off the main drag, there's another large cinema in **Las Americas Mall.** All three have multiple theaters and show new movies.

SHOPPING

Cancún's malls are sleek and spectacular; no bargaining here (at least in most businesses). In downtown Cancún you'll find streetside shopping marts, often fronted by touts urging you in with their favorite come on. Some of these people can be downright rude. You won't find vendors on the beach—it's illegal, and the law is enforced. Almost all businesses in Cancún accept credit cards and dollars, but it's wise to carry pesos just in case, especially for the little vendors.

Cancún is a phenomenal place to find arts, crafts, and textiles from all over Mexico. We have seen the yarn and beaded artwork from Tarahumaran Indians, shiny silver jewelry and sculpture from Taxco, and bright weavings from Chiapas.

Shopping Centers

The newest shopping centers are not just for shopping, they are truly entertainment centers with excellent restaurants. You can't miss the monolith mall known as Forum by the Sea.

Forum by the Sea

Right on the beach, this lovely mall comes with enough activities to keep everyone entertained for hours. The shops come in all sizes and descriptions and are surrounded with a good sprinkling of eateries and bars. Restaurants come in all varieties, including Italian **Mama Romas** and Japanese **Suschi Ito** and an immense **Hard Rock Café** with old-fashioned American hamburgers. A food court is open until 5 A.M. in case you get hungry after a long night of dancing. Watch the Huichol Indians do traditional intricate beadwork (for sale, of course), or shop for Mexican ceramics, pewter ware, women's clothes, jewelry, or a large selection of gifts. If all of this shopping makes you thirsty, stop in at the **Beer Factory** and try a stout, or pilsener, or Coyote pale ale. You can also have a snack of wood barbecue.

La Isla Mall is a showcase for a variety of entertainment. Set up like an island of shops surrounded by canals of water, the mall includes a terrific aquarium with nearly every aquatic creature in the Caribbean. The **Cinemark La Isla** shows all the newest Hollywood movies in their many auditoriums. Check out the good Mexican food at **Las Casitas de las Margaritas.** Or dine at the unique **Modern Art Café.** Or grab a little gnash at the **Super Deli** and top it off with an ice-cream cone at **Haagen Dazs.**

La Mansión-Costa Blanca is a small, exclusive mall featuring unique boutiques, several of the city's top restaurants, a money exchange, and a bank. The shops at **El Parian** are constructed around a small garden off to one side of the Convention Center.

Plaza Caracol is conveniently located in the hub of the hotel zone, and is elaborately finished with marble floors and lots of windows. The two-story mall holds more than 200 shops and boutiques.

Even more good shopping is found at: **Plaza la Fiesta,** a huge one-floor department store featuring Mexican crafts; **Plaza Lagunas,** at the center of the hotel zone; **Plaza Nautilus,** a modern, two-story plaza; **Terramar,** opposite the Fiesta Americana Hotel; **Kukulcán Plaza,** a two-story, air-conditioned establishment near Casa Turquesa that also holds a bowling alley and movie theaters; **Plaza México,** on Av. Tulum, which specializes in Mexican crafts; **Plaza Safa,** a lovely arcade that fronts Av. Tulum; and **Tropical Plaza,** next door to Plaza México.

Crafts Markets

In the hotel zone, next to the Convention Center, **Coral Negro** is a collection of approximately 50 stalls selling handicrafts from all parts of Mexico. **Ki Huic,** downtown on Av. Tulum, is Cancún's main crafts market, with more than 100 vendors. **Plaza Garibaldi,** also downtown at the intersection of Av. Tulum and Uxmal, contains several stalls of serapes, tablecloths, traditional clothing, onyx, and other handcrafted items.

NEARBY TOURS AND DAY TRIPS

Taxi Tours
One way to make sure you see the sights you want to see around Cancún without having to follow a group itinerary is to hire an English-speaking taxi driver for an hour or a day. Rates start at US$13 per hour if you stay within the Cancún limits. The hourly price increases the farther you travel. For information, contact the taxi drivers' union, tel. 988/3-1840 or 3-1844; or ask at your hotel.

Water-Taxi Route
The water taxi is called the **Agua Bus,** tel. 988/3-3155. What a great idea! An open boat with a sun cover travels from dock to dock along the lagoon. It's a great way to get a new view of Cancún. From the water the taxi meanders through Nichupté Lagoon and picks up every hour from the following docks: **La Boom, Jardine del Arte, Carlos and Charlies, Aquatours, Plaza Zocalo, Marina Punta Este, Plaza La Isla, Restaurante/Museum La Destileria, Marina Barracuda, Restaurante Crab House, Marina Rey,** and **Marina Agua Fun.** There are several boats, so pickups are frequent. One local told us it was faster to go the distance from one end of the hotel zone to the other by water taxi than by auto taxi because of all the road traffic. It takes an hour and 10 minutes for a round trip according to the Agua Bus people. Hop on and pay US$3 per trip or buy a multiple-trip pass for US$15 per day or US$35 per week. The stops may change—ask before you buy your ticket.

Note: Though it's been tried, a trip on this boat to nearby Isla Mujeres can get pretty rough!

Cancún Trolley
A colorful trolley takes visitors on a trolley ride (on rubber wheels) around the main street of Cancún with a guide who talks about sights along the way. Coffee or beer and snacks are included for US$10 per person.

Agua World
This water park in the hotel zone on Paseo Kukulcán opposite the Melia Cancún Hotel, tel. 988/5-2288, offers all the water toys you could ask for, plus jungle tours, diving trips, and deep-sea fishing trips. It's also the departure point for the *Cancún Queen* paddleboat dinner/party cruise.

OUT OF TOWN BY SEA AND ROAD

Boat Tours to Isla Mujeres
A variety of boat tours go from Cancún to nearby Isla Mujeres. You can ride in a glass-bottom boat and slowly drift above flamboyant undersea gardens, take a musical cruise that lets you dance your way over to the small island, or enjoy cruises based on any number of other themes and activities. These tours often include snorkeling, and the necessary equipment is furnished (though there may be an added rental charge).

The **Crucero Tropical Cruiser Morning Express** includes a continental breakfast, snorkeling at Garrafón, time for shopping, lunch at the Pirate's Village on the island, and an open bar. The boat is air-conditioned and departs from the Playa Langosta dock at 10:30 A.M., returning at 4:30 P.M. Fare is US$5 per person; tel. 988/3-3268.

The B/M *Carnaval Cancún,* tel. 988/4-3760, a large triple-decker, serves an onboard buffet lunch with an open bar. It stops for snorkeling and allows time for shopping in downtown Isla Mujeres. Called the **Caribbean Funday** tour, the boat leaves the Fat Tuesday pier daily. Fare is US$50, plus US$5 for snorkel gear. The same ship is used for the evening Caribbean Carnaval cruise to Isla Mujeres, which includes a buffet dinner, open bar, and Caribbean floor show for US$60 per person.

Atlantis is a submarine that takes visitors to the edges of Manchones Reef to view the fish and coral, and to the nearby wreck of the SS *Elizabeth*. It's *almost* like being in scuba gear and swimming the reef. The boat then proceeds to Isla Mujeres beach where you can go swimming or just relax in the restaurant and bar. *Atlantis* departs from Cancún's Playa Linda hourly. For more information call 988/3-3021.

Dolphin Express offers another good day trip to Isla Mujeres. The all-inclusive journey takes you to Pirate Village to see and swim with the dolphins. Continental breakfast and lunch at the village are included. The trip fare is about US$30; to swim with the dolphins is about another US$110 depending on whether you are just touching them or swimming with them. Departure time from Playa Langosta Pier is 10 A.M.; return is at 4:30 P.M. For reservations, call 988/3-3283 or 3-1488.

For information on getting to Isla Mujeres on your own, see "Getting There" in the Isla Mujeres section.

Cancún Xcaret Ecoarchaeological Park

One of the most popular day trips from Cancún goes to **Xcaret,** a man-made eco-park a half-hour drive south of Cancún. Wildly decorated air-conditioned buses depart between 9 and 10 A.M. from the Xcaret terminal on Paseo Kukulcán across from Plaza Caracol, next to the Fiesta Americana Coral Beach Hotel, and return in late afternoon. The tour costs US$79 and includes transportation and park entrance along with a chance to see birds, dolphins, butterflies, and more. Diving, horseback riding, and dolphin activities within the park are not included in the admission. Tours, including the ruins of Tulum with a stop at Xcaret, are also available. Call 988/3-0654 or 3-0743 for information.

Isla Holbox

Leave the car fumes, the shopping carts, the crowded cafés, the postage-stamp-size spots on the beach, the tall glass buildings, the loud music—yes, leave them way behind. Get out of town and go to Isla Holbox ("whole-bowsh"). Holbox is located off the eastern tip of the northern Yucatán Peninsula and is one of the last obscure islands in Mexico. A fishing village, nature preserve, and bird refuge, Holbox harbors mangrove swamps and marks the division between the Gulf of Mexico and the Caribbean Sea.

Just 1,500 people live on this 25-mile-long island. Most of the men are fishermen here, and the junior high school offers fishing-technique classes for the kids! What a practical idea for a fishing town. You'll see few cars here, as the streets are sand. Only recently did they progress from a one-telephone-line town to a telephone for everyone who wants it. Tourism here is just a tiny sparkle on the horizon. This is a great

place—and time, at least for now—to find a secluded fishing village or that elusive desert-island ambience. The islanders are still not accustomed to tourists, and your presence will likely be greeted with curious stares and friendly advances.

Getting There

To get to Holbox you have two choices—drive to the coast and hop on a boat, or fly (with **AeroSaab,** tel. 987/3-0804, email: info@aerosaab.com) via commuter plane from Playa del Carmen. The airport on Holbox is just grass outlined with conch shells—fine for small planes. If you're interested in flying in on your own single-engine plane, go online and visit www.holboxisland.com. Both the **Flamingo Hotel** and **Puerto Holbox Hotel** offer package trips from Playa del Carmen airport, including an overnight at Holbox. AeroSaab also gives one-day air tours around and to the island, with lunch and an exploratory trip with an island guide.

If you're driving, go west from Cancún toward Mérida on the old Highway 180 (not the *autopista*) to Kilometer 80 and turn north, through Kantunil Kin. If you miss that, there's another side road heading north near Nuevo X-Can. Your ultimate destination is Chiquila—don't hesitate to ask locals for directions. The paved road heads north to Kantunilkin past small ranches and pueblos and after about 65 miles arrives at the fishing community of Chiquila on the north coast.

Chiquila is the departure point for the eight-mile car ferry to Isla Holbox. There are five roundtrip shuttles per day; the first leaves Chiquila at 6 A.M. and the last leaves Holbox at 4 P.M. (US$3 one way; check current schedule before you go). Alternatively, consider hiring a local fisherman to take you across on a private boat (more expensive).

A few *palapa* restaurants on the Chiquila beach serve cold drinks and super fish and lobster lunches. A day tour of Isla Holbox takes about four hours. There are no hotels in mainland Chiquila. On Holbox, however, camping is permitted and there are several new hotels on the beach.

What to Do

Some would say there is little to do in Holbox, and it's true, this island is not set up as a tourist mecca. But if you want some peace and quiet, this is the place to go. An eclectic little town, one of its main attractions is the **hammock house,** where women gather and hook up their hammock frames and weave away. There's also a workshop run by Victor Vasquez, a local instrument maker. Vasquez teaches children to make and play guitars, violins, mandolins, and a variety of other string instruments. If you're in town for a couple of days, you're bound to hear the youngsters sing and play.

As nice as this little village is, the real draw here is nature, especially the birds. Among many other species, you'll find pelicans, frigates, cormorants, and flamingos.

This is a great fishing haunt (and fishermen leave here vowing to keep it a secret). The catch is always good, and the fish seem to always be big. It's also a wonderful place to just stroll the shore, as the long white beaches are full of crabs, sea birds, and shells (lots of whole conch shells). This is a fine place to relax and enjoy the beauty of nature.

Nearby Places to See
When you get tired of watching the birds, fishing, swimming, hunting for shells, or watching dolphins, ask about a trip to **Yalahau Spring.** This place was a stopping point for pirates who came to fill their barrels with fresh water. Today locals take visitors to swim in this *ojo de agua,* or eye of the water, which bubbles up from its underground spring.

Accommodations US$50–100
Villas Flamingos, tel. 800/538-6802, is a group of 19 *palapa*-topped bungalows with hammocks on the patios, hardwood floors, ceiling fans, private bathrooms, and hot water. It's right on the beach and there's a swimming pool on the grounds. Room rates range from US$80–95 (US$55–70 in summer) and include a continental breakfast. Ask about off island tours.

Hotel Faro Viejo, Av. Juarez y Playa S/N, tel. 987/5-2217, email: faroviejo@prodigy.net.mx, is another beachfront hotel with a view. Rooms include air-conditioning, fans, and private baths. There's also a restaurant and bar; golfcart and bike rental and tours are available. Tour options include going around the island, visiting out of the way beaches for shelling, going on fishing trips, going to Yalahau Spring, or flying to other Maya sights on the peninsula.

Esmeralda Hotel, tel. 988/5-1811, email: esmeralda@esmeralda-hotel.com, is a *palapa* hotel just steps away from the beach with nice rooms, air-conditioning, fans, lovely vistas, good food, and a bar. Rates range from US$65–120.

Accommodations US$100–150
About one kilometer out of town on the beach, the **Villas Delfines,** U.S. tel. 800/555-8842, fax 988/4-6342, email: delfines.holbox.com, is a charming *palapa* resort. Its restaurant serves great seafood, and the comfortable rooms include private baths. Still, it's a little pricey at US$100. If you stay here, keep your eyes open for the pod of dolphins that is often seen just offshore.

Out-of-Country Destinations
Tikal: The Guatemalan airline **Aviateca** operates a one-day tour that takes you by air from Cancún to the spectacular Maya ruins of Tikal, in the Guatemalan highlands. The plane departs Cancún at 6 A.M. and lands at Flores, about a 20-minute drive from the ruins. You get five hours to explore Tikal, which many consider to be the most spectacular of the Maya sites. Wildlife is abundant; spider monkeys swing from the treetops along heavily wooded paths, and parrots fly overhead. Vendors sell Guatemalan crafts and folk art in the ruins parking lot for prices far lower than those at Cancún shops, where Guatemalan crafts have overshadowed those from Mexico. The plane returns to Cancún at 6 P.M. For information, contact your hotel tour desk or Aviateca at Plaza Mexico, Av. Tulum 200, tel. 988/4-3938 or 7-1386, U.S. tel. 800/327-9832.

Other airlines flying from Cancún to Flores include Mexicana airlines, tel. 988/4-2000; and Aerocaribe, tel. 988/4-2000, with flights on Tuesday, Thursday, Saturday, and Sunday.

Flights are also available from Cancún to **Cuba.** The U.S. State Department will not help Americans who go there and get into trouble, but many folks take the chance. Flight information is easy to get at any of the many travel agencies scattered about Cancún.

From Cancún you can fly to **Belize City** on Aerocaribe. Planes leave Tuesday, Thursday, Saturday, and Sunday. I've heard that the flight is canceled if there aren't enough passengers. From Belize City it's easy to rent a car or hop a bus to the Maya sites, or to find a boat to take you to the many beautiful offshore cays.

Aviateca, Plaza Mexico, Av. Tulum 200, tel. 988/4-3938 or 7-1386, also offers extended tours of Guatemala and flights to **Guatemala City.**

SERVICES AND INFORMATION

Medical Information
Most hotels in Cancún can provide the name of a doctor who speaks English. For serious problems contact American-owned **American Medical Care Center,** (tel. 988/3-0113, after hours 7-1455). American physician and owner Mike McFall has established a good reputation for treating and helping visitors. For other health questions call the American Consulate, tel. 988/4-2411.

Pharmacies are tourist-oriented and at most of them a little English is spoken. They are available everywhere, in all of the malls, and hotel delivery service is usually available. The pharmacy at Caracol Plaza in the hotel zone, tel. 988/3-1894 or 3-2827, is open daily 9 A.M.–10 P.M. If you should have an emergency and need to order a prescription and can't get a delivery (which is highly unlikely), go through the your hotel concierge or manager to arrange for a pick up (there will be a fee). If you don't speak Spanish, someone in your hotel should be able to help you out.

Post Office and Telegrams
The post office is on Av. Sunyaxchen (west of Av. Tulum) at Av. Xel-Ha, tel. 988/4-1418. It's open Monday–Friday 8 A.M.–7 P.M. and Saturday 9 A.M.–noon. Call the telegraph office at 988/4-1529.

Consulate Representatives
The **U.S. Consular Office,** Plaza Caracol, Third Floor, Kukulcán Blvd. (Kilometer 9), tel. 988/3-0272, keeps hours Monday–Friday 9 A.M.– 1 P.M. and 3–6 P.M. The **Canadian Consulate** is at the same address, tel. 988/3-3360, and is open Monday–Friday 9 A.M.–5 P.M.; for emergencies outside business hours call toll free 800/706-2900. The **French Consulate** is at Instituto Internacional de Idiomas, Av. Xel-Ha 113, tel. 988/4-6078, and is open Monday–Friday 8–11 A.M. and 5–7 P.M.

The consular representative of **Spain** is in the Oasis Building on Kukulcán Blvd. (Kilometer 6.5), tel. 988/3-2466, and is open Monday–Friday 10 A.M.–1 P.M. The **Italian Consulate** is downtown at 39 Alcatraces Street, Retorno 5, tel. 988/4-1261, and is open daily 9 A.M.–2 P.M.

Tourist Information
The **state tourist office** is on Av. Tulum at the Plaza Municipal Benito Juárez, next to the Multibanco Comermex, tel. 988/4-8073, and is open Monday–Saturday 9 A.M.–5 P.M. *Cancún Tips* is a helpful, free tourist information booklet available in hotels and shops; the publishers also operate tourist information offices in Plaza Caracol, Plaza Kukulcán, the Convention Center, and at Playa Langosta Pier. The chamber of commerce, tel. 988/4-4315, is also a good source of information. Booths with tourist information signs abound along Av. Tulum and Paseo Kukulcán; be warned—most are operated by time-share companies offering free tours and meals in exchange for your presence at a timeshare presentation.

Easter Break and Legal Matters
In recent years, the college crowd has descended upon Cancún during Easter break (shades of Florida). The city fathers do not like this unleashed orgy of pleasure. Now, young people are handed a document that spells out the rules. The legal age for drinking alcohol is 18. Under-aged drinkers who are caught are tossed into jail and treated like adult prisoners. And that *ain't* a pretty picture. Purchase, possession, and consumption of drugs is illegal. Public nudity is also illegal, although you will find nude sunbathers on some of the out-of-the-way beaches along the Riviera Maya coast to the south and on Isla Mujeres.

Immigration
Remember that you must turn in your Mexican visitor's card when you leave the country. The card can be good for 30–90 days. If you need an extension (*before* your card expires), go to the main immigration office at Av. Nader 1 downtown, tel. 988/4-1749, fax 988/4-0918; open Monday–Friday 8:30 A.M.–noon. You will be asked to leave your card and pick it up the following day. A second immigration office at the airport, tel. 988/4-2992, can also answer questions and provide assistance.

Tours and Travel Agencies

With the advent of the tour guide's union, tours around the area are supposed to be the same price at all agencies; however, that's not always the case. If you're feeling spunky, try a little bargaining. All the larger hotels in Cancún have travel agencies available to help you with your travel needs locally and internationally. Many more are scattered about the city. Most offices close 1–3 P.M. then reopen till 7 or 8 P.M.

Turismo Aviomar, Av. Yaxchilán downtown, tel. 988/4-8831, fax 988/4-5385, offers many tours of the city and surrounding area in modern air-conditioned buses. The agency can make reservations for party boats to Isla Mujeres and arrange most of your vacation plans. The **American Express** office is downtown at Av. Tulum 208 (at Calle Agua), tel. 988/4-1999. Two other good firms are **Intermar Caribe,** Av. Bonampak at Calle Cereza, tel. 988/4-4266, fax 988/4-1652; and **PTT Travel,** Av. Cobá 12-20, tel. 988/4-8831.

Mayaland Tours, tel. 988/7-5411 or 988/7-2450, offers many day trips and packages that begin in Cancún and continue on to Chichén Itzá, Uxmal, Palenque, Mérida, and more. Some of the packages include hotels and autos—a real bargain. Their modern, air-conditioned, double-decker buses have friendly and knowledgeable guides and onboard attendants. Most travel agencies and tour desks in town have information and can make your reservations. **Yucatán Central Reservations,** U.S. tel. 800/555-8842, specializes in all parts of the Yucatán Peninsula and can create custom trips—including hotel and airline reservations—for visitors.

GETTING THERE AND AROUND

By Air

The international airport is 20 kilometers (12 miles) south of Cancún. Along with everything else around this young city, the airport continues to grow and add to its facilities each season. It now has two runways, but no storage lockers; most hotels are willing to check your tagged luggage for you.

Airlines serving Cancún include: **Mexicana,** Av. Cobá 39, tel. 988/7-4444, airport tel. 988/6-0120; **Aeromexico,** Av. Cobá 80, tel. 988/4-

---

TO GET MARRIED IN CANCÚN

The rules for getting married in Mexico are different in each city. Call the concierge or the wedding coordinator at the hotel where you will be staying for specific details. Commonly you will need:

_ A copy of your tourist cards or visas
_ Certified birth certificates or passports
_ Blood tests within 15 days of the wedding (the type of tests required can vary from city to city)
_ Certified copy of final divorce decrees if applicable (you must wait at least one full year from final decree). If widowed, bring certified copy of deceased spouse's death certificate.
_ The names, addresses, ages, nationalities, and tourist-card numbers of four witnesses (some cities require Mexican witnesses, often available at the Civil Registry office for a fee)
_ Money to pay the cashier at the city hall
_ Filled-out application given to you by the judge

Very important: allow *at least* two to five days before the wedding.

3571, airport tel. 988/6-0018; **Continental,** airport tel. 988/6-0040; **Lacsa,** Av. Bonampak at Av. Cobá, tel. 988/7-3101, airport tel. 988/6-0014; and **Aviacsa,** Av. Cobá, tel. 988/7-4214 or 7-4211. **Aerocaribe** and **Aerocozumel,** Av. Tulum 29, tel. 988/4-2000, airport tel. 988/6-0083, offer daily flights to and from Isla Cozumel. **Aviateca,** airport tel. 988/6-0155, flies to Guatemala. Several airlines run charter flights to Cancún from major U.S. gateways at reduced fares. Ask your travel agent to check out this option.

Car rentals, taxis, and *colectivos* are available at the airport. The *colectivo* vans are cheaper than taxis and they *will* be filled to capacity. Buy your ticket near the baggage pickup for US$15. It's always a good idea to watch each person remove his or her luggage on the way to your hotel, just to avoid a mix-up. When you depart from Cancún, you will have to take a taxi since the *colectivos* only run one way. Depending on the number of people in the cab, it will cost US$10–15 from downtown, about US$20 from the hotel zone. Be sure you set aside

US$17 for departure tax to be paid at the airport.

By Bus

Buses operate daily between Cancún, Mérida, and Chetumal, linking smaller villages en route. The bus terminal is downtown on Av. Tulum. Call or go to the terminal for complete schedules—they change frequently. You will find the first- (**ADO**) and second-class (**Autotransportes del Caribe**) bus stations next door to each other, across from the Hotel Plaza Caribe at the intersection of Avs. Tulum and Uxmal and at Av. Pino, a small side street off Uxmal. These buses run frequently and fares are cheap. Try to buy your ticket well ahead of your departure since the traffic is heavy.

Playa Express on Av. Pino, offers air-conditioned minibus and regular bus service between Cancún, Playa del Carmen, Tulum, Felipe Carrillo Puerto, and Chetumal. The minibuses do not have large luggage compartments. Right across the street, **Interplaya** operates minibuses between Cancún and Playa del Carmen (with stops at all the beach areas) every half hour from 5 A.M.–10 P.M. **InterCaribe** runs first-class, nonstop buses to Mérida and Chetumal.

Caribe Express, on Av. Pino, around the corner from ADO, tel. 988/7-4174, runs between Cancún, Chetumal, Campeche, and Mérida. These first-class luxury buses are the 747s of the road, featuring air-conditioning, earphones, TV, music, bathrooms, and an attendant who will serve you drinks and cookies.

Expresso de Oriente, on Av. Uxmal, tel. 988/4-5542 or 4-4804, offers deluxe service between Cancún and Mérida. Eleven buses run daily nonstop; others stop in Playa del Carmen, Tulum, and Valladolid. Reservations must be confirmed two hours before departure or they will be canceled.

By Car

Car rentals are available at Cancún International Airport and many hotels. Most companies rent jeeps, mid-size sedans, and Volkswagen bugs (personal favorite), and accept credit cards. You may find that you get the best rates by reserving your car in advance through U.S.-based agencies, though some of the small local agencies offer great deals when business is down.

The 320-kilometer, four-hour drive from Mérida to Cancún is on a good highway (Highway 180) through henequen-dotted countryside, past historic villages and archaeological ruins. The new toll highway cuts 30–60 minutes off the drive, though the straight, high-speed, eight-lane road is somewhat monotonous. The tolls from Cancún to Mérida are not cheap and change often. It can be anywhere from US$15 and up. New roads are going in along the Cancún-Tulum corridor (now known as the Riviera Maya); it's not certain whether they will be free or not. Right now the free Highway 307 from Cancún to Chetumal (343 kilometers) is a four-hour drive along a well-maintained four-lane road as far as Playa del Carmen (two more lanes are slowly gaining). One friend who lives in Puerto Morelos told us that he has watched the road being built under three different presidents. It's great where it's finished. The road runs parallel to the Caribbean coast.

DRIVING DISTANCES FROM CANCÚN

Airport:	20 km
Akumal:	104 km
Aventuras (playa):	107 km
Bacalar:	320 km
Chemuyil:	109 km
Chetumal:	382 km
Chichén Itzá:	192 km
Club Med:	25 km
Cobá:	167 km
Kohunlich:	449 km
Mérida:	312 km
Pamul:	92 km
Playa del Carmen:	65 km
Puerto Juárez:	2 km
Puerto Morelos:	32 km
Punta Sam:	7 km
Tulum:	130 km
Valladolid:	152 km
Xcaret:	72 km
Xelha:	123 km

ISLA MUJERES

Considered by some to be the Bohemian Outpost of the Caribbean, this tiny island is still a great escape. Finger-shaped Isla Mujeres lies 13 kilometers (eight miles) east of Cancún across Bahía Mujeres. Just off the tip of this small island is the famous Honduran Reef that meanders to the Bay of Honduras. The island is small—just eight kilometers (five miles) long and 400 meters at its widest point—but many visitors return year after year to spend a few hedonistic days relaxing or diving on the island's outlying reefs.

Though the overflow of tourists from Cancún and Cozumel is noticeable, the island is relatively quiet, especially in the off-season (June and September are really low key!). The easygoing populace still smiles at backpackers, and travelers can easily find suitable lodging in all price ranges, though in the budget category it's getting harder.

Isla Mujeres harbors a large naval base, so you'll see many ships in its port. (Note that the Mexican navy does not like people photographing the base, ships, or on-duty sailors, so if you're struck with the urge to photograph *everything,* ask someone in charge first.) Before tourism, fishing was the island's prime industry, with turtle, lobster, and shark the local specialties. Today the turtle is protected—with a few specific exceptions, it is illegal to hunt them or take their eggs. Stiff fines face those who break this law.

The weather here is about the same as on the entire coast. Hurricanes are not common, but Isla Mujeres is nevertheless prepared; all the hotels know just what to do should a hurricane blow ashore.

History

One legend says the name Isla Mujeres ("Island of Women") comes from the buccaneers who stowed their female captives here while conducting their nefarious business on the high seas. Another more prosaic (and probably correct) version refers to the large number of female-shaped clay idols found on the island when the Spaniards arrived. Archaeologists presume the island was a stopover for the Maya Indians on their pilgrimages to Cozumel to worship Ix Chel, female goddess of fertility and an important deity to Maya women.

SIGHTS

Orientation

The "city" of Isla Mujeres, at the north end of the island, is 10 blocks long and five blocks wide. On Av. Hidalgo, the main street, you'll find the central plaza, city hall, police station, cinema, *farmacia,* and a large supermarket. Most streets are really only walkways, with no vehicles allowed (although they frequently squeeze by anyway). The ferry dock is three blocks from the plaza; if you're traveling light, you can walk to most of the hotels when you get off the ferry. Otherwise, taxis queue up along Av. Rueda Medina close to the ferry dock.

Garrafon Park

The park is five kilometers (three miles) south of town. Garrafon is now a privately owned site. Since being taken over by the Xcaret and Xelha people, Garrafon has undergone major changes with major investment. The new owners are doing their best to revive the reef that has been trampled for years by careless tourists and tour boats. The park has been totally renovated with broad sloping lawns, trees, a swimming pool, ramps, and lots of steps. The large restaurant at the top of the cliff offers a fantastic view of the sea. Look for an ice-cream shop, money exchange, and gift shop. A two-tiered entry fee is rather costly—general adults (US$10), children (US$6). The all-inclusive fee (includes lunch, drinks, locker, towels, and snorkeling gear) for adults is US$39, children US$27. Daily snorkel gear rental is US$8. It's a beautiful place to spend the day snorkeling, swimming in the pool, eating good food, exploring, and browsing the gift shop.

The snorkeling at Garrafon has been heralded for years. It's great for beginners, thanks to a close-in coral reef, little swell, and water only a meter deep for about five meters offshore (after which the bottom drops off abruptly to six meters). Brazen Bermuda grubs gaze at you eye-to-eye through your mask, practically begging to have their picture taken. Swim past the reef and you'll see beautiful angelfish that seem to enjoy hanging around a coral-encrusted anchor and a couple of antiquated ship's cannons. This is a good place to introduce children to the undersea world.

The close-in reef has been roped off to prevent swimmers from touching or climbing. For years it's been a favorite attraction, harboring myriad sea creatures. It has suffered from thousands of people abusing the reef, taking it for granted; even the fish flee the tourist hordes, while in years past they just looked back at you through your mask. With cooperation from the public and the work of the marine biologists, it won't take too long for the coral to rejuvenate.

You are asked to observe and enjoy from within the ropes. Sunscreen is not permitted in the water, as it contains chemicals toxic to these fragile creatures. An ecological sun lotion that will not harm the fish and coral is available at the gift shop.

The park is open 8 A.M.–5 P.M. Note: Some snorkelers are not happy having to wear a life vest while snorkeling (the vest is provided).

Maya Ruins

At the southern tip of the island, an ancient Maya temple once used as a coastal observation post stands guard on a cliff overlooking the sea. The occasional hurricane has caused immense damage over the years. Right now it is still in its most recent renovation. These ruins were first seen and described by Francisco Hernández de Córdoba in 1517. Legends are varied. One says that the temple was devoted to the worship of Ix Chel, goddess of fertility. Another says it was used for making the sophisticated astronomical observations that were part of Maya daily life. Still another claims it was used to watch for incoming storms and human intruders. Today it offers a magnificent view of the sea.

In the past you could ask the caretaker's permission to climb up into the lighthouse (it's 10 meters high and worth the climb for the view). And until the Garrafón Park management gets organized, it's doubtful that will change. If you do go up there, tip the caretaker. Sometimes you have to call for him, since he might be behind his house hoeing his garden of tomatoes, peppers, and watermelons. This is a magnificent spot to see both the open sea on the windward side of the island and, leeward, the peaceful Bahía Mujeres.

To get there, continue south from El Garrafón

on the main road until you see the lighthouse road going off to the right. Park your vehicle in the small clearing near the lighthouse and follow the dirt path to the ruins. If traveling by taxi to the Maya ruin, ask the driver to wait while you look around. Or let him go—you can walk back to Garrafón and catch a taxi to town (until 5 P.M.).

Tortugranja Turtle Farm

This low-key, no-frills sea turtle sanctuary is located on Carretera Sac Bajo, on the beach south of the Cristalmar Resort and Beach Club. During the nesting season, one section of sand is fenced off as the hatchery, where the turtles dig their nests and lay their eggs. Eggs are collected from their nests and put into protected incubation pens. After they hatch, they are placed in three large pools to grow in a protected environment until they are at least a year old and can be safely released into the sea. An experimental holding area in the sea is roped and netted to keep adult turtles close by and within easy reach of the hatchery beach for the summer. This insures they will come to *this* shore to lay their eggs under the watchful eye of marine biologists. Once the laying season is over, they are released back to the open sea. Staff at the farm give information (in Spanish) and let you examine the smaller turtles up close. On the grounds you'll find restrooms, great ice-cream bars, and a gift shop (proceeds from T-shirt sales and the small admissions charge go to the care of the turtles).

Swim with Dolphins

Dolphin Discovery, on the Sac Bajo Peninsula, has as its main attraction a big saltwater pen holding six dolphins where you can swim for a fee. First you'll watch an instructive video explaining where you can and cannot touch the dolphins. Then you join these marvelous animals in the water. It appears to be a frolic, dolphins jumping over you, under you, pulling you, and swimming with you. A trainer is in charge at all times, directing you and the dolphins. Cost is US$110; for an extra fee you can purchase a video of your entire swim. A restaurant on the premises offers a buffet lunch 11 A.M.–1 P.M.

Beaches

The closest beach to downtown is **Playa Norte,** also called Coco Beach and Nautibeach (perhaps

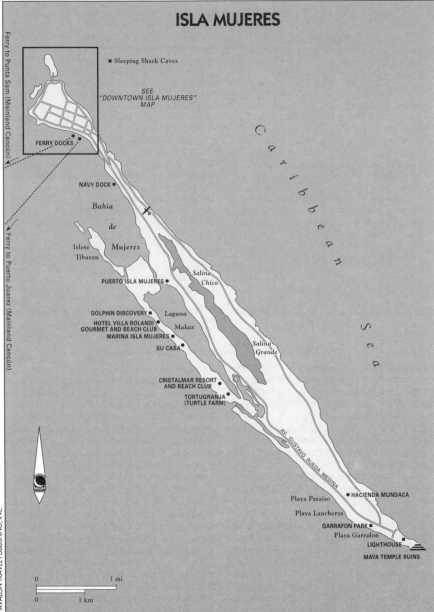

ISLA MUJERES

■ Sleeping Shark Caves

SEE
"DOWNTOWN ISLA MUJERES"
MAP

FERRY DOCKS ■

Ferry to Punta Sam (Mainland Cancún)

Ferry to Puerto Juárez (Mainland Cancún)

NAVY DOCK ■

Bahía

de

Islote
Tiburón

Mujeres

PUERTO ISLA MUJERES ●

*Salina
Chico*

Laguna

DOLPHIN DISCOVERY ■
HOTEL VILLA ROLANDI
GOURMET AND BEACH CLUB ●
MARINA ISLA MUJERES ■
SU CASA ●

Makax

*Salina
Grande*

CRISTALMAR RESORT
AND BEACH CLUB ●

TORTUGRANJA
(TURTLE FARM) ●

AV. GUSTAVO RUEDA MEDINA

C a r i b b e a n

S e a

■ HACIENDA MUNDACA

Playa Paraíso

Playa Lancheros

GARRAFON PARK ■
Playa Garrafón
LIGHTHOUSE
MAYA TEMPLE RUINS

0   1 mi
0   1 km

© AVALON TRAVEL PUBLISHING, INC.

HACIENDA MUNDACA

There's something *juicy* about legends and myths, especially when it involves a real-life person. Somehow his persona, whether famous or infamous, just keeps on growing! A touching local legend from the mid-1800s tells of a swashbuckling, slave-trading pirate, Fermín Mundaca de Marechaja, who fell in love at a distance with a lovely woman on Isla Mujeres. Mundaca was an old man, she was young, and he saw her only once. Her name may have been Prisca Gómez (a.k.a. *Trigueña* or "Brunette"), and depending on which version of the story you hear she was either a visitor from Spain or a native of the island. After 10 years of plying the seas and buying and selling slaves, and, it is whispered, discovering gold, Mundaca retired to this small island and built a beautiful hacienda to woo this woman who didn't know he existed. Sadly, he was unsuccessful. All of his efforts were fruitless—she married another and moved to Mérida and the high life, leaving the heartsick slave-trader and his fortune behind to live the last of his lonely life here on the island. Fate can be fickle—and perhaps just. If you're a romantic, stroll through the overgrown property, see the old archway, take a look at the well, and see if you feel a haunting melancholy in the once-gracious gardens of this deserted estate.

But that's not the end of the story. There's more! Mundaca became a bitter and aloof old man, and all the local fishermen believed he had lots of gold hidden somewhere. He was not very popular. The fishermen spied on him. They whispered that with the help of a young man, Mundaca found a rugged cave on a rocky cliff of the rough south coast to bury his booty. The story was repeated so many times it took on a life of its own. Who knows if it was true—alas, the locals never located the cave or the gold.

In the early 1900s, however, a couple of visiting American college kids paid a taxi fare with some strange-looking coins—gold coins. They went back to the states and told a tale of treasure. Other Americans came back searching for this treasure, and they ravished the remains of Mundaca's hacienda. The only hint of any worth was a golden globe that remained for years on the gate to the once-lovely estate.

The government plans to restore Hacienda Mundaca and make it into a park. Right now, it's not much more than trails through the bush. To get there from downtown, follow the main highway south approximately 4.5 kilometers (2.7 miles) to a signed turnoff to the left.

It sounds as though Mundaca was bitter even at the end—he must have written his own epitaph before he died: *As you are I was. As I am you will be.*

---

because of the topless women?). It's on the lee side of the island at the north edge of town. Here you can relax in the sun and swim in a blue sea that's as calm as a lake. In this shallow water you can wade out 35 meters and still be only waist deep. At the west end of the beach are *palapa* cafés serving both soft and hard beverages.

You'll find lots of activity in front of Las Palapas Chimbo beach café. When around, a Tarzan-like man rents sailboards, water skis, and bright-yellow three-wheeled "bikes" that float. Prices are always open to negotiation, especially in the off-season.

At the south end of the island, toward Garrafón on the main road out of town, are **Playa Paraíso** and **Playa Lancheros,** quiet beaches where people formerly swam and rode the backs of giant sea turtles. Today the turtles are protected by law from such indignities, but you can still come here to enjoy the sun, sand, and sea. An open *palapa* restaurant specializes in seafood.

Isla Contoy

Bird lovers especially will enjoy a trip to Contoy. A national bird sanctuary, Contoy is 24 kilometers (14 miles) north of Isla Mujeres and is home to herons, brown pelicans, frigates, and cormorants, among other species. The island's only structures are a three-story viewing tower, remnants of old informational displays explaining the island's ecology, and old bunkhouses once used by biologists. The rest of the island is lush tropical jungle surrounded by crystal-clear water. Recently reopened to the public, Contoy was closed for a while as biologists worried its popularity was ruining the local ecology. The earlier you can get to the island, the more bird activity you will see.

Day trips to the island leave from Mujeres. Check with the tourist office at Av. Hidalgo 6 or with the Boatman's Cooperative next to the ferry pier, tel. 987/7-0036. You'll see many signs over tiny offices that advertise trips to Contoy. Many of the boats are slow and have wooden seats, so if comfort is a necessity double check which boat you'll be on. Even if you are on a slow boat, you'll forget all about it as the verdant island with hundreds of birds soaring in the wind comes into view. Exploration of the small island is left to you with plenty of time to enjoy swimming or snorkeling in the warm, shallow waters. Most of the tours serve fresh fruit on arrival. Often a lunch of fresh barbecued fish (tic 'n chix style) caught on the way, Spanish rice, bread, soft drinks, and beer is served on the beach.

WATER SPORTS

Snorkeling and Scuba Diving
Snorkelers on Isla Mujeres have many choice locations from which to choose. **Garrafón** is a good introduction to the underwater world. Another good option is the east end of **Playa Norte,** where visibility can be up to 33 meters (109 feet) near the wooden pier (occasionally the sea gets choppy here, clouding the water). The windward side of the island is never good for snorkeling as the sea is seldom calm; don't snorkel or even swim on the windward side on a rough day— you'll risk being hurled against the sharp rocks. An open wound caused by coral laceration often becomes infected in this humid climate.

The dive shops on the island sponsor excursions to nearby reefs. A lot of press has been devoted to Isla Mujeres's **Sleeping Shark Caves.** Ask at the dive shop for detailed information. Although some divemasters will take you in among the sluggish though dangerous fish, others feel that it isn't a smart dive. Bill Horn, experienced diver and owner of Aqua Safari Dive Shop on Isla Cozumel, warns that there's always danger when you put yourself into a small area with a wild creature. In a cave, even if a large fish isn't trying to attack, the swish of a powerful tail could easily send you crashing against the wall. Reasons given for the sharks' somnambulant state vary with the teller: salinity of the water or low carbon dioxide. Divers must dive to depths of 150 feet or more to see the sharks, which may or may not be around. Local divemasters say that divers have a 30 percent chance of spotting the sharks. Between Cancún and Isla Mujeres, experienced divers will find excitement diving **Chital, Cuevones, La**

Bandera, and **Manchones Reefs.**

Scuba diving and snorkeling trips or rental equipment can be arranged at **Carnavalito Dive Shop,** tel. 987/7-0118; **Mexico Divers,** tel. 987/7-0131; and **La Bahía Dive Shop,** tel. 987/7-0340. All three are on Av. Rueda Medina in the vicinity of the ferry docks. These shops are qualified, reliable, and offer excellent service. Remember, always check out the divemaster's certification and approach with caution the divemaster who doesn't ask to see yours.

Fishing
Deep-sea fishing trips can be arranged through any of the marinas. Spring is the best time to catch the big ones: dorado, marlin, and sailfish. The rest of the year you can bring in good strings of grouper, barracuda, tuna, and red snapper. **Mexico Divers,** on Av. Rueda Medina next to the boat dock, tel. 987/7-0131, offers a day-long deep-sea fishing trip that includes bait, tackle, and lunch. The **Boatmen's Cooperative,** on the waterfront just north of the ferry pier, tel. 987/7-0036, and the **Club de Yates,** on Av.

dive boat, Isla Mujeres

Rueda Medina next to the Pemex station, tel. 987/7-0211 or 7-0086, also offer deep-sea fishing trips and boat rentals.

Dock Facilities

The marinas in Isla Mujeres are getting more sophisticated, with many services available. **Pemex Marina** in the bay offers electricity, water, diesel, and gasoline. You'll find a mechanic at the navy-base dock, tel. 987/7-0196. **Laguna Makax** offers only docking facilities. In boating emergencies, call the Coast Guard ("Neptuno") on VHF channel 16.

ACCOMMODATIONS

You'll find a surprising number of hotels on this miniscule island. Besides the few luxury-class establishments, most are simple, family-run inns. Many are downtown near the oceanfront.

Under US$50

Low-priced hotels are no longer as easy to find here as they once were. Look at budget places carefully before paying your money—what can be clean and friendly one season can go downhill the next. And at any lodging in this category, hot water can be an elusive, unreliable item.

The youth hostel, **Poc Na,** Av. Matamoros 91, tel. 987/7-0090, fax 987/7-0059, offers clean, dormitory-style rooms with fans, communal baths and toilets, and either mattresses or hammocks. The cafeteria is simple with few choices, but its food is adequate and inexpensive. Rates start at US$5 for a mattress and sheet, and US$1 for a towel, with a US$7 deposit required for all rentals. Each space comes with a locker—bring your own lock.

For another peso saver, take a look at the simple, multistoried **Caribe Maya,** Av. Madero 9, tel. 987/7-0190. Old but clean, the 20 rooms (under US$50) each have private bath and thrift-store furnishings; some have air-conditioning, the rest have fans. Air circulation is better on the upper floors.

Hotel El Isleño, Calle Vicente Guerrero at Madero, tel. 987/7-0302, shouldn't be your first choice for low-priced accommodations (under US$50), since cleanliness is not its hallmark. But if the other places mentioned are full, check here.

US$50–100

On the oceanfront, the **Hotel Vistalmar,** Av. Rueda Medina s/n, between Abasolo and Matamoros, tel. 987/7-0209, fax 987/7-0096, is really spartan, but offers a friendly ambience and good location. Most of the clean rooms have ceiling fans and private bathrooms with hot water. At the end of the day, guests gather at the tables and chairs out on the big common balconies—a good place to meet fellow travelers. A small restaurant overlooks the sea and serves simple but tasty meals. Rates are US$50–100.

Marina Isla Mujeres, tel./fax 987/7-0594, on Sac Bajo, is a private little resort on the waterfront with 10 efficiency suites (US$45–65), each including a kitchenette, a living room, a bathroom, a bedroom, air-conditioning, and a fan. Rates include complimentary breakfast. It's out of town, but it's pleasant.

Su Casa, Miriam of Su Casa, south of town on

Yucatecan boatmen keep a sharp watch for the reef between Isla Mujeres and Isla Contoy. Hundreds of ships over the past 400 years have been wrecked on the reef, which parallels the Caribbean coast for some 250 kilometers.

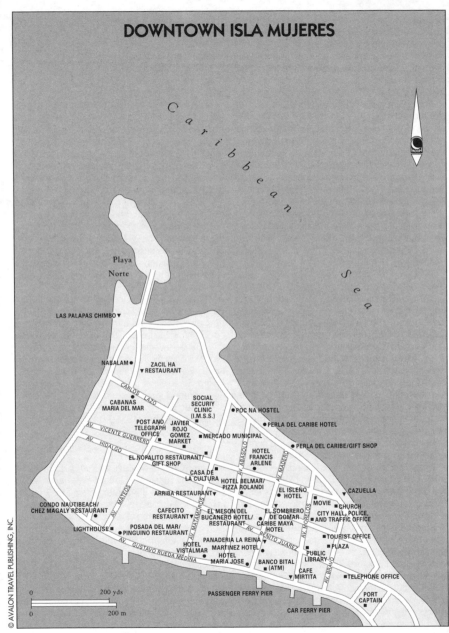

DOWNTOWN ISLA MUJERES

Caribbean Sea

Playa Norte

LAS PALAPAS CHIMBO ▼

NABALAM ●   ZACIL HA
▼ RESTAURANT

CARLOS LAZO

CABANAS
MARIA DEL MAR

SOCIAL
SECURIY
CLINIC
(I.M.S.S.)

● POC NA HOSTEL

POST AND
TELEGRAPH
OFFICE

JAVIER
ROJO
GOMEZ
MARKET

■ MERCADO MUNICIPAL

● PERLA DEL CARIBE HOTEL

AV. VICENTE GUERRERO

AV. HIDALGO

EL NOPALITO RESTAURANT/
GIFT SHOP

● PERLA DEL CARIBE/GIFT SHOP

HOTEL
FRANCIS
ARLENE

AV. ABASOLO

AV. MADERO

CASA DE
LA CULTURA

HOTEL BELMAR/
PIZZA ROLANDI

ARRIBA RESTAURANT ▼

EL ISLEÑO
HOTEL

CAZUELLA ■

AV. MATEOS

AV. MATAMOROS

CONDO NAUTIBEACH/
CHEZ MAGALY RESTAURANT

CAFECITO
RESTAURANT ▼

EL MESON DEL
BUCANERO HOTEL/
RESTAURANT

EL SOMBRERO
DE GOMAR
CARIBE MAYA
HOTEL

MOVIE ■
■ CHURCH
CITY HALL, POLICE,
AND TRAFFIC OFFICE

AV. MORELOS

LIGHTHOUSE ■

POSADA DEL MAR/
PINGUINO RESTAURANT

HOTEL
VISTALMAR

PANADERIA LA REINA ●
MARTINEZ HOTEL ●

BENITO JUAREZ

■ TOURIST OFFICE

■ PLAZA

AV. GUSTAVO RUEDA MEDINA

HOTEL
MARIA JOSE

BANCO BITAL
● (ATM)

PUBLIC
LIBRARY

CAFE
▼ MIRTITA

AV. BRAVO

■ TELEPHONE OFFICE

0   200 yds

0   200 m

PASSENGER FERRY PIER

CAR FERRY PIER

PORT
CAPTAIN

© AVALON TRAVEL PUBLISHING, INC.

Laguna Mekax, U.S. tel. 845/339-6694, Mexico tel./fax 987/7-0180, is a delightfully low-key, nine-room resort right on its own beach. It's rustic, private, peaceful, and exudes a happy ambience. Each fan-cooled room (US$65) has a bedroom, sitting area, and small kitchen. It's walking distance to Dolphin Discovery.

Facing the windward side of the island, **Hotel Perla del Caribe,** Av. Madero 2, tel. 987/2-0444, fax 987/7-0011, U.S. tel. 800/258-6454, offers pleasant rooms with private bathrooms and air-conditioning or fans. Rooms (US$78) have terraces and balconies, so be sure to ask for one facing the sea. Other amenities include a snack bar and pool. The hotel's rough-water beach is good for sunbathing and walking; swim only when the sea is calm. The concrete *malecón* walkway along the backside of the island is conveniently close to La Perla. Credit cards are okay. Prices drop considerably during the low season.

El Mesón del Bucanero, Av. Hidalgo 11, tel. 987/7-0210, email: bucanero@QROO1.telmex.net.mx, is a small hotel above the sometimes-noisy Bucanero restaurant. The rooms (US$67) are pleasant and clean with private bathrooms, fans, air-conditioning, and cable TV. Some have refrigerators and hot water.

At **Hotel Francis Arlene,** on Av. Guerrero near the Casa de la Cultura, tel./fax 987/7-0310, the owners keep a close eye on the condition of the immaculately clean though simple rooms (US$50), which have air-conditioning or fans, tiled baths, and good mattresses. Some rooms have refrigerators, toasters, and coffeemakers, and some have stoves. Some rooms are cheaper at certain times of the year.

Posada del Mar, Av. Rueda Medina 15A, tel. 987/7-0212, fax 987/7-0266, is an older complex with your choice of bungalows or hotel rooms. Some are very attractive and comfortable; however, you should ask to see your room before you pay. Prices are US$57–67 in the off season, rooms come with full breakfast. Many customers return each year—a good sign. You can go swimming in the bay across the street or in the hotel's own lovely pool, which is fed by a stone, colonial-style aqueduct. A low-key *palapa* bar—where swings substitute for barstools and hammocks hang in the shade—sits next to the pool; ask bartenders Romie or Miguel for a Maya Sac-

rifice, a drink that lights up the *palapa* with flames and fun! The restaurant Pinguino, at the front of the property, offers tables overlooking the sidewalk and beach and a big bar in back.

Cabañas María del Mar, Av. Carlos Lazos 1 (on Playa Norte), tel. 987/7-0213 or 7-0179, fax 987/7-0173, began providing visitors with simple bungalows many years ago. It has since grown into one of the island's larger complexes. You have a choice of simple bungalows or more upscale hotel rooms. Rates range US$80–100. Most of the rooms are on the beach, with ceiling fans, air-conditioning, terraces, refrigerators, and purified water. Ask to see your room before you pay, as some are nicer than others. Look for screens on the windows. Facilities include a pool, restaurant, bar, and game room.

Hotel Belmar, Av. Hidalgo at Abasolo (above Pizza Rolandi), tel. 987/7-0430, fax 987/7-0429, offers 10 nicely decorated rooms with air-conditioning, tile floors, and satellite TV; the master suite even has its own hot tub and kitchenette. Rates range US$60–75.

Media Luna Hotel, located very close to Nabalam on Half Moon Bay, tel. 800/833-5971, is a new multistory hotel offering 18 rooms with a pool right on the beach. This is the rough side of the island—swimming is not suggested. Nevertheless, it's only a two-minute barefoot walk to North Beach where the water is very calm. Rooms have either two double beds or one king bed, refrigerators, air-conditioning, fans, large balconies with hammocks, and great views. Rates range from US$50–112, depending on the room and the season.

US$100–150

Nabalam, on Calle Zazil at Playa Norte #118 (just up the road from Cabañas María del Mar), U.S. tel. 800/555-8842, Mexico tel. 987/7-0279, fax 987/7-0436, offers 30 comfy rooms in a superb location on the white-sand beach. Its two-story white stucco buildings face the sea, and all rooms are junior suites with sitting areas, dining tables, air-conditioning, fans, and patios or balconies. Rates range from US$90–170. Folk art and photographs from Chiapas, along with Maya carvings, decorate the rooms and public spaces; landscaped trails lead to the restaurant and beach. Hammocks hang under the palms beside comfortable lounge chairs in a small garden facing the beach. The hotel's restaurant, Zacil Ha, gets glowing reviews, and the *palapa* bar is a popular happy-hour hangout for tourists as well as local expats.

Though Isla Mujeres has long been known for its low-key, glitz-free atmosphere, a couple of flashy resorts have now been built here. Two are on the island's south end; either take a taxi back and forth to town, rent a golf cart, or ride a bike. We've heard rumors that there will soon be a large **Sol Melia Hotel** on this lovely little island.

Puerto Isla Mujeres, tel. 800/400-3333, is tucked away where you'll never see it unless you go looking for it. Along with slips for luxury yachts, it offers beautiful hotel rooms and condos for US$105–225. Everything is sprawled along the shore. The atmosphere is tranquil and private. Sun worshiping is the favorite pastime of most guests, and meals are served at tables next to the large circular pool. The bungalows are luxuriously furnished. In high season prices are in the premium range, but in low season, this is one of the best bargains in the Yucatán. There's no beach on the premises; however, the staff offers a small boat to take you to a private beach.

US$200 and up
A really lovely (and pricey) place to check out is **Hotel Villa Rolandi Gourmet and Beach Club.** It offers 20 beautifully furnished suites, in Isla's southern section on the Cancún side of the island, tel. 987/7-0500, email rolandi@kuartos .com. Each oceanfront suite includes a balcony Jacuzzi, air-conditioning, marble bathrooms, continental breakfast, and many small amenities guaranteed to make life sweet. Also included in the price is an á la carte lunch or dinner. And yes, you'll find the same good Italian Swiss food that has made Rolandis successful for many years. Enjoy a fitness center, fine pool, and white beach. Roundtrip transportation is provided on the hotel's power catamaran from Cancún's Playa Linda to the Rolandi's private dock. Suite prices range from US$310–US$380 for two people, depending on the time of year. Prices during holidays are higher.

La Casa de los Sueños, on Carretera Garrafón, tel. 987/7-0651, fax 987/7-0708, U.S. tel. 800/551-2558, is an intimate, luxurious, non-smoking resort with its own beach, "infinity" pool, nine rooms and suites, and graceful surround-

ings. Breakfast and bikes are included in the rates. Light lunches are available. Each room (US$250) has a terrace or balcony with an ocean view, marble bathrooms, and air-conditioning. Rates include breakfast. The modern Mexican architecture sings with bright colors and beautiful pottery; an art gallery is planned. This is a really lovely place. Note: two *big* dogs are permanent residents of the resort; some visitors have written to complain.

Condos
For the visitor who plans to stay a week or two, two-bedroom condos are available on the beach at **Cristalmar Resort and Beach Club,** south of town on the Cancún side of the island, U.S. tel. 800/555-8842, Mexico fax 987/7-0007. The apartment/suites have one or two bedrooms (US$115 and US$125 respectively). Each is air-conditioned and comfortable, with lots of tile and a color TV. Breakfast, lunch, and dinner are served by the pool near the *palapa* bar, which stays open all day. Taxis to town are about US$5. You can snorkel, sun, and swim; fishing and scuba diving can be arranged through the front desk. Hacienda Gomar is next door and the snorkeling is great under Gomar's dock, where large schools of colorful fish enjoy the shade. Prices go way down in the low season.

Note: Cristalmar is a family resort par excellence. We observed a wonderful family gathering here that included an 83-year-old great grandma, grandparents, eight adult siblings, and their brood of kids ages 3–17. . . 35 people in all. The gentleness shown by the entire hotel staff was remarkable, even when the little ones were dashing about, maybe yelling a little too loud, splashing in the pool, or bringing in their day's catch of fish for the chef to cook. Even the pool-cleaning guy interrupted his chores to help the little city kids who had never seen coconut trees and thought coconut came out of a package. He helped them climb the tree and capture the big yellow nut, then he split the coconut, explained the juice, and showed them how to clean it. During the holidays, Cristalmar puts out piñatas for the kids to attack and demolish, releasing a shower of candies and confetti inside. No wonder this is a favorite destination for families, year after year.

FOOD

As is the case elsewhere in the area, seafood is the highlight of most restaurant menus on Isla Mujeres; in fact, the fish is caught right in the front yard. Dozens of simple, informal indoor and outdoor cafés and a number of small fast-food places sell *tortas,* tacos, and fried fish. If you've never had a fish taco this is the place to try one.

Arriba

Vegetarians and health-food fans are in luck at this great second-story restaurant on Hidalgo between Abasalo and Matamoros. The salads of fresh veggies and cucumber-dill dressing are worth celebrating, as are the vegetable kabobs and tempura served with wasabi and soy sauce. Fish and poultry dishes are prepared with a minimum of oil; potatoes are sautéed with jicama, onions, and herbs. The Caribbean rice with ginger, vegetables, and egg is a meal in itself. Try the watermelon margarita or avocado pie for a real change of pace. Look for the blue-and-white trim and narrow stairway on Hidalgo. Open for lunch and dinner.

Cafecito

As the name implies, Cafecito, on Calle Juárez at Matamoros, serves great cappuccino and espresso, along with wonderful crepes filled with fresh fruit and ice cream. Breakfast choices include fresh waffles, fruit plates, and eggs—you may find yourself starting every day here—while at dinner the chef goes all out with specialties that include a sublime shrimp curry (good, but expect to wait for your food). Glass-topped tables cover pretty arrangements of sand and shells, and soothing jazz plays softly in the background. Part of this small café's charm is its status as a gathering place for world travelers of all ages and interests. Open 8 A.M.–noon and 6–10 P.M.; closed Thursday and Sunday nights. Moderate prices.

Red Eye Café, not too far from North Beach on Hidalgo, is a fine little food stop that opens at 6 A.M. and serves breakfast and lunch. If you like German food, stop and check out the bratwurst and homemade breads.

Pinguino

Sunsets are superb from the porch tables looking out to sea at Pinguino, the Posada del Mar's restaurant on Av. Rueda Medina, tel. 987/7-0300. The chef does marvelous things with lobster here; if you're going to splurge, this is the place to do it. Plan on spending the evening and start with an appetizer of nachos or a seafood cocktail, then move on to the feast. Pinguino is also good for huge breakfasts of *huevos rancheros,* yogurt, and granola. Moderate prices.

El Mesón Del Bucanero

On Hidalgo, this large outdoor café serves good seafood and Yucatecan specialties for breakfast, lunch, and dinner. Prices are reasonable—a breakfast of bacon, eggs, beans, and toast runs about US$3.50. Good fried fish and *chilaquiles.* Moderate Prices.

Miramar Restaurant

It's always nice to discover a café with good food, good service, and a nice ambience. That's the Miramar. It's nothing fancy, but the open-sided, *malecón* café provides great views of the harbor. You can see the ferries come and go and watch the fishermen cleaning their catch and tossing scraps to the waiting pelicans. Seafood dominates the menu; try the whole fried fish (about US$7), a very *tipico* dish.

Pizza Rolandi

This small café, on Av. Hidalgo between Madero and Abasolo, tel. 987/7-0430, has been serving good food here for years and has an efficient staff. It's one of the few places in town with a satellite dish, which they are willing to tune to such luxuries as NFL playoff games. The café serves beef, great fish, pastas, calzone, and pizza. Be sure to try their garlic bread; it's great with beer. Service is inside or in the center patio. Moderate prices.

Bistro Francaise

Superb seafood is the hallmark of this café on Matamoros, and for good reason: Diane, the owner, hails from Montreal and is a former fish broker who inspects every fish and shrimp that comes into her restaurant. Breakfasts here are also tasty; try the excellent crepes or the French toast made with freshly baked bread. Among the dinner specialties are filet mignon and shrimp curry. Moderate prices.

Chez Magaly

Caribbean food with a European flavor is the specialty of Chez Magaly, on Av. Rueda Medina at Playa Norte's Nautibeach Condos, tel./fax 987/7-0436. Sit by the sea and enjoy tender steaks, superb shrimp and lobster, authentic Caesar salad, and outstanding service. Sipping a tequila sunrise while watching the sunset is the *only* way to end a tropical day—or to begin a romantic candlelight dinner. Closed Monday. Expensive.

Cazuela M&J

This little place serves a great breakfast omelette with just about anything you want. The *chaya* omelette with cheese is delicious. They also offer small casseroles, *cazuela,* with all kinds of goodies. Really friendly people gather at M&Js, including the owners. Open for breakfast and lunch, it's located on a little hill behind a church on the backside of the island with a great view of the sea.

Zacil Ha

The Zacil Ha, part of the Nabalam hotel, on Calle Zazil at Playa Norte, tel. 987/7-0279, email: nabalam@cancun.rce.com.mex, is another of the island's good, if expensive, restaurants. Check out the popular happy hour in the *palapa* bar.

Others

Restaurante El Sombrero de Gomar, on the corner of Hidalgo and Madero, tel. 987/7-0142, gives visitors an ice-cream parlor on the street floor and colorful Mexican-patio ambience on the second floor. The food is good, especially the barbecued meats and kabobs. Everyone, even the waiter, seems to be having a good time—it's a real Mexican party. It's a little pricey, but it's worth it. Open 7 A.M.–11 P.M.

On Playa Norte, try **Las Palapas Chimbo,** an open-air beach café serving simple but tasty fish dishes. As the evening goes on the music gets louder and can last through most of the night.

Café Mirtita, on Av. Rueda Medina near Morelos, serves great brewed coffee and good simple food. A small fan mounted at each table ensures your comfort. This old standby consistently puts out good hotcakes, egg dishes, sandwiches, and simple hamburgers with all the trimmings (US$4). It's very clean and reasonable, and features friendly, quick service.

Ciros, an old-time dining spot that at one time served the best food in town, was recently rejuvenated. Today, if anything, the food is even better than ever. Fish has always been a favorite here.

Anyone who likes crepes with mushrooms and hollandaise better check out **El Nopalito,** Av. Guerrero 70 (near Matamoros), tel. 987/7-0555, a small café attached to the folk-art shop, El Nopal. You'll find homemade bread, yogurt, muesli, and lots of good sandwiches. The moderately priced café is run by Anneliese Warren, who speaks English, German, and Spanish and loves to talk about her island. The café is open daily for breakfast and Monday–Friday for dinner.

Groceries

If you prefer to cook your own meals, you can buy groceries at several places in town. The **mercado municipal** opens every morning till around noon. It has a fair selection, considering that everything must come from the mainland. Well-stocked supermarkets with liquor and toiletries include: **Mirtita,** Av. Juárez 14, tel. 987/2-0127, open 6 A.M.–noon and 4–6 P.M.; and the larger **Super Betino,** Av. Morelos 5 (on the plaza), open 7 A.M.–9 P.M. **La Melosita,** Av. Hidalgo 17 (at Abasolo), is a mini-supermarket open 10 A.M.–midnight, with candies, piñatas, film, cigarettes, gifts, and snacks. **Panadería La Reina,** on Av. Madero, makes great *pan dulce.* It's open 6 A.M.–noon and 5–8 P.M. Fresh pastries appear on the shelves at 5 P.M.

ENTERTAINMENT AND SHOPPING

Nightlife

Little Isla Mujeres isn't the nightlife capital of Mexico. Those who need to be "entertained" will not find the numerous clubs, shows, fireworks, and other glitzy coddling that is everywhere in Cancún. In fact, the reason many folks come to Isla Mujeres is to avoid all that and to instead stroll around the plaza, watch the moon reflect off the water, buy hot *elote* (corn) and sweets from the vendors, and watch families at play, observing the respectful relationships between the very young and old. This is the real Mexico.

Evening activities here might include taking in a Spanish-language movie at the theater (on Morelos near the plaza) or dancing in the plaza during special fiestas. You might check out the **Casa de la Cultura** on Av. Guerrero, where classes are offered in a variety of subjects, including folk dancing, aerobics, and drawing. The Casa also has a library with a book exchange.

Those who want to party will find lively groups of people and often live music at **Las Palapas Chimbos.** Many of the little night spots often find a guitar in the audience and wind up with fun music into the wee hours.

A Great Event

The free, 12-day **Isla Mujeres International Music Festival** takes place on the plaza beginning the second weekend in October. The island rocks with bands and dancers from everywhere. Hotel reservations are suggested. The plaza comes alive with music, and housewives set up tables to sell all kinds of homemade goodies, from savory to sweets.

Shopping

You'll find several excellent folk-art shops on Isla Mujeres. **La Loma,** Av. Guerrero 6 (near La Perla del Caribe Hotel), sells carved wooden masks from Guerrero, wooden animals from Oaxaca, lacquered boxes and trays, textiles from Guatemala, and a huge display of hand-crafted jewelry. **El Nopal,** at the El Nopalito restaurant, has some beautiful embroidered dresses and shirts, as well as crafts from all over Mexico. T-shirts bearing the images of Maya gods are featured by the hundreds at **Casa del Arte México** on Av. Hidalgo; check out the fine limestone carvings as well. Gorgeous jewelry and precious gems are displayed at **Van Cleef and Arpels** and **Rachat and Rome,** both near the ferry pier.

SERVICES

Money

Banco Bital, on Rueda Medina between Madero and Morelos, will change money Monday–Friday after 10 A.M. The bank also has an ATM machine on site and another on Av. Hidalgo at Madero. Money is returned in pesos, up to an equivalent of around US$200. It's not unusual for the machines to run out of cash, so get money during banking hours. Though banks always give the best exchange rate, many *casas de cambio* are reasonable, perhaps charging an extra US$.60 per US$100 over the bank rate. You'll see *cambio* signs here and there; an easy one to find is across the street from Banco Bital near the ferry (frequently its rate is comparable to the bank's).

Many, but not all, stores, hotels, and restaurants in Isla accept credit cards.

Medical Services

For medical treatment, call Dr. Greta Shorey, tel. 987/7-0443, a Briton in charge of the island's Red Cross. We've never had occasion to use her but have heard great reviews from a couple of readers. Another local doctor, Dr. Salas, also has a good reputation.

You'll find well-stocked *farmacias* at Av. Juárez 2 and on Av. Francisco Madero at Hidalgo.

In the United States, for good guidance in choosing a hotel or purchasing airline tickets, and for local transportation information, call Isla Mujeres specialists at tel. 800/555-8842.

Isla Mujeres port

Other Services

A limited selection of **newspapers and magazines** can be found on the corner of Juárez and Bravo. The **post office** is at Av. Guerrero 13 and is open weekdays 9 A.M.–9 P.M.; Saturday, Sunday, and holidays 9 A.M.–noon. **Tim Pho** on Av. Juárez, does laundry by the kilo. Bring it in separated or all your white socks might come back pink.

GETTING THERE

Passengers-only Ferries

Two types of passenger boats travel from Puerto Juárez to Isla Mujeres. The modern, air-conditioned, enclosed ferries charge about US$3.50 one way and make the crossing in less than 30 minutes. The older open ferries charge about US$1.75 each way and make the trip in 45 minutes. Buy your ticket on board for either boat. At least one boat leaves every hour from Puerto Juárez to Isla Mujeres 6 A.M.–8 P.M. (there is one more that leaves at 11:30 P.M.; however, this is often filled with islanders and if the boat is overloaded, you could be left behind). Ferries leave from Isla Mujeres to Puerto Juárez 5 A.M.–6 P.M. At the foot of the dock in Puerto Juárez you'll find a tourist information center sponsored by the municipal government, with bilingual employees and a restroom (small fee). The office is open sporadically, and during the off season it's hard to find help.

From Playa Linda Pier in the Cancún hotel zone, a more comfortable boat, the **Shuttle Express,** tel. 988/3-3448, leaves four times a day for the island. The fare is about US$13 roundtrip. This may not be as costly as it sounds when you consider that taking a taxi from the hotel zone to Puerto Juárez can cost almost as much roundtrip as the shuttle. A bus to Puerto Juárez—Ruta 8 from Av. Tulum—is a lot less; however, allow extra time and travel light.

Note: Be aware of the time the last passenger boat leaves Isla Mujeres. If you haven't got a hotel reservation you might have to sleep on the beach, and it can rain any time of year.

Car-and-Passenger Ferries

A car ferry leaves Punta Sam (five kilometers north of Puerto Juárez) daily and carries passengers and cars to Isla Mujeres. You really need a good reason to bring a car; the island is short, with narrow, one-way streets. RVs can travel on the ferry, but there are very few places to park once you're there and there are no hookups.

The trip on the ferry from Punta Sam takes 45 minutes. Arrive at the ferry dock an hour before departure time to secure a place in line; tickets go on sale 30 minutes in advance. The ferry departs from Punta Sam six times daily 7 A.M.–8 P.M., and from Isla Mujeres six times daily 6 A.M.–7 P.M. Fare for an ordinary passenger car is about US$6 (more for RVs) and about US$2 for each passenger. Walk-on passengers are permitted. Please note, the bathroom situation is deplorable. The car-ferry schedule tends to run on time.

Those traveling the Peninsula by bus will find it easier to make ongoing connections in Puerto Juárez than in Punta Sam.

GETTING AROUND

Mujeres is a small and mostly flat island, and in town you can walk everywhere. The eight-kilometer (five-mile) distance from one end of the island to the other is a fairly easy trek for the practiced hiker, but in this heat, any others should choose another way to get around. Other options include taxis, bicycles, rental cars, golf carts, and motorcycles.

Cars, Carts, Mopeds, and Bicycles

If you want to see the outer limits of the island, the transport du jour is the golf cart, which travels at a top speed of about 15 kilometers per hour. The carts offer a little more protection than mopeds and provide shelter from the sun and rain. Rental cars are beginning to appear on the island as well. Most hotels can arrange rentals, or you can check with the shops scattered all over downtown. Rental carts cost about US$60 per (24-hour) day, US$50 per eight-hour day, or US$14 per hour—but negotiate! Mopeds are about US$35 for 24 hours, US$23 for eight hours, or US$8 per hour. Bikes go for about US$7–10 for eight hours. All of these prices are just guidelines—remember that old saying, "everyone has their price," and this might not be it. Again, negotiate.

By Taxi

Taxis are plentiful and easy to get; fares are posted at the taxi stand. The main taxi stand is on Av. Rueda Medina next to the ferry dock; service is available 24 hours (tel. 987/7-0066). Taxis deal strictly in pesos, and fares double after midnight. A two-hour tour around the island in a taxi—including stops to watch the lighthouse keeper making hammocks and to inspect the Maya temple on the south tip—costs around US$20 per trip for up to three passengers.

KATHY ESCOVEDO SANDERS

RIVIERA MAYA
AND ISLA COZUMEL
RIVIERA MAYA

SOUTH FROM CANCÚN

For decades after the Spaniards came, the ancient Maya structures at Tulum, Cobá, Akumal, and Xcaret remained deserted, serving as jungle gyms for the thorny iguana in the middle of the bush. Through centuries of neglect and tropical weather, the ruins grew moss, clutching vines, lacy ferns, and tall trees from cracks and crevices in the stone. It wasn't until the 1970s that change came when a trickle of tourists were lured by a few hotels perched on white sand and the remarkable aqua sea. Located on the Caribbean, Tulum, Xcaret, and Xelha have been popular diversions ever since. Historians and archaeologists believe that in pre-Cortesian times, these ports were used as nautical lookouts along the Riviera coast. Today the structures and surrounding land are clear and the same locations welcome daily busloads of curious tourists.

Now called the Riviera Maya, the stretch of coast between Cancún (officially between Playa Secreto) and Tulum is reached via paved Highway 307. The road parallels the sea (the two new lanes are still only partially completed) and each month a new attraction opens along the way. In addition to the ancient structures travelers find myriad resorts on beautiful beaches, nature reserves, and growing villages—not to mention the sea that defines this flamboyant part of the world. The Riviera Maya has come to life. Rival hotels as grand as anything in Cancún are still hidden from the public on isolated beaches.

RIVIERA MAYA

Cancún
180

307

CROCOCUN CROCODILE FARM ■

Puerto Morelos
JARDÍN BOTÁNICO ■ **FERRY DOCK**
Punta Brava

Caribbean
TRES RÍOS ★

Sea
CABAÑAS CAPITÁN LAFITTE ●

0   5 mi
307
0   5 km   Punta Bete

SHANGRI-LA CARIBE RESORT ■ ■ **COCO BEACH CLUB**

LAS PALAPAS CABAÑAS RESORT ●

San Miguel
○ Playa del   de Cozumel
Carmen
○ Xcaret   *Isla*
Cozumel
**TURTLE NESTING
GROUNDS**
Paamul ● **CAMPING**

Puerto Aventuras   **OMNI PUERTO AVENTURAS HOTEL**
MARINA ⌐ **CEDAM MUSEUM**
⌐ **CLUB OASIS**

● **EL DORADO RESORT AND SPA**

Actun
Chen   **CENOTE**
Caves   **(DIVING)**
★ ○ Akumal
AVENTURAS   *Bahía Akumal*
AKUMAL   Playa Chemuyil
307 ○ Playa Xcacel

*Parque
Nacional
Xelha*
Caribbean
**XELHA
RUINS**   *Sea*
○ Playa Tankah
▼ **CASA CENOTE RESTAURANT/HOTEL**
▲▲ **TULUM RUINS**

Tulum ○

Top Cobá (Archaeological Site and Hotel)

Nature reserves and activity centers such as Tres Ríos and Actun Chen have, of course, been here for eons. But until tourist interest accelerated on the Riviera they remained hidden and in their natural state with nary a road to get there. There are scores of caves and cenotes in Quintana Roo, and only today, with the new one-lane tracks, are visitors discovering them. They are becoming maybe *too* well known. Hordes of people arrive in crowded vans or convoys of jeeps and make visits to hidden rivers, pristine beaches, towering tropical trees, and the jungle animals that live among them. Others prefer to trek past sparkling stalactites or dive in cenotes where before only the blind fish lived.

CrocoCun

As the road approaches Puerto Morelos, look along the seaward side of the highway (about 1.6 kilometers north of Morelos) for the turnoff to this fascinating little crocodile farm —really a tropical mini-zoo. Here you'll observe crocodiles—from babies to full-grown adults—and learn how they breed and hatch. Hang onto the kids! Actually, the kids can handle the babies at certain times of the year and feed them. It's a fun place for youngsters and the young at heart and anyone who loves exotic nature—boas, colorful parrots, deer, and more. Come feed the animals. Admission: US$10 adult, US$6 children 8–12. Snacks available.

Maroma Resort, tel. 987/4-4730, is 20 miles south of Cancún International Airport. The entrance, from the Highway 307, is almost impossible to find. But that's just the way they like it. This exclusive Moorish-style resort is intimate (36 rooms), beautifully appointed, and tranquil—at least for now (new hotels are springing up nearby). This is a great place relax while surrounded by nature's excellence: soft sand, the silky sea, and the powder-blue sky. Rates range from US$306–720.

PUERTO MORELOS

The entry road to Puerto Morelos is about a 17-kilometer drive south of Cancún. Turn left when you see the large gas station/rest-stop complex. From the highway it's a couple of kilometers further. This is a small village on the north end of Highway 307. For decades the town had limited accommodations, few places to eat, friendly people, a beautiful beach, and easy access to the rich reef. It really was a hidden wonder known only by divers. We used to call it the beach town with the leaning tower (actually an old light house). Today it still leans but it's no longer in use. The town has a certain tranquil air about it—perhaps that's why it's fast becoming the meditation center of the coast. Anyone looking for yoga, channeling, spas, rebirthing, or a chance to rest the spirit while enjoying nature, will find everything they need at Puerto Morelos. Many expats have found this tranquility desirable and have built lovely homes on the edge of the village.

After a lot of hard work, mostly by the locals, the small town and offshore area has been designated a **National Reef Park.** Accommodations have grown and Puerto Morelos has been "discovered," and along with it's peaceful mood, lack of tourists, and easy access to the sea. At one time its only claim to fame was the vehicle ferry to Cozumel, but divers brought low-key attention using the town as a base for exploring the rich coastline and reef. Will it change now that a couple of large hotels are moving in? The town is working hard to keep out the largest, a 3,000 room hotel. There goes the neighborhood. Who would even want to stay in a 3,000-room hotel? Another new hotel, **Ceiba Del Mar Hotel and Spa,** tel. 800/552-4550, has 140 rooms, a size the town can handle gracefully. Check it out—it is lovely.

The Plaza

A short walk through town reveals a central plaza, shops, a cantina, and several fine restaurants. The little plaza is a gathering place for locals and offers two (ecological) dry-compost public restrooms. In the winter the town holds a Sunday *tianguis* (flea market) on the plaza—always fun to browse through someone else's old "treasures."

Food

Circling the main plaza, several good cafés serve excellent seafood and typical Mexican dishes. On the oceanfront just south of the plaza, **Los Pelicanos** serves good hamburgers and great shrimp cocktails at the beach *palapa.* Another waterfront favorite, **Restaurant Las Palmeras,** serves excellent fresh seafood in a pleasant atmosphere; their *pulpo Mexicano* (octopus) is delicious, as is the conch in garlic sauce. **Palapa Pizza** is a popular hangout by the plaza, next door to the Alma Libre Libros. Nearby **Deli and Café de la Plaza,** tel. 987/1-0513, is a tiny (three tables) natural foods store offering special fruit juice and sandwiches made on special breads.

Speguetonni, Av. Javier Rojo Gomez, serves good Italian food, is clean, and has good service. It's just two blocks from the plaza. Try **Che Carlitos** at Casita del Mar Hotel, tel. 987/1-0522,

This tranquil dock offers great fishing.

OZ MALLAN

QUEEN CONCH

A popular, easy-to-catch food beautifully packaged—that's the problem with the queen conch (pronounced "conk"). For generations inhabitants of the Caribbean nations have been capturing the conch for their sustenance. The land available for farming on some islands is scant, and the people (who are poor) have depended on the sea—especially the conch—to feed their families. Even Columbus was impressed with the beauty of the peach-colored shell, taking one back to Europe with him on his return voyage.

The locals discovered a new means of making cash in the 1970s—exporting conch meat to the United States. The shell is also a cash byproduct sold to throngs of tourists looking for local souvenirs. An easy way to make money, except for one thing: soon there will be no more conch! In recent years the first signs of overfishing have become evident; smaller-sized conch are being taken, and fishermen are finding it necessary to go farther afield to get a profitable catch.

It takes three to five years for this sea snail to grow from larva stage to market size. It also takes about that long for planktonic conch larvae carried into fished-out areas by the currents to replenish themselves. What's worse, the conch is easy to catch; large (shell lengths get up to 390 cm) and heavy (about three kilograms), the mollusk moves slowly and lives in shallow, crystalline water where it's easy to spot. All of these attributes are contributing to its demise.

Biologists working with various governments are trying to impose new restrictions that include closed seasons, minimum size of capture, a limit on total numbers taken by the entire fishing industry each year, limited numbers per fisherman, restrictions on the types of gear that can be used, and, most important—the cessation of exportation. Along with these legal limitations, technology is lending a hand. Research has begun, and several mariculture centers are now experimenting with the queen conch, raising animals in a protected environment until they're large enough for market or grown to juvenile size to be released into the wild.

A new research center at Puerto Morelos is in operation and recently released its first group of juvenile conchs to supplement wild stock. This is not always successful. Sometimes one group of larvae will survive and the next 10 will not—for no clear-cut reason. In the wild, not only does the conch have humans to contend with, it also has underwater predators: lobsters, crabs, sharks, turtles, and rays.

The conch is not an endangered species yet, but it must be protected for the people who depend on it for life.

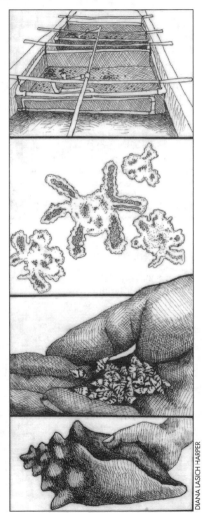

DIANA LASICH HARPER

for an Argentinean flavor and their special *churrasco* and pasta.

Johnny Cairo Restaurant, on the beach south of the plaza at the Hacienda Morelos hotel, is the fanciest in town restaurant. You never know what exciting things are being prepared, or if there might be a special party on the beach to watch a meteor shower or who knows what? This is a don't-miss restaurant. The owner is a former Ritz Carlton chef, and it shows!

Around the corner from the plaza the **Posada Amor Restaurant** serves authentic *mole poblano* and other regional dishes at moderate prices.

There's a supermarket near the plaza for groceries. On Wednesdays you can buy fresh vegetables from vendors near the Catholic church.

Shopping

Stop at **Arte Maya** to see unique artwork being created. The finished product consists of brightly painted metal cut-outs in a variety of sizes and designs—bracelets, wall hangings, etc. Started some 17 years ago by the late Armando Fernández in his home, the shop now has a staff of craftspeople. You'll see Fernández's work in upscale shopping centers in Cancún. The prices are better here!

Another gift shop that displays the arts and crafts of locals is **Artisolo** on Av. Rojo Gomez. You'll find ceramics, silver and gold jewelry, and other art pieces.

Anyone who has traveled the peninsula knows that good bookstores with many English language books are scarce. With a 20,000-title inventory, **Alma Libre Libros,** Av. Tulum #3, tel. 987/1-0264, is the exception. Expat owner Jeanine Kitchel returns to the States each year to shop for used books, then brings them back to stock her shelves. FYI, she has gathered a small collection of medical books (for lending—not for sale). You never know when you will have a medical emergency. Those living in Puerto Morelos especially, appreciate this service. The book store also carries some new books and a few children's books. Open 10 A.M.–1 P.M. and 6 P.M.–9 P.M.

Services

No bank here, but you will find an ATM machine (at the gas station on the highway near the entrance road). **Marand Travel** (opposite Posada

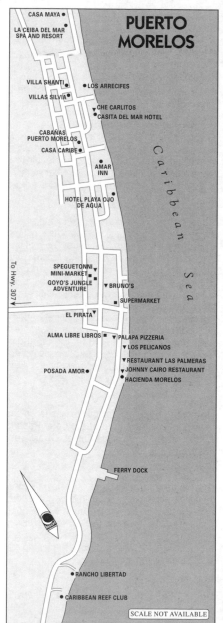

PUERTO MORELOS

CASA MAYA
LA CEIBA DEL MAR SPA AND RESORT
VILLA SHANTI ● ● LOS ARRECIFES
VILLAS SILVIA ▼ CHE CARLITOS
● CASITA DEL MAR HOTEL
CABAÑAS PUERTO MORELOS
CASA CARIBE ●
AMAR INN
HOTEL PLAYA OJO DE AGUA
Caribbean Sea
To Hwy. 307
SPEGUETONNI MINI-MARKET
GOYO'S JUNGLE ADVENTURE ▼ BRUNO'S
■ SUPERMARKET
EL PIRATA ▼
ALMA LIBRE LIBROS ■ ▼ PALAPA PIZZERIA
▼ LOS PELICANOS
▼ RESTAURANT LAS PALMERAS
POSADA AMOR ● ▼ JOHNNY CAIRO RESTAURANT
● HACIENDA MORELOS
FERRY DOCK
● RANCHO LIBERTAD
● CARIBBEAN REEF CLUB
SCALE NOT AVAILABLE

Amor) cashes traveler's checks and can answer questions.

A liquor store, pharmacy, and car repair shop are within walking distance of downtown. The Laundromat is about two blocks from the police station on Av. Ninoes Heroes. A Catholic church and an Adventist church offer services in the village.

Snorkeling and Scuba Diving

Puerto Morelos's most spectacular attraction is its reef, which begins 20 km north of town. Directly in front of the village, 550 meters offshore, the reef takes on gargantuan dimensions—between 20 and 30 meters wide. For the scuba diver and snorkeler this reef is a dream come true, with dozens of caverns alive with coral and fish.

Snorkeling is best done on the inland side of the reef, where the depth is about three meters. Expect visibility of up to 25 meters. The reef has long been a menace to ships; early records date losses from the 16th century. One wrecked Spanish galleon here is a boon for divers; its coral-crusted cannons are clearly visible from the surface five meters above.

Scuba divers find good service at the PADI-affiliated **Wet Set** dive shop at the Caribbean Reef Club Hotel, tel. 987/1-0198 (at the far end of town past the ferry dock). The shop also offers snorkeling, fishing, and other water sports. Several hotels offer good dive shops as well.

Fishing

Onshore fishing is only fair off the pier. Deep-sea fishing can be arranged at the hotel Posada Amor or through Maranda Travel. Or ask your hotelier.

Jungle Tours

Goyo's Jungle Adventure, Av. Rojo Gomez, tel. 987/1-0463, email: goyo@goyosjungle.com, offers a chance to see the bush with a good guide who loves the area. He'll tell you the history of this jungle and let you know which herbs and roots do what for the body. For a longer trip ask about their "Deep Jungle Tour."

Accommodations

Under US$50: Hotel Ojo de Agua, tel. 987/1-0027, Av. Javier Gomez, email: info@ojo-de-agua.com, offers 36 modern rooms overlooking

a beautiful beach just north of town. It's just a short walk to from restaurants and the plaza area. The rooms have comfortable beds, kitchens, ceiling fans, and air-conditioning, and range from US$30–45 depending on the season. Other amenities include a restaurant, solarium, a dive shop and pool, and free use of their kayak. There's also a great view. Stop at the restaurant for dinner and try the tasty paella.

Simple **Posada Amor,** tel. 987/1-0033, fax 987/1-0178, is a friendly, family-run, 20-room hotel. Rooms (US$25–40) have ceiling fans and shared baths (some private baths) with hot water. There's a communal patio good for meeting other independent travelers. The lighthearted decor is mosquito-netting tropical. Nonguests can take a hot shower for US$3. Try the all-day Sunday buffet in the family-run restaurant in front.

Amar Inn, 987/1-0026, had at one time been a lovely colonial-style house on the beach. It was destroyed during Hurricane Gilbert, but feisty Ana Maria Almada rebuilt it and it has again been around for a long time. Originally run by Ana Maria, a fine lady who made staying at the simple inn fun, it is now run by her daughter, Ana Luisa Aguillar, who is following in her mother's footsteps. The main house has four rooms (US$50 with breakfast) with fans and refrigerators and views of the sea. There are also three very simple *palapa* bungalows right on the sand (US$25 for the two smaller ones, US$35 for the larger).

US$50–100: Hacienda Morelos, one block south of the plaza, tel. 987/1-0015, overlooks the beach. The upstairs rooms are especially nice, offering a great view of the sea. All rooms (US$75) have cooling ocean breezes, mini-refrigerators, immaculate white decor, and bathtubs with showers—a rarity in these parts. A small pool and sunbathing area sit right above the beach and an enclosed parking lot is out front. The main entrance to the hotel is also at the highly rated **Johnny Cairo** restaurant, one of the best in town.

The **Casa Caribe,** U.S. tel. 763/441-7630, Mexico tel. 987/1-0459 email: casacaribe@puertomorelos.com.mx, is a small hotel (six rooms with private bathrooms) a few steps from the beach. It's run by American expats. Each room is distinct with its own decor and stylish *talavera* tile. One bathroom is a spunky red. Tile floors, fans, refrigerators, coffeemakers, and private outdoor areas make this a charming spot. Choose from two rates: US$70 per day or US$400 per week (a bargain).

South of the ferry dock, **Rancho Libertad** tel. 987/1-0181, email: rancholibertad@puerto morelos.com.mx, is a *palapa* hideaway on the beach next to Caribbean Reef Club. Twelve two-story cabañas (US$65–75, including a nice buffet breakfast) have hanging beds and offer private baths, hot water, ceiling fans, air-conditioning (in some), mini-refrigerators, and coffeemakers. Queen-sized beds are upstairs; double beds are downstairs. There is also a full range of spa services, including massage, and a room for retreats and workshops. Adults only, except in June, which is family month. Finally, you'll find great African-style *djembe* and conga drums for sale here. They're built on site, and sell for US$150–$600.

US$150–200: Casa Maya, U.S. tel. 415/882-1155, Mexico tel. 987/1-0264, email: casamaya @yahoo.com, is a lovely house on the beach meant for romance or relaxation. Just steps from the beach and a five-minute walk from downtown, this two-bedroom, two-bath beach house sleeps six (US$155 per night for four, US$15 per additional person, ask about their weekly rate). This is one of the better bargains in this area. The rooms are airy and have tile floors. There's also a fully stocked kitchen, daily maid service, lots of terrace space, and garden areas. If you really want to relax, spend an hour watching the koi fish in their pond. The American owners are very involved with the town and own the **Alma Libre Libros** bookstore. Not surprisingly, the library in their house is well stocked.

All-inclusive Resorts: South of the ferry dock on an isolated stretch of white-sand beach, nude sunbathers might enjoy the **Caribbean Reef Club,** tel. 987/1-0191, U.S. tel. 800/3-CANCUN, fax 987/1-0190, email: info @caribbeanreefclub.com. (If you live anywhere except the U.S and Canada, call 714/964-8453.) This all-inclusive, couples-only, clothing-optional resort has hotel rooms, studios (with kitchens), and fourth-floor penthouses facing the sea. Rooms include cool tile floors, terraces, fans, air-conditioning, and satellite TV. There's a private pool, plus the largest hot tub on the Peninsula that accommodates 30 adults. There's also a 3,000 square-foot *palapa* ideal for parties, a friendly bar, and a beachfront restaurant with great seafood and an excellent selection. Rates start at US$290 per couple per night for a hotel room in the high season; studios for two are US$325. A one-bedroom penthouse is US$400, US$90 per extra person. The à la carte menu, drinks, all nonmotorized water sports, taxes, and tips are included in the price. Diving equipment is available next door at the **Wet Set** dive shop, and guests receive free use of Windsurfers, sailboats, and more.

If you're passing through town and just want to spend the day at the Caribbean Reef Club, it will cost you US$150 (10 A.M.–10 P.M.); food, drinks, and all activities are included.

Other Rental Properties

At **Villa Shanti,** owners Jack and Jean Loew have created a secluded, comfortable yoga retreat in their eight-apartment villa just a block from the beach. Jean Loew offers yoga classes twice a week and week-long yoga retreats in the high season. Guests are treated to the classes as well as to shiatsu therapy. Each apartment has a bedroom, modern bathroom, kitchen, air-conditioning, and fan; outside there's a barbecue area, swimming pool, and large *palapa* strung with hammocks. The Villa is also used by groups for yoga, rebirthing, channeling, and healing retreats. For information on reservations and upcoming retreats, contact the Loews at P.O. Box 464, Glen, New Hampshire 03838-0464 (May 1–November 30); or, between December 1 and April 30, in Mexico at tel. 987/1-0040, fax 987/1-0041.

Bill and Connie Bucher have two properties for rent: **Cabañas Puerto Morelos,** which consists of three one-bedroom units with sitting areas and kitchens; and **Villa Amigos,** a two-bedroom, two-bath house (the master bathroom has a bathtub—rare in these parts) with a full kitchen and outside patio. For rates and information tel./fax 763/441-7630 in the United States, or 987/1-0004 in Puerto Morelos.

Vicki Sharp also offers two rentals: **Los Arrecifes,** consisting of eight nicely furnished apartments, each with separate bedroom and full kitchen on a great windswept beach north of town; and **Casa Miguel,** a beautiful guesthouse closer to town. For rates and information call 987/1-0112, fax 988/3-2244. If you decide not to go with her, she can tell you about other rental properties in the area.

Villas Clarita is a two-story, Spanish-style building five blocks from town offering four one-bedroom apartments—each with a kitchen and either a balcony or patio. There are also separate one- and two-bedroom cabañas set around a swimming pool. For rates and information call 987/1-0042 in Puerto Morelos.

Villa Latinas, tel. 987/1-0075, has seven furnished apartments for rent by the week or month.

Camping

No one minds if campers spread their sleeping bags north and south of the lighthouse away from town, houses, and hotels. The beach is free and this is a relatively safe, peaceful place. Choose a high spot so you'll stay dry. It can get gritty if the wind picks up and buggy (mosquitoes) if it's very still.

Puerto Morelos has one of the best gas station/rest areas on Highway 307 (just across from the entrance into town). Though gas availability has become more reliable and stations are placed reasonably close to each other (others are at Tulum, Playa del Carmen, and Felipe Carrillo Puerto), top off your tank whenever you can. The Puerto Morelos station also has two markets, a public Ladatel phone, an ATM machine, restrooms, and a restaurant.

Getting There

Buses from north and south stop at Puerto Morelos frequently. From Cancún it's about a 40-minute drive, from Chetumal about five hours. Hitching is reasonably easy from the larger towns (Chetumal, Cancún, Felipe Carrillo Puerto, Playa del Carmen); try Highway 307 where the service roads enter the towns.

Ferry to Cozumel

The vehicle ferry to Isla Cozumel departs Puerto Morelos daily beginning at 6 A.M. Check the schedule the night before. Be at the dock two or three hours early to get in the passenger-car line. It also expedites things to have correct change and your car's license number in hand when you approach the ticket window. The tick-

et office is open 5 A.M.–6 P.M. The trip takes two hours and can be a rough crossing, so take your Dramamine if you tend to get seasick, I don't recommend this ferry for passenger-only travel, as it doesn't have that "cruise-ship" ambience.

Note: In Puerto Morelos on Christmas Eve, the ferry boat company throws a *tipico* Christmas party with a big buffet dinner, drinks, and piñatas for the kids. It goes on until the last dog leaves. And, of course, it's all free.

Jardín Botánico

On the way to Punta Bete, just a couple of kilometers south of Puerto Morelos, you'll find a lovely botanical garden, study center, and tree nursery spread over 60 hectares (150 acres). Three kilometers of trails wind through a wild natural atmosphere under a canopy of trees, past specimens (labeled in English, Spanish, and Latin) of the Peninsula's plants and flowers. Habitats range from semi-evergreen tropical forest to mangrove swamp. Look for the epiphyte area, with a variety of orchids, tillandsias, and bromeliads. As you wander around you'll also find a re-creation of a Maya *chiclero* camp (showing how chicle was harvested to be used in chewing gum), some small ruins from the postclassic period, and a contemporary Maya hut illustrating day-to-day life—from cooking facilities to hammocks. Be prepared: Wear good walking shoes, cover up your arms and legs, and use bug repellent. The jungle is full of biting critters at certain times of year, especially after a good rain.

The garden is open daily 9 A.M.–5 P.M. Admission is US$3 and includes a map of the area. You can hire a guide for an additional US$5.

PUNTA BETE

Tres Ríos

A few miles north of the Capitan Lafitte turnoff, look for the sign to Tres Ríos, another park where an effort has been made to preserve the natural rivers, flora growth, and wildlife, while bringing in tourists to experience it all. Enjoy a canoe or kayak paddle—the park's waterways are lovely with leafy limbs draping the sun-dappled river. Where Río de la Selva meets the sea, a small palapa play area has been installed on the sand and a *palapa* restaurant sits on stilts next to a gift shop, dive shop, and parking area. The park's volleyball court was busy the whole day we were there. Everything except snorkeling gear, lockers, and reef trips is included in the entrance fee of US$16 for adults, US$8 for children.

Continuing south on the highway you'll soon arrive at Punta Bete, a four-kilometer stretch of beach and a complete tropical fantasy. Swaying palms hover over the pure white sand and gentle blue waves run across the shore. Getting in and out of the water here can be hazardous to your feet, due to rocks and coral scattered on the sea floor and in the sand. Shoes, sandals, or diving booties help. The rocky bottom makes a perfect snorkeling area 10–20 meters offshore.

As recently as 1965, no tourists visited this part of the coast. At that time Quintana Roo was only a federal territory and there wasn't even a road to this white-sand beach. Family groups, mostly descendants of the Chan Santa Cruz Indians, tended their small, self-sufficient *cocales* (miniature coconut plantations). In recent years, yellowing disease destroyed most of the tall coconut palms. A short, new species of palm, resistant to the devastating disease that began in Florida, has now been planted. Today most of the old *cocales* are small tourist centers.

Cabañas Capitán Lafitte

This all-inclusive beach resort, tel. 800/538-6802 or 303/674-9615, fax 303/674-8735, draws a large repeat clientele with fine service, good food, and a wonderful location. The stucco oceanfront cabañas have double- and king-size beds, hot water, ceiling fans, and private baths. Other amenities include a swimming pool, game room, and coffee delivered to your room each morning. Every afternoon between 5 and 6 P.M., look for a flock of small, colorful parrots that flies over the pool. A nice outdoor bar near the pool is a great place to talk over the day's activities with fellow travelers.

A full dive shop on the premises has a good selection of rental equipment, including sailboards. The management provides transportation by skiff to nearby Lafitte Reef, an exciting snorkeling destination.

Successful anglers can have their catch prepared by the restaurant chef. Hands off the large, handsome turtles you may see, and don't expect to find turtle soup or conch ceviche on the menu; the management makes it clear that they support the preservation of these endangered species.

Rates—US $200 double occupancy, children 4–10 US$40 per night, children three and under free—include a full breakfast and dinner. Room rates go up on holidays. During high season it's best to make reservations. No credit cards or personal checks are accepted; cash and traveler's checks only. Car rentals are available.

Kailuum II

The pioneer of high-style safarilike tent-living on

Tres Ríos, where the river meets the sea

OZ MALLAN

Playacar Xaman Ha
Condominiums

the beach describes the original Kailuum from the 1970s. After a siege of hurricanes did them in, **Kailuum II,** tel. 800/538-6802, email: info @turqreef.com, has emerged better than ever in a slightly different location on the beautiful Caribbean. All the nice little attributes of the old *tentalapa* resort are still intact, including the honor bar (**you** mix them the way **you** want them, and **you** keep track of how many you drink). Enjoy near-gourmet cuisine with a Yucatecan flavor in a romantic candlelit sand-floor dining room with a soaring *palapa* roof. The entire resort is lit with candles, gas lanterns, and flaming torches. Roomy tents (US$120) include comfortable beds, pillows and linens (no camping cots here), daily maid service, two tile bathhouses with hot water, individual shower stalls, and private toilet stalls. Everything is spotless. Each tent has a shady *palapa* roof and a porch with hammocks facing the sea—perfect for lazy afternoons with a cold drink and a good book. Rates include breakfast, dinner, tips, and tax, and are less during the summer months. No credit cards are accepted (remember, no electricity). Ask about the roundtrip transfer from Cancún International Airport for US$80 per couple. Kailuum is closed September and October. Adults only (over 16 is fine).

Getting There

When driving south from Cancún on Highway 307, the Capitan Lafitte turnoff is 30 miles south of Cancún International Airport. You can't miss the large sign. Turn left onto the narrow dirt road. About two kilometers down the road there's a guard post; go under the arch. If you turn right the road brings you to **Kailuum II.;** if you continue straight toward the sea you'll come to the heart of **Capitan Lafitte.**

Back on Highway 307, it's approximately eight kilometers from the La Fitte sign farther south to **Shangri-La;** shortly beyond that is **Las Palapas.** A taxi from Cancún costs US$55–65 for up to four passengers. From Playa del Carmen (six miles south), taxi fare is less. Heading south from Puerto Morelos, a couple of good minibuses run from Cancún to all the resort towns along the Riviera Maya. They leave from the ADO bus station. Ask for directions when making reservations. And remember, hotels offer a roundtrip transfer for US$80 per couple.

Xcalacoco

Some budget travelers prefer to skip the all-inclusive, marble palaces along this beautiful beach and head to **Paradise Point Resort,** fax 651/762-8284, email: paradisepoint1@juno.com. To find it, follow Highway 307 south to the Punta Bete exit at Kilometer 296, then turn east on a white singletrack road leading 2.2 kilometers to the sea. Look for the Paradise sign and you'll find nine cabañas located on the beach close to the sea. There's also a camping area (about US$5, bring bug repellent and mosquito netting). These were formerly Novelo's cabañas. The new owners have refurbished the cement structures (US$45), and though they are still simple, they are very comfy with either king beds or two doubles, tile floors, private bathrooms, hot water, solar lighting, and front-porch hammocks. There's no restaurant on the premises, but there are three close by.

Coco Beach Club is just a short distance north of Shangri La Caribe. It has good food, beach umbrellas, and sun beds, and offers snorkeling, changing room, showers, and restrooms. Stop for a drink or Argentinean-style lunch for a change of pace. No animals please.

Shangri-La Caribe Resort

On its own entry road 62 kilometers south of Cancún, Shangri-La Caribe, U.S. tel. 800/538-6802 or 303/674-9615, email: info@turqreef.com, is an almost-luxurious resort and a perfect place to kick back. Stucco-and-*palapa* bungalows, each with private bath, hold comfortable beds, fans, tile floors, hot water, and balconies or patios with hammocks. The beachfront bungalows are just steps from the sea. Here every room has an ocean view. Rates, including breakfast, dinner, taxes, and tips: US$180–240 (depending on room style and proximity to the beach), children 4–10 US$40, children three and under free. No credit cards. Other amenities include two swimming pools, a poolside bar and grill, a dive shop, gift shop, and car-rental desk. A large, circular *palapa* serves as a gathering place during the cocktail hour and is a great place to meet fellow travelers, have a drink, or shoot a game of pool after dinner. Breakfast and candlelit dinner are served in a lovely open-air dining room; the food is great and you can usually expect a Mexican fiesta once a week with music and Mexican food. The grounds are well kept and the staff are friendly.

The **Cyan Ha** dive shop is open seven days a week, offers rentals and lessons, and has a PADI-certified divemaster. Beginners should ask about trips to the shallow reefs of Chenzubul—a perfect place to enjoy a secure but exciting introduction to the Caribbean underwater world and its exotic inhabitants. All swimmers will enjoy exploring nearby Cenote Jabali. Car rentals are available here.

Las Palapas Cabañas

Just south of Shangri-La Caribe, Las Palapas Cabañas Resort, Calle 34 N., U.S. tel. 800/467-5292, Mexico tel. 987/3-0582, fax 987/3-0458, email: palapas@playadelcarmen.com, is on the beach. The location is idyllic. Its 50 units (in two-story *palapa*-roofed buildings) are comfortable, clean, and upscale. Rates (US$175–207) include breakfast, dinner, tax, and tip, prices vary depending on the time of year and room location. No credit cards—cash or traveler's checks only. Hammocks hang on the front porches and small desks face windows looking out to landscaped walkways or the beach. The large pool is great for swimming laps, while the white-sand beach seems to go on forever—you can easily walk the shore to Playa del Carmen (watch out for sharp shells). Two restaurants serve Mexican, seafood, and Continental meals and often feature German dishes for the German tour groups that frequently stay here. The management and staff go out of their way to make your stay comfortable. Many guests spend a week or more.

PLAYA DEL CARMEN

Not too many years ago, your stroll through Playa del Carmen would have been escorted by smiling children, chattering dogs, little black pigs, and incredibly ugly turkeys; you might even have seen the milkman delivering milk from large cans strapped to his donkey's back. No more. The small town that we writers used to describe as a "sleepy fishing village" has today exploded into a large Caribbean resort. At the time of our first trip there were maybe a thousand people; today there are 60,000 and maybe since I typed this sentence it has added another 100.

With its population increasing nearly 20 percent annually, Playa del Carmen is the fastest-growing area in Quintana Roo. Tourists crowd the streets, and the milkman has been replaced by mini- and super-markets with modern refrigeration and hi-tech freezers. Ferries from Cozumel come and go all day, and luxury cruise ships anchor close by in the bay.

Though high-rises are still absent, the town is sprawling farther north as more and more visitors return for a permanent stay. And classy hotels and condos are spreading along the beach south of the dock; in fact, there you'll find a whole new community called **Playacar,** which holds an 18-

hole golf course, **Aviary Xaman Ha,** Maya ruins, a few restaurants, several new hotels, and even a small private school.

Nature endowed Playa del Carmen with a broad, beautiful beach—one of the Peninsula's finest. The beaches are usually crowded near the ferry dock and play host to a conglomeration of independent travelers: archaeology buffs, students of Maya culture, backpackers, adventure seekers, and sun lovers. The cooler early hours are best for walking along the beach. Warm afternoons are perfect for swimming and snorkeling, snoozing in a shady hammock, or watching the magnificent frigate bird make silent circles above you, hoping to rob another bird of its catch.

Despite the growth, Playa still has the feeling of a Mexican town. Unlike Cancún or Puerto Aventuras, which were invented by hotel people, this is just a tiny village that grew. The growth may have been too fast to suit some, and without a whole lot of planning, but at least the streets are paved and the sand and sea are still lovely!

The waterfront's brick-lined pedestrians-only *malecón* and Avenida 5 are always bustling with people, noisy with laughter, a variety of music, and storekeepers inviting passersby in to inspect their wares. The *malecón* has a low wall that makes a perfect perch for people-watching or stargazing. Avenida 5, one block west of the *malecón,* has lots of cafés, hotels, money changers, and shops. Avenida 5 continues to grow and that's a good thing; it improves as it spreads north. Check out the trendy shops and fine cafés offering top-quality food and products. Not quite as honky tonk as the southern end of the avenida. Investigate it all and the little side streets offer even more businesses to look into. Though not as inexpensive as it once was, much of the town is still a bargain compared to Cancún; however, if you're looking, you'll find many upscale hotels and restaurants just north and south of town that almost match the prices of Cancún.

Note: The persistent old rumor that there will be an international airport in Playa has been heating up lately. Who knows, it may come to pass. But for now a single air strip satisfies the needs of the commuter who hops in and out of Playa del Carmen, to and from Cozumel and other sites of interest to people exploring the Yucatan peninsula and its Maya Sites. There are at least two small commuter planes with of-fices at the airport or next door: **AeroSaab,** tel. 987/3-0804, email: info@aerosaab.com; and **AeroFerinco,** 20th Av. south next to the airport, tel. 987/3-1919, email: yourwings@aeroferin co.com. Both airlines offer charter tours, including trips to Maya sites in the Yucatán, and many other options, even if it's just a chance to look at the coast of Quintana Roo from above. Aero-Ferinco charges US$15 for the one-way flight to Cozumel. AeroSaab makes trips to Isla Holbox.

ACCOMMODATIONS

Under US$50
For Playa del Carmen's **CREA youth hostel,** follow the signs off the main street about one kilometer (about a 15-minute walk from the bus station). Bunks in fairly new, clean, single-sex dorms cost US$8 per person, and simple cabañas (most sleeping up to four) rent for US$17 per night. Amenities include a dining room with reasonably priced food, a basketball court, and an auditorium. Too bad it's not closer to the beach.

Mom's Hotel, Av. 30 at Calle 4, email: tel. 987/3-0315, combines a bed-and-breakfast with rooms and apartments. It offers simple, pleasant accommodations (about US$30), air-conditioning, fans, private bathrooms, secure parking, a pool, restaurant, bar, lots of books, Internet access, and really nice staff.

Tree Tops Hotel, Calle 8, tel. 987/3-0351, email: info@treetopshotel.com, has a jungle patio with birdsong, and a relaxing atmosphere.

REEFS OF THE SOUTH COAST OF QUINTANA ROO

La Moncha	Moe Che
La Moncha Chica	Chenzubul
Puenta Maroam	El Esfuerzo
Cerebros	Sabalos
Los Arcos N & S	Barracuda
El Cofre	Wrecki
Xcalacoco N & S	Mama Viva

PLAYA DEL CARMEN

↑ To Airport and Cancún

307

AV. CONSTITUTIONES
AV. CONSTITUTIONES

CALLE 16

EL TUCAN CONDOTEL

CHICHAN BAAL KAH HOTEL

SAN FRANCISCO
DE ASSIS

CALLE 14

CALLE 14

MOSQUITO BLUE HOTEL/
RED EYE

BED AND BREAKFAST BAAL
NA KAH/CAFÉ POKARA

CALLE 12

CALLE 12

MAYAN PARADISE HOTEL

BEER
BUCKET

HOTEL/CAFE DA GABI

CALLE 10

YOUTH
HOSTEL

MEDIA LUNA
TIRED FROG

SASTA

ATOMIC INTERNET CAFÉ

ALBATROS ROYALE

CALLE 8

YAXCHE MAYA CUISINE

PELICANO INN

RINCON DEL SOL
SHOPS/LA PARILLA

HOTEL ALEJARI

CALLE 6

AV. 45
AV. 40
AV. 35
AV. 30
AV. 30
AV. 25
AV. 20
AV. 15
AV. 10
AV. 5

PHONE/
FAX

LA RAYA
CAPT. TUTIX

CALLE 4

PARKING

SABOR

PEZ VELA

CALLE 2

CINEMA

POLICE STATION/
POST OFFICE

PARKING

BUS STATION

WALKWAY/MALECON

THE COFFEE PRESS
GIFT SHOP

TACOLOTE/MASCARAS

AV. JUAREZ (PRINCIPAL)
AV. JUAREZ (PRINCIPAL)

HOSPITAL

WATER
STORE

TELEPHONE

Plaza

BAKERY

SELVA
TOURS

LOS MOLCAS HOTEL/
RESTAURANT

FERRY TO COZUMEL

BANK

SEÑOR
FROG

AERO FERINCO

AERO SAAB

CONTINENTAL PLAZA
PLAYACAR

PLAYACAR XAMAN HA
CONDOMINIUMS

PLAYA DEL CARMEN
AIRPORT

RUINS

307

AVIARY XAMAN HA

SCALE NOT AVAILABLE

↓ To Xcaret and Tulum

© AVALON TRAVEL PUBLISHING, INC.

Rooms (US$45–$78), with private baths, vary from really rustic with thatch-roof bungalows and beds draped in mosquito netting to modern and air-conditioned with fans. Everything is near the beach and within walking distance of town.

On the outer edge of the busy town center, **Hotel Da Gabi,** Calle 12 just off Av. 5, fax 987/3-0048, is a fine little hotel with just a few fan-cooled rooms, 100 meters from the beach. The per-night price of US$45 includes breakfast. The excellent Italian restaurant on site serves homemade fettuccine, ravioli, and brick oven–baked pizza. It's a good value for delicious foods, especially Monday–Thursday. Check out the menu specials.

US$50–100

Hotel Alejari, on Calle 6, tel. 987/3-0374, fax 987/3-0005, is a hidden little gem in a garden setting. The duplexes and studios (US$65) are clean and simple with air-conditioning or fans, tile floors, hot water, and private bathrooms; some include kitchenettes. Beach access is available through the back gate, and the reception office has a public phone.

Bed and Breakfast Baal Na Kah, on Calle 12 just off Av. 5, email: mta@webtelmex.net.mx, occupies a delightful three-story building one block from the beach. The house has a comfortable "great room" and common decks have good views. Although guests have access to the main kitchen, continental breakfast is served downstairs at the Café Pokara. Occasionally proprietors Kathy and Mino throw impromptu dinner parties where guests meet and mingle. Interesting people seem to be attracted to Baal Na Kah. Each room in the house is different in design and size, and each has a private bathroom, decorated with *talavera* tile. The floors are all *saltillo* tile. Each room has its own price, but ranges from US$52–98. Reservations are advised as this well-priced hostel stays pretty full.

Albatros Royale, three blocks north of the plaza at Calle 6 and Av. 5, U.S. tel. 800/538-6802, Mexico tel. 987/3-0001, is one of the nicest hotels along this stretch of beach. Owner Sam Beard, an American expat, knows how to offer his guests comfort without exorbitant rates. The Royale's two-story buildings face each other across a landscaped pathway leading to the

beach. Hammocks are strung by the front door or on the balcony of each room, and guests tend to congregate on patios for card games and conversation. Tile floors and fans keep the 31 rooms cool and comfortable. Rooms are US$85; the price drops to US$44 in the summer.

Mosquito Blue, at Av. 5 between Calles 12 and 14, tel./fax 987/2-1245, offers a pool, a big outdoor movie screen, and well-kept, attractive rooms with air-conditioning, modern bathrooms, and cable TV for US$86. The open-air lounge is cool and comfy with a stylish two-story *palapa* roof. The French and continental cuisine is good. The hotel within walking distance of the very busy beach. Ask about the connection to the **Fisherman's Village Beach Club** in Playacar; it welcomes Mosquito Blue guests and even gives a discount on drinks and food.

Chichan Baal Kah, Calle 16 Norte, U.S. tel. 800/538-6802 or 303/674-9615, Mexico tel. 987/3-0040, is a charming hotel in a shady residential neighborhood— a welcome change from the hustle and bustle of downtown Playa. The quiet little hotel offers seven kitchen-equipped suites (US$80), each sleeping three people (no children under 16 allowed) The kitchens all have juicers—there's almost always a basket of oranges around—and table service for six. Full maid and linen services are provided. Other amenities include a small swimming pool, a sun deck with barbecue facilities, and an honor bar. Early-bird coffee service and bikes are available.

The white stucco, Spanish-style **Pelicano Inn,** U.S. tel. 800/538-6802, is a real treat. Each room has a private bathroom, a hammock, and a balcony with views of the sea. King-size beds are available, and rates include a breakfast buffet. There's no air-conditioning, but there are fans. Rates are US$68–90, depending on the time of year.

El Tucan Condotel, Calle 14 just off Av. 5, is an exotic place with its own cenote and waterfall near the outdoor bar where it's always cool under the thick trees and plants. The pool is set in a sunny spot, and there are two dining rooms. The rooms are condos with private bathrooms and living, dining, and kitchen areas. The rooms upstairs are the nicest. Always check your room before you settle in to make sure you have screens, on the first floor you can invite mosquitoes with the windows open. Rates are US$88 for two with air-conditioning up to US$219 for a three-bedroom with breakfast. Everyone we have heard from rave about the breakfast (and we agree: it's a full breakfast that's fresh with a good variety of everything). The other comment seems to be the hotel needs a little TLC. If you plan to cook, there's very little in the kitchen to cook with (pots, silverware, etc). Also, several people have said the desk clerk didn't have records of prepayment or exactly the accommodations they expected to be in. Just in case, come with all receipts of payment, and have a name and number contact. These situations have always been worked out, it just took a little time. People do like the place, the quiet location, the staff, and the great breakfast. Their beach club is a short walk away on a good beach.

US$100–150
Mayan Paradise, Av. 10, tel./fax 987/3-0933, offers 40 rooms (US$143) with kitchens, air-conditioning, TVs, and *palapa* ambience. Amenities include a great pool, beautiful landscaping, and a good restaurant. Though not on the beach, the hotel has its own beach club and shuttle service; ask at the desk. Breakfast is included.

Near the Continental Plaza Playacar, **Playacar Xaman Ha Condominiums,** Yucatán Reservations, tel. 800/555-8842, are handsomely designed. There are grassy areas around the pool and condos are either on or close to the beach. A five-minute stroll from shops and cafés near the ferry dock, units have one to three bedrooms, a living room, and a fully equipped kitchen (some also have washer and dryer). Our second-floor unit had a balcony with comfy lounges overlooking the pool. This is a quiet place, great for families or small groups. Prices begin at about US$130 per night for a one-bedroom condo, depending on time of year. Each condo is owned by a different person, so furnishings and prices vary. The managing staff does a good job of matching people and their preferences. Upper-floor units have the best balconies and views.

US$150–200
Continental Plaza Playacar, tel. 987/3-0100, fax 987/3-0105, U.S./Canada tel. 800/882-6684, was the first hotel south of the dock. The five-floor establishment holds 188 rooms and 16 suites, all with air-conditioning, satellite TV, private terraces overlooking the Caribbean, tile bathrooms and floors, and comfy beds. The per-night rate is US$196 (US$98 in summer). Common-area amenities include a beautiful pool and lounge area, several dining rooms and bars, and a spacious, attractive lobby (check out the striking painting of the birds and animals of Quintana Roo). Scattered around the grounds are many Maya ruins that were carefully preserved as the hotel was being built. Reservations are a must, since the hotel is often filled with large

This relaxed family enjoys living out of their camper on the beach for several months each year.

OZ MALLAN

tour groups. If you have children and you're staying at a nearby hotel, stop in for a nice buffet breakfast—they offer one free child's buffet for each paying adult.

All-inclusive Resorts South of Town

From here south there are many fine all-inclusive, upscale hotels along the Riviera Maya coastline. Many are big names, such as Oasis, Palace Resorts, Barcelo, Bahia Principe. They range from US$70–200 per person per night (although one of the Palace Resorts goes for US$600 per night). They all have wonderful beaches and offer great activities. Meals and drinks are included in the rates. For more information call Yucatán Reservations, tel. 800/555-8842.

OTHER PRACTICALITIES

Food

New restaurants are springing up even faster than hotels in Playa del Carmen. Around the central plaza several of the old timers are still here. Small cafés serve a variety of good inexpensive Mexican, Italian, and seafood dishes.

Tacolote, on the first block off the beach, across from the plaza, is modeled after a café by the same name in Cancún (but has different owners). Beloved for its many varieties of tacos and heaping platters of fajitas, it can get very noisy.

Máscaras, on the first block off the beach across from the plaza, serves Italian food. Try the pizza and pasta baked in a brick, wood-burning oven, or the spinach cannelloni. The fresh limeade, served in bulbous glasses with lots of purified ice, is tasty. Everything served goes well with a margarita or a cold beer.

There are three great places on Avenida 5. **Nuestra Señorita Carmen** is a popular budget spot serving grilled fish and Yucatecan meals priced under US$5. Nearby **Media Luna** is a popular indoor/outdoor vegetarian café that's always trying new recipes. The fruit drinks are terrific. For a real Mexican experience, try **La Parilla.** Expect live music, great Mexican food, and lots of people.

Yaxche Maya Cuisine Restaurant, 8th St. between 10th Av. and 5th Av., is easy to recognize: When you see a façade that looks like a Maya ruin, you're there. This is a place for good

food with a Maya twist. Several cafés advertise the same, but somehow this one is more of a show and the food really is good. From hors d'oeuvres to entrées to drinks, owner Alberto Lizaola puts his Maya thumbprint on it (even though he's not Mayan). Try the peppers stuffed with *cochinita pibil* (spicy pork) or anything with *chaya* (a vegetable that looks a lot like spinach). The fruit/*chaya* water is very tasty. Prices are moderate.

If you're a **Señor Frog** fan, you'll find him at the foot of the ferry dock. The same Mexican menu and live music make for quite a party.

Another party spot is **Red Eye,** next to Mosquito Blue at Av. 10 and Constituyentes (you just have to look a little bit to find it). It offers food for the soul and the body. Taiwanese and Brazilian specialties include rice, shrimp, and coconut.

Across from Media Luna, you find **Tasta,** a fine little coffee shop with fresh beans and good cappuccino. Try their croissants, bagels, or falafel.

If you need the Internet, try the **Atomic Internet Café,** on 8th St. between 5th and 10th Av. And for a good book and a good sandwich on a fresh baguette, stop in at **La Libreria,** also on 8th St. between 5th and 10th Av.

Johnny Cairo, at the Quinta Mija Apartments, serves up good gourmet food in a low-key atmosphere. Former Ritz Carlton chef John Gray and his partner, George Cairo, serve great contemporary-American cuisine. Try offerings like scallops and shrimp on a bed of polenta or roast duck with tequila/chipotle sauce. Or, if you're tired of making decisions, be really daring and order the demonstration dinner (about US$50), a great meal for a special evening. They have another restaurant in Puerto Morelos right on the beach where they put on special dinners such as Full Moon Parties on the beach, with tiki torches and bonfires, Super Bowl parties, and what ever else they think up.

The Coffee Press, 2nd St. between 5th Av. and the beach, is a neat little place for breakfast and lunch. Come read one of their many books while you munch on pastries and sip coffee or tea.

Two **bakeries** on Avenida 5 are **Sabor** and **Mr. Baguette,**. Both places serve light snacks and cold drinks in addition to the regular bakery fare.

Locals will find every traditional pastry eaten for every Maya/Mexican holiday at **Yaxche Maya Restaurant.**

If you're cooking for yourself, check out the huge **San Francisco de Assis** supermarket on the 30th Street. It has everything and then some!

Playa Nightlife

You can definitely find music and dance spots in this small town. A few favorites are **Calypso Dancing Bar,** for salsa, merengue (no cover, just buy drinks); **La Raya; Disco Bar; Capt. Tutix;** and the **Blue Parrot Bar.** The music is loud and the dancing goes on into the wee hours of the morning (or as long as anyone is still there to listen). The Blue Parrot, Capt. Tutix, and La Raya are on the beach. The **Beer Bucket** is another spot worth checking out.

Shopping

In the colonial-style **Rincón del Sol** center, Av. 5 at Calle 8, are several shops selling carved masks, T-shirts, Guatemalan textiles, and other clothes. Among them, **La Catrina** is filled with shells, figurines, and *papeles picados,* the tissue-paper cutouts Mexicans string up for fiestas; **Luna Maya** features one-of-a-kind jewelry from Guadalajara; and **El Vuelo de los Niños Pájaros** carries handcrafted papers made from bark, as well as a good selection of Latin American CDs and cassette tapes.

La Playense, on Av. Juárez (Principal), offers gifts of all kinds—check out the woodcarvings. Get your photo supplies at **Omega** on Av. Juárez across from the bank. If you need to send a fax, go to **Computel,** Av. Juárez at Av. 5, which has copy machines and long-distance phone service as well.

Meeting the Maya of Today

A tour group in Playacar called **Alltournative Expeditions,** 987/3-2036, email: tour@alltour native.com, offers ecotours in combination with visits to the jungle and ruin sites. One tour takes small groups of visitors to **Pac Chen,** a Maya village of about 25 families 50 miles inland, not too far from Coba. Visitors have an opportunity to meet the Maya, in their thatch roof houses, meander the flower lined village paths, see the small school house, and speak to the children who love to show everyone their beehives in hollow logs.

After wandering Pac Chen, trek to a large peaceful lagoon nearby where you are free to swim or rappel down into a very deep cenote—42 feet to the water. On our tour, the village women prepared a lunch with a Maya flavor; most ingredients were brought by the guide—there's no electricity in the village, hence no refrigeration. They prepared chicken in *achiote,* rice, beans, melon, and served packaged rolls (where were the tortillas?) along with chilled soda and bottled water.

The fee for the tours is US$90 per person. The village is like a living museum, and with its

Maya boys at Pac Chen

OZ MALLAN

share of the money from the tours, the village has been able to improve the quality of life.

Services

Banco del Atlántico, Av. Juárez at Av. 10 (three blocks from the ferry dock), and **Bancomer,** Av. Juárez at Av. 25, both cash traveler's checks and advance cash on credit cards. Money-changing hours are Monday–Friday 10 A.M.–12:30 P.M. The **post office** is on Av. Juárez in a small building between the police station and the mayor's office.

At **La Palma** laundry on Av. 5 you can either do it yourself (after 6 P.M.) or have it done for you. Laundry service is provided all day and usually takes three to four hours.

Transportation

By Taxi: A taxi from Cancún International Airport to Playa del Carmen costs US$55–65. If there are several passengers, you can get a good deal—just bargain with the driver before you start your journey. A taxi from Carmen to Tulum (with three passengers) runs about US$25–30 roundtrip. Nonmetered taxis meet the incoming ferry at Playa del Carmen and are available for long or short hauls; again, make your deal in advance.

By Ferry: Two types of passenger ferries travel between Playa del Carmen and Isla Cozumel. The faster **MV *Mexico*** is air-conditioned and makes the trip in about 30 minutes; fare is about US$7.50 per person one way. The slower open-air boats take about 45 minutes; fare is about US$3. Between the two, ferries depart just about every hour 6:30 A.M.–8 P.M. You can request a specific ferry, but invariably you will get a ticket on the next boat out. (This is a way to keep all the ferries in business, including the older ones.)

The ferry crossing is usually a breeze. However, the calm sea does flex its muscles once in a while. If you're prone to seasickness, delay your departure till the next day—the sea seldom stays angry for long. Young boys with imaginative homemade pushcarts or men with three-wheel *triciclos* meet incoming ferries at the dock to carry luggage for a small fee. Because of the ferry traffic, this is also a good place to try **hitchhiking** north or south.

By Bus: Three bus lines provide this small town with the best bus transportation on the coast. Buses going north to Cancún travel the 65 kilometers in 50 minutes. **Autotransportes del Caribe** carries passengers to and from Cancún in a small bus that makes six daily trips. Seats are reserved; buy your ticket a half hour in advance. **ADO** bus company offers at least one first-class reserved bus daily between Playa and Cancún. **Playa Express** mini-buses run to Cancún nonstop throughout the day, but have minimal room for luggage. Check at the bus station for the current bus schedule for service from Playa del Carmen to Cancún.

ADO operates three luxury express buses to Mérida daily; the buses have air-conditioning, bathrooms, and refreshments. Other buses travel to and from Chetumal and other points south. Ask about public transport to local sights. Often your hotel can set you up with vans or mini-buses from your hotel to Tulum, Xelha Lagoon, and Coba.

By Plane: You can fly from Play to Cozumel via **AeroFarinco,** U.S. tel. 987/3-0574, Mexico tel. 800/MAGICAL, email: yourwings@aeroferinco.com. The office is located in the Playa del Carmen airport. Make reservations a day in advance—they don't fly every day. Business hours are 6:30 A.M.–8:30 P.M. Usually flights leave Playa at 1 P.M., and the one-way fare is US$15. The trip takes about 10 minutes.

Getting Around Town: This is a walking town, especially since they keep extending the pedestrian walkways. If you must drive, and the streets are getting busier every year, note that the road going to the ferry dock is closed to all vehicle traffic; watch the signs and follow the traffic to the parking lot north near the bus station. Most streets go one way in a confusing system. Parking is severely limited. Street signs are beginning to appear, but most locals give directions by using landmarks. Once you're off the main paved entry road into town, you'll find the streets are still bumpy, but they improve a little each year. In short, park wherever you can and rely on your feet to get you around town. Remember, don't park too close to a corner or the cops will remove your license plate, and to get it back you'll have to pay a large fine. If you're taking the ferry to Isla Cozumel for the day, park your car at the public parking lot by the bus station. Fees are posted.

XCARET ECOARCHAEOLOGICAL PARK

Xcaret is about an hour's drive south of Cancún and one kilometer off the highway toward the sea. The small port, called Pole during the post-classic period (A.D. 1200–1500), was an important trading center and Maya ceremonial center. Maya pilgrims en route to Isla Cozumel to worship the goddess Ix Chel used Xcaret as a jumping-off point; historians say the Maya would spend several days here praying for a safe crossing before boarding their wooden canoes.

Today the site draws pilgrims of another sort: fun-seekers coming to frolic at Xcaret's natural history–oriented theme park. Though some visitors have compared Xcaret to Disneyland (and the crowds can often feel comparable), park developer Miguel Quintana says it's much more. Here the family fun centers around some decidedly serious ecological endeavors.

Maya Archaeology

Archaeologists under the direction of the Instituto Nacional de Antropología e Historia continue to excavate the site, which is rich with Maya history. Several ruins in the park's developed area have been restored, and according to archaeologist Tony Andrews, dozens more structures are scattered throughout the surrounding bush; so far 60 buildings and remnants of hundreds of platforms have been found. The work will probably take another six or seven years to complete. In the evenings the stone temples located in the middle of the park are lit with torches and make an impressive sight.

Natural History Studies

Other scientists here are studying the region's fauna, including turtles, manatees, bats, and butterflies. Study areas are all open to the public and include educational exhibits. The immense screened-in butterfly enclosure, for example, offers exhibits that explain how butterflies develop and illustrates different species and the plants they prefer.

Swimming with Dolphins

Of all the natural-history programs here, the most popular involves the chance to swim with the park's dolphins. A limited number of visitors each day are given the opportunity to pay about US$65 to swim with the graceful animals. Trainers supervise the entire event, first showing a video to all "swimmers," then providing instructions on in-the-pool interaction. There's something really special about touching and talking to these creatures while looking them straight in the eye. I've heard this is a wonderful therapy for children and adults who suffer from hard-to-treat mental illnesses. Perhaps these animals sense a problem.

Swimmers must reserve a time slot for their swim. Make your reservations in advance at a travel agency; otherwise, it's on a first-come-first-served basis starting first thing in the morning at the dolphin area. This means when the park gates open there's a mad rush to get there. If you're not a good runner or get turned around in the park, you're liable to be disappointed. And note that if you take the Xcaret bus from Cancún, you'll arrive too late to sign up. If you're staying in Cancún and want to swim with the dolphins, rent a car and get to Xcaret early, before the 9 A.M. opening.

It's fun to spend an entire day at Xcaret.

If you miss out, don't worry—you can also swim with dolphins at Xelha and Puerto Aventuras.

Trivia Note: the dolphins are really smart. We watched one of them trying to steal fish out of the trainers "reward" cooler when the trainer turned her back for a moment.

Underground River

What used to be an underground river here has been made into a "floating adventure." Openings were made in the earthen ceiling of an underground cavern to let in light and circulate air (a couple of cenotes were destroyed in the making). People are given life jackets and, starting at the entrance of what was once considered a sacred cenote, they spend 20–30 minutes floating along the underground river, admiring coralline deposits and unusual little fish until they reach the other end, 1,000 feet south. Many visitors say the float alone is worth the price of park admission.

Snorkeling

The *caleta* (small bay) at Xcaret provides beginning snorkelers, especially children, with a perfect learning spot. The water is shallow and there's little current, though to enter the water you must either climb over rocks or jump off a small wooden platform. But it's not necessary to go much beyond the limestone shoreline to discover colorful denizens of the sea. Resident schools of parrot fish and blue and French angelfish almost always put in an appearance. About the only problem is fighting off the tourists; come early in the day and you might have the small bay almost to yourself.

Entertainment and Food

Nighttime activities are not to be missed. In addition to the recreation activities, the park offers a variety of first-class entertainment. A living-history presentation leads you on a mystical walk through a tunnel where you'll view ancient Maya ceremonies. A *charreada* (Mexican rodeo) is presented daily in late afternoon, and at night the park puts on an incredible show in the stone amphitheater. The nightly show changes frequently—it might include classical music, ballet, or just about anything—but it's always a good show in an exotic setting. Note: anyone who suffers from claustrophobia better think twice about the underground tunnel walk on a busy night—it gets very crowded.

You're not allowed to bring food into the park, but several restaurants on the grounds offer different menus. Go to the seafood café and taste the excellent coconut fried shrimp—a real treat! None of the restaurants are particularly cheap.

Around the Park

Trails meander throughout the lushly landscaped park, past orchid-covered trees, a large variety of tropical plants, and ferns from all over southern Mexico. A stroll along the breakwater gives you a view of the regal dolphins. Large, informative plaques placed about the park explain just about everything.

Facilities include a dive shop offering equipment rental and lessons, a gift shop, spotlessly clean restrooms with lockers and changing stalls, and a stable with some fine rental horses for riding through the jungle surrounding the beach.

Information

Tickets: You have several options to choose from. If you arrive after 4 P.M. for the evening entertainment, you must pay the full amount, but this ticket will get you in the next day for the entire day. If you think you'll be coming back more than once or twice, ask about their multiple-entrance tickets. The single-ticket price right now is about US$39, and is good for entry to the living-history presentation, good snorkeling spots, and a lovely sandy beach adjacent to placid aqua water—everything except swimming with the dolphins and diving gear and diving trips. Everyone is welcome to sit and watch the dolphins and the swimmers without charge.

Sunblock: Do *not* apply any type of sunblock before coming to Xcaret. When you arrive and pay for your ticket, they will ask you to exchange your sunblock for a special biodegradable variety that won't pollute the water.

Hours and Directions: The park is open October–March 9 A.M.–9 P.M., April–September 9 A.M.–10 P.M. If you're driving, look for the only high hill on Highway 307 (at Kilometer 72, six kilometers south of the Playa del Carmen turnoff) and a very large sign, where you'll find the park entrance. Bus tours to Xcaret from Cancún are available (see the Cancún section, above). For more information, call 988/3-0654 or 8/3-0743.

sandy, but the shallow water here harbors the prickly sea urchin—look before you step, or wear your shoes while you're wading.

The Quintana Roo coast offers miles and miles of pristine dive spots, and the waters here at Pamul are ideal. The water is crystal clear, allowing you to examine the fascinating life within the shallow tidal pools cradled by rocks and limestone. Snorkeling is better the closer you get to the reef 120 meters offshore. On the way the sea bottom drops off to about eight meters, and its colorful underwater life can absorb you for hours.

Turtles

If it's a bright moonlit night in July or August, you may be treated to the unique sight of large turtles lumbering ashore to lay eggs in the sand. If you're here 50 days later it's even more exciting to watch the tiny hatchlings (about eight centimeters in diameter) dig out of their sandy nests and make their way down the beach to begin life in the sea. Much has been written about protecting the turtles of the Caribbean from humans, but nature in the form of egg-eating animals provides its own threat to this endangered species. On the beach of Pamul, more than half the eggs are scratched up from the sand and eaten by small animals that live in the adjacent jungle. However, marine biologists are taking a larger part in protecting the eggs and hatchlings by digging them up as soon as they are laid and reburying them in a protected area until they hatch.

Accommodations

Cabañas Pamul, a small hotel on the beach, offers simple and inexpensive but clean cabañas with electricity between sunset and 10 P.M., hot and cold water, and shared bathrooms.

Camping

The campground at the south end of the hotel has room for 15 RVs. All spots have electricity and water; eight are large pads with sewer hookups (US$13), and seven will accommodate small trailers (US$5). You can use the showers and toilets in the hotel. The camping fee is about US$6 per person, which includes bathroom privileges. And those large palapa roofs you see are to shelter RVs, pretty nice.

Float for 20–30 minutes on the surface of an underground river at Xcaret.

OZ MALLAN

CALICA DOCK

Just south of Xcaret is the dock used for decades by the large Calica company to ship limestone products to the United States. The dock has now been pulled into use by cruise ships. Usually the ships stay docked for the day, and taxis and tour buses take passengers to sightsee on this part of the Riviera Maya. It's feasible to hire a taxi for the day and visit many of the sights along this coast. You can try haggling over the price before you take off, but the taxis are really "unionizing" their fee schedule.

PAMUL

A small beach worth exploring (beachcomb here for shells, coral, and interesting jetsam), Pamul is in some places steep and rocky, in others narrow and flat. The south end of the beach is

GIANT TURTLES

At one time the giant turtle was plentiful and an important addition to the Indian diet. The turtle was captured by turning it over (no easy matter at 90–100 kilograms) when it came on shore to lay its eggs. Any eggs already deposited in a sandy nest on the beach were gathered, and then the entire family took part in processing this nourishing game. First, the parchmentlike bag of unlaid eggs was removed from the body, then the undeveloped eggs (looking like small, hard-boiled egg yolks). After that, the meat of the turtle was cut into strips to be dried in the sun. The orange-colored fat was put in calabash containers and saved for soups and stews; it added rich nutrients and was considered an important medicine. The Indians wasted nothing.

Today CIQRO, a protective organization, along with the government, keep a sharp lookout along the coast for egg poachers during the laying season. Turtle-egg farms are being developed to ensure the survival of this ancient mariner. Sadly, today's poacher travels the entire coast, and each beach is hit night after night. The turtle can lay as many as 200 eggs in an individual nest or "clutch." One beach may be the instinctual home for hundreds of turtles (at one time thousands) that return to the site of their own hatching each year.

Turtles can live to be a hundred years old, which means they can lay a lot of eggs in their lifetime. But as the poachers steal the eggs on a wholesale basis, the species could eventually be wiped out entirely. If caught, poachers are fined and can be jailed—though the damage has been done. When released they usually return to their lucrative habits. In

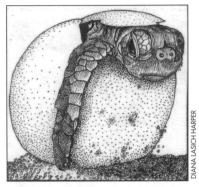

DIANA LASICH HARPER

most Mexican marketplaces a ready market for these eggs exists among superstitious men who believe the eggs are an aphrodisiac.

The survival of the giant sea turtle lies within the education of the people—locals and visitors alike. Shoppers will see many sea-turtle products offered for sale: turtle oil, tortoise-shell combs, bracelets, rings, buttons, carvings, and veneer inlaid on furniture and jewelry boxes, plus small stuffed, polished hatchling paperweights. **Note:** It is against the law to bring these products into the United States and other countries. If discovered they will be confiscated. Sadly, many travelers are not even aware of the law, and often the products get by the inspectors. If tourists refused to purchase these products, the market would dry up—a big step toward preserving these gentle lumbering beasts.

Food
Los Arrecifes, the café/bar on the beach, is quite nice, and a great place to watch the sunset in the bar-swings. The kitchen offers fresh-caught seafood, good breakfasts, and hamburgers and such at reasonable prices. All water and ice is purified and the veggies and fruits are bathed in Microdin. It's open 8 A.M.–8 P.M.

Other Practicalities
A small cenote provides water for Pamul; boil water before drinking, unless you're at the restaurant. Otherwise, buy bottled water (you'll find a mini-super across the highway from the entrance road). Los Arrecifes has a dive shop on the premises where you can arrange a three-hour snorkeling trip to the reef for US$30 per person.

PUERTO AVENTURAS AND VICINITY

One of the most ambitious developments on the Riviera Maya, Puerto Aventuras—a few minutes south of Akumal—includes residential housing, time shares, hotels, all sorts of resort amenities, and a large marina.

Boating

At the marina, yachtsmen will find everything they need: gas and diesel, marine supplies and minor repairs, purified water and ice, bait, 24-hour radio monitoring and medical services, restrooms and showers, car rentals, travel agencies, a shopping center, yacht club, hotels, and restaurants. Boat access into the marina is through a carefully planned channel, well marked for navigation and ready with an escort service through the reef 24 hours a day. Some of the marina's waterways are left from the days of the Maya, simply improved and opened to the sea. In other cases they are totally man-made. The marina can hold almost 300 boats with a maximum length of 120 feet and a maximum draft of 10 feet.

Diving

Puerto Aventuras is a favorite hub for world-class diving. Ten different well-known dive sites are just minutes away, and the beauty of the Caribbean along this coast is legendary. The water is full of curious creatures.

Mike Madden's Dive Center, Apdo. Postal 117, Playa del Carmen, Quintana Roo 77710, Mexico, tel. 987/3-5129 or 3-5131, offers scuba instruction, night dives, daily reef dives, cavern trips, snorkeling, and cenote diving (as well as jungle adventures and deep-sea fishing). Trips are available to little-known dive spots such as Canyonland Reef, Chanyuym Reef, Xpu-Ha, Xaac, and Xaac Chico.

Madden has been involved in some unusual adventures that have placed his name in the *Guinness Book of World Records.* In 1987 he was the leader of the expedition that discovered and surveyed Nohoch Cave, the world's longest known underwater cave system. Today visitors can explore Nohoch (whose name means "huge" in the Maya language) with Madden's dive guides or other area guides, if trained for cavern diving. Permanent guide lines have been placed along more than 13 kilometers of passageways to ensure that divers will be able to find their way out of the cave, as well as to provide a baseline for further surveys. Some of the cave's vast chambers are as much as 300 meters wide and are majestically beautiful, with sparkling columns, brimstone pools, stalagmites, stalactites, cave pearls of pristine white limestone, and blue passageways channeling off in all directions. One room has six feet of airspace overhead, allowing even beginning snorkelers to view the breathtaking visions of this marine wonder.

Another cavern trip offered by Madden's Dive Center is called the Indiana Jones Adventure. The trip goes to **Nohoch Nah Chich** ("Giant House of the Birds"), named for the bats that lived in the cave. Part of the giant cave system can safely be reached from a cenote on the property of a local farm family. A jeep takes you within three kilometers of the cenote; from there you hike in. Trekkers have a chance to visit with the family; they still get their water from the cenote. There's a 15-minute guided tour of the cenote for snorkelers (after which snorkelers can go back in and spend as much time as they wish). This is a fascinating trip for snorkelers since the underwater caves are usually accessible only to scuba divers. The group departs at 9:30 A.M. and returns at 2:30 P.M. Cost is about US$38; no children under 10. You can find a short article and photo on one of the caves in the September 1990 issue of *National Geographic* magazine.

Note: Cavern diving is dangerous and different from open-sea diving. It requires highly specialized training. The danger of getting lost within this subterranean and subaquatic world is very real; hundreds of untrained divers have lost their lives in underwater caves over the years.

Golf and Tennis

Puerto Aventuras has a tennis court and a nine-hole, tournament-quality golf course. Golf carts are available for rent.

CEDAM Museum

Artifacts recovered from the sunken ship *Mantanceros* can be seen at the CEDAM Museum on the waterfront. CEDAM (an acronym for Conservation, Ecology, Diving, Archaeology, and Museums) is a nonprofit organization. The *Mantanceros* was a Spanish merchant ship that left Cadiz, Spain, in 1741, headed for the New World. Loaded with trade goods, it foundered and sank on the reef two kilometers north of Akumal. No one knows for certain why the ship sank, since there were no survivors. Research suggests the ship probably engaged in battle with a British vessel and then drifted onto the treacherous reef now known as Punta Mantanceros. For more detailed information on the finds of the *Mantanceros,* read *The Treasure of the Great Reef,* by Arthur C. Clarke. Beginning in 1958, CEDAM spent several years salvaging the *Mantanceros.* Artifacts retrieved and on display here include belt buckles, cannons, coins, guns, and tableware.

Accommodations

The **Omni Puerto Aventuras,** tel. 987/3-5100, fax 987/3-5102, has undergone a massive renovation. The luxurious hotel faces the marina on one side and a shimmering white beach and the translucent water of the Caribbean on the other. All rooms have tile floors, king-size beds, beautiful colors, regional decor, and first-class amenities. The first-floor rooms have private patios with hot tubs; the second- and third-floor rooms have balconies with private hot tubs and marina and partial ocean views. Each room has a "magic" box in the wall through which complimentary breakfast is delivered each morning. All types of water-sports equipment are available. Other amenities include a swimming pool, pool bar, lobby bar, beach *palapa* bar, and the excellent **Da Vince** dining room. The all-inclusive rate is US$360; those who stay five nights or longer receive credit at several restaurants in the Marina.

Club Oasis is a great all-inclusive destination. The grounds are large, with the sea and the marina nearby and pools right at hand. All rooms (US$85 per person) are nicely appointed, with comfortable beds, air-conditioning, and balconies. Several dining areas are available, and the breakfast buffet—including fresh eggs cooked to order—just doesn't quit.

Food

Several cafés are at the marina. **Solo Mío** makes good Italian food, including pizza. What used to be **Carlos 'n Charlie's** is now **One for the Road,** offering good Mexican food. Need a cigar? Or a good cuppa coffee? Try **Coffee Bar and Tobacco Shop. Richard's Steak House** serves the best (imported) beef steaks and brochettes around. For ice cream check out **Mexico Lindo.**

Shopping and Services

Along the walkway by the marina channels you'll find most everything you need, including cafés, a Laundromat, a small medical service for emergency first aid, a beauty parlor, a travel agency, a money changer, a taxi stand, **Videorama** (what would the kids do without video games for a week?), and several markets that carry sundries as well as groceries, ice, and drinks. You can rent a car for a day at your hotel; also ask about bike rentals.

Katenah Bay

Continuing south, the highway soon passes Katenah Bay, a curved slice of white sand washed by crystal-clear water. Here you'll find the beautiful premium/all-inclusive **El Dorado Resort and Spa,** Kilometer 95, tel. 800/511-4848. Guests at the El Dorado are pampered with good service and have a choice of three restaurants (Italian, Mexican, or continental) and a couple of bars. Rates include use of the pool, tennis court, sea kayaks, paddleboats, bicycles, and snorkeling equipment, as well as all gratuities. The rooms are really junior suites; some have hot tubs on their balconies or patios, some have ocean views. The "Spa" part is a little misleading, but the resort does offer a beauty and nail shop, massage, and aromatherapy, all for an extra fee. Taxis and car rentals are available. The resort has a dive service on the premises and good snorkeling just offshore. Rates begin at US$97–190 per person double occupancy, depending on season and room (best rates run April 5–December 19). No children under 18 permitted.

AKUMAL BAY

About 100 kilometers (60 miles) south of Cancún, the crescent of intensely white sand at Akumal Bay is home to an ever-growing resort that survives nicely without the bustling activity of Cancún (although it gets busier each year). The traveler desiring the tropical essence of Yucatán *and* a dash of the good life will appreciate Akumal, which offers a wide range of hotel rooms, dining, and activities. During the off-season you'll have little difficulty finding a room here. However, if you travel between December 1 and April 15, you should reserve well in advance.

The barrier reef that runs parallel to the Quintana Roo coast protects Akumal Bay from the open sea and makes for great swimming and snorkeling. Proximity to the reef and easy access to the unspoiled treasures of the Caribbean make it a gathering place for divers from all over the world. For the archaeology buff, Akumal is 10 kilometers (six miles) north of Tulum, one of the few walled Maya sites on the edge of the sea. In Maya, Akumal means "Place of the Turtle," and since prehistoric times the giant green turtle has come ashore here in summer to lay its eggs in the warm sand.

History
Akumal was a small part of a sprawling working coconut plantation until 1925, when a *New York Times*–sponsored expedition along the then-unknown Quintana Roo coast stumbled on the tranquil bay. It was another 33 years before the rest of the outside world intruded on its pristine beauty. In 1958 Pablo Bush and others formed CEDAM, a renowned diver's club, and introduced Akumal as the "diving capital of the world." Soon the word was out. The first visitors (divers) began making their way to the unknown wilderness. At that time, the only access to Akumal was by boat from Cozumel. A road was built in the 1960s. Since then, Akumal has continued to grow in fame and size each year. Though many people come here, it still remains a beautiful, tranquil place to study the sea and stars.

Flora
Akumal is surrounded by jungle. In March, bright red bromeliads bloom high in the trees, reaching for a sun that's rapidly hidden by fast-growing vines and leaves. These "guest" plants that find homes in established trees are epiphytes rather than parasites. They don't drain the sap of the host tree, but instead sustain themselves with rain, dew, and humidity; their leaves absorb moisture and organic requirements from airborne dust, insect matter, and visiting birds. The bromeliad family encompasses a wide variety of plants, including pineapple and Spanish moss. The genus seen close to Akumal is the tillandsia, and the flame-red flower that blooms on the tops of so many of the trees here is only one variety of this remarkable epiphyte. While searching for bromeliads, you undoubtedly will see another epiphyte, the orchid. Sadly, these are fast disappearing along with the jungle.

Dive Shops
Akumal Dive Center offers a three-day dive-certification course as well as a four-hour resort course that culminates in one escorted dive on the reef. If you decide to take a resort course from any dive shop, check to make sure that you'll be making the dive with a divemaster. The Akumal Dive Center is fully PADI certified. For advance dive information, contact Akutrame Inc., P.O. Box 13326, El Paso, TX 79913 USA, tel. 915/584-3552 or 800/351-1622, Canada tel. 800/343-1440. The shop also rents kayaks and sailboards.

Akumal Dive Shop is the original dive operation at Akumal. Still right on the beach, they offer certification for full training in cave and cavern diving. Cenote diving is gaining popularity every day. Often the dive into a cenote takes you into a deep cave. These caves are carefully chosen. It is stimulating and dangerous if you don't know what you are doing. The dive shop offers sailing, reef diving, and lessons for the whole family. For more information tel. 987/5-9032 or email: akumal@cancun.com.mx.

Snorkeling
Calm swimming areas are ideal for snorkeling. A good spot within wading distance is the rocky area on the north end of the bay. Floating along the surface of the water and looking through your private window into the unique world below can be habit-forming along this coast. Take it slow and easy, and you won't miss anything. Search the rocks and crevices that you'll drift over, even the sandy bottom—what may look like a rocky bulge on the floor of the sea may eventually twitch an eye and turn out to be a stonefish hiding in the sand (hands off—it's deadly).

Within walking distance of Akumal (about a kilometer), **Yalku Lagoon** is worth a snorkel for the many fish you'll see in a quiet hideaway (at least it used to be a hideaway—today more and more people have discovered this small lagoon). Parrot fish gather here in numbers and make a multicolored glow just below the surface. A current of fresh water flows into the three- to four-meter deep lagoon; the visibility is about five meters. To care for the lagoon and lessen the impact of an increasing number of visitors (30,000 in 1996), a neighborhood organization of Akumal residents (Vecinos de Akumal) has taken on the task of protecting and maintaining the entrance to Yalku. Stone paths are now in place and there is an ecologically friendly toilet on site. Guards are on duty to instruct and ensure that suntan lotions and trash do not contaminate the waters. Plans are for biological studies and monitoring of the lagoon. This is a fine example of how a caring community can safeguard its local treasures and preserve their beauty for future generations. Admission to the lagoon is US$5 adults, US$2.50 children.

Accommodations

The hotels in Akumal proper are mostly on the beach, except for **Las Casitas** and **Canon Suites.** Villas and condos are also available for rent on Half Moon Bay, just a short distance north of Akumal Bay.

The old thatch huts once used by the CEDAM diving club (completely remodeled and nicely furnished) now form the core of **Club Akumal Caribe Villas Maya.** The bungalows (US$103) have been spruced up with private baths, tile floors, fans, small refrigerators, and air-conditioning; even the lighting has been improved for readers. Plenty of water sports are available, along with tennis and basketball courts. Nearby is the Club's three-story **Beachfront Hotel,** which offers 21 rooms (US$125), each with full bath, compact refrigerator, and small porch or balcony. The rooms look out on the Caribbean and the garden area, which has a swimming pool and pool bar. They're also just a few steps from the sea, Lol Ha restaurant, and all the other facilities of Akumal. Note: This hotel really took care of me when I slipped and broke both ankles while trekking south of Akumal. Laura Bush (one of the owners) even brought her family doctor to take a look and administer care and advice.

If you're with young children, ask about the **Children's Activity Center.** This is a baby sitting type service that's fun for the kids. Ask at the Club Akumal Caribe Villas Maya for details about price, age, hours, and activities.

Club Akumal's **Cannon House Condos** lie on a separate beach around the point north of Akumal Bay. One has two bedrooms, two bathrooms, a fully equipped kitchen, and a living room with two sofa beds. Another one is a studio. The Club has four smashing villas on Half Moon Bay. Each villa has an enormous living room, fully equipped kitchen, dining room, one or two upstairs bedrooms, an ocean view, tasteful furnishings, a large terrace with barbecue grill, daily maid service, and air-conditioning; each is a little different and a swimming pool is shared by the four individual villas. For prices, reservations, and information on all of Club Akumal's facilities, including meal and dive packages, contact Akutrame Inc., P.O. Box 13326, El Paso, TX 79913 USA, tel. 915/584-3552 or 800/351-1622, Canada tel. 800/343-1440.

Las Casitas Akumal, at the east end of Akumal Beach, U.S. tel. 800/5-AKUMAL, email: mexvac@aol.com, has airy, furnished condominiums with two bedrooms, two baths, living room, kitchen, and patio. Daily maid service is included. The newer condos are more spacious and cheaper than the older ones. Everything is walking distance to restaurants, a grocery store, a dive shop, the sandy beach, and the beach bar. The bay is right at your front door. Rates range from US$195–US$230. Take a look at the canons mounted along this arm of the bay— they were salvaged by divers.

Food

Akumal regulars know that the old **Lol Ha Restaurant** burned to the ground a while back. Now it has reopened with a stunning new structure yet still with a romantic *palapa* ambience looking out on the sea. You can expect excellent seafood and both Mexican and American specialties; at breakfast time the basket of homemade sweet rolls still comes immediately when you sit down, and the orange juice is still fresh-squeezed. It's open for breakfast and dinner (by candlelight). Ask about the box lunches—the sandwiches are good. Twice a week the restaurant has live entertainment: Wednesday nights you'll find flamenco dancing and Friday the Playa Cultural Dance group performs colorful, regional dances.

Adjacent to Lol Ha is the **Snack Bar Lol Ha,** serving lunch from noon to 5:30 P.M. With the best hamburgers on the beach, really good guacamole, and the tasty Maya treat *tacos cochinita,* this is one lively place most of the day, but es-

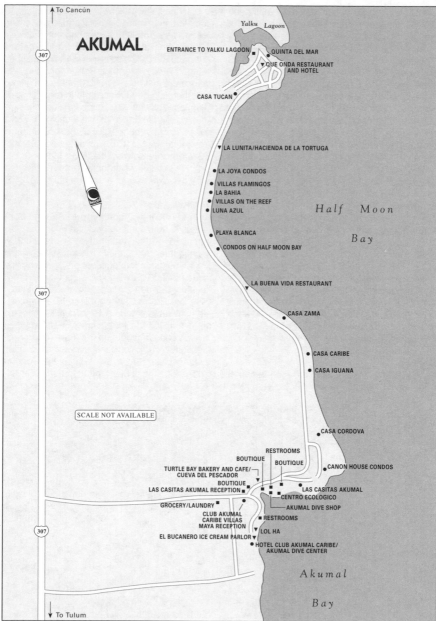

To Cancún

Yalku Lagoon

AKUMAL

307

ENTRANCE TO YALKU LAGOON ● ● QUINTA DEL MAR

▼ QUE ONDA RESTAURANT
AND HOTEL

CASA TUCAN ●

▼ LA LUNITA/HACIENDA DE LA TORTUGA

● LA JOYA CONDOS

● VILLAS FLAMINGOS

● LA BAHIA

● VILLAS ON THE REEF

● LUNA AZUL

Half   Moon

● PLAYA BLANCA

Bay

● CONDOS ON HALF MOON BAY

▼ LA BUENA VIDA RESTAURANT

307

● CASA ZAMA

● CASA CARIBE

● CASA IGUANA

SCALE NOT AVAILABLE

● CASA CORDOVA

RESTROOMS

BOUTIQUE

BOUTIQUE

TURTLE BAY BAKERY AND CAFE/
CUEVA DEL PESCADOR

● CANON HOUSE CONDOS

BOUTIQUE

LAS CASITAS AKUMAL RECEPTION ■

● LAS CASITAS AKUMAL

CENTRO ECOLOGICO

GROCERY/LAUNDRY ■

AKUMAL DIVE SHOP

CLUB AKUMAL
CARIBE VILLAS
MAYA RECEPTION

■ RESTROOMS

▼ LOL HA

307

EL BUCANERO ICE CREAM PARLOR ▼

HOTEL CLUB AKUMAL CARIBE/
AKUMAL DIVE CENTER

Akumal

Bay

To Tulum

pecially so at happy hour (4–5 P.M.—half-price drinks). The bar serves drinks 11 A.M.–11 P.M. Nearby, try the **Lol Ha Pizzeria,** which serves pizza and other tasty Italian specialties.

Kids discover great ice-cream cones at **El Bucanero Ice Cream Parlor.** Just before the main entrance arch to Akumal, a small general store called **Super Chomak** sells a good selection of groceries, cold drinks, liquor, beer, ice, sundries, fresh fruit, vegetables, meat, frozen chicken, and fresh-baked *pan dulce* (get here early in the morning for the baked breads). Attached to the store is a small fast-food restaurant selling tacos, *tortas,* and all kinds of good Mexican food. Open 7 A.M.–9 P.M.

Shopping

Two gift shops, the **Akumal Bazaar** and **Boutique Sayab,** sell a little of everything: typical Maya clothing, leather sandals, shawls, postcards, pottery, original Maya art and reproductions, black coral and silver jewelry, and a good selection of informative books (in English, French, and German) about the Peninsula and the Maya.

In Plaza Ukana (near the arch entrance) you'll find a couple of stores: **La Rosa,** selling women's clothing and accessories, and a **camera store** that also processes film.

Services

Laundry service is available around the corner from Super Chomak—leave your clothes before 9 A.M. for next-day pickup. The closest **bank** is 36 kilometers north at Playa del Carmen. A convenient **gas station** is at the junction of Highway 307 and the Tulum ruins road, 24 kilometers south. Stations are also found in Playa del Carmen and Puerto Morelos. Remember, the gas stations are just that, with no mechanics. However, there's a good **mechanic** in the village of Tulum on Highway 307. He doesn't have a sign but is easy to find (on the left side of the road going south) by the many cars parked under a large metal awning. Prices are reasonable.

Stamps are sold at the Villas Maya lobby, and mail is taken from there to the post office every day except weekends and holidays.

Transportation

By Taxi: Taxis will bring you to Akumal from Cancún or from the ferry docks at Playa del Carmen. Arrange the price before you start. The average fare from Cancún to Akumal is around US$45–55 (up to four passengers; they say this price is controlled by a taxi drivers' union). From Playa del Carmen it's approximately half that.

By Car: From Cancún it's an 80-kilometer, one-hour drive south on Highway 307 to Akumal. From Mérida take Highway 180 east to Cancún and turn south on 307 (both good two-lane highways), which passes the entrance road to Akumal. Car rentals are available in Cancún and Mérida, and at the Capitán Lafitte, Shangri-La, and Puerto Aventuras resorts, all fairly close

Akumal beach

OZ MALLAN

CEDAM AND THE BIRTH OF AKUMAL

In 1958 a small group of Mexican divers was salvaging the *Mantanceros*, a Spanish galleon that sunk off the Palencar reef in 1741. These men, originally Mexican frogmen active during World War II, were first organized in 1948 and called themselves CEDAM (Club de Exploración y Deporte Acuáticos de Mexico—a nonprofit organization). This was not the typical fun-and-games type of dive club; its members were dedicated to the service of country, science, and humanity.

While diving the *Mantanceros* they camped on the beaches of Akumal, two kilometers south of the dive site. This bay, part of an enormous copra plantation owned by Don Argimiro Arguelles, was (and still is) a deserted crescent beach of white sand edged by hundreds of coconut palms. Then the only way in and out of Akumal was by ship. As owner and captain of the ship leased by the divers as a work boat, Don Argimiro spent much time with the group. It was during one of those relaxed evenings around the campfire that Akumal's destiny was sealed. Arguelles sold Pablo Bush (organizer of the charter group of CEDAM) the bay and thousands of acres of coconut palms north and south of Akumal.

Pablo Bush's tropical lagoon had no airstrip nearby, and even if there had been one, there would have been no road to reach it. So for 12 years the creaky vessel, SS *Cozumel,* plied the waters between the island of Cozumel and Akumal, carrying divers, drinking water, and supplies. The only change to the environment was the addition of typical *palapa* huts built for the divers.

The CEDAM organization, in the meantime, was gaining fame and introducing Cozumel and the Yucatán to the diving world. Visiting snorkelers and scuba divers were entranced, and the word soon spread about the exotic Mexican Caribbean coast.

In 1960 the idea of promoting tourism began to circulate, but Quintana Roo was still a territory. Pablo Bush and other movers and shakers began talking

road and airport. The government began listening. But governments move slowly, and it was three governors and two presidents later that the road was finally completed. In the meantime, Cancún was born, Quintana Roo became a state, and finally Akumal bloomed. The beautiful bay continues to grow. Today several hotels, restaurants, dive shops, and many other services make visitors (not only divers) feel welcome.

In 1966, CEDAM International was born and gave new meaning to the initials: Conservation, Ecology, Diving, Archaeology, and Museums. Akumal is the main headquarters for both CEDAM groups in the Caribbean and international symposiums and seminars are still held here for the active divers of the world. CEDAM has had an active part in archaeological exploration in several cenote dives during which early Maya artifacts were retrieved.

In 1968 (before Cancún), the owners of Akumal formed the Club de Yates Akumal Caribe, A.C. (A.C. stands for Civil Association, a nonprofit). They turned over 5,000 acres of land to the government and donated the Cove of Xelha for a national park. The aim was to open the isolated area to tourists, and in so doing jobs became available to the local residents. CEDAM provided housing, food, electricity (added in 1982), running water, a school for the children, and a first-aid station with a trained nurse. Up until this time, the sparse population lived in the shadow of their ancient ancestors—few were ever exposed to modern civilization—and hauled in water from deep wells eight miles inland.

In 1977 a fire destroyed one of the original large *palapa* structures built on the beach; the closest fire protection then was in Cancún. The only communication even today is by shortwave radio. Although it's still rather primitive (who knows for how long), all who visit Akumal fall in love with its slow, rustic way of life and tropical beauty. Houses are springing up, and though many more visitors come today, the wide beaches are still never *too* crowded.

to Akumal. Highway 307 is good, and the side roads (though rough and potholed) are drivable.

By Bus: Local buses frequently pass the Akumal turnoff, going both north and south throughout the day. Ask the driver to drop you off (it's not a regular stop); from the highway it's about one kilometer to town—a hot haul if you're carrying

luggage. The bus from Playa del Carmen to Tulum makes the trip several times each day. Ask the driver what time you must be on the highway to be picked up.

Chichén Itzá Tours
Mayaland Tours offers tours from Akumal to

Quinta del Mar is a beautiful villa on Half Moon Bay

Chichén Itzá. Tour buses pick you up at your hotel and take you to and from the ruins. Lunch is provided at the Mayaland Hotel, where you can also use the swimming pool. Free beer, wine, and soft drinks are served on the bus back to your hotel. The tours run on Monday, Wednesday, and Friday and cost US$66 per person. For information contact Mayaland's Cancún office, tel. 988/7-2450, fax 988/7-2438, U.S. tel. 800/235-4079.

HALF MOON BAY

There are many condos and villas for rent around the bend at Half Moon Bay. It's only about a kilometer from the main entrance to Akumal.

Near the entrance to Yalku Lagoon, **Quinta del Mar,** U.S. tel./fax 415/559-0708; email: exw@earthlink.net, is a striking villa that faces the sea and can accommodate six or eight people. The beautiful white stucco structure is set in a garden with cooling breezes and is decorated with colorful weavings, paintings, and pottery. Daily maid service is provided by Mercedes and her husband, Alejandro, caretakers who live in a small cottage on the property. If you wish, Mercedes and Alejandro will prepare meals (extra fee). The villa has four bedrooms, four and one-half baths, a living room, dining room, fully equipped kitchen, tile floors, and lots of windows to bring in the luxuriant outdoors. A comfortable terrace on the ground floor offers stunning views of the Caribbean, and a path leads to the steps

that go into the sea. Quinta del Mar is within walking distance (one kilometer) of the dining rooms and shops of Akumal Beach. Rental fees vary widely depending on time of year and number of guests but for three bedrooms and three and one-half baths the weekly rate begins at US$1,700. For four bedrooms the rate starts at US$2,200. From there the price goes up depending on season.

Caribbean Fantasy is a group that handles many villas on Half Moon Bay. Contact them at tel. 800/523-6618 or email: caribbfan@aol.com. Rates range from US$140–$3,000 per night. There are many choices.

Food
Around the bend on Half Moon Bay, look for **La Buena Vida Restaurant,** a two-story *palapa* offering a tropical atmosphere. The sandy first-floor bar has swinging seats and a fun happy hour. The upstairs dining room makes a delicious hamburger, and the flan is always firm and tasty with fresh coconut. Also on the menu are turkey and fish dishes. La Buena Vida is on the beach south of Vista del Mar condos and is open 7 A.M.–11 P.M.

Also on Half Moon Bay you'll find **La Lunita,** a fine little dinner house on the ground floor of the Hacienda de la Tortuga condos. It serves good lobster and tasty fish, inside or out. Closed Sunday.

If you're in the mood for Italian, try the neat little **Que Onda** restaurant one block from the entrance to Yalku Lagoon. It's an outdoor café run by *real* Italians preparing *real* Italian food. The lasagna is very tasty, as is the bruschetta, and the pastas are served with light sauces. Prices are not cheap, but everything is well-prepared. Open for dinner.

Actun Chen

On the opposite side of the road to the entrance to Akumal, look for a sign for the Actun Chen nature preserve. Located 16 kilometers north of Tulum, the 985 acres of rainforest that is Actun Chen is relatively virgin. The forest was stormed by chicle hunters at the beginning of the century, but has seen very little traffic since. Now, however, it's open to tourists, who are invited to follow a guide along an established path. For anyone who has never trekked through a nature preserve, this should be fun, especially the caves. There are three caves in the area, one of which is easlily accessible and included on the tour. The stalactites and stalagmites are stunning. A 12-meter deep crystalline cenote lies near the end of the walk. A small zoo and outdoor café are close to the exit.

Actun Chen cave

The paths are lined with trees and bush where small animals scurry and hide. Wild turkeys strut their luminescent gray, turquoise, and red feathers, looking for the dog food put out for them. The caretakers place cut fruit out to feed the few wild monkeys that live in the trees. Don't put your purse down, or the monkeys will swipe it. Roll up your car windows or you may have an extra passenger when you leave. Sometimes the little beggars have to be chained up because they are too friendly. Open 9 A.M.–5 P.M.; the last cave tour begins at 4:30 P.M.

Aventuras Akumal

Just south of Akumal, Aventuras Akumal, tel. 800/552-4550, is an isolated, upscale resort on a breathtaking turquoise bay ringed by a white-sand beach. Modern, comfortable villas, condos, and hotels perch along the water's edge. One of the highlights is **De Rosa Villa**, with condos or villas with one and two bedrooms (all lovely) just steps away from the sea. You can snorkel, literally, in your front yard. The accommodations are upscale and comfortable, with spacious living quarters and modern amenities including a sauna, a rooftop bar, and, in most units, fully equipped kitchens. The resort has a small restaurant. Units are available by the night or week. It's really a must to have a car for this area because there is no public transport to this isolated little peninsula jutting out into the Caribbean.

Owner Tony DaRosa is also an avid diver and offers cenote dive packages as well as conventional scuba and snorkeling trips; all include accommodations.

Hiking the Coast

If you're a hiker or bird-watcher, take the old dirt road that runs parallel to the shoreline from Chemuyil to Xelha, about five kilometers in all. The road edges an old coconut grove now thick with jungle vegetation. Just after dawn, early birds are out in force looking for the proverbial worm or anything else that looks tasty. If at first you don't see them, you'll surely hear them. Look for small, colorful parrots or brilliant yellow orioles; you may even see a long-tailed motmot. If you decide to hike to the mouth of Xelha Park, bring your snorkeling gear, especially if you get there before all the tour buses. Remember: Don't wear sunscreen or bug repellent into the water. There is an admission fee of about US$20; ask about the all-inclusive prices that include lunch and snacks at the park.

PARQUE NACIONAL XELHA

Snorkeling

By midday the body count grows—many, many bodies lying face down in the turquoise sea, floating in the lagoon, plastic air tubes at attention. These are snorkelers at Xelha (shel-HAH) Lagoon, where the warm and clear water invites you to don mask and fins and experience a remarkable undersea world inhabited by rare and beautiful tropical fish.

Xelha is protected by the 250-kilometer-long Honduras Reef, the longest reef in the Western Hemisphere. Open to the sea only through a small opening in the reef, the multifingered lagoon is a safe harbor for many species of fish. Vast schools of inch-long silver stripers sail gracefully in and out of the reefs in large clouds. The rainbow parrot fish spends a lot of time grazing on the reef—that's the crunching sound you often hear when diving or snorkeling. Yellow striped sergeant majors dart here and there, always looking for a handout. The lagoon is strictly off-limits to fishermen.

In addition to the fascinating fish, the lagoon holds other features of interest. Many underwater caverns punctuate the lagoon's edge; in one you'll see the remains of a decaying Maya temple altar. Little islands, narrow waterways, and underwater passages make for marvelous snorkeling amid the beautiful coral formations and fish. This is truly a diver's paradise.

All snorkeling gear—masks, fins, large floating tubes, and underwater cameras—can be rented. Life jackets are loaned to anyone who needs them. Guided water tours are available.

Other Activities

You don't dive or snorkel? Don't despair. Sparkling white sand has been brought in to cover the sharp coral that edges the lagoon, creating a sunbathing beach along part of the shoreline. Sun chairs and showers are available. In addition, small platforms extend over the turquoise sea, providing convenient observation points. You can spend a lazy hour or three in the sun, lying on these platforms and enjoying the myriad colors undulating just below the surface of this natural aquarium.

Another attraction at Xelha is the river adventure. Hop a small tram that takes you to the head of the river about a kilometer inland; from there you can snorkel or tube back to the lagoon, watching plentiful birdlife along the way.

Others might prefer just strolling the grounds; a path leads to *palapa* sunshades and beach chairs on the sand overlooking the open sea. Another area holds a hammock grotto under a shady *palapa*—a perfect place for a snooze.

Certain areas of Xelha are off limits for swimming, but not for looking. The lagoon is surrounded by tropical vegetation and palm trees here and there; the place is swarming with many varieties of birds, butterflies, iguanas, and lizards.

Practicalities

Sunscreen: Despite its commercial aspects, the park is wholly devoted to saving the lagoon's natural treasures. Marine biologists have been working for almost two years to clean up the lagoon and revitalize fish reproduction. Because the lagoon is surrounded by reefs and shoreline, it takes longer for the ocean to wash out the impurities of civilization. The management insists that you do not wear your own tanning lotions; they provide you with their own formula, which is safe for the lagoon's sealife.

Facilities: Five restaurants are scattered about the property; one specializes in seafood, another in Mexican cuisine. You'll also find ice-cream stands and gift shops.

Hours: Xelha is open daily 8 A.M.–6 P.M. Buses from Cancún are available. The best time to explore Xelha and have it all to yourself is right when the gate opens, before the tour buses arrive with loads of cruise-ship passengers.

RUINAS DE LA XELHA

Across the highway and about 200 meters south of Xelha lies a small group of archaeological ruins. Be prepared for a bit of a stroll from the entrance. The structures are mostly unimpressive except for the **Templo de Pajaros** ("Temple of the Birds"). Protected under a *palapa* roof, one wall still shows remnants of paintings and it's possible to make out the tails and outlines of the original art depicting birds and Chac (the Maya rain god). A young boy is always available to guide you around, and is certainly worth a dollar or so.

Continuing along a dirt path farther into the jungle, you'll find an enchanting cenote surrounded by trees covered with bromeliads, orchids, and ferns. A few swallows put on a graceful ballet, swooping and gliding low over the water, stealing a small sip each time. Thick jungle and vines surround the crystal-clear water and it's a perfect place for a swim.

PLAYA TANKAH

Between Xelha and the turnoff to the Tulum ruins is Playa Tankah, where you'll find a cenote called Cenote Tankah. The cenote is located almost at the end of the road behind the Casa Cenote Restaurant Hotel. The Cenote Tankah is one of the deepest along the Caribbean coast. Just offshore, the snorkeling is superb; you'll discover the fresh-water bubbles where the cenote empties into the sea, and you might spy a family of shy manatees (they once visited regularly but now come back only occasionally). The white-sand beach here is a great place to spend the day.

Casa Cenote Restaurant

For many years this was almost the only life on the beach. We have enjoyed great lunch stops here, along with cooling swims in the crisp cenote water and the tepid sea, hoping that the manatees will show up (they never have), and a relaxing chat over a grand plate of nachos with the interesting people who find this little gathering place next to the cenote. It is no longer isolated, from the turnoff road you'll find hotels and private villas, and we hear there's a neat little B&B somewhere along here, but haven't found it yet. Don't hesitate to investigate. Our favorite is still Casa Cenote. An American expat first built and runs the restaurant, which has one of the broad *palapa* roofs in the area. Sunday-afternoon barbecues are a big hit with visitors as well as expats living around Tulum and Akumal. All settle in for the afternoon over heaping plates of great food and good camaraderie. The regular menu features homemade potato chips, nachos with all sorts of toppings, great burgers, and marinated chicken.

Casa Cenote Hotel

And now the hotel! (Actually delightful bungalows.) Look for the Casa Cenote sign between Xelha and Tulum, then follow the dirt road east along the coast until you spot the *palapa*. What a nice place to wake up in the morning—with a sparkling blue sea at your doorstep and coffee delivered to your door (thanks to owners Peggy and Gary). The rooms are cool and comfy with a small sitting area, large beds, tile floors, and Maya glyphs decorate. Colors are relaxing, and a five-speed ceiling fans and ocean breeze keeps it cool. Rates are US$150 including breakfast and dinner or lunch.

ISLA COZUMEL

The Caribbean isle of Cozumel has something of a split personality. The lee (west) side of the island faces a calm sea ideal for swimming, diving, water-skiing, sailboarding, beachcombing, or relaxing in the sun. This is the island's developed side, where the small seaside town of San Miguel de Cozumel (the island's *only* town) concentrates offices, shops, banks, markets, hotels, and restaurants. The island's east coast is another world, relatively devoid of people but dotted with isolated coves and beaches—some with placid water, others with spectacular crashing surf. Clear water and the proximity of at least 20 live reefs make snorkeling a must, even for the neophyte. Between the coasts, the island's overgrown interior holds Maya ruins ripe for exploration and accessible by motorcycle, bike, car, or foot.

The friendly people of Cozumel accept the growing number of visitors who come each year. The island's lively discos and steady influx of divers and cruise ships make it a more upbeat place than Isla Mujeres, yet Cozumel still lacks the jet-set feeling of Cancún—perhaps because it's a real town where fishing and diving flourished long before outsiders arrived. But guess what else has arrived? A traffic light! There goes the town.

Land and Climate

Cozumel is 47 kilometers (29 miles) long, 15 kilometers (nine miles) wide, and lies 19 kilometers (12 miles) offshore across a channel nearly a kilometer deep. The island's high point measures a scant 14 meters (45 feet) above sea level. So far only 4 percent of the island has been developed.

Temperatures are warm year-round, with daytime highs averaging 27° C (81° F). The heaviest rains begin in June and last through October. It's possible for rain to fall almost every day during that time, but the usual afternoon shower is brief and causes minimal interruption of travel or activities. Occasionally, however, the skies can open up and let loose torrents. During wet months, expect high humidity. November through May is generally balmy, with daytime highs averaging 25° C, lower humidity, and an occasional cool evening. But remember, tropical climes can change from mellow to wild and back again very quickly.

Fauna

Iguanas and other lizards skitter through Cozumel's brush. The iguana, more visible than the others because of its size and large population, is often seen sunning atop rocks along the east shore or even in the middle of the warm paved road that parallels the beach, although with the growth of tourism and its obligatory traffic, road-sunning is almost a thing of the past. Though the iguana is said to move slowly, the traveler with a camera has to be lightning fast to capture it on film; once it spots a human, the timid iguana slips quickly into its underground burrow or up the nearest tree. The iguana found in Cozumel is commonly shades of dark green. It can grow up to two meters long, including its black-banded tail, and has a comblike crest of scales down the middle of its back.

Armadillos, deer, small foxes, and coati also call the Cozumel jungle their home.

Marinelife is abundant in the waters surrounding the island. Brilliantly colored fish—from tiny silver bait fish traveling in cloudlike schools, to the grim, thick-lipped grouper—lurk in and around graceful, asymmetrical formations of coral with names like cabbage, fan, and elk. You'll see rainbow-hued parrot fish, yellow-and-black-striped sergeant majors, French angelfish, yellow-tailed damselfish, and shy silver-pink squirrel fish with their big, sensitive-looking eyes. In shallow coves, daring Bermuda grubs come up out of the water to eat from your hand; watch the teeth!

SAN MIGUEL DE COZUMEL

San Miguel has a relaxed, unhurried atmosphere, though it's no longer the sleepy fishing village it once was. The town offers a large selection of restaurants from budget to gourmet, as well as hotels in every price range. Grocery

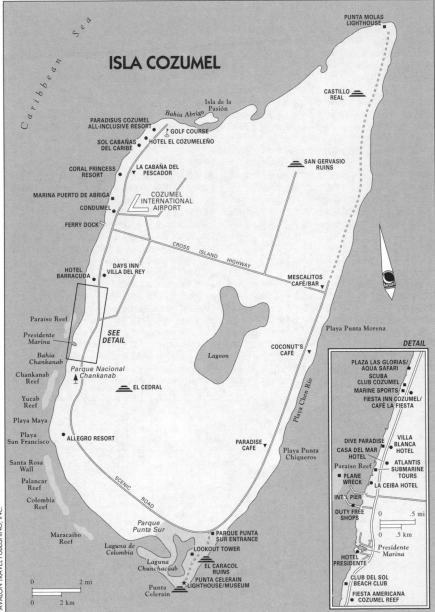

ISLA COZUMEL

Caribbean Sea

PUNTA MOLAS
LIGHTHOUSE

CASTILLO
REAL

Isla de la
Pasión

Bahía Abrigo

PARADISUS COZUMEL
ALL-INCLUSIVE RESORT
GOLF COURSE
HOTEL EL COZUMELEÑO
SOL CABAÑAS
DEL CARIBE

SAN GERVASIO
RUINS

CORAL PRINCESS
RESORT
LA CABAÑA DEL
PESCADOR

MARINA PUERTO DE ABRIGA
CONDUMEL
COZUMEL
INTERNATIONAL
AIRPORT

FERRY DOCK

CROSS ISLAND HIGHWAY

HOTEL
BARRACUDA
DAYS INN
VILLA DEL REY

MESCALITOS
CAFÉ/BAR

Paraíso Reef

Presidente
Marina

Bahía
Chankanab

Playa Punta Morena

SEE
DETAIL

COCONUT'S
CAFÉ

Chankanab
Reef

Parque Nacional
Chankanab

Lagoon

DETAIL

Yucab
Reef

EL CEDRAL

Playa Maya

Playa Chen Río

PLAZA LAS GLORIAS/
AQUA SAFARI
SCUBA
CLUB COZUMEL
MARINE SPORTS
FIESTA INN COZUMEL/
CAFÉ LA FIESTA

Playa
San Francisco

ALLEGRO RESORT

Santa Rosa
Wall

PARADISE
CAFE

DIVE PARADISE
VILLA
BLANCA
HOTEL

Palancar
Reef

Playa Punta
Chiqueros

CASA DEL MAR
HOTEL
ATLANTIS
SUBMARINE
TOURS

Colombia
Reef

Paraíso Reef
PLANE
WRECK
LA CEIBA HOTEL

SCENIC ROAD

INT'L PIER

DUTY FREE
SHOPS

.5 mi

Maracaibo
Reef

Parque
Punta Sur

PARQUE PUNTA
SUR ENTRANCE

.5 km

Laguna de
Colombia

LOOKOUT TOWER

Presidente
Marina

Laguna
Chunchacáab

EL CARACOL
RUINS
PUNTA CELERAIN
LIGHTHOUSE/MUSEUM

Punta
Celerain

HOTEL
PRESIDENTE

CLUB DEL SOL
BEACH CLUB

FIESTA AMERICANA
COZUMEL REEF

0   2 mi

0   2 km

© AVALON TRAVEL PUBLISHING, INC.

stores, trendy curio shops, banks, cyber cafés, a post office, telegraph office, dive shops, and anything else you might need are available. The main street, known either as the *malecón* or Av. Melgar, extends 14 blocks along the waterfront. The main dock is at the foot of Av. Juárez, in the center of town.

Plaza del Sol, the large central plaza, boasts modern civic buildings and imposing statues of the late Mexican president Benito Juárez and a great general named Andreás Quintana Roo. The surrounding streets are closed to vehicular traffic, making the plaza a pleasant place to stroll, shop, and enjoy the island's tranquility. In spring, masses of orange *framboyán* (poinciana) flowers bloom on the surrounding shade trees, under which local townspeople gather for festivals, religious celebrations, and friendly chats. Cafés and gift shops surround the plaza.

ARCHAEOLOGICAL SITES

Cozumel was one of the most important ports of trade for the postclassic Putún Maya seafarers. The island was a major producer of honey and contained the most important pilgrimage destination on the Peninsula's east coast. Women from throughout Mesoamerica traveled to Cozumel to worship at the shrine of Ix Chel ("She of the Rainbow"), goddess of childbirth and medicine. Twenty-four archaeological sites have

been discovered on the island, which was occupied from A.D. 0 on. The island's indigenous population grew significantly after A.D. 800 and reached its peak in 1400.

Most ruins on the island are of the "oratorio" type: small square buildings, low to the ground, with short doors that led early Spaniards to believe the places were once inhabited by dwarfs (a now discredited myth). El Cedral is the exception; though the temple is small, major ceremonies were probably held on this site. Several of the ruins are easily reached by car or motorbike.

El Cedral

Just beyond Playa San Francisco on the main highway leaving town, a paved road takes off to the left and ends 3.5 kilometers (2.1 miles) further at El Cedral. Small and not enormously impressive, this is the oldest Maya structure on the island. Amazingly, it still bears a few traces of the paint and stucco applied by the original Maya artist. But the deterioration indicates that hundreds of years have passed it by. A tree grows from the roof, its thick, exposed roots tangled in and around the stones. Fat iguanas with bold black stripes tracing their midsections guard the deserted, mold-covered site, where sounds of cows blend with the songs of countless birds and the resonant buzz of unseen insects.

Located in what is now a small farm settlement, El Cedral was used as a jail in the 1800s. Right next to it is a rustic, modern-era stucco

Hummingbirds are seen everywhere in the Yucatán bush. The tiny bird was an important part of Maya art and religion.

DIANA LASICH HARPER

church painted vivid green. Go inside and take a look at two crosses draped with finely embroidered lace mantles—a typical mixture of Christianity and ancient belief, which some believe is associated with the Talking Cross cult.

San Gervasio

San Gervasio is a well-preserved and recently reconstructed group of structures. Travel east on Av. Juárez (the cross-island highway), then turn left (north) on a dirt road (look for the San Gervasio sign) and follow it approximately 10 kilometers (six miles) until it dead-ends at the site's entrance. The silence of these antiquities looming in the midst of dense brush, with only birds singing in the tall trees, overwhelms the visitor with an image of what it must have been like centuries ago when only the Maya visited.

Three building groups are visible at San Gervasio; these are connected by trails built along the old Maya causeways. The structures are mainly small temples and shrines built on platforms around a plaza. In the middle of one causeway is the Temple of Ix Chel, a small but well-preserved building that was probably a shrine, although the connection to the goddess is not certain. Archaeologists at San Gervasio have recently found a grave containing 50 skeletons as well as some Spanish beads, leading them to believe that these were victims of a European disease brought by the conquistadors.

San Gervasio is open 8 A.M.–5 P.M.; admission is US$4.50. A snack bar sells cold drinks. Be prepared; guides will offer their services for US$10–12 or more for two people. That's a bit pricey considering you can do just as well in this small area by first getting solid information and a site map at Cozumel's museum (downtown).

AROUND THE ISLAND

Following the scenic road south from San Miguel will take you past many beautiful beaches and sights of interest. The road loops back up the east side of the island and meets the cross-island highway, where a left turn will take you back to San Miguel. The following points of interest are listed in that order: north to south down the west side of the island, then south to north up the east side.

Parque Nacional Chankanab

Chankanab, nine kilometers (5.5 miles) south of San Miguel, is a national park centered around a lagoon containing more than 60 species of marine life, including an assortment of fish, crustaceans, turtles, and coral. The lagoon is shallow, and at one time swimmers could go from the lagoon to Chankanab Bay (on the sea) through underwater tunnels; the tunnels have collapsed and no longer assure safe passage. Swimming in the lagoon is now prohibited.

As you stroll the grounds of the shady park, you'll discover lovely stone Maya reproductions. A small pond—a crystal-clear natural aquarium—is surrounded by a botanical garden of 352 species of tropical and subtropical plants from 22 countries, as well as those endemic to Cozumel.

Also within the national park boundaries, Chankanaab Bay is a popular beach for sunbathers, swimmers, divers, and snorkelers. The snorkeling here is excellent—the bay's showy sea creatures have no fear of humans, and limestone caves near the shoreline make for great exploring. A sunken boat, rusty anchors, coral-crusted cannons, and an antiquated religious statue all make for eerie underwater sightseeing. Adventurous scuba divers can check out the coral reef, close offshore at depths of 2–16 meters. Note that the word Chankanab means "little sea" in Maya, probably because the bay can get surgy.

Park facilities include a floating barge that allows swimmers a place to haul out and catch the rays; a well-equipped dive shop offering rentals, air, sales, and instruction; several gift shops; a snack stand; and two *palapa* restaurants. The park is open daily 9 A.M.–5 P.M. Most people come to spend the day—it's a great place for the kids. Park admission is about US$8.50, which includes use of shade *palapas*, freshwater showers, dressing rooms, and lockers.

Playa Corona

South of the national park, Playa Corona makes a pleasant place to spend an afternoon. Here you'll find a white-sand beach, workout equipment, good swimming and snorkeling, and an outdoor café serving fresh fish and cold *cerveza*.

Playa San Francisco

Continuing south, you'll soon come to Playa San Francisco. This 3.5-kilometer (2.1-mile) stretch of

SAN MIGUEL DE COZUMEL

Caribbean Sea

To Playa del Carmen

MAIN DOCK AND FERRY

GUIDO'S
PANCHO'S BACKYARD/ CINCO SOLES
MUSEO COZUMEL/ MUSEO RESTAURANT
CINEMA COZUMEL
CARLOS'N CHARLIE'S
BAKERY ZERMATT
MEXICANA AIRLINES
SPORTS PAGE
EL PORTAL
HARD ROCK CAFÉ

LAS PALMERAS
THE PLAZA
NIÑOS HEROES MONUMENT
Benito Juarez Park
PLAZA DEL SOL
SAN MIGUEL CHURCH
ARTS AND CRAFTS MARKET
HOTEL MARY CARMEN
CASA DENIS
LA COCINA ECONÓMICA MI CHABELITA
HOTEL EL MARQUÉS
LOS COCOS
LA CUCCINA ITALIANA
ALFALFA'S
PEPE'S GRILL
TELEPHONE OFFICE
LA CHOZA
HOTEL AGUILAR
SAFARI INN/AQUA SAFARI DIVE SHOP
VILLAS LAS ANCLAS
THE WAFFLE HOUSE
DECOMPRESSION CHAMBER
POST OFFICE
CASA MEXICANA

To Hotel Barracuda and Acuario Restaurant

CALLE 10 NORTE
NORTE
CALLE
8 NORTE
10 AVE
5 AVE
CALLE
6 NORTE
NORTE
4 NORTE
15 AVE
CALLE
2 NORTE
NORTE
AVENUE BENITO JUAREZ
20 AVE
CALLE
1 SUR
DR. A. RODADO SALAS
SUR
CALLE
3 SUR
SUR
GRAL. R. MELGAR
5 AVE
CALLE
SUR
5 SUR
10 AVE
SUR
25 AVE
7 SUR
20 AVE
9 SUR
15 AVE
CALLE 11 SUR

SCALE NOT AVAILABLE

© AVALON TRAVEL PUBLISHING, INC.

busy beach has two open-air restaurants, dressing rooms, a bar, gift shops, a volleyball net, wooden chaise lounges, and snorkeling-equipment rental (US$7 per day). During the week it's relatively quiet, but during busy seasons and on weekends it's inundated with tourists, many brought by bus from cruise ships that anchor in the downtown harbor. San Francisco is also a popular Sunday destination for local citizens. Fresh fish and Mexican specialties are served to the accompaniment of loud, live music, romping kids, and chattering adults. The bay is usually filled with dive boats attracted to nearby San Francisco Reef.

Continuing South to Parque Punta Sur

Continuing south, between Playa San Francisco and Punta Sur you'll find several other beach clubs, among them **Playa Sol Beach Club** (snorkel shuttles US$15/hour), **Playa Mac,** and **Punta Francesa,** which lies on a lovely tip of land by the sea and serves a buffet noon–4 P.M.

Along this road you'll come to signs directing you to **Parque Punta Sur** and a turnoff south that meanders to the entrance to the park. Parallel to the coast behind sand dunes, the road eventually ends at **Punta Celerain Lighthouse** (the southernmost tip of Cozumel). All along this road, turnoffs lead east to beautiful isolated beaches.

Part way down the road is El Caracol ruins, where a small, conch-shaped structure has been restored. According to archaeologists, it was built A.D. 1200–1400 as both a ceremonial center and navigational guide; the Maya keeper used smoke and flames in the equivalent of a modern-day lighthouse. One of the docents at the town museum explains how the small openings at the structure's top act as a foghorn when a hurricane wind blows through them. Behind this small building, a dirt path over a sand dune goes to another beach great for swimming, sunbathing, and beachcombing. This might qualify as myth, but an old man told us that when Hurricane Janet hit the coast, the winds set off the "Maya foghorn" and islanders were able to warn the folks living in Playa del Carmen.

Parque Punta Sur Entrance

This natural attraction on the island is called Parque Punta Sur (admission US$10). A colorful bus is available at the entrance to take you through the park, or you can rent bikes and golf carts and discover the park on your own. This southern section of the island has harbored two isolated lagoons, **Laguna de Colombia** and **Laguna Chunchacaab,** that few people ever saw unless they climbed to the top of Punta Cerlerain, the old lighthouse that still does its duty. The park harbors a beautiful array of birds, crocodiles, and other small tropical creatures that still live free. Visitors find a fine little navigation museum, a tall wooden viewing tower where you can study life in the lagoon. The viewing

Chankanab Lagoon

OZ MALLAN

tower offers a spectacular view of the red lagoons that invite birds of every variety to stop along their migrating paths. You never know what you'll see off in the distance; you might even see flamingos. Binoculars are available if you don't have your own.

An **interpretation center** exhibits pictures of the area. Docents that know a lot about the southern point and its wildlife are there to fill you in with historical tidbits and natural-history information. There are restrooms here, electric cart and bike rentals (with motors), and a souvenir shop.

At the café near an improved beach on the east coast, you'll find changing rooms, restrooms, and a parking area for your rental vehicles. The managers of this project have many new attractions planned including another restaurant, a snorkeling center, and, what sounds fascinating, night trips to view nocturnal wildlife with the help of night goggles and boats to cross the lagoons. The preservation of wildlife is said to be the most important part of the park. Time will show us the benefits or the damage to this beautiful 100 hectares of untouched treasures of nature.

Punta Celerain

The lighthouse is four kilometers (2.4 miles) from the main road. From a distance it stands tall, white, and regal and for years a small army base with soldiers on guard wandered the point. A strong surf crashes over an irregular black limestone shore in great clouds of misty surf, spraying tall geysers through jagged blowholes. At one time there was a friendly family at the lighthouse and on Sundays they sold visitors fresh fried fish and beer.

After leaving the park, back on the paved road and turning up the east shore, a large sign warns of the consequences of taking turtle eggs. The turtles are a protected species, and they come to shore here in large numbers during the summer to lay their eggs. You might find a soldier (with tent) stationed by the sign; in addition to guarding against poachers, this coastal watch keeps tabs on the boating activity between Cozumel and the Yucatán coast—illegal drug runners on their boats try to get through here undetected.

Playa Punta Chiqueros
to the Cross-Island Highway

Swimming is idyllic at Playa Punta Chiqueros, a protected cove with crystalline water and a white-sand beach. A small restaurant/bar, the **Paradise Café,** sits on the edge of the lovely crescent bay. You can camp on the beach—with a tent or a vehicle—but there are no facilities. If you're driving an RV, check with the restaurant owners before you park.

A bit farther north, at **Playa Chen Río,** you might find space for a tent and a few camping vehicles on a broad flat area next to the beach (ask).

At the east end of the cross-island highway you'll find the tiny **Mescalitos Café** facing the sea. Expect a couple of daily seafood specials. You can rent a horse here if you like or an ATV (all-terrain vehicle).

North of the Cross-Island Highway

To visit beaches on this part of the east shore, you'll need a motorcycle, ATV, or four-wheel drive for the unpaved sandy road. If you rent a jeep for this trip, make sure the four-wheel drive hasn't been disengaged by the rental agency (almost all agencies do this to conserve gas). Because of its condition, the 24.5-kilometer (14.7-mile) road is seldom used, and few people see these beautiful beaches. If you decide to hike along this coast, you'll make better time in many areas walking on the road rather than on the rocky limestone shore between sandy beaches.

The first two beaches north of the cross-island highway, **Playa Santa Cecilia** and **Playa Bonita,** are good beachcombing spots, and Playa Bonita is a good camping beach (no facilities). Hard-core adventurers can follow trails west from the road to various little-known Maya ruins, abandoned cenotes, and caves; this kind of jungle trek requires carrying all essentials. This is not an easy hike. From the Maya site at **Castillo Real** to the north, there are no more sandy beaches before the lighthouse on Punta Molas. Many ships have sunk along this violent shore, and cannons and anchors are occasionally found to prove the legends.

WATER SPORTS

Snorkeling

Snorkeling and diving are the most popular outdoor activities on Cozumel. If you can swim but haven't tried snorkeling, Cozumel is a great place to begin. It's easy to find a fascinating marine environment close to shore; in many cases you need only step out of your hotel. Along the lee side of the island almost all the beaches are ideal snorkeling sites. If it's your first time, practice with a snorkel and mask while sitting in shallow, calm surf with your face underwater, breathing through the snorkel that protrudes above the surface. (Or use your bathtub to learn before leaving home.) Once you're accustomed to breathing with the tube, the rest is simple. Wear fins—they make it easier to maneuver in the water.

A few easy-to-reach snorkeling sites include Bahía Chankanab, Playa San Francisco, and the beaches at the Hotel Presidente Intercontinental and La Ceiba Hotel (where there's an underwater plane wreck). One other spot that's seldom used any more is north of town at **Isla de la Pasión.** This tiny island in Bahía Abrigo offers secluded beaches and a rocky shoreline good for underwater exploring. It's now a state reserve without cafés, restrooms, or other facilities. Ask at a dive shop for information.

Rental equipment is available at hotels and dive shops. Dive shops also offer boat trips to offshore reefs.

Scuba Diving

If you've always wanted to learn to scuba dive, here's the place to do it. A multitude of dive shops and instructors offer certification, or instruction sufficient for one dive. Make sure to find a qualified instructor; ask for his or her qualifications and accident record, and ask around town for more information about the person (try the harbormaster). It's your life.

Offshore fringing reefs make good simple dives for the neophyte; caves and crevices line the shore, and coral heads rise to within three meters of the surface. Experts can find boat trips geared to wall diving, night diving, and deep diving. In winter, a wetsuit top is suggested; the rest of the year a bathing suit will suffice.

Note: Since 1980, a refuge has protected marine flora and fauna on the west coast of Cozumel from the shore up to and including the Drop-Off (El Cantil). It is illegal to fish or to remove any marine artifacts, including coral, from the area. And all divers should be aware that

Punta Celerain Lighthouse

even touching a delicate coral reef kills it. Take care not to scrape your equipment or push off from the coral with your feet. Do your part to protect and save the area for future generations of divers to enjoy.

DIVE SITES

Plane Wreck

A 40-passenger Convair airliner—engines removed—reposes upside down on the seabed, 100 meters off the La Ceiba Hotel pier. It was purposely sunk in 1977 for the Mexican movie production of *Survive II,* and now it affords schools of fish shady hiding places on the white sandy bottom. The water's clarity allows a clear view of the wreck, as well as multicolored sponges and huge coral heads. A 120-meter trail has been marked with underwater signs pointing out the various types of marine life on La Ceiba reef. The visibility is up to 30 meters, and the average depth is 9–17 meters.

Paraíso Reef

About 200 meters off the beach just south of the International Dock (between the Presidente and the dock), North Paraíso Reef can be reached either by boat or from the beach. It averages 9–17 meters deep and is a site of impressive star and brain corals and sea fans. The south end of the reef, farther offshore, is swarming with sealife. This is a good spot for night diving.

Chankanab Caves and Reef

For easy-access diving, go to Chankanab Lagoon Park; along the bay shore, steps are carved from coral for easy entry. Three large underground caverns here are filled with hundreds of fish of all varieties. Striped grunt, snapper, sergeant majors, and butterfly fish are found in all three caves. Dives average 5–12 meters.

A boat is needed to dive Chankanab Reef (sometimes referred to as Outer Chankanab Reef), several hundred meters offshore south of Laguna Chankanab. Night diving is good here at depths of 8–15 meters, where basket starfish hang out with octopi and jail-striped morays. At the drop-off, stunning coral heads are at a maximum depth of 10 meters; in some spots coral is within three meters of the surface. Coral heads are covered with gorgonian and sea fans; striped grunt and mahogany snapper slowly cruise around the base. This is a good location for snorkelers and beginning divers.

Tormentos Reef

This medium-depth reef features innumerable coral heads in 8–12 meters of water above a sandy bottom. The heads are decorated with fans, gorgonians, and sponges. With little current, you can get excellent photos. Great numbers of invertebrates prowl the sandy bottom; look for flamingo tongue shell, arrow crab, black crinoid, coral shrimp, and sea cucumber. The farthest section of the reef drops to 21.5 meters, where you'll see deep-sea fans, lobsters, and immense groupers.

Yucab Reef

One kilometer south of Punta Tormentos, Yucab Reef is fairly close to shore, shallow (good for beginners), and alive with such beauties as queen angelfish, star and brain corals, sponge, and sea whip. The coral reef is about 120 meters long,

with an average depth of nine meters, and coral heads about three meters from the floor. When there's a current it can be two or three knots.

Tunich Reef

A half-kilometer south of Yucab—directly out from Punta Tunich—this deeper reef (15–24 meters) has about a 1.5-knot current or more, and when it's stronger you could be swept right along to Cuba! The reef is loaded with intricately textured corals, and the water activity attracts manta rays, jewfish, and barracuda. It's a good reef to spot shy moray eels. Just south of here you'll find **Cardona Reef.**

San Francisco Reef

Another popular boat-dive site, San Francisco Reef is one kilometer off Playa San Francisco. The abbreviated (half-kilometer) coral reef runs parallel to shore and is teeming with reef fish of many varieties and brilliant colors. Depths average 17–19 meters.

Santa Rosa Wall

This sensational drop-off, which begins at 22 meters and just keeps going to the black bottom of the Caribbean, really gives you a feeling for the ocean's depth. Strong currents make this a drift dive and a site for experienced divers only (watch your depth gauge). You'll discover tunnels and caves; translucent sponges; stony overhangs; queen, French, and gray angelfish; white trigger fish; and many big groupers.

Paso del Cedral

This flat reef with 22-meter, gardenlike valleys is a good wall dive. In some places the top of the reef begins 15.5 meters from the surface. Sealife includes angelfish, lobster, and thick-lipped grouper.

Palancar Reef

The reef most associated with Cozumel is actually a five-kilometer series of varying coral formations about 1.5 kilometers offshore. Each of these formations offers a different thrill. Some drop off dramatically into winding ravines, deep canyons, passageways, or archways and tunnels with formations 15 meters tall-all teeming with reef life. Depths vary; at the south (deep) end, the top of the reef begins at 27 meters.

Horseshoe, considered by some to be the best diving in the Caribbean, is a series of coral heads forming a horseshoe curve at the top of the drop-off. The visibility of 66–86 meters, plus a solid bronze, four-meter-tall, submerged modernistic sculpture of Christ, make this a dramatic photo area. The statue, created especially for the sea, was sunk on May 3, 1985 with great pomp and ceremony and the presence of Ramón Bravo, a well-known Mexican TV reporter and diver. The much-discussed reef lives up to its good press. Just south of here find **La Francesa Reef.**

Colombia Reef
Several kilometers south of Palancar, Colombia Reef is a deep-dive area, with the top of the reef at 25–30 meters. In addition to undersea canyons and ravines, here the diver may encounter giant sea turtles and huge groupers hiding beneath deep coral overhangs. Water temperature averages 23° C (73° F) in winter and 27° C (81° F) in summer; when the water cools down, you'll see spotted eagle rays here. This reef is best for experienced divers, as there's usually a current. Visibility is 50–66 meters.

Maracaibo Reef
At the island's southern tip, this reef offers an exhilarating experience for the experienced diver. It's considered by most to be the ultimate challenge of all the reefs mentioned. At the deepest section, the top of the wall begins at 37 meters; at the shallow area, 23 meters. Unlike at many other reefs, coral formations here are immense. Be prepared for strong currents and for who-knows-what pelagic species, including shark. Dive boats do not stop here on their regular trips and advance reservations are required for this dive.

Other Good Diving Areas
North of San Miguel, **Barracuda** and **San Juan Reefs** are for experienced divers only—currents can be as fast as six knots. In that kind of current a face mask could be ripped off with the wrong move. It's definitely a specialty dive (somewhat like a roller coaster!). Check with Aqua Safari for more information; reservations are necessary for their trips to these reefs. One of the new favorite dive sites is around an old U.S. mine sweeper 84 feet beneath the surface near Tormentos Reef. The Mexicans have owned it since 1962, and it was sunk in 2000 to create an artificial reef. Check with your divemaster; it takes special training to dive a wreck, and only those who are advanced PADI open-water divers and 15 years old can be trained.

Dive Trips and Lessons
Many of the reef dives mentioned may be arranged through one of the dive shops in town, through the boatmen's co-op, or by some of the hotels that have their own equipment and divemaster. All equipment is provided and sometimes lunch and drinks are provided, too. Shop'

Cozumel's reefs make it a favorite divers' destination.

OZ MALLAN

galleon

around to find an outfit that suits your needs, level of diving experience, and pocketbook (prices vary). Scuba lessons for certification or a resort course for one-day dives are available at most of the same shops. Be sure to check the qualifications and track record of the dive shop and divemaster you choose.

Aqua Safari, Av. Melgar at Av. 5 Norte, U.S./Canada tel. 529/872-0101 or 872-3101, Mexico tel. 987/2-0101, email: dive@aquasafari.com (also in the Plaza Las Glorias hotel, tel. 987/2-3362), enjoys an excellent reputation for safety, experience, good equipment, and happy divers who return year after year. Aqua has its own fleet of boats and offers two-tank morning dives, one-tank afternoon dives, and evening dives; they operate daily except Sunday, Christmas, and New Year's Day. Aqua Safari Dive Shop hours are 8 A.M.–1 P.M. and 4–6:30 P.M.

Other reputable Cozumel dive shops include: **La Ceiba Del Mar Aquatics,** 987/2-0379, located at La Ceiba Hotel and Casa Del Mar Hotel; **Scuba Cozumel,** 987/20853, across the street

from the **Galápagos Dive Club;** and **Dive House,** at the Fiesta Americana, 987/2-1953, which comes highly recommended.

Underwater Photography

The clear waters around Cozumel allow outstanding photographs. Even the little throw-away cameras do a pretty good job.

Dive Safety

Because of the growing influx of divers to Cozumel from all over the world, the small island continues to increase safety services. All reputable shops require divers to show their certification card and state the date of their last dive. If they don't require a card, I'd question their integrity. Some shops require divers who haven't been in the water for a while to go through a checkout dive so divemasters can ascertain their ability.

At affiliated dive shops, US$1 per dive day is added to divers' fees to help support the SSS (Servicios de Seguridad Sub-Acuática). This donation is like having an insurance policy; it entitles the distressed diver to make use of Cozumel's hyperbaric chamber, marine ambulance, and fully trained personnel (each facility offers 24-hour service). All divers are welcome to use these services, but nonparticipants pay regular commercial rates, so inquire about affiliation before choosing a dive shop. The decompression chamber is on Calle 5 Sur near Av. Melgar, tel. 987/2-2387.

FISHING

Cozumel boasts good deep-sea fishing year-round. Red snapper, tuna, barracuda, dolphin, wahoo, bonito, king mackerel, and tarpon are especially plentiful March–July, which is also the high season for marlin and sailfish. You can hire a boat with tackle, bait, and guide for US$125–825, depending on length of excursion, size of boat, number of people, and season. Arrangements can be made at the boatmen's co-op, tel. 987/2-0080, or by contacting Club Náutico de Cozumel at Marina Puerto de Abrigo Banco Playa (Apdo. Postal 341, Cozumel, Quintana Roo 77600, Mexico), tel. 987/2-0118. You can also just visit the marina in mid-afternoon when the boats are returning from the day's fishing trips; talk with boat captains and their customers, choose a boat to your liking, and negotiate the fee on the spot. The main marina is just north of town; a smaller one is by the Presidente Cozumel hotel.

Glass-bottom Boats
Even nondivers can get a close-up view of Cozumel's flamboyant underwater realm on a glass-bottom boat tour. Small boats cruise along the lee side of the coast, and bigger motorized launches travel farther out to the larger reefs. Prices vary accordingly. Ask at your hotel, one of the dive shops, or Fiesta Cozumel, tel. 987/2-0831, whose *Nautilus IV* is the island's newest tour boat. Called a floating submarine, the boat actually has a glass-enclosed area below deck for viewing shallow reefs.

LAND-BASED ACTIVITIES

In the Saddle
Sea Horse Ranch, tel. 987/2-1958, offers horseback expeditions into the Cozumel bush, where you will see off-the-beaten-track Maya ruins and even the Red Cenote. English-speaking guides explain island flora and fauna. Regular tours are offered Monday–Saturday; reservations are necessary.

Golf and Tennis
A new golf course and country club is just about finished as we go to press. So by the time you have this book the course should be filled with duffers and champs. We have no information other than it's a Jack Nicklaus design and will be quite trendy. Let us know how you like it if you find it open.

ACCOMMODATIONS

Downtown Hotels
Under US$50: For 20 years, the Anduze family has been running the fine old **Hotel El Marqués,** Av. 5 Sur on the plaza, tel. 987/2-0677, fax 987/2-0537, a great downtown option. Rooms have eclectic furnishings, air-conditioning, and small in-room refrigerators; the third-floor rooms

have good views. Rates are US$35–45. Los Cocos Restaurant is on the premises.

Hotel Aguilar, Calle 3 Sur (one block from downtown), tel. 987/2-0307, fax 987/2-0769, email: haguilar@cozunet.finned.com-mx, is another oldie still serving the traveler well. The simple rooms (US$34–40) have air-conditioning and fans. There's also a pool. It's three blocks from the plaza. No credit cards are accepted—send your deposit in traveler's checks.

Hotel Mary Carmen, Av. 5 Sur 4, tel. 987/20581, is a pleasant and simple hotel just a stone's throw from the plaza, discos, restaurants, shops, and all other downtown activities. The 28 rooms (US$40) are clean and surround a nicely tended garden.

US$50–100: Hotel Flamingo, on Calle 6 Norte about five blocks north of the *malecón,* tel. 987/2-1264, U.S. tel. 800/806-1601, offers large, clean rooms, some with balconies, and a pleasant Mexican ambience. Rates range from US$59–69. This is a good value. Ask about packages.

A half mile from town, on the waterfront **Hotel Barracuda,** tel. 987/2-0002, fax 987/2-0884, is another old standby. A favorite with divers, the hotel is right on the beach and boasts its own pier, rinse tanks, gear-storage lockers, dive shop (**Dive Paradise**), and restaurant. The 20 simple rooms (US$84) have two double beds, air-conditioning, and balconies. Rent scooters and cars on site.

Villas Las Anclas, Av. 5A Sur 325, tel. 987/2-1955, fax 987/2-1403, is another small and well-priced complex with seven efficiency apartments (US$70 per night). Each has air-conditioning and nice furnishings; the complimentary continental breakfast is delivered to your door (and the coffee is excellent). No credit cards.

Days Inn Villa del Rey, Av. 11 Sur 460, U.S. tel. 800/DAYS-INN, Mexico fax 987/2-1692, is a simple, clean, downtown hotel with 43 air-conditioned rooms (US$55; some have kitchenettes) and a pool. It's four blocks from the ocean and five blocks from the plaza.

Casa Mexicana, on the Malecon next door to the post office, casamexicana@cozumel.net, fax 987/22339, is the new kid downtown. It's a honey, but if you aren't familiar with Cozumel, you need to know there are no nice beaches downtown. But Casa Mexicana is a great hotel

Aqua Safari boats wait for passengers for an all-day dive trip.

OZ MALLAN

facing the ocean. An escalator (yes, on our little island) takes you up to a large lovely lobby where you get checked in. The hotel offers king or double beds, air-conditioning, satellite TV, complimentary full American breakfast, bar, concierge service, elevators (making it handicap friendly), swimming pool, and a complete gym. Rooms with an ocean view have balconies. Rates are US$85–130, depending on time of year and rooms. Up to two children under the age of 12 may stay for free with their parents.

US$100–150: North of town, **Sol Cabañas del Caribe,** Carretera San Juan, Kilometer 4.5, tel. 987/2-0411, fax 987/2-1599, U.S. tel. 800/336-3542, offers nine simple little cabañas in addition to standard hotel rooms. Each unit (US$121) has air-conditioning, simple furnishings, and comfortable beds, and there's a pool. The windsurfing shop at the hotel is operated by one of Mexico's top windsurfing champions and is a great place to learn; kayaks are available for rent as well.

Also on the north side of town is **Coral Princess Resort,** tel. 987/2-3200, fax 987/2-2800, U.S. tel. 800/253-2702, with fully equipped condos overlooking the beach. The 139 rooms (US$139) are quite lovely. Guests may stay on a nonsmoking floor if they prefer. There is a children's program, two pools, and beach volleyball. Rooms have air-conditioning and kitchen facilities (optional).

US$150–200: Fiesta Inn Cozumel, on the Chankanab road at Kilometer 1.7, tel. 987/2-2899, fax 987/2-2154, U.S. tel. 800/FIESTA1,

offers 180 well-decorated rooms (US$168) across the street from the beach. Amenities include a large pool away from the road and a *palapa* on the beach serving drinks and snacks. Room service is available until 11 P.M.. The hotel's Los Arcos dining room serves a breakfast buffet for US$9 and a dinner buffet for US$12.

Plaza Las Glorias, on Chankanab road at Kilometer 1.5, tel. 987/2-2000, fax 987/2-1937, U.S. tel. 800/882-6684, is right on the beach and features an in-house diving service through Aqua Safari Dive Shop. Amenities include air-conditioning, a pool, a private dock for divers, good entry into the ocean for snorkelers, and a fine dining room. The hotel is walking distance to town. Rates start at US$193.

Fiesta Americana Cozumel Reef, just south of town on the Chankanab road (at Kilometer 7.5), U.S. tel. 800/343-7821, Mexico fax 987/2-2688, is one of the island's newer hotels. It sits on the land side of the street, but beach access is simple—a pedestrian bridge leads from the hotel over the road to a beach club, which has a pool, restaurant, dive shop (**Dive House**), and boat dock. Rooms are US$175.

US$200 and up: Hotel Presidente Intercontinental, tel. 987/2-0322, email: cozumel @interconti.com, U.S. tel. 800/327-0200, is probably the island's nicest hotel and sits on one of the best beaches on the San Miguel side. Visitors find a relaxed and jovial atmosphere, 260 air-conditioned rooms, a pool, beautiful grounds and public rooms, and several dining rooms that serve delicious meals with music. Be sure you try

El Caribeno, the open-air *palapa* café overlooking the sea. Rooms (US$220) are well decorated in pastel colors and priced according to location; some are upstairs with a "partial" view of the sea, others have a full view, some have private balconies, and some (the most expensive) offer private patios opening onto the beach. All sea sports are available. Snorkeling is great here and just a few steps from the hotel. Easy car rentals and taxi service.

Hotels for Divers

Most of the hotels in Cozumel encourage their dive clientele, but some hotels go out of their way to accommodate divers. One such hotel is the 12-room **Safari Inn,** downtown on Av. Melgar, above Aqua Safari Dive Shop and across from the Safari boat dock (Apdo. Postal 41, Cozumel, Quintana Roo 77600, Mexico), tel. 987/2-0101, fax 987/2-0661, email: dive @aquasafari.com. The three-story hotel is modern with large rooms and tile floors. However, there is no elevator. Rooms (US$45) are simple and clean and have air-conditioning. Stay here and you'll be just three blocks from downtown. Dive/hotel packages are available.

The **Scuba Club Cozumel,** formerly called the Galápagos Inn, two kilometers south of town, tel. 987/20853, a dedicated divers' hotel, offers comfortable spacious rooms, a great shop, a generous row of hammocks by the beach, and a very good restaurant called **The Fat Grouper** (stop by even if you're not staying here). The club deals only with dive packages and is often full with groups from U.S. dive shops. For information on dive packages contact the dive shop (**Scuba Cozumel**) at the hotel, tel. 800/847-5708. Ask about handicap diving facilities.

La Ceiba Hotel, on the edge of town, U.S. tel. 800/435-3240, Mexico fax 987/2-0065, welcomes divers. A submerged airplane lies just offshore in front of the hotel and is a popular site for shore dives. The hotel offers comfortable rooms, a pool, air-conditioning, and **Del Mar Aquatics,** an on-site dive shop. Room rates are US$148–160.

All-inclusive Resorts

El Cozumeleño, at Playa Santa Pilar, U.S. tel. 800/437-3923, Mexico tel. 987/2-0050, email: hotelcoz@cozumel.czm.com.mx, is a multistory hotel right on the sand, with the blue Caribbean at its feet. The 254 rooms are nicely decorated and have air-conditioning and private balconies. Keeping cool is easy; in addition to the sea, guests have use of two pools, tennis courts, sailboats, and personal watercraft. Deep-sea fishing nearby can be arranged in-house. Dining is a delight on the beautiful sea-view terrace. Rooms are US$125 per person (double occupancy, all-inclusive).

South of Playa San Francisco, **Allegro Resort,** tel. 987/2-3433, fax 987/2-4508, U.S. tel. 800/858-2258, offers rooms in modern, two-story, *palapa*-roofed villas. Everything is included in the daily price—meals, drinks, tax gratuities, tennis, and a host of nonmechanized water sports. Dive packages are available at the dive shop, and great dive spots are just minutes from shore. Guests enjoy all the splash sports, plus Sunfish sailers, pedal boats, and one free scuba lesson in the pool. Daytime and nighttime activities include aerobics, cocktail parties, and theme nights. Town is a US$12 cab ride away. The hotel is often filled with tour groups. Rooms are US$194 for two people.

Paradisus Cozumel All-inclusive Resort, tel. 987/2-0411, fax 987/2-1599, U.S. tel. 800/336-3542, is a five-star hotel at the far north end of the island, about a 15-minute drive from town. Amenities include marble-tile floors, pastel-decorated rooms with private balconies, 24-hour room service, direct-dial phone service, air-conditioning, satellite TVs, mini-bars, tennis, two pools, and a dive shop. Dining is exquisite, with a choice of continental haute cuisine or typical Yucatecan specialties. At this one, all-inclusive *really* includes everything. Double rooms are US$350 per night.

Condos

Condos have not taken over the Cozumel shoreline—at least not yet! One of the finest is the small and intimate **Condumel,** a 20-minute walk or five-minute cab ride north of town (Attn. Sara, Apdo. Postal 142, Cozumel, Quintana Roo 77600, Mexico), tel. 987/2-0892, fax 987/2-0661, U.S. tel. 800/262-4500. Condumel has its own beach and swimming dock where iguanas sunbathe with the visitors. The condos each have air-conditioning, one bedroom with a king-size bed, a folding couch, and a kitchen ready for the cook. A few basic food items, including beer and purified water, are chilling in the fridge in case you don't want to go shopping right away. Owner Bill Horn also manages the Aqua Safari dive shop and will arrange diving trips and equipment. Rates start at US$129 for up to four people.

Bed-and-Breakfasts
Tamarindo, Calle 4 Norte 421 (between Avs. 20 and 25), tel./fax 987/2-6190, email: Tamarind@Cozumel.com.mx, is a pleasant bed-and-breakfast about five blocks from the plaza and four blocks from the ocean. Breakfast is served on the patio; some rooms have air-conditioning, and there's a community kitchen. Rates range from US$36–51.

B&B Caribo, 799 Av. Juárez, U.S. tel. 800/830-5558, is another nice little place away from downtown, about eight blocks from the sea. The house was the former home of a Mexican doctor, and the proprietors—a couple of American expats—have really fixed it up. Some rooms have air-conditioning, some have fans, a couple have kitchens, and a couple share a bathroom. A lovely fountain and colorful flowers contribute to a charming atmosphere, and the breakfast is good. Rates range from US$70–90. Along with everything else, the bed-and-breakfast offers "special" weeks when stays are coupled with seminars by experts on a variety of topics; call for the upcoming program.

Palapas Amaranto, Calle 5 Sur between Avs. 15 and 20, tel. 987/2-3219 (mornings only), email: amaranto@cozumel.com.mx, is a comfortable and colorful bed-and-breakfast. The three thatched-roof bungalows include air-conditioning and fans, and there's a swimming pool. It's 3.5 blocks from Aqua Safari Pier. Rates range from US$45–55 and include breakfast.

Island Camping
Cozumel has no campgrounds with facilities. However, hidden coves and isolated beaches on the island's east side make great primitive campsites. Bring everything needed to camp, including water. Don't expect even a tiny *tienda* at which to buy forgotten items. If you ask the tourist office about beach camping, they'll tell you to get permission from the navy, which occupies the large building south of town (on the ocean side across from the Costa Brava café

and hotel). You can also request permission for camping at **Mescalitos Bar, Balneario Popular,** and **Paradise Café,** all on the east side of the island. None of these places have camping facilities of any kind, but they might let you stay on their property.

FOOD

Cozumel's fast-food stands and restaurants fit all budgets. Seafood is exquisite and fresh, and Yucatecan specialties simply must be tasted! *Camarones con ajo* (shrimp with garlic), *caracol* (conch), and tangy ceviche (fish or conch marinated in lime, vinegar, chopped onions, tomatoes, and cilantro) are all tasty treats. *Huachinango Veracruz* (red snapper cooked with tomatoes, green pepper, onions, and spices) is popular, and snapper is caught off the reef year-round (eat it a few hours after it's caught). Fresh seafood is sold in most cafés.

Inexpensive Cafés
Budget-class **La Cocina Económica Mi Chabelita,** two blocks from the plaza heading inland on Calle 1 Sur to Av. 10 Sur, offers ample servings of *pescado frito* (fried fish) and *carne asada* (grilled meat) for about US$4. **Casa Denis,** the yellow house just up Av. Juárez from the plaza, has a few tables set out by the street and more in a back garden. Have a cold beer and empanadas stuffed with fish for under US$6. **Comida Casera Toñita,** on Rosado Salas, is a great find for its *comida corrida,* the fixed-price afternoon meal that covers both lunch and dinner and fills you up for about US$6.

Prowl around on the back streets away from the sea toward the middle of the island—more and more small cafés are opening up, and prices are usually cheaper than at those near the ocean. **Las Tortugas,** Av. 10 Norte 82, serves good tacos.

El Portal, an open café facing the waterfront, serves tasty family-style food. A sturdy breakfast of bacon, eggs, beans, and toast costs about US$5. Open for breakfast, lunch, and dinner. **Las Palmeras,** at the foot of the pier in the center of town, has been serving good food for many years and is always busy; moderate prices.

Mexican and American Entrees

Once you discover **Los Cocos,** Av. 5 Sur one block from the plaza, you'll probably return frequently. It's open for breakfast and lunch. Cream cheese muffins? Oh yes.

La Misión, Av. Juárez 23, is beloved by hungry divers who devour huge portions of fresh fish, *carne asada,* and fajitas—all prepared in the open kitchen by the front door. **Mr. Papa's,** Av. Melgar at Calle 8 Norte, is another favorite for hearty eaters, especially on the nights they offer the all-you-can-eat barbecued chicken dinners.

For the zany crowd, **Carlos 'n Charlie's,** north of the plaza on Av. Melgar, tel. 987/2-0191, is a lively restaurant specializing in fun. Beer-drinking contests are held nightly. **El Capi Navegante,** on Av. 10 Sur, tel. 987/2-1730, serves good seafood, and you can usually find a coupon for a free margarita in the tourist brochures.

Yearning for an American hamburger and a football game? Go to the **Sports Page,** a video bar/restaurant (usually a good money exchange also) on the corner of Calle 2 Norte and Av. 5, tel. 987/2-1199. Try a taste of "Americana" with hamburgers, steaks, or sandwiches. And if you happen to be in Cozumel in January, rest easy—you'll be able to watch the Super Bowl right here.

Mexican-food lovers pack **La Choza,** on the corner of Av. 10 Sur and Rosado Salas. The simple little café with oilcloth-covered tables, painted cement floor, and Mexican wood furniture is always crowded with returning aficionados. Lately we've been hearing mixed reviews on the food.

In an old building on the waterfront, **Pancho's Backyard,** Av. Melgar 27, continues to offer a gracious atmosphere reminiscent of vintage colonial Mexico. The tableware is *típico* pottery, but guaranteed lead-free. The *carne asada* is tasty, as is the shrimp brochette, served at the table on a unique charbroiler. The jicama salad is served with a delicious orange-and-coriander dressing and is refreshing on a hot summer night.

Casa Denis has expanded onto the Calle 1 Sur pedestrian walk. It offers a great outdoor atmosphere.

Museo Restaurant is a nice little outdoor café on the roof of the Museo Cozumel. It's a pleasant, airy place to sit and enjoy a meal while watching the boats cruise past. And yes, the museum is good as well.

More Expensive Cafés

Pepe's Grill, a half block south of the plaza on Av. 5 Sur, has long been noted for its relaxed atmosphere and sunset view from the nautical-style second-story dining room. If you're in the mood for a good prime rib and salad bar, this is the place. It's open for dinner only, with main courses (à la carte) running US$12 and up. The service is excellent.

Lobster, lobster, and more lobster is what you'll find at **La Cabaña del Pescador,** north of town. Diners choose their lobster at the front counter; then it's weighed and priced accordingly—about US$15–20 for a hefty lobster tail served with bread, potato, and vegetables. There's nothing else on the menu except drinks, and the place is packed in the high season. Recent remodeling has added a little more space. Outside, geese mill about the garden and pond. The restaurant is open for dinner only; full bar, no reservations.

A half kilometer south of town, **Acuario Restaurant,** Av. Melgar at Calle 11 Sur, serves elegant fish and lobster dinners with cocktails. Walls are lined with huge aquariums filled with tropical fish, including a few brightly colored eels. It's open noon–midnight.

Hard Rock Café on Av. Melgar is another trendy choice for fun and food.

Gourmet

For a romantic, candlelight dinner go to **Arrecife** at the Hotel Presidente Intercontinental. The lusciously elegant dining room serves scrumptious lobster, savory beef, immense shrimp, and other delectable entrées in an elegant linen-and-crystal atmosphere. A little costly, but worth it.

Italian

At **La Cuccina Italiana,** on Av. 10 Sur between Rosado Salas and Calle 1, owner Paolo and family offer delicious authentic Italian food and a variety of wines, all at good prices. **Prima Trattoria,** Rosado Salas 109, specializes in northern Italian seafood dishes and handmade pastas served in a charming rooftop garden. **Guido's** (formerly Rolandis), Av. Melgar 22, offers Swiss-Italian specialties and good pizza, lasagna, calzone, and salads, plus beer and great sangria. The outdoor patio/dining room is a pleasant place to be on a balmy Caribbean evening; indoor dining is also available. The name has changed but the food certainly has not.

For Vegetarians
Alfalfa's, on Calle 1 Sur in the garden of the Casa San Miguel bed-and-breakfast, serves breakfast, lunch, and dinner and offers vegetarian dishes and other healthy meals. Try the scrumptious veggie tacos. Open Monday–Saturday 9 A.M.–9 P.M.

Breakfast Time
The Waffle House is on the *malecón,* next door to Aqua Safari Dive Shop. The made-to-order waffles are a real treat and even replace tortillas as the base for the savory *huevos rancheros.* Other breakfast options include eggs, hash browns, and homemade whole wheat toast. The restaurant also serves great cold coffee drinks, tasty pastries, lunch, and excellent linen-napkin dinners with moderate prices.

Coffeehouses and Bakeries
How times have changed! Ten years ago in Cozumel it was hard to find any coffee except instant. Today the town is overrun with fine coffeehouses. The **Coffee Bean,** in Plaza Orbi on Calle 3 Sur, offers gourmet coffees, pastry, and lunch. **Esquisse,** Rosado Salas 200, serves tasty Mexican coffees, hot and cold, and great French pastries. It also holds a Mexican art gallery and a shop with magazines, postcards, posters, and crafts. Between 8 and 11 A.M. it offers two-for-one coffees.

Bakery Zermatt, Calle 4 Norte at Av. 5, serves great Mexican pastry, bread, and pizza by the slice. You'll find another bakery a block north of the plaza at Calle 2 Norte, and a third on the corner of Calle 3 Sur and Av. 10. If you notice the aroma of roasting beans, follow your nose to **Café Caribe,** Av. 10 Sur 215, the original coffee shop in town. It's a great place for a pastry and a basic cuppa joe or a superb cappuccino, Irish coffee, mocha, or other concoction. Open 8 A.M.–noon and 6–9 P.M.

ENTERTAINMENT

Discos are popular in Cozumel; at night the town jumps with lively music. Dancing continues till morning at **Neptuno,** Av. Melgar at Calle 11

Food is performance art at many restaurants.

Sur, and **Scaramouche,** Av. Melgar at Rosado Salas. The **Presidente, Plaza las Glorias, La Celba,** and **Melía** hotels have music at cocktail hour and often during dinner. **Joe's Lobster Pub,** Av. 10 Sur 229, presents live salsa and reggae after 8 P.M. **Carlos 'n Charlie's** is just a fun place to be well into the night.

Special Events
The **Billfish Tournament** is held every year in May, bringing fishing enthusiasts from all over—especially boaters from the United States who cross the Gulf of Mexico to take part in the popular event. **Carnaval,** a movable fiesta usually held in February, is a great party with street parades, dancing, and costumes—all with a tropical flavor. Another popular event is the celebration of the patron saint of San Miguel, held the last week of September.

Cinemas
Cinema Cozumel is on Av. Melgar (the *malecón*) at Calle 4 Norte; **Cine Cecilio Borgues** is on

Av. Juárez at Av. 35 (show time 9 P.M. at both). Sometimes American films are shown with their original soundtracks and Spanish subtitles, but most are Spanish-language films.

Museo de la Isla de Cozumel

The town's small nonprofit museum is on the waterfront north of the plaza in an old building that once housed a turn-of-the-century hotel. Informative exhibits cover island wildlife, coral reefs, and artifacts of historic Cozumel. The museum also offers a bookstore, library, and a pleasant outdoor café overlooking the sea. It's closed on Saturdays. A small admission fee is charged.

The Plaza

On Sunday evenings local citizens and tourists meet in the central plaza. Families—sometimes three generations—gather around the white gazebo to hear Latin rhythms and tunes of the day played by local musicians. A few women still wear the lovely white *huipiles,* while men look crisp and cool in their traditional *guayaberas* and best white hats. Children, dressed as miniatures of their parents, run, play, and chatter in front of the band. It's hard to say who does the best business—the balloon man or the cotton-candy vendor. This is a nice place to spend an evening under the stars, meeting the friendly folk of Cozumel.

SHOPPING

You can buy almost anything you want in Cozumel. Gift shops are scattered all over town. You'll see black coral jewelry, pottery of all kinds, and typical Mexican clothing and shoes. A few trendy fashion houses carry the latest sportswear, T-shirts, and elegant jewelry. Take a look at **Los Cincos Soles,** in the same building as Pancho's Backyard restaurant on Av. Melgar, for handsome tableware and glassware.

Talavera, Av. 5 Sur 141 near the plaza, sells gorgeous hand-painted dishes.

The gift shops of some hotels carry a limited selection of English-language reading material. **La Belle Ondine,** Av. Melgar at Calle 4 Norte, has an unpredictable selection of books

and also sells maps of the coastal area. Several excellent jewelry shops line Av. Melgar; check out the stunning selection of precious and semiprecious gems at **Casablanca** and **Van Cleef.**

INFORMATION AND SERVICES

Tourist Information and Consulates

The tourist office is at Plaza del Sol, second floor, facing the plaza; tel./fax 987/2-0972, and is open Monday–Friday 8:30 A.M.–3 P.M. An information booth in the plaza, tel. 987/2-1498, is an on-again, off-again affair. When open it's a font of information, usually staffed by someone who speaks English. A complete list of hotels in every price bracket is available, along with maps of the island and any general information you might need. The closest U.S. consular office is in Cancún, tel. 988/4-2411.

Money

The four banks in town are all near the main plaza; exchange dollars or traveler's checks 10 A.M.–12:30 P.M. Since the advent of the cruise ships, almost everyone in town will accept dollars. But there have been complaints that cruise-ship passengers often are taken advantage of with the exchange; know your rates and count your money.

Communication

The Calling Station, Av. Melgar 27, corner of Calle 3 Sur, tel. 987/2-1417, offers good services. Come here to make long-distance calls in private air-conditioned booths, send faxes, or rent videos, VCRs, or video cameras. The long-distance phone office is on Calle 1 on the south side of the plaza; open 8 A.M.–1 P.M. and 4–9 P.M. Several new Ladatel phone booths are in town near the plaza; dial 09 to place collect calls with an international operator. Long-distance calls can be made from many hotels as well. Calling collect will save you a good part of the added tax. Don't use the phones that say you can dial direct to the United States because they can be as high as US$30 to start with. The **post office** is on Melgar, close to Calle 7, and is open Monday–Friday 9 A.M.–1 P.M. and 3–6 P.M. The **telegraph office** is in the same building, tel. 987/2-0106 or 2-0056, and is open Monday–Friday 9 A.M.–8:30 P.M., Saturday–Sunday 9 A.M.–1 P.M.

Laundromats

Lavandería Mañana, Av. 11 #101, tel. 987/2-0630, charges by the kilo; open Monday–Saturday 7 A.M.–8 P.M., usually one-day service. Pickup service on request. A self-serve laundry, **Margarita Laundromat,** is at Av. 20 #285, tel. 987/2-2865. **Express Laundry,** on Av. Salas between Avenidas 5 and 10 Sur, tel. 987/2-2932, has self-service machines and dry-cleaning service.

Medical Services and Pharmacies

In the event of a medical emergency, contact your hotel receptionist for an English-speaking doctor. **Hospital y Centro de Salud,** Av. Circunvalación, tel. 987/2-1081, is a small clinic with a doctor on duty and is open 24 hours a day. The **Medical Specialties Center of Cozumel,** Av. 20 Norte 425, tel. 987/2-1419, has a 24-hour clinic and access to air ambulance services. Pharmacies include **Los Portales,** on Calle 11 Sur, tel. 987/2-0741; **Farmacia Joaquín,** on the plaza in front of the clock tower, tel. 987/2-0125, open 9 A.M.–1 P.M. and 5–9 P.M.; and another in Centro Comercial on the north side of the plaza. If still in need of help, call the U.S. consular office in Cancún, tel. 988/4-2411. Three dentists are listed in Cozumel's Blue Guide: Z. Mariles, tel. 987/2-0507; T. Hernández, tel. 987/2-0656; and Escartín, tel. 987/2-0385.

GETTING THERE

By Ferry

Passenger ferries come and go to Playa del Carmen from the downtown dock in San Miguel. Two types travel between Playa del Carmen and Cozumel. The faster **MV *Mexico,*** is air-conditioned and makes the trip in about 30 minutes; fare is about US$7.50 per person, one way. The slower open-air boats take about 45 minutes; fare is less. Between the two, there is a ferry departing just about every hour. The earliest leaves Cozumel and Playa at 4 A.M. The last ferry leaves Playa at 11 P.M. and Cozumel at 10 P.M. Check the schedules posted at the ferry pier.

Car ferries use the international pier across from the Fiesta Americana Sol Caribe Hotel, where cruise ships dock. Arrive a few hours early and be prepared with exact change and your car license number when you approach the ticket window or you may lose your place in line and miss the boat. The car ferry departs once a day for Puerto Morelos on the mainland. Check the schedule at the international pier or call 987/2-0950.

By Air

Air travel from various points on the Yucatán Peninsula is becoming more common. Close by there are flights from Mérida and Cancún to

Cozumel's Museum and rooftop restaurant

Cozumel (Aerocaribe). Right now it's possible to fly between Cozumel and Playa del Carmen on AeroFerinco (call toll free in Mexico, 800/magical; or call 987/3-0636) in about 10 minutes. The fare is US$15 one way. You must contact the airline the day before. They don't have a regular schedule, although we were told that the plane usually flies at 1 P.M. (Check with your hotel tour desk.) International flights arrive from the United States via several airlines. Remember that schedules change with the season. Airlines serving Cozumel include Aerocaribe/Aerocozumel, tel. 987/2-3456; American Airlines, U.S. tel. 800/433-7300; Continental, tel. 987/2-0847; and Mexicana, tel. 987/2-2945. Charter flights are available from major U.S. gateways in the high season; ask your travel agent for information.

Cozumel International Airport is approximately three kilometers from downtown San Miguel. Taxis and minibuses meet incoming planes. Taxi fare to town is US$8 per person in a *colectivo* that will take you to your hotel; it's more for the return trip in a private taxi. When departing, an airport-use tax (about US$12) is collected. This tax applies to all international Mexican airports, so hang onto US$12 for each international airport city where you plan to stay 24 hours or more. Although there's a *casa de cambio* (money-changer) at the airport, change your money in town, as banks and some shops (when you're making a purchase) give the best exchange rates, with hotels notoriously giving the worst. Cozumel International Airport has many small duty-free shops with a good selection of gifts. Reading materials, especially English-language pictorial books about the area, are found here and there. The airport has a dining room upstairs, and on the ground level there's a snack bar, but they're usually not open before the earliest flight departs.

Travel Information in the United States
For a knowledgeable travel agent, call **Four Seasons Travel** from anywhere in the United States (tel. 800/555-8842). They specialize in Mexico's Caribbean coast and will work with you to create a vacation that best suits your needs, whether it's to Cozumel, Cancún, Isla Mujeres, or low-key resorts along the entire Quintana Roo coast and Yucatán Peninsula.

GETTING AROUND

Getting around on the island is easy; it's flat and the roads are maintained. It's easiest in the city of San Miguel. The roads are laid out in a grid pattern with the even-numbered *calles* to the north of the town plaza, odd-numbered *calles* to the south; numbered *avenidas* run parallel to the coast. There is now a public bus running along Avenida Melgar and to the hotels north and south of town on the leeward side. The schedule was erratic on our last visit; ask about it at your hotel. All of downtown San Miguel is easily reached on foot.

Several transportation options exist for exploring the outlying areas of the island on your own—which everyone should do! Escorted tours around the island are available through any travel agency or your hotel. Avenida Juárez begins in downtown San Miguel at the dock and cuts across the middle of the island (16 kilometers), then circles the south end. The road around the north end of the island isn't paved. Walking the flat terrain is easy, but distances are long.

By Bicycle or Motorbike
The 70 kilometers of paved island roads are easily explored by bicycle, available for about US$15 per day at most hotels and at **Ciclissimo,** tel. 987/2-1593.

Golf carts, mopeds and 125cc motorcycles are the most popular vehicles on the island, but some risks are involved. Helmets are now required by law on the island (a definite improvement that helps prevent serious injury). Be conscious of the vehicles around and behind you when on a motorbike, and get out of the way of impatient taxi drivers. Mopeds and motorcycles are available for rent at most hotels and at rental shops all over town; cart rates are around US$35–40 per day. Remember to bargain; at certain times of the year you'll get a discount.

By Car
Cozumel has two stations. The first is five blocks from downtown at Avenida Juárez and Avenida 30 and is open daily 7 A.M.–midnight. The second is on the same street but on the opposite side. Cozumel has government-sponsored Green Angel motorist assistance. If your car

should break down on the coastal highway, stay with it until they come by with gas, parts, or whatever help you need to get you on your way. The Green Angels cruise only on paved roads and only during daylight hours.

Car rentals run approximately US$45–80 daily and are available at: AutoRent at La Ceiba Hotel, tel. 987/2-0844; Budget at the airport, tel. 987/2-0903; Hertz at the airport, tel. 987/2-1009; Rentador Cozumel, Av. 10 Sur, tel. 987/2-1120; and National Inter Rent, Av. Juárez 10, tel. 987/2-1515.

By Taxi

Taxis will take you anywhere on the island and are available by the day; agree on a price before your tour begins. Expect to pay in the neighborhood of US$60 for four hours. Traveling with a local cabbie is often a real bonus since drivers know the island and its hidden corners better than most guidebooks. Remember, when the cruise ships arrive, many of the taxis are busy with passengers at the ferry pier and the international pier, leaving the rest of the visitors high and dry. Ask at your hotel for ship times if possible and plan your movements around it. The same goes for the larger shopping centers; they are jammed when the ships are in port.

For taxi service it's usually a matter of standing on the sidewalk and waving your arm, or waiting on Avenida Melgar at the foot of the downtown dock—taxis queue along the sidewalk on the waterfront. The taxi office is on Calle 2 Norte, tel. 987/2-0236 or 2-0041, and any hotel will call a taxi.

KATHY ESCOVEDO SANDERS

TULUM AND THE SOUTHERN CARIBBEAN COAST

TULUM ARCHAEOLOGICAL ZONE

Seven kilometers south of Akumal on Highway 307, Tulum is one of Mexico's best-known archaeological sites, largely due to its seaside location. Perched on a cliff 12 meters above the sea, Tulum was part of a series of Maya forts, towns, watchtowers, and shrines established along the coast as far south as Chetumal and north past Cancún. Measuring 380 by 165 meters, it's the largest fortified Maya site on the Quintana Roo coast, though it's small compared to other archaeological zones. Tulum means "Wall" in Mayan; the site is enclosed by a sturdy stone wall three to five meters high and several meters thick. Within its confines, 60 well-preserved structures reveal an impressive history.

History

Originally called Zama ("Sunrise"), the site was occupied from A.D. 1200 on, when Mayapán was the major power and this part of Quintana Roo was the province of Ecab. Many of Tulum's buildings—none especially elegant—show late Chichén Itzá, Mayapán, and Mixtec influences.

The Spanish got their first view of this noble, then-brightly-colored fortress when Juan de Grijalva's expedition sailed past the Quintana Roo coast in 1518. This was the Spaniards' first encounter with the Indians on the new continent, and according to ships' logs, the image was awe-inspiring. One notable comment in the log of the Grijalva expedition mentions seeing "a village so large, that Seville would not have appeared larger or better."

Tulum evidently outlasted the conquest; the Temple of the Frescoes contains several fine wall paintings, one of which portrays a rain god astride a four-legged animal that is almost certainly a horse. Horses only arrived with the Spanish.

In 1850 Tulum was inhabited by a group of Maya known as the Chan Santa Cruz, members of a "Talking Cross" cult. The Spanish had taught the Indians Catholic rituals, many reminiscent of Maya ceremonies; even the cross reminded the Maya of their tree of life. They believed that the gods spoke to the Maya priests through idols.

In order to manipulate the Indians, a clever revolutionary half-caste, José María Barrera, used an Indian ventriloquist, Manuel Nahual, to speak through the cross. At a cross in a forest shrine called Chan, near what is now known as Felipe Carrillo Puerto, a voice from the cross urged the Indians to take up arms against the Mexicans once again. Bewildered, impressed, and never doubting, they accepted the curious occurrence almost immediately. The original cross was replaced with three crosses that continued to "instruct" the guileless Indians from the holy, highly guarded site.

The political-religious Chan Santa Cruz group grew quickly and ruled Quintana Roo efficiently. These well-armed, jungle-wise Indians successfully kept the Mexican government out of the territory for 50 years. Even the British government in British Honduras (now known as Belize) treated this group with respect. Around 1895 the Indians requested that the Territory of Quintana Roo be annexed by British Honduras, but the Mexican government flatly refused and sent in a new expeditionary force to try once again to reclaim Quintana Roo.

The Mexican army was doomed from the outset. They fought not only armed and elusive Indians but constant attacks of malaria and the jungle itself. The small army managed to fight its way into the Indian capital of Chan Santa Cruz, where they were trapped for a year. The standoff continued until the Mexican Revolution in 1911, when President Porfirio Díaz resigned.

Four years later the Mexican army gave up and the capital was returned to the Indians, who continued to rule Quintana Roo as an independent state—an embarrassment and ever-present thorn in the side of the broadening Mexican Republic. This small, determined group of Indians managed to keep their independence and culture intact while the rest of the world proceeded into the 20th century. But life in the jungle was tough, and with famine, a measles epidemic, malaria, and 90 years of fighting, the Chan Santa Cruz population was reduced to 10,000. Weary, in 1935 they decided to quit the fight and were accorded the recognition given to a respected adversary. When their elderly leaders signed a peace treaty, most of the Chan Santa Cruz agreed to Mexican rule. This was one of the longest wars in the Americas.

One of the few pure Chan Indian villages left in 1935 was Tulum, and today many residents are descendants of these independent people. Even after signing the treaty, the Indians still maintained control of the area and outsiders were highly discouraged from traveling through. They say a skeleton imbedded in the cement at the base of one of the temples at Tulum is the remains of an uninvited archaeologist—a warning to other would-be intruders.

All of this has changed. With foresight, the Mexican government in the 1960s recognized the beautiful Quintana Roo coast as a potential tourist draw, and the new state entered the 20th century. The advent of roads and airports has paved the way for the rest of the world to visit the unique ruins of Tulum—the most visited of all the Maya ruins.

The Structures

Tulum is made up of mostly small, ornate structures with stuccoed gargoyle faces carved onto their corners. In the **Temple of Frescoes,** looking through a metal grate you'll see a fresco that still bears a trace of color from the ancient artist. Archaeologically, this is the most interesting building on the site. The original parts of the building were constructed around 1450 during the late postclassic period, and as is the case with so many Maya structures, it was added-to over the years.

Across the compound, a small *palapa* roof protects the carved **Descending God.** This winged creature is pictured upside down and is thought by some historians to be the God of the Setting Sun. Others interpret the carving as representing the bee; honey is a commodity almost

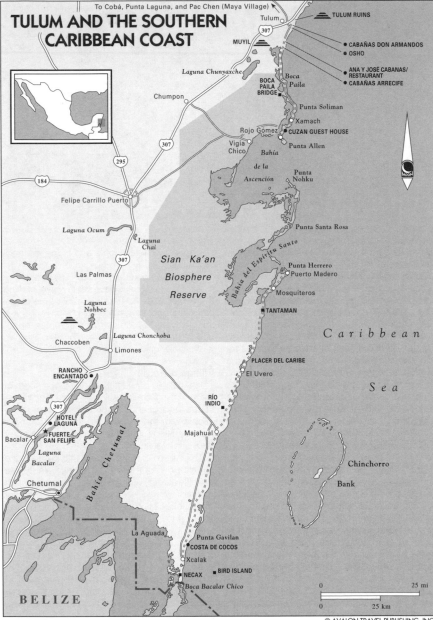

TULUM AND THE SOUTHERN CARIBBEAN COAST

To Cobá, Punta Laguna, and Pac Chen (Maya Village)

Tulum

307

TULUM RUINS

MUYIL

CABAÑAS DON ARMANDOS

OSHO

Laguna Chunyaxche

Boca
Paila

ANA Y JOSÉ CABANAS/
RESTAURANT

CABAÑAS ARRECIFE

BOCA
PAILA
BRIDGE

Chumpon

307

Punta Soliman

Xamach

Rojo Gómez

CUZAN GUEST HOUSE

Vigia
Chico

Bahía
de la
Ascención

Punta Allen

Punta
Nohku

295

184

Felipe Carrillo Puerto

Punta Santa Rosa

Laguna Ocum

Laguna
Chai

Sian Ka'an

Bahía del Espíritu Santo

Punta Herrero

Puerto Madero

307

Biosphere

Reserve

Las Palmas

Mosquiteros

Laguna
Nohbec

TANTAMAN

Caribbean

Chaccoben

Laguna Chonchoba

Limones

Sea

RANCHO
ENCANTADO

PLACER DEL CARIBE

El Uvero

307

HOTEL
LAGUNA

RÍO
INDIO

FUERTE
SAN FELIPE

Bacalar

Laguna
Bacalar

Majahual

Chinchorro

Chetumal

Bahía Chetumal

Bank

La Aguada

Punta Gavilan

COSTA DE COCOS

Xcalak

NECAX

BIRD ISLAND

Boca Bacalar Chico

BELIZE

| 0 | | 25 mi |
| 0 | | 25 km |

© AVALON TRAVEL PUBLISHING, INC.

El Castillo, Tulum

OZ MALLAN

as revered on the Peninsula as maize. Visitors are no longer allowed to climb this ruin to view the carvings.

El Castillo is the site's most impressive structure; the large pyramid stands on the edge of a 12-meter limestone cliff overlooking the sea. The building, in the center of the wall on the east side, was constructed in three different phases. A wide staircase leads to a two-chamber temple at the top; visitors are no longer allowed to climb this stairway, but the view from the hill on which the Castillo stands encompasses the sea, the surrounding jungle (with an occasional stone ruin poking through the tight brush), and scattered clearings where small farms are sprouting up.

Entrance and Visitor's Center

Along with a large parking lot, the new Tulum Visitor's Center houses restaurants, restrooms, a museum, and a bookstore. There's also a ticket office for the Inter-Playa bus, and sometimes there's music. Sometimes the *Voladores* (the native pole flyers) put on their show; and the Inter Playa bus brings visitors to Tulum all day long. The bus depart from Cancún and Playa del Carmen starting at 7:30 A.M.; the last bus leaves Tulum on the return trip at 4:40 P.M., (the site closes at 5 P.M.).

At the entrance, you catch a shuttle to the ruins (US$1.50 roundtrip), thereby avoiding the 10-minute walk, or hire a guide from the Licensed

Guides' Organization. The guides cost about US$25–30 for four people and come well recommended.

The site is open daily 8 A.M.–5 P.M. At 8 A.M., most of the tour buses have yet to arrive, making the cooler early hours a desirable time to explore and photograph the aged structures. Admission is US$3.50 per person (plus about US$5–10 to bring in your camcorder. Parking is available for US$1.50.

Village of Tulum

Tulum pueblo is on Highway 307, just south of the turnoff to the archaeological zone. The village has always been the home of stalwart Maya people with the courage to preserve their ancient traditions; today they've chosen to enter the world of tourism.

The stretch of Highway 307 that parallels the pueblo now has a row of glaring streetlights down its middle, while its shoulders are crowded with storefronts. Restaurants and open-air gift shops selling Mexican handicrafts are multiplying, and food stores now have refrigerators and freezers. Many small markets, fruit stands, trinket shops, and *loncherías* line the highway. Charlie's is a good place to stop for lunch. A plaza and kiosk have been built a bit north of the traditional center but seem barren most of the time. Dirt roads extend ever farther into the jungle as additional humble homes are built to house workers for the nearby resorts.

Accommodations: A few little hotels have gone up along the roadway just past the Tulum archaeological sites; however, most of the Tulum-area accommodations and campgrounds are in the Tulum Archaeological Hotel Zone, which is at the north end of Boca Paila/Punta Allen Road, a few kilometers south of the ruins (see "Boca Paila/Punta Allen Road," below).

A budget-priced hotel is at the intersection of Highway 307 and the old Tulum access road (just north of the new entrance), a 10-minute walk from the ruins. Nearby, the **Hotel Acuario,** tel. 984/5-1181, Cancún tel. 988/6-5106, is newer and again, pretty simple. Most of the 27 rooms have air-conditioning. There's also a pool, but often it's not filled. Some rooms are large enough for six people (US$25). This hotel can get really noisy and busy with large tour buses stopping in the parking lot. Car rentals and restaurant are on the premises.

BOCA PAILA/PUNTA ALLEN ROAD

This road intersects Highway 307 across from the Cobá turnoff and in three kilometers comes to a T intersection. Here a cluster of signs marks the area on either side of the intersection as the **Tulum Archaeological Hotel Zone.** If you turn left (north) you'll find a few hotels and campgrounds fairly close to the ruins. If you turn right you can follow this road (Boca Paila)

all the way to Punta Allen, past a string of bohemian-style cabañas.

If you're planning to drive south to Punta Allen on Boca Paila Road, make sure your gas tank is full. If necessary go back to Highway 307 and fill your gas tank at the Tulum Pemex station since there's not another one to be found on the 57-kilometer coastal road. Start out early in the morning so that if Punta Allen's village **Rojo Gómez** is not for you, you'll have time to go back. It takes about three hours to reach Punta Allen from Tulum. The challenging road passes through Sian Ka'an Biosphere Reserve, an enormous nature reserve. At the end of the peninsula you'll come to Rojo Gómez, often called Punta Allen, a tiny fishing village. (In a pinch you can buy a little drum of gas in Rojo Gómez; ask at Socorro's Store.)

This route holds few attractions for tourists looking for glitz. But explorers, naturalists, bird watchers, artists, snorkelers, scuba divers, kayakers, and fishermen love the beautiful beaches, blue-green sea, humble accommodations, bird-filled wetlands and islets, and the mysterious canals where the Maya left their mark. Pilgrims will revel in the area's isolation and lack of commercialism. If they ever *really* pave and fix this road, that will be the end of this natural desert-island atmosphere!

Though the first part of the Boca Paila Road—where many beachside hotels are located—is paved and smooth, don't be fooled. It soon be-

Tulum

OZ MALLAN

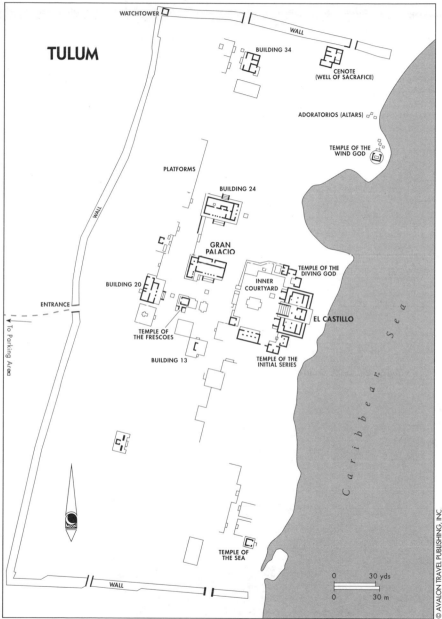

TULUM

WATCHTOWER

WALL

BUILDING 34

CENOTE
(WELL OF SACRIFICE)

ADORATORIOS (ALTARS)

TEMPLE OF THE
WIND GOD

PLATFORMS

BUILDING 24

GRAN
PALACIO

TEMPLE OF THE
DIVING GOD

INNER
COURTYARD

BUILDING 20

EL CASTILLO

ENTRANCE

To Parking Area

TEMPLE OF
THE FRESCOES

BUILDING 13

TEMPLE OF THE
INITIAL SERIES

WALL

C a r i b b e a n   S e a

MOON

TEMPLE OF
THE SEA

WALL

0   30 yds

0   30 m

© AVALON TRAVEL PUBLISHING, INC

comes potholed, ridged, and rugged even before you pass the last hotels. Even though it's slow-going, bumpy, and uncomfortable, any vehicle can handle this road when it's not raining. Four-wheel drive may be necessary if the rains have been particularly heavy.

Note: RVs are not permitted on the road.

Tulum Hotel Zone and South

If you turn north at the T intersection, you'll come across **Cabanas Don Armando,** a beach spread with small rooms, some with shared toilet facilities, others with private bathrooms, a restaurant, and a wide beach often frequented by topless Europeans. Rooms with a bathroom are US$30. It's simple and very economical, but the beach and sea are worth a million. It's run by a large and friendly Mexican family that we have watched grow up over the years. Camping with your own gear is about US$4 per person. The large restaurant serves great Mexican/Yucatecan food, and is also a gathering place for beach-goers.

Also north from this intersection you'll find two popular, usually full combination cabaña/campgrounds. **Santa Fe** and **El Mirador** sit side by side on the beach immediately south of the Tulum ruins. Bring drinking water, bug repellent, and mosquito netting. If you're camping it helps to have a tent; when the wind blows it gets mighty gritty on this beach. The Santa Fe has a cafeteria, and its popular **Bar Marley** is reggae central.

El Mirador, tel./fax 987/1-2092, now offers 30 rooms. Some, like the sand-floored hammock cabaña, are tiny and cheap (US$11). A cabaña with a real floor and two beds is US$22 (half that in the summer). Toilets and showers are shared, except in the *suite,* which accommodates four with two beds and three hammocks (US$150). A simple, pleasant sit-down restaurant up some steps offers diners a view of the sand and Caribbean Sea. There's also a nearby dive shop, and a reef lies just offshore.

South of the T intersection more simple cabañas and basic hotels line the beach. In the past these places were much beloved by travelers seeking seclusion and tranquility, but today the seclusion is almost nonexistent. It's more like a funky little beach town with a wonderful carefree atmosphere. There is no electricity here,

so most people depend on gas lanterns or small generators for at least part of the day. (Although there was power here for a while, it was knocked out by a hurricane.) Until power is returned, visitors must rely on the night sea breezes to keep cool in their rooms. Just about no one accepts credit cards. Some sell bottled water (water from all other sources here must be boiled or otherwise purified). There is a market, a public phone, small eat-abouts, and a great feeling of mutual adventuring. And by the way, if you think isolation means "cheap," think again—a few places are true bargains, but prices are escalating.

Another good place to stay is **Hotel Piedra Escondida,** tel./fax 987/1-2217, a small resort right on the beach offering eight clean rooms in two-story cabañas. It's simple but pleasant—some even say dreamy—with a full-service bar and restaurant on the premises and hot and cold water (US$90, cash only).

Hotel La Perla, tel. 987/1-2382, Quebec tel. 450/434 3717, email: laperlatulum@hotmail.com, has great beach access. It boasts eight rooms, each with white-tile bathrooms and showers, hot water, and generator-powered electricity 5–11 P.M. (US$65). A bar and restaurant are on the premises.

In the same area, rustic **Zamas,** U.S. tel. 415/387-9806 or 800/538-6802, email: zamas @compuserve.com, is a low-key, thatched-hut resort developed by friendly Americans. Five kilometers south of Tulum, the 15 thatched rooms have electricity for lights, but no other appliances. Rooms are on both sides of the road, which means some are not right on the sea, but close (garden view, US$80; beachfront, US$105). In the middle of nowhere this tiny tropical restaurant **Zamas,** formerly called Que Fresca, has an authentic stone pizza oven, and the pizza and gnocchi are great. The restaurant and bar are open 7:30 A.M.–9:30 P.M..

Nohoch Tunich has been around for decades, even when there was little else around, but today it is bigger and better than ever, with 18 rooms. Still rustic, the simple resort is just what a lot of people want. The rooms are stucco and thatch (except for the cabañas, which are all thatch), and beds are netted to protect against little flying critters. Prices vary depending on what you want, but range from US$20–25 at the low end, to a cabaña with a private bathroom for

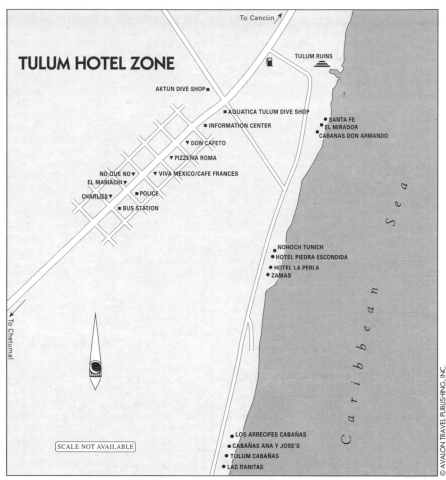

TULUM HOTEL ZONE

To Cancún ↗

TULUM RUINS

AKTUN DIVE SHOP ■

■ AQUATICA TULUM DIVE SHOP
■ INFORMATION CENTER

● SANTA FE
● EL MIRADOR
● CABANAS DON ARMANDO

▼ DON CAFETO

▼ PIZZERIA ROMA

NO QUE NO ▼   ▼ VIVA MEXICO/CAFE FRANCES
EL MARIACHI ▼

CHARLIES ▼   ■ POLICE

■ BUS STATION

● NOHOCH TUNICH
● HOTEL PIEDRA ESCONDIDA
● HOTEL LA PERLA
● ZAMAS

Caribbean Sea

To Chetumal ↙

SCALE NOT AVAILABLE

● LOS ARRECIFES CABAÑAS
● CABAÑAS ANA Y JOSE'S
● TULUM CABAÑAS
● LAS RANITAS

US$50, to US$75 at the high end. You'll find a restaurant (serving Mexican and Italian food), a market, and public telephone on the premises.

Maya Tulum (Apdo. Postal 99, Tulum, Quintana Roo 77780, Mexico, tel. 987/4-2772, U.S. tel. 888/515-4580, email: reservations@mayatulum.com) is really a meditation center (yoga retreats, some lead by Baron Baptiste, are common), but everyone is welcome. You'll find cute and simple cabañas with hanging double beds, mosquito netting, screenless shutters, and shared bathrooms and hot showers. A few deluxe rooms offer private bathrooms. Rates range from US$75–119. The dining room, a striking building with an enormous *palapa* roof, serves mediocre meals but good guacamole. There's no meat here—just vegetarian specialties and fresh seafood served with a sparkling view of the beautiful bay. The entrance to **Reserva de la Biosfera Sian Ka'an** is just across the street.

Heading south through the reserve, you'll come to several resorts on this road. **Cabañas Ana y José** (Apdo. Postal 15, Tulum, Quintana Roo 77780, Mexico, tel. 988/7-5470, email:

JUAN VEGA

L ocal legend has it that during the height of the post-Caste War conflict, Juan Vega was kidnapped by the Maya Indians as a young child. His entire family and young companions were put to death, but, because he was carrying religious books and could read, he was spared. The Maya had a curious acceptance of the Christian religion. Because of certain similarities, they managed to weave it into their own beliefs and would listen attentively to Vega's preaching.

Although Vega was a captive, he was given tremendous respect and spent his entire life in the village, marrying a Maya and raising a family of mestizos in the village of Chumpon. Vega (nicknamed "White King of the Maya") operated a chicle business at Muyil. Chumpon is referred to by knowledgeable outsiders as the "Jungle Vatican." Vega saved the lives of many captured Mexican soldiers. They were doomed to death by the Maya until he stepped in and read the laws of the Christian God from his worn books.

In 1961, Quintana Roo was still a no-man's land without roads and Vega was seriously ill; through a fluke, archaeologist Pablo Bush heard about Vega. Bush, acting quickly, used a small plane to spot the hidden jungle village and a helicopter to pick up the sick man (by foot it was a three-day expedition into the village). Juan Vega was rescued—but only after he asked the chief's permission to leave. After surgery and a long stay in a Mexico City hospital, the newspapers gave an account of Vega, and a soldier who had once been saved by Vega came to visit him. A recovered Vega had one request while in Mexico, to visit Abuelitas (the Virgin of Guadalupe). When able, he made his pilgrimage to the shrine and then happily returned to his isolated village and family in Chumpon. Juan Vega lived in Chumpon until his death a few years later.

some with Yucatecan flair. Try the fish *cymbals* with *chaya.*

Down the road from Ana y José's at Kilometer 9, **Las Ranitas,** tel. 987/7-8554, email: lasranitas@pa.com.mx, is an upscale version of the rest of the small bungalow resorts along this dirt road. This was formerly the home of a French filmmaker, who added bungalows and then moved to a quieter place on this Caribbean. Set on a great white-sand beach, there are 16 classy rooms and a restaurant serving fine Mexican food with a French touch. Rooms (US$150, breakfast included) are attractive and airy, and the grounds are inviting with views of the sea, a swimming pool, a tennis court, and hammocks beneath shady palms.

Cabañas Tulum, tel. 987/1-2009, email: savana2tulum-mexico.com, offers 32 rooms (US$50–60) with beds, hammock hooks on the front porch, bathrooms, ceiling fans, and electricity from sunset until about 10 P.M.. There's a restaurant on the premises and a white beach hosting topless sunbathers.

Also along this road are many other budget-priced bungalows worth checking out. Take a look at **Cabañas Arrecife,** reasonably modern and very clean, with well-kept grounds and—usually—an abundant water supply (boil your drinking water or buy bottled).

SIAN KA'AN BIOSPHERE RESERVE

About six kilometers south of the Tulum ruins on Boca Paila Road is the entrance to Sian Ka'an Biosphere Reserve. From here to road's end at Punta Allen, you'll be entirely within the reserve. In the Maya language, Sian Ka'an means, "Where the Sky is Born."

You'll usually find a guard at the reserve entrance; ask him about road conditions ahead (RVs are not permitted). Admission to the reserve is free, but you are asked to sign yourself in and then back out when you leave. The guard will offer to sell you a short but informative book about the reserve. Continuing south from the entrance gate, you'll encounter an army checkpoint with a small group of soldiers. Stop and smile—they're just kids doing their job, looking for drug and arms runners. They may or may not ask you to get out of the car and open your trunk.

anayjose@cancun.com.mx), seven kilometers south of Tulum, is one of the few hotels in the area that offer 24-hour electricity (via solar panels) and a swimming pool. Its two-story tile-roofed buildings house 15 rooms (US$80–105), all nicely appointed with private tile bathrooms and freshwater showers. A colorful screened-in and sand-floored *palapa* restaurant overlooks the sea and serves three good meals a day,

No matter what you decide to do in the reserve, it's a good idea to always travel with a flashlight, bug repellent, sunscreen, hat, and walking shoes that can survive in the water.

Flora and Fauna

A wide variety of plants thrive in the reserve, including four species of mangrove and many medicinal plants. Birdlife is abundant—over 300 species at last count. Toucans and parrots reside in the jungle year-round, and bird-watchers flock to **Laguna Chunyaxche,** a watery stopover for migrating flamingos, herons, and egrets.

Bird Island, a small island in Laguna Chunyaxche, hosts two species of crocodile found in estuaries throughout the preserve. Another notable reptile here is the boa constrictor, which can grow to lengths of over four meters (13 feet). Mammals that live in the jungle include monkeys, raccoons, foxes, and various rodents.

Local waters are rich in lobster, and not too long ago, wildlife groups in association with the local lobster cooperative and the Mexican equivalent of the National Science Foundation studied the way the Yucatecan fishermen handled the spiny crustaceans. The Rojo Gómez villagers don't use lobster traps as we know them, but instead create artificial platform habitats from which the lobsters can come and go. The lobsters grow sheltered in these habitats, and when they reach a predetermined size, the fishermen take them by hand.

Fishing

Many consider this Mexico's best place for fly-fishing. Bahía Ascensión is one of the Caribbean's richest permit and bonefish fishing grounds (all catch and release). In May and June the targets include tarpon, barracuda, and snook. In years past, visitors looking for fishing guides had to ask local fishermen to take them fishing, but today many small guiding outfits are found in the area. Ask around Rojo Gómez or check with Cuzan Guest House.

Hiking

For the hardy type with lots of time, walking the 57-kilometer road from Tulum to Punta Allen can be high adventure. Plan at least two weeks (that is, if you take time to smell the flowers and float in the silky sea). Along the way, the sea sometimes disappears behind sand dunes, but it's never that long a trudge through the brush to dozens of fine beaches where you might be seduced into staying a while. Here and there you'll find coconut trees on which to sling your hammock—a tropical paradise. Be sure to carry mosquito netting for your nights under the stars. And be prepared for long stretches with nothing but empty beach and an occasional *ranchito* surrounded by thick jungle. Several large luxury homes are going up along this stretch of coast, all with heavy-duty fences; take the hint.

Restaurants are *nada* until you reach Rojo Gómez; come prepared with your own victuals and water. Before you start out remember that once you reach the end of this peninsula, you either have to hoof it back, make arrangements with a villager for a ride, or catch the irregularly scheduled bus between Rojo Gómez and Felipe Carrillo Puerto.

Muyil

One of the larger Maya sites within the Sian Ka'an Biosphere Reserve is Muyil, also known as Chunyaxche. Situated near Laguna Chunyaxche on the edge of a karstic limestone shelf, the site was at one time an ancient Maya seaport. It has been the subject of a study conducted by Tulane University and the Quintana Roo Regional Center of INAH. Along with mapping the site to determine its size and settlement pattern, graduate students from Tulane and villagers from Chumpon have been excavating for ceramics in order to ascertain the settlement's dates of occupation.

The potsherds dug up at the area indicate that Muyil was settled about A.D. 1 and occupied continuously until the Spanish conquest began. The report's author, archaeologist Elia del Carmen Trejo, notes that since no Spanish ceramics have been identified and because there is no mention of a settlement at Muyil in books from the period, the population of Muyil likely perished in the 40 years following the conquest. A large *sacbe* (roadway) at Muyil runs at least a half kilometer from the site center to near the edge of the lagoon. The western half of the road runs through mangrove swamp.

Six structures are spaced along the roadway approximately every 120 meters. They range from two-meter-high platforms to the large *castillo,* one

Trekkers find many campsites along Quintana Roo's Caribbean coast.

OZ MALLAN

of the tallest structures on the Yucatán Peninsula's east coast. All but the westernmost of the structures face westward, away from the lagoon. The Maya always oriented their structures with precise reference to the positions of the sun and Venus. Orientation of the roadways between the structures suggests that the residents were always supposed to pass these structures along their north side; no one knows why.

The *castillo,* at the midpoint of the *sacbe,* stands 21 meters above the lagoon's water level. At the summit is a solid round masonry turret, which is unique to ancient Maya structures. From there it's possible to see the Caribbean.

Muyil is about 25 kilometers south of Tulum; look for the signs. The ruins are open daily 8 A.M.–5 P.M. The entrance fee is about US$3.

Tours
Amigos de Sian Ka'an, tel. 984/8-1618 or 8-1693, email: sian@cancun.com.mx, offers an eco-tour into the reserve—by car on unpaved roads and by boat through the coastal lagoons. For US$58 the tour takes you through tropical forest to the ancient Maya seaport remains of Muyil-Chunyaxche. Guests meet at Ana y José Cabana (below Tulum, near the entrance to the reserve) at 9 A.M. and are returned at 4 P.M.

Rojo Gómez (Punta Allen)
Rojo Gómez (also called Punta Allen) is a small fishing enclave on a finger of land overlooking Bahía de la Ascención. The village offers what a lot of the Quintana Roo coast has lost: an end-of-the-road ambience. Only a few simple businesses operate here, and the sand streets are easy to mistake for beach with palm trees scattered here and there. It's a tiny little village where the villagers still carry on some of the old Maya customs. One January, we stumbled on a small fiesta sponsored by the local market. It was low key, but probably the highlight was the pig-head dance, and music, and families dancing modern, all in the dirt road in front of the market. Everything was sponsored by the **Tres Reyes** store, with free beer, soda pop, food, and of course the *música!* This quaint small town culture is fading away in the larger cities along the peninsula.

Our first experience in Punta Allen was about 15 years ago. There was not much here then, but we were able to spend the night in a thatch tipi with a sand floor and shared bathrooms. That wasn't the only thing we shared—hermit crabs with cockeyed shells on their backs and beady eyes that glowed in the light of our flashlight (there was no electricity here then) kept finding their way under the door to join us. We sent them on their way many times, but they loved our tipi and kept coming. So we crawled into our hanging netted bed and went to sleep surrounded by the clicking sound of crabs pacing around the perimeter of our tipi the entire night. We shared our meals in fisherman Armando's house and enjoyed delicious lobster. But that has all changed now.

Maya construction using chit *palm*

Accommodations: Old-timer **Cuzan Guest House,** tel. 983/4-0358 (answering machine in English), fax 983/4-0383, email: flshcuzan @aol.com, has held firm through just about everything: hurricanes, a bad entry road, even modernization. The simple but charming stucco and wooden *palapa* cabañas each have two double beds, a private bath, solar light, and hot water. They can be very hot during warmer times of the year, but their front porches are great and include hammocks. There's a fine little restaurant that serves good local specialties and cold drinks (including *cerveza*). Ask about bargain fishing packages. Kayaks and bikes are available for rent. For information contact Armando's wife, Sonia Lilvik, Apdo. Postal 24, Felipe Carrillo Puerto, Quintana Roo 77200, Mexico. There are no communications at Punta Allen, so all telephone, email, and fax goes to Felipe Carrillo Puerto, a 2–3 hour trip. So it could be 10 days before you hear back. If writing, allow a week or so for answers.

Fishing and Eco Tours
Nearby **Ascension Bay** is a large playground for wading fishermen. It consists of 20 square miles of uniformly shallow water famous for its flats of white sand. Fly fishermen catch permit, bonefish, tarpon, and ladyfish. There's great fishing out near the reef as well. Call Cuzan Guest House for more fishing information.

Tropicales Aventuras de Sian Ka'an
Right next to Cuzan, look for the Holtzmans at Tropicales. There you'll find Jim, who has been fishing forever and is a great guide. He offers fishing, trekking, kayaking, biking, camping trips; whatever you can think up, Jim can bring it together. The trips entail complete immersion in the nature and life of this isolated part of Mexico. Ask about package deals—week-long trips to the Sian Ka'an's estuaries, lagoons, and caves. Getting in touch may take awhile, tel. 983/4-0358 (answering machine in English), fax 983/4-0383, email: Yucatan@boreal.org. Again, there are no communications at Punta Allen, so all telephone, email, and fax goes to Felipe Carrillo Puerto, a 2–3 hour trip, and it could be 10 days before you hear back.

If you're just wandering and you find yourself in Punta Allen, you'll find several small hostels in addition to the accommodations listed above. Most are inexpensive with spartan features and pleasant staff.

Food: A few small cafés in town serve basic Mexican meals with fresh fish and lobster as the centerpiece. **Tres Reyes** is a combination grocery store, *tortilleria,* and café. The **Cuzan Guest House Dining Room** (open to the public) is a laid-back *palapa* hut in the sand that serves pretty good à la carte food. Don't bother with the steak; instead, stick to the great seafood and the Mexican specialties.

Several markets in town offer a fair selection of grocery items, and **Panaderia Lupita,** about a block from the town square, makes good bread.

Getting There
This is the "adventure part" of the trip. The main road to Punta Allen is dirt (they all are), rutted, and potholed. It can be rough, especially after a heavy rain when it's not uncommon to find large lakes on the road. But this is the Sian Ka'an, and despite the inconveniences the countryside

can be quite interesting. You'll see a variety of birdlife and, if you look carefully, many unusual animals. Plan on two–four hours from Tulum depending on road conditions. Leave early in the morning and give yourself time to return if you find Rojo Gómez is not your cup of tea—not everyone is enthralled with the end-of-the-road ambience and the lack of luxuries. Most who make the trip love desert islands, where ever they are.

Another means of access that we have yet to try is via a dirt road (also through Sian Ka'an) from Felipe Carrillo Puerto. According to those who have traveled it, the road is subject to the same poor conditions as any other, but a canopy of trees shades the way and there's very little traffic. The road was formerly a railway for small trains shipping chicle, copra, and wild game from Ascension Bay to Felipe Carrillo Puerto. From Felipe Carrillo Puerto, it's a two-hour road trip to the *playon* boat landing where Cuzan Guest House will meet you and ferry you 20 minutes through old Maya channels, beautiful mangroves, and lagoons (frequented by huge flocks of migratory birds in winter) to their beach. Cuzan takes reservations for a taxi that takes guests from Felipe Carrillo Puerto through the reserve. The taxi runs about US$55 per person, or you can drive your own car. Check with Cuzan for road directions. Remember if you drive your own car you must leave it in this isolated area for the length of your stay.

FELIPE CARRILLO PUERTO

Highway 307 from Tulum to Chetumal passes through Felipe Carrillo Puerto, a small colonial city with some of the richest history in Quintana Roo. When the Caste War was going badly for the Maya, three clever Maya leaders—one a ventriloquist—reintroduced the "Talking Cross" to the Indians near Felipe Carrillo Puerto. The talking cross dictated tactical orders to cult followers—who called themselves the Chan Santa Cruz ("People of the Holy Cross")—and predicted victory in the Maya fight against the Spanish. Felipe Carrillo Puerto became the capital of the Chan Santa Cruz; at that time, the city, too, was named Chan Santa Cruz.

When the war was over, the fathers and grandfathers of many of today's *antiguos,* or oldtimers, rejected the peace treaty negotiated between their leaders and the Mexicans. They took their families into the jungle and began new villages, continuing their secretive lifestyle and calling themselves *separados.* Here in Felipe Carrillo Puerto, named for a patriot who stood up for the working class people of the area, many *antiguos* still cling to the belief that one day the Maya will once again control the Quintana Roo coast.

Little English is spoken in Felipe Carrillo Puerto, and other than its historical significance, the town holds nothing in the way of tourist attractions. Ask about the "Wooden Church," an open church where the three crosses still remain, complete with a live-in guard on the premises to protect the beloved crosses. Nevertheless, it's still a typical Mexican town and worth a look around. Whether your next stop is north or south, be sure to fill up at the Pemex gas station; it sells Magna Sin unleaded gas, and the next station with unleaded gasoline is 98 kilometers away.

Accommodations
Hotel Esquivel, located across the street from the church and the plaza, tel. 983/4-0344, fax 983/4-0313, is quite old and has historical significance. The 18 rooms (US$10–16) have private bathrooms and hot water. These are simple and rustic rooms out of the past, painted and decorated with care. Still part of the hotel, another eight rooms at the **Casona** across from the hotel have private baths, hot water, air-conditioning, television, and a garden. These rooms rent for less than US$20. Just drop in—you will probably find a room available, not always the case with many towns along Highway 307. Felipe Carrillo Puerto is *not* a real tourist town— at least not yet. But if you're interested in the beginnings of Quintana Roo, this is a great place to snoop around. It's been the real heart of Quintana Roo since the time of the caste war. The Esquivel family were one of the founders of the city. This property was at one time a hacienda, and the Casona was the family quarters. If you like history, talk to Maria Elena Vargas, Senor Esquivel's widow. She speaks a little English and is very knowledgeable.

Services

There are a couple of places in town to stop for lunch. **Mirador Maya Café** is across from the **Pemex Gas Station** on the second floor. It's a simple family-operated café with *salbutos* and quesadillas for less than US$2, hamburgers for US$1.50, instant coffee, and a TV in the dining room. **Faisan y Venado** is another place for simple Mexican food at budget prices.

XCALAK PENINSULA

This low-lying limestone shelf—bounded by Bahía Espíritu Santo on the north, Bahía Chetumal on the south, and the Caribbean Sea on the east—holds a mosaic of savannas, marshes, streams, and lagoons, dotted by islands of thick jungle. The coastline is a series of sandy beaches and dunes interrupted by rocky promontories, some of which connect with the offshore Belize Reef. A few still-healthy coconut plantations from the early 20th century dominate the shore.

Maya sites have been discovered on the peninsula's shores and in its jungles, but little is known about the area's preconquest history; the peninsula was already abandoned when the Spaniards unsuccessfully tried to settle Bahía Espíritu Santo in 1621. Later, however, the peninsula became a sanctuary for Indian refugees fleeing Spanish control in the interior, as well as a haven for pirates, British logwood cutters, and Belizean fishermen.

In 1910 the village of Xcalak (shka-LAK), at the peninsula's southern tip, held a population of 544; a few additional people were scattered among the *cocales* (small coconut plantations) and ranchos along the coast. In the ensuing years, the population fluctuated. The major industries—*cocales* and fishing—have been disrupted several times with the onslaught of major hurricanes and, more recently, the yellowing disease that has decimated the state's coconut trees.

Only in recent years has a rough dirt road opened the isolated peninsula to home builders and a few (so far) small resorts. Tracts of land along the coast are rapidly being bought up by developers and individuals seeking a last bit of undisturbed paradise. In 1993 the government of Quintana Roo began working with a major tourism developer to study the peninsula and ways it could be enhanced by tourism without destroying its fragile ecology.

Xcalak Peninsula is going to be the "new" but controlled Playa del Carmen, with a marketing label of "La Costa Maya." The government is taking precautions to stem what could be runaway development. Hotels will not be built higher than the palm trees (we've heard that before!), septic systems will be tightly regulated, and a limit will be imposed on the number of rooms at each resort. Hopefully the authorities will stick to their guns, and everyone will cooperate to keep this area pristine for generations.

Overland to Xcalak

Just south of Limones, a paved road breaks off Highway 307 and meanders east for 57 kilometers through varied scenery to a dead end. Much of the land along the road has been cleared of jungle, and small *ranchitos* are scattered about. In some areas mangrove swamps line the highway and are home to a variety of birds, including hundreds of egrets and the graceful white heron. However, in drought years so little rain falls that many of the swamps dry up and the birds go elsewhere. The remaining trees are covered with green and red bromeliads, orchids, and ferns.

About 55 kilometers down this road there's a turnoff to the north leading to Uvero and Placer, home to a few small and increasingly popular diving destinations. Just two kilometers past this turnoff is Majahual and the sea. A military camp guards the point, but again, they're just a bunch of kids trying to decide who might be a drug runner. Before you reach the coast look for signs to Xcalak and turn south on a newly paved road and continue another 66 kilometers to Xcalak. The road cuts right through the jungle and is teeming with animals.

A 4,500-foot runway is in place; commuter flights will eventually begin on a limited basis. A new cruise dock in Majahual was being planned. Haste is made very slowly on this end of Quintana Roo, compared to the Cancún end.

Xcalak Village

The tiny fishing village of Xcalak lies just a short distance from a channel that separates Mexico from Belize's Ambergris Caye. It was founded in 1900 as a military base for a project to dredge a canal across the southern end of the peninsula. The project never got off the ground and instead a small rail line was laid between Xcalak and La Aguada on Chetumal Bay.

Visitors will find a few hotels, small grocery stores, and simple cafés. **Commacho's** has been around forever and serves simple meals for lunch and dinner.

Electricity in the village is wind-generated and works pretty well. When the wind stops, generators take over. Bring flashlights and batteries to get around after dark.

Diving and Fishing

Diving is the area's most popular activity; many divers go across the reef to breathtaking **Chinchorro Bank,** 26 kilometers off the coast, where there's crystal-clear water, a huge variety of colorful fish, delicate coral, and three sunken ships clearly visible from above.

Catch-and-release fishing for tarpon, bonefish, barracuda, and snook is also popular around here, and most of the area's hotels can arrange fishing trips.

Peninsula Accommodations

As you drive through the small village of Xcalak, you'll see a couple of spartan hotels. North of "downtown," however, along the old beach road, you'll find more accommodations. Some—the real pioneers in this isolated part of Quintana Roo's coast—have been around for a long time. Others are brand new. Most are quite nice with simple, modern facilities and attractive decor. Credit cards are generally not accepted and there is no bank in Xcalak, so bring extra cash (especially pesos).

Sin Duda, U.S. tel. 888/881-4774, is a pleasant little inn next door to Sand-Wood Villas. Its twin two-story buildings are connected by walkways and imposing stairways to a roof deck providing a 360-degree view of jungle, lagoon, sea, and reef. Three of the rooms are doubles; the fourth includes a kitchen, a living room, and a bedroom (US$64–104, including breakfast). Families are welcome. Transportation is available into Xcalak for dinner.

The peninsula's first resort, located 2.9 kilometers north of the village, was **Costa de Cocos,** U.S. tel. 800/538-6802, a fine little resort catering mostly to fishermen and divers. The resort features a dining room and eight wood- and thatch-roofed bungalows—each with tile showers, warm water, and lots of comfortable touches. It's all set on the palm-studded, tropical-paradise oceanfront (US$98–120 per person, double occupancy, including breakfast and dinner). Chinchorro Bank, a one-hour boat ride away, is a favorite diving destination. Guided trips to hidden caves and rich fishing grounds are becoming very popular. A trip from here to **Bird Island** is a fine day trip, as are naturalist-led kayaking trips to the "back-water."

Breakfast and dinner are included in the room rates, which start at US$75. Diving, fishing, snorkeling, and all other excursions are extra. It is suggested that guests bring along a supply of favorite snacks, since shopping in town is limited. Beer and soft drinks are sold on site; liquor isn't, but feel free to bring your own. Once on the new paved road drive south exactly 52 kilometers and you'll see the sign for Costa de Cocos on a gravel road.

Sand-Wood Villas, U.S. tel. 952/898-1667, Mexico tel. 983/1-0034, email: esanders @isd.net, is a comfortable and immaculate fourplex about 10 kilometers north of town. Each unit has a living room, kitchen, two bedrooms, two bathrooms, hot water, and ceiling fans. You can bring your own food, eat in the *palapa* restaurant on the property, or buy groceries from a grocery truck that comes four times a week. Purified water and ice are supplied. A 23-foot-long *panga*, a canoe, and kayaks are available for guests to use. Diving is close by (contact **Adventures Chinchorro**). Behind the villas there is fishing in Laguna San Julia.

Tierra Maya is really a honey, U.S. tel. 800/480-4505, Mexico tel. 983/1-0404, email: fantasea@xcalak.com. It is a beautifully constructed two-story building on the beach, with six spacious rooms (US$65–75), each nicely furnished with all the comforts of home, including 24-hour electricity, refrigerators, air-conditioning, fans, and private baths. There's a nice little restaurant on the property. The American owners, avid divers, split their time between the States and Xcalak. They've been diving the area for years and offer trips to local reefs as well as river trips, birding excursions, and fly-fishing.

The self-sustained resort takes most of its electrical power from the sun. Telephone service is available.

Villas Guacamaya, tel. 983/1-0334, guacamaya@pocketmail.com, a few miles north of the village on the old coast road, has great diving right off the property. Behind the villas there's good fishing in Laguna San Julia. The airy rooms (US$70, no credit cards) have private baths and access to the communal kitchen and are all nicely appointed. On the second floor there is an apartment with private bath, kitchen, and sitting room. This is a nice choice if you want to be away from the busy tourist areas of northern Quintana Roo yet have the Caribbean at your doorstep.

BACALAR AND VICINITY

Back on Highway 307, heading south from Limones, you'll come to Bacalar, a small enclave beside beautiful, multihued Laguna Bacalar. The lagoon is enjoyed by locals and visitors alike.

Fuerte San Felipe

This 17th-century fort was built by the Spanish for protection against the bands of pirates and Maya that regularly raided the area. It was destroyed in 1858 during the brutal Caste War. The star-shaped stone edifice has been restored, and cannons are still posted along the balustrades overlooking Laguna Bacalar. Originally, the moat was filled with sharp spikes; today it's filled with flowers and plants. The fort has a diminutive museum displaying metal arms used in the 17th and 18th centuries. A token assortment of memorabilia recalls the history of the area. The museum is open daily except holidays and charges a small entry fee.

Cenote Azul

A circular cenote, 61.5 meters deep and 185 meters across, filled with brilliant blue water, this is a spectacular place to stop for a swim or a canoe ride, or for lunch at the outdoor restaurant (where the adventurous gourmand can taste the jungle creature called *tempescuinkle*). Wanna-be entrepreneurs (children 6–12) in the area may request an admission fee to visit Cenote Azul (unofficial, of course) and will make quite a fuss until you give them a few pesos. In many remote areas, locals (most of whom live at a subsistence level) are now seeking their share of the tourist dollar.

Accommodations

Near Cenote Azul, built into the side of a hill overlooking Laguna Bacalar, is **Hotel Laguna** (Av. Bugambilias 316, Chetumal, Quintana Roo 77000, Mexico, tel. 983/4-2206 or 4-2205), with clean rooms and private baths. Each room (US$45) has a fan and a beautiful view. The dining room serves tasty Mexican food at moderate prices. A small pool (filled only during high season) and outdoor bar look out across the unusually hued Lagunas de Siete Colores ("Lagoons of Seven Colors"). A diving board and ladder make swimming convenient in the lagoons' sometimes blue, sometimes purple, sometimes red water; fishing is permitted, and you can barbecue your catch on the grounds. Ask about a bungalow including kitchen facilities. Reserve in advance during the high season and holidays. To find the hotel, turn left off Bacalar's main street and follow the shore south.

Rancho Encantado tel. 983/1-0037, U.S. tel. 800/505-MAYA or 505/758-9790, email: reservations@encantado.com, is an enchanting mini-resort on the edge of Bacalar Lagoon. The 12 attractive, comfortable *casitas* feature native hardwoods and Mexican tile, and each holds a small sitting room, ceiling fan, coffee pot, bathroom, and a small porch with a hammock and a view of the garden or lagoon. Facilities include a lagoonside spa and massage area, kayaks for guest use, and a large *palapa* where visitors enjoy a tropical buffet breakfast and candlelit dinner, both included in the room rates. Also available is a private villa with three bedrooms, 2.5 baths, and private dock. It's on the waterfront a short distance away. Rates range from US$150–245.

Encantado is a favorite of bird lovers. The grounds are a lush Eden of tropical shrubs, coco palms, and fruit trees—all just a few steps from the lagoon shore. Flocks of parakeets and a huge variety of other birds flit from tree to tree. Bird-watchers should talk to Luis, the manager, who keeps a list of birds you can expect to see and hear on the grounds. He's a font of information and an excellent nature photographer.

Other activities that can be arranged include archaeology and sightseeing tours of the area and scuba trips to Chinchorro Banks.

Camping
On the edge of the lagoon, **Laguna Milagros Trailer Park** accepts both RVers and tent campers for about US$7 per person. Amenities include restrooms, showers, sun shelters, a narrow beach, a small store, and an open-air café.

CHETUMAL AND VICINITY

Chetumal is the capital of Quintana Roo and the gateway to Belize. The city lacks the bikini-clad, touristy crowds of the north, instead presenting the businesslike atmosphere of a growing metropolis.

The population is a handsome mixture of many races, including Caribe, Spanish, Maya, and Anglo. Schools are prominently scattered around town. Though sea breezes help, the climate is generally hot and sticky. The most comfortable time to visit is the dry season, November–April. Copious rainfall in the region creates dense jungle with vine-covered trees, broad-leafed plants, ferns, and colorful blossoms. The forests here are noted for hardwood trees such as mahogany and rosewood. Orchids grow liberally on the tallest trees. Deer and javelina roam the forests.

Those interested in Maya archaeology will find several Maya sites off Highway 186 west of Chetumal.

A Walk through Town
Chetumal is a good city to explore on foot; a 10-minute walk takes you from the marketplace and most of the hotels to the waterfront. Wide, tree-lined avenues and clean sidewalks front small variety shops. Modern sculpted monuments stand along a breezy bayside promenade, while the backstreets harbor pastel-colored, worn wooden buildings with an old Central American/Caribbean look.

At the city center, note the **Monument to the Mestizo,** an interesting sculpture symbolizing the joining of Spanish shipwrecked sailor Gonzalo Guerrero and a Maya princess—the birth of the Mestizos. Heading down Av. de los Héroes

Rancho Encantado

toward the bay, you'll pass **Altamirano Market,** a typical Mexican market place and a great place to practice your bargaining techniques, and **Museo de la Cultura Maya,** a fine large museum where leafy jungle penetrates half the spectacular main exhibit hall.

Numerous small shops and a few upscale department stores line Av. Héroes. At the southern end of the street near the sea you'll come to the walkway to **La Bandera Square,** where Sunday concerts and city celebrations are held, and the newly renovated **Palacio de Gobierno.**

The waterfront lacks beaches, but Boulevard Bahía makes for a fine bayfront stroll; along it you'll find cafés, monuments, a lighthouse, and, hopefully, a cooling breeze. The modern shell-shaped structure is the **Palacio Legislativo.** Just northwest of the Palacio in a wooden colonial-style building is a handmade model of **Payo Obispo,** as Chetumal was called in the 1930s.

Accommodations
Although Chetumal is not considered a tourist re-

sort, its status as the state capital and its location on the Belize border make it a busy stopover for both Mexicans and Belizeans. Arrive as early in the day as possible to have your choice of hotel rooms. During the holiday season it's wise to reserve in advance. Most of the hotels are within walking distance of the marketplace, downtown shops, and waterfront.

The low-priced hotels are for the most part friendly. All have hot water and some have air-conditioning (most are fan-cooled). Some are clean, some aren't; look before you pay. **Casa Blanca Hotel,** Av. Alvaro Obregon 312, tel. 983/2-1248, fax 983/2-1658, is simple. The clean

rooms are a bargain (under US$50) and have fans or air-conditioning.

Hotel Caribe Princess, Av. Alvaro Obregón 168, tel. 983/2-0520, is very clean and offers rooms with air-conditioning and TV for less than US$100.

Hotel Los Cocos, Av. Héroes 134 (at Calle Chapultepec), tel. 983/2-0544, fax 983/2-0920, has pleasant air-conditioned rooms (US$58), a pretty garden, a large, clean swimming pool, a bar with evening disco music, and a quiet dining room with a friendly staff and a varied menu. The lobby holds a car-rental desk and one of the best travel agencies in Chetumal. Nearby,

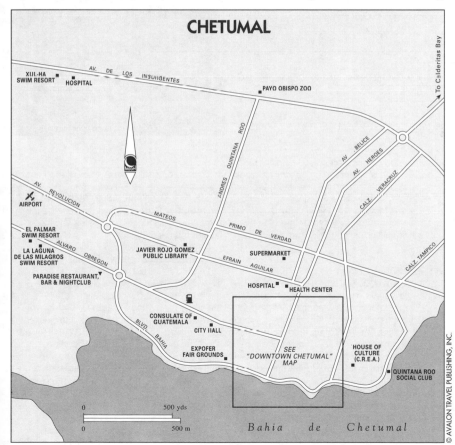

CHETUMAL

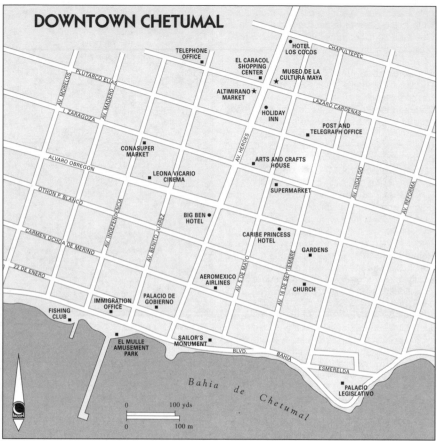

DOWNTOWN CHETUMAL

Labels on map:

TELEPHONE OFFICE

HOTEL LOS COCOS

CHAPULTEPEC

EL CARACOL SHOPPING CENTER

MUSEO DE LA CULTURA MAYA

PLUTARCO ELIAS

AV. MORELOS

I. ZARAGOZA

AV. MADERO

ALTIMIRANO ★ MARKET

HOLIDAY INN

LAZARO CARDENAS

POST AND TELEGRAPH OFFICE

AV. HÉROES

CONASUPER MARKET

ALVARO OBREGON

ARTS AND CRAFTS HOUSE

LEONA VICARIO CINEMA

OTHON P. BLANCO

SUPERMARKET

AV. HIDALGO

AV. REFORMA

AV. INDEPENDENCIA

BIG BEN HOTEL

CARMEN OCHOA DE MERINO

AV. BENITO JUAREZ

CARIBE PRINCESS HOTEL

GARDENS

22 DE ENERO

AV. 5 DE MAYO

AV. 16 DE SEPTIEMBRE

AEROMEXICO AIRLINES

CHURCH

IMMIGRATION OFFICE

PALACIO DE GOBIERNO

FISHING CLUB

EL MULLE AMUSEMENT PARK

SAILOR'S MONUMENT

BLVD.

BAHIA

ESMERELDA

Bahia de Chetumal

PALACIO LEGISLATIVO

0   100 yds

0   100 m

© AVALON TRAVEL PUBLISHING, INC.

Food

Holiday Inn, Av. Héroes 171, is probably the nicest hotel in town. Amenities include air-conditioning, a swimming pool, a good restaurant, and a bar with evening entertainment. Rates range from US$75–120.

Food

Emiliano's, Av. San Salvador 557 (at Calle 9), tel. 983/7-0267, is easily comparable to the best seafood houses in Cancún. Start with the shrimp or conch pâté, followed by shark empanadas, then the freshest ceviche, *pulpo en su tinto,* and *chiles rellenos* stuffed with seafood. It's the perfect spot for a long lunch or celebratory dinner. A three-course meal will run about US$20–30,

though you can get by much cheaper (e.g., a heaping platter of *arroz a la marinera,* rice mixed with seafood, runs about US$8). Open for lunch and dinner.

Several fast-food cafés line Av. Alvaro Obregón. For seafood try **El Pez Vela;** for chicken go to **Pollos Sinaloa.**

Events

Chetumal hosts an **auto road race** in December. Open to drivers from all over the globe, it's gaining prominence in the racing world. Hotel reservations should be made well in advance.

Windsurfing is popular on both Bahía Chetumal and Laguna Bacalar; state competitions are held in both areas yearly. For more information, write to the Secretaría de Turismo, Palacio de Gobierno 20, Chetumal, Quintana Roo 77000, Mexico.

Transportation

By Air: Chetumal's small modern airport still has only a few flights each day. The rental-car offices and café at the airport seem to be open only when flights are expected. An airport van provides transportation to hotels or downtown. Check out **AeroFerinco** and **AeroSaab**, both out of Playa del Carment, provide commuter service. **Aerocaribe, Aeroméxico, Bonanza,** and **Mexicana** serve the city less frequently.

By Bus: First- and second-class buses from points all over Mexico arrive throughout the day at the new and modern-looking Chetumal bus station, Salvador Novo 179 (on the highway, 20 blocks south of town). Taxis to town are available from the station. With the expanding road system, bus travel is becoming more versatile and is still the most inexpensive means of public transportation to the Quintana Roo coast.

Buses run between Chetumal and Mérida (5.5 hours), Mexico City (22 hours), Cancún, and Campeche. Check with a travel agent for a pickup point in Chetumal; it's usually at one of the hotels. Fares and schedules change regularly. To Cancún costs about US$17. **Omnibus Caribe Express,** tel. 983/2-7889, offers deluxe service to Cancún and Mérida.

Novelo's and **Venus Bus** offer frequent buses into Belize (US$2–7). You will have to get off the bus when you go across the border into Belize. Have your passport handy, as sometimes this takes a while.

By Car: A paved road connects Mérida, Campeche, Villahermosa, and Francisco Escarcega with Chetumal. The cross-peninsula highway from Chetumal to Escarcega can be filled with potholes. Highway 307 links all of the Quintana Roo coastal cities. There's little traffic, and the route's four gas stations are well spaced (top off at each one).

CROSSING INTO BELIZE

Across the Río Hondo from Chetumal lies the country of Belize, which makes an easy side trip for the explorer, archaeology buff, diver, or the

children's parade on the first day of spring, Chetumal

just-plain-curious. Belize is easily reached from Chetumal by taking a Novelo or Venus bus or taxi over the Río Hondo bridge.

There's rarely a problem crossing the border as long as you show a valid passport. If you look poor you'll be asked to show money or proof of onward travel. If driving, you must buy insurance with Belizean dollars; moneychangers are waiting for you as you cross the border. Their rates seem comparable to bank rates. U.S. citizens and most others don't need visas, but citizens of a few countries do; check with your embassy before leaving home.

Tours

Henry Menzies Travel and Tours, Box 210, Corozal Town, Belize, tel. 42/2725, takes visitors back and forth across the border all the time. Henry is a good, honest guide/driver who knows the border-crossing ropes and will take you anywhere in Belize.

International Expeditions, One Environs

a camping tour

OZ MALLAN

Park, Helena, AL 35080 USA, tel. 800/633-4734 or 205/428-1700, offers several good theme trips with small groups. The 11-day **Naturalist Quest** expedition is led by a knowledgeable naturalist who takes the group into the country's Jaguar Sanctuary and Howler Monkey Sanctuary. Other expeditions visit the country's Maya archaeological sites, offshore cayes, or nearby Costa Rica.

Further Reading
For details about traveling in Belize, including accommodations, restaurants, attractions, diving, and everything else you ever wanted to know about the country, pick up a copy of *Moon Handbooks: Belize,* published by Avalon Travel Publishing.

KATHY ESCOVEDO SANDERS

INLAND ARCHAEOLOGICAL ZONES

Maya ruins and other sites of archaeological and historical interest are favorite attractions (after the beach, of course) for most visitors. Noteworthy areas are located in the states of Quintana Roo, Yucatán, and Campeche—all easy trips from Cancún and the cities along the Riviera Maya coastline. Look into the different options. In some cases, a day trip is enough. For those sites further away you may want enough time to really absorb what you're seeing and spend a night or two. To explore further, take a local bus, rent a car, go with a tour group, or hire a car and driver for two or three days. Many travel agencies and hotels in Quintana Roo offer day trips to outstanding pre-Cortesian Maya sites.

COBÁ AND VICINITY

From Tulum and the main coastal highway 307, head inland for 42 kilometers and you will pass first through the tiny town of Cobá. This road travels past a few ranchitos and over many *topes* (speed bumps) that will put a hole in the bottom of your car if you don't slow down. On the way, you'll have the opportunity to take a couple of side trips, or stop at the growing number of souvenir shops.

COBÁ

The early Maya site of Cobá covers an immense area of some 50 square kilometers. The ancient city was begun in A.D. 600, and thousands of Maya are believed to have lived here during the classic period. Only in recent years has the importance of Cobá come to light; now archaeolo-

COBÁ AND VICINITY 183

gists are convinced that in time it will prove to be one of the largest Maya excavations on the Yucatán Peninsula. More than 5,000 mounds have yet to be uncovered.

Distances between groupings of structures are long (in some cases one–two kilometers), and each group of ruins is buried in the middle of thick jungle. All along the paths are unexcavated mounds overgrown with vines, trees, and flowers. Watch for signs and stay on the trails.

The fact that the jungle hasn't been cleared away here nor all the mounds uncovered adds a feeling of discovery to any visit. Come prepared with comfortable shoes, bug repellent, sunscreen, a hat, and, of course, water.

Ancient Highways

The remains of more than 50 *sacbe* (roads) crisscross the entire Peninsula, and there are more here than in any other location. The roads pass through what were once outlying villages and converge at Cobá—an indication that this was the largest city of its era. One such *sacbe* is 100 kilometers long and travels in an almost straight line from the base of Nohoch Mul (Cobá's great pyramid) to the town of Yaxuna. Each *sacbe* was built to stringent specifications: a base of stones one–two meters high, about 4.5 meters wide, and covered with white mortar. However, in Cobá some ancient roads as wide as 10 meters have been uncovered. Archaeologists have also discovered the mines where

ancient workers excavated the sand used to construct the roads, and a massive stone cylinder that was used to flatten the roadbeds.

The Pyramids

Cobá's highest pyramid, **Nohoch Mul,** is the tallest pyramid on the Peninsula (42 meters—a 12-story climb!). The view from the top is spectacular, and a small temple there bears a fairly well preserved carving of the Descending God. **La Iglesia,** the second-highest pyramid at the site (22.5 meters), also offers splendid views of the surrounding jungle and Lake Macanxoc from its summit. Many offering caches of jade, pearls, and shells have been found in La Iglesia and other temples.

Scientists believe there may be a connection between the Petén Maya (who lived hundreds of kilometers south in the Guatemalan lowlands) and the classic Maya who lived in Cobá. Both groups built pyramids that are much taller than those found in Chichén Itzá, Uxmal, or elsewhere in the northern part of the Peninsula.

Other Highlights

Numerous carved stelae dot the site; some are covered by *palapas* to protect them from the elements. One temple is named **Conjunto Las Pinturas** because of the stucco paintings that once lined the walls. Minute traces of the paintings, in layers of yellow, red, and blue, can still be seen on the temple's uppermost cornice. This

ruins at Cobá

OZ MALLAN

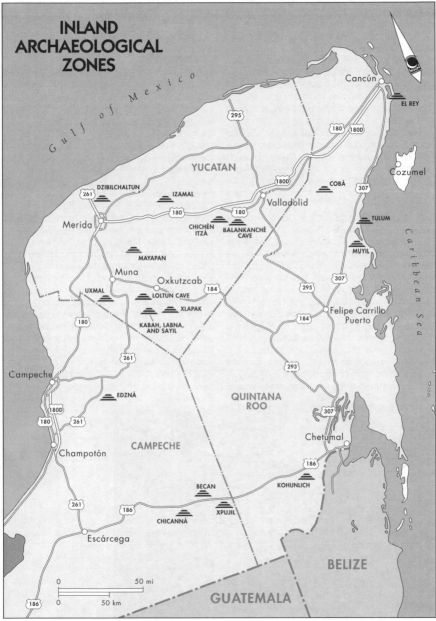

If you look on the ground, you'll almost certainly see long lines of cutter ants. One double column carries freshly cut leaves to the burrow, and next to that another double column marches in the opposite direction, empty jawed, returning for more. The columns can be longer than a kilometer. The work party usually slashes the same species of leaf or blossom until the plant is completely stripped. It's amazing how far they travel for food! The vegetation decays in their nests, and the mushrooms that grow on the compost are an important staple of the ants' diet. The determined creatures grow up to three centimeters long.

People

Cobá today holds a fraction of the population it had at its peak. Because of its (up till now) isolation from outsiders and low profile, traditional Maya ways are still common in the area.

The locals live in communities on both sides of the lake, planting their corn with ceremony and conducting their family affairs in the same manner as their ancestors; many villages still appoint a calendar-keeper to keep track of the auspicious days that direct them in their daily lives. Residents near the ruins operate small artisans' shops and restaurants and typically speak a smattering of Spanish. The community on the far side of the lake has a small clinic and a basketball court that serves as the town plaza. The communities have electricity, but no telephone service; the only phone in the area is cellular. But don't hesitate to ask about a telephone, as things are changing rapidly.

Accommodations

A couple of modest inns are on the highway, south of the turnoff to the archaeological zone on what could be called the main street of Cobá. **Bocadito's** cabins (US$10) on Calle Principal are plain and clean; each has a private bathroom, cold water, tile floors, two double beds, and a place for a hammock. There's a quaint gift shop on the premises where you can buy typical souvenirs, many of which were made by the Maya. There's also a simple restaurant. This is a popular stop, so get here early to ensure a room. If you can, try to make reservations (tel. 987/6-3738). It helps if you can speak Spanish.

The one upscale hotel in Cobá, **Villa Arque-**

OZ MALLAN

A roof has been placed over this carved stela to help preserve it from nature's constant attack.

small building is well preserved, and bright green moss grows up the sides of the gray limestone.

Flora and Fauna

Cobá in Maya means "Water Stirred by the Wind." Close to a group of shallow lakes (Cobá, Macanxoc, Xkanha, and Zacalpuc), some very marshy areas attract a large variety of birds and butterflies. The jungle around Cobá is good for viewing herons, egrets, and the motmot. Once in a while, even a stray toucan is spotted. Colorful butterflies are everywhere, including the large, deep-blue *morphidae,* as well as the bright yellow-orange barred sulphur.

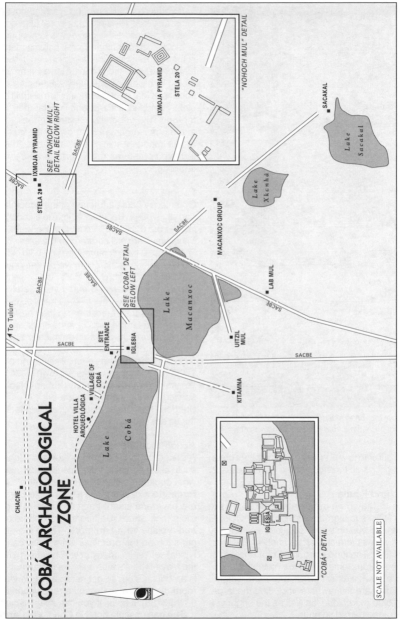

COBÁ ARCHAEOLOGICAL ZONE

CHACNE

To Tulúm

SACBE

HOTEL VILLA ARQUEOLÓGICA

VILLAGE OF COBÁ

SITE ENTRANCE

IGLESIA

Lake Cobá

KITAMNA

Lake Macanxoc

UTZIL MUL

SEE "COBÁ" DETAIL BELOW LEFT

MACANXOC GROUP

LAB MUL

SACBE

Lake Xkcnhá

SACAKAL

Lake Sacakal

STELA 20

IXMOJA PYRAMID

SEE "NOHOCH MUL" DETAIL BELOW RIGHT

SACBE

IXMOJA PYRAMID

STELA 20

"NOHOCH MUL" DETAIL

IGLESIA

"COBÁ" DETAIL

SCALE NOT AVAILABLE

© AVALON TRAVEL PUBLISHING, INC.

ológico, U.S. tel. 800/258-2633, is part of a chain that has placed hotels at various archaeological zones in Mexico. Each hotel is a clone of the other and includes a well-equipped library with many volumes containing histories of the area and the Maya people. This little sister of the Club Med resorts has an entirely different personality from what you might think. First of all, you pay for everything separately, and the food is more costly than at any other restaurants around (some say it's also a lot better, some don't agree). The decor is a pleasant white-stucco and red-tile Mexican.

The villa has small but attractive rooms, air-conditioning, a shallow swimming pool, an outdoor bar, and dining. Rates (US$47 per person) include breakfast and dinner. The restaurant food is fairly good *típico* and American, and a gift shop carries reproductions of Maya art. It's hard to predict seasonal highs since groups from Europe are bused in all year long; reservations could be important even though the hotel is often quiet and empty.

Food

Old-timer **Bocadito's** (at the hotel) offers good *típico,* inexpensive food, simplicity, and pleasant surroundings. A three-course *corrida comida* runs about US$4. Try one of the Maya specialties like *cochinita pibil.* An à la carte menu is available. Open 7 A.M.–9 P.M. The bus stops here—see the schedule of departures and prices posted on the wall. Close by, a small market carries purified water, cold sodas, and a few groceries and sundries.

Across the street from Bocadito's, a small café, **Restaurante La Sazon Mexicano,** offers a pleasant atmosphere and serves a nice meal for less than US$3 (opens at 7 A.M.).

A number of outdoor cafés are adjacent to the entrance to the ruins. In Cobá you'll find the cafés clean and pleasant. The food, though limited in choice, is *típico* and can be quite good.

Near the Villa Archaeológico, look for **Nicte Ha,** a small cafí serving a good toast-and-coffee breakfast starting at 8 A.M. What's fun about this place is proprietor Victor Kinil's occupation of feeding the crocodile that floats in the nearby lake. Nicte Ha means "flower of the water," and the flowers of this water are the eyes of the croc, who drifts along with only his eyes showing. Vic-

tor calls him a cannibal because his favorite food is raw chicken and chicken bones. The beast is fed every few days on the beach near the water.

Shops and Services

Small gift shops carry the usual, including carved wooden jaguar statues, hammocks, and pottery depicting the Maya gods. One shop advertises their bathroom (there's also a public restroom across from the entrance to the ruins site).

Tourist services are beginning to appear along the road from Tulum to Cobá. There are small markets with cold drinks at most settlements, and a full-blown rest stop called **Lolche.** You can't miss it—look for the wooden statue of a rifle-bearing campesino next to a large parking lot. Designed with tour groups in mind, Lolche has a snack bar with cold soda, bottled water, and sandwiches; clean restrooms; and a huge souvenir shop with rows and rows of pottery, masks, hammocks, and woodcarvings. Open daily during the daylight hours.

Transportation

Getting to Cobá is easiest by car. A 31-kilometer road provides a good **shortcut to Valladolid,** Chichén Itzá, and Mérida; from Cobá look for the signs that say Chemax where the intersection gives you the choice of Cancún or Valladolid. Those heading southeast from Cobá to Tulum and the coast highway will find good road all the way.

If traveling by local bus, your schedule is limited to two or three buses a day. Northwest-bound buses run to Cobá (en route to Nuevo X-Can and Valladolid) from Playa del Carmen and Tulum; make sure your bus actually goes into Cobá along its route. Some buses go to the entrance of the ruins; most stop on the main road by Bocadito's (a schedule and tickets are available here). Some southeast-bound buses from Valladolid to Tulum and Playa del Carmen stop at Cobá; again, make sure the bus actually goes into the town. (If you're planning to spend the night, make reservations or get there very early in the day.) You'll often run into travelers on the trail at the Cobá ruins who are willing to give you a ride. Organized bus tours are available from hotels and travel agencies in Cancún, Playa del Carmen, and Cozumel.

PUNTA LAGUNA

Look for the cutoff road from Cobá toward Nuevo Xcan and Highway 180. Fifteen kilometers northeast of Cobá, you'll pass Punta Laguna, a forested area where spider monkeys can occasionally be seen and howler monkeys occasionally heard. Locals from the nearby Maya village have built a small *palapa* hut on the side of the road and another by a nearby lagoon. At either place, for a small fee a Maya guide will take you through the forest to look for the monkeys; the rough trail passes small deteriorating stone structures built by the Maya. Increasing tourist activity in the area is sure to drive the monkeys away eventually. For now, however, few people stop here, and the monkeys—as well as colorful birds—can be seen in the early morning and at dusk.

We heard that divers in nearby Cenote Calaveras recently discovered 43 skeletons. So far we have not heard if archaeologists have studied the skeletons, or if any other artifacts were found like at the Sacred Cenote at Chichen Itza. We'll keep you posted.

At the roadside hut entrance to Punta Laguna (pay a small fee here) you'll find Maya villagers selling jars of honey taken from their own hives. Consider buying some and supporting their local economy.

CHICHÉN ITZÁ AND VICINITY

Chichén Itzá is one of the finest Maya archaeological sites in the northern part of the Peninsula. Largely restored, the site is about a three-hour drive from Cancún and about two hours from Mérida. It's a favorite destination of those fascinated with Maya culture.

Restoration, begun in 1923, continued steadily for 20 years. After a long hiatus, workers are now once again uncovering and reconstructing buildings on the site. Still, even today, there are enough unexcavated mounds remaining to support continued exploration for many years.

HISTORY

Two distinct styles of architecture—now known as "Old Chichén" and "New Chichén"—are represented at the site. According to scientists, the Old Chichén buildings were constructed by the Maya between the 5th and 12th centuries (late-classic period). Scientists disagree, however, on the origin of the New Chichén structures.

Because these newer buildings bear a remarkable similarity to those in the ancient Toltec capital of Tollan (today called Tula), 1,200 kilometers away in the state of Hidalgo, some scientists believe the Toltecs invaded and ruled Chichén Itzá for 200 years, building new structures and adding to the many already in place. Most researchers, however, believe the Toltecs never ruled at Chichén Itzá, and that the people who built the "Old Chichén" and the "New Chichén" were the same: Maya.

Topiltzin Quetzalcoatl

The traditional theory formulated by Ralph Roys holds that in the 9th century, Chichén Itzá was a typical late-classic city of the northern region, featuring Puuc-influenced architecture and hieroglyphs commemorating important political events. The remnants of this era may be seen in structures like the Nunnery and the Akab Dzib in the "Old Chichén" part of the site. During the 10th century, when Yucatán was embroiled in terminal-classic wars and political strife, a king named Topiltzin Quetzalcoatl in the far-off Toltec capital of Tula (just north of Mexico City) was expelled from his realm after a power struggle with the warrior caste. He was last seen departing from the Gulf coast on a raft of serpents headings west.

In A.D. 987, the same year as his departure, *The Books of Chilam Balam* recorded the arrival on Yucatán's shores of a king named Kukulcán, identifying him, like Tolpiltzin Quetzalcoatl, with the Feathered Serpent. Kukulcán gathered an army that defeated the Puuc city-states of northwestern Yucatán and made Chichén Itzá his capital, rebuilding it in a mixed Toltec-Maya style. These Toltec traits include reclining *chac mool* figures, warrior columns, skull platforms, feathered serpents, and the cult of Tlaloc. As in Tula, hieroglyphs were absent from the art. Reliefs showed

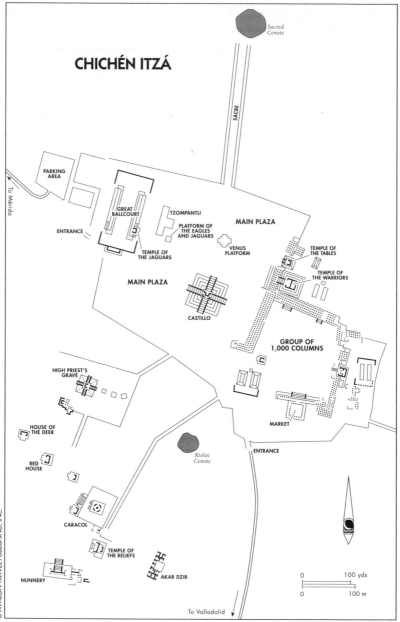

CHICHÉN ITZÁ

Sacred Cenote

SACBE

PARKING AREA

To Mérida

GREAT BALLCOURT

TZOMPANTLI

ENTRANCE

PLATFORM OF THE EAGLES AND JAGUARS

MAIN PLAZA

TEMPLE OF THE JAGUARS

VENUS PLATFORM

TEMPLE OF THE TABLES

TEMPLE OF THE WARRIORS

MAIN PLAZA

CASTILLO

GROUP OF 1,000 COLUMNS

HIGH PRIEST'S GRAVE

HOUSE OF THE DEER

MARKET

RED HOUSE

Xtoloc Cenote

ENTRANCE

CARACOL

TEMPLE OF THE RELIEFS

AKAB DZIB

NUNNERY

To Valladolid

N

0   100 yds

0   100 m

© AVALON TRAVEL PUBLISHING, INC.

bloody battle scenes celebrating the Toltec victories. After dominating northern Yucatán for more than two centuries, the Toltec abandoned Chichén Itzá in 1224, perhaps after an invasion.

Putún Maya

Another theory holds that Chichén Itzá was first settled by the Itzá, a tribe of Putún Maya seafarers. In the 9th century, they fought and defeated the Puuc cities centered around Uxmal and the eastern power of Cobá and carved out a territory in central Yucatán. The Itzá gave the city its current name, "The Well of the Itza." They settled around the sacred cenote and built monuments to commemorate their victories and legitimize their rule. The sacred cenote's depths received not only human sacrifices (male and female, adults and children) but offerings from throughout Mesoamerica.

The city-state of Chichén was ruled by a Putún Maya–style joint government. In other Maya cities, hieroglyphs are always associated with a sole ruler who needed to legitimize his claim to power; they are absent at Chichén Itzá because the form of government is different, not because they were Toltecs. The Putún Maya were far-ranging traders and probably built the central Mexican cities of Cacaxtla and Xochicalco, thus Chichén's central Mexican connection. There was a Toltec influence, but Chichén Itzá probably influenced Tula more than the other way around. Perhaps the traits we regard as definitively Toltec—*chac mools,* warriors columns, etc.—actually came from Yucatán. It is certain that Chichén Itzá was a more grandiose "Toltec" city than Tula itself.

After an internal revolt toppled the Itzá, Chichén Itzá was abandoned for good.

Later at Chichén Itzá

Though Chichén Itzá was most likely abandoned toward the end of the 13th century, Maya were still making pilgrimages to the sacred site when Montejo the Younger, the Spaniard who played a role in ultimately subjugating the Maya, settled his troops among the ruins of Chichén Itzá in 1533. Although they placed a cannon on top of the pyramid of Kukulcán, the Spaniards were unable at that time to conquer the elusive Indians, and after a year left Chichén Itzá for the coast. The pilgrimages continued.

Today, a different breed of pilgrim comes to Chichén Itzá from all over the world to walk in the footsteps of great rulers, courageous ball players, mysterious priests, and simple peasants.

Note: In 1988, UNESCO declared Chichén Itzá a **Heritage of Humanity** site.

SIGHTS

So far 18 structures have been excavated, and many of those have been restored. The former uses for these buildings are not truly understood. Archaeologists can only study and guess from the evidence that has been found.

Temple of the Warriors

On a three-tiered platform, the Temple of the Warriors stands next to the impressive **Group of a Thousand Columns**—reminiscent of Egypt's Karnak. Today the number of columns is approaching 1,000 as archaeologists continue to reconstruct. Many of the square and circular stone columns have carvings still in excellent condition. In 1926, during restoration, a subtemple found underneath was named **Chacmool Temple.** The former color on the columns of the inner structure is still slightly visible.

Close to the Thousand Columns on the east side of the plaza is a cleverly constructed sweat house with an oven and a channel under the floor to carry off the water thrown against the hot stones. Indian sweat houses are used for religious and health reasons and are still used today throughout North America. Archaeologists are working behind this area to uncover structures buried by jungle mounds. Within this area is a market with a rectangular courtyard surrounded by columns. Some speculate this courtyard was covered with palm thatch and used as a marketplace.

The Platforms

Strolling the grounds, you'll find the **Platform of Venus** and **Platform of Tigers and Eagles.** The flat, square structures, each with low stairways on all four sides, were used to stage ritual music and dancing, and, according to Diego de Landa (infamous 16th-century Franciscan bishop), farce and comedy were presented for the pleasure of the public.

OZ MALLAN

*Group of a Thousand Columns from the top of
Temple of the Warriors*

Temple of the Bearded Man

At the north end of the ball court sits the handsome Temple of the Bearded Man. Two graceful columns frame the entrance to a small temple with the remains of decorations depicting birds, trees, flowers, and the "earth monster." It's doubtful whether anyone will ever know if the unusual acoustics here were used specifically for a display of histrionics, or if it's just by chance that while standing in the temple you can speak in a low voice and still be heard a good distance down the playing field, well beyond what is normal (much like in the dome of St. Peter's Cathedral in Rome). Was this the "dugout" from which the coach whispered signals to his players downfield? Some believe that only members of the upper class actually watched the game and that the masses remained outside the walls and listened.

Great Ball Court

Of several ball courts at Chichén Itzá (some ar-

chaeologists say nine), the most impressive is the Great Ball Court, the largest yet in Mesoamerica. On this field, life-and-death games in the tradition of the Roman Colosseum were played with a 12-pound hard rubber ball. The playing field is 135 meters by 65 meters, with two eight-meter-high walls running parallel to each other on either side. On these walls, note the reliefs that depict the ball game and sacrifices. The players were obliged to hit the ball into carved stone rings embedded in the vertical walls seven meters above the ground using only their elbows, wrists, or hips. The heavy padding they wore indicates the game was dangerous; it was also difficult and often lasted for hours. (In Diego de Landa's book, written in the late 1600s, he mentions in two different places, "The Indians wore padding made of cotton with salt padding.") The winners were awarded jewelry and clothing from the audience. The losers lost their heads. Another theory is that the *winners,* too, were granted the "privilege" of losing their heads.

Temple of the Jaguar

The upper Temple of the Jaguar was constructed A.D. 800–1050 on the southeast corner of the ball court. To get there you must climb a steep stairway at the platform's south end. Two large serpent columns, with their rattlers high in the air, frame the opening to the temple. The inside of the room is decorated with a variety of carvings and the barely visible remnants of what must have been colorful murals.

Sacred Cenote

Today's adventurer can sit in the shade of a *palapa* terrace and enjoy a cold drink near the sacred cenote. This natural well is 300 meters north of Kukulcán. The roadway to the sacred well is an ancient *sacbe* constructed during the classic period. The large well, about 20 meters in diameter with walls 20 meters above the surface of the water (34 meters deep), is where the rain god Chac supposedly lived; to con him into producing rain, sacrifices of children and young adults were made, evidenced by human bones found here. On the edge of the cenote is a ruined sweat bath, probably used for purification rituals before sacrificial ceremonies.

In 1885 Edward Thompson was appointed United States consul in nearby Mérida. A young writer greatly interested in the archaeological zones surrounding Mérida, he eventually settled in Chichén Itzá and acquired the entire area, including an old hacienda (for only US$75). For many years he had studied Diego de Landa's account of human sacrifice still going on at the time of the Spanish conquest. Stories of young virgins and valuable belongings thrown into the well at times of drought, over hundreds of years, convinced him there was treasure buried in the muddy cenote bottom. During 1903–07, with the help of Harvard's Peabody Museum, he supervised the first organized dive into the well. Fewer than 50 skeletons were found, mostly those of children, male and female. Precious objects of jade, gold, and copper, plus stone items with tremendous archaeological value, were also dredged from the muddy water.

Thompson set off an international scandal when he shipped most of these important finds to the Peabody Museum by way of diplomatic pouch. He was asked to leave, and for years (1926–44) a lawsuit continued over the booty. Ironically, the Mexican court ruled in favor of the Peabody Museum, claiming that the Mexican laws concerning archaeological material were inadequate. After the laws were toughened up, the Peabody Museum, in a gesture of friendliness, returned many (but not all) of the artifacts from Chichén Itzá's well of sacrifice.

The next large-scale exploration of the well was conducted in the 1960s and sponsored by the National Geographic Society with help from CEDAM (a Mexican organization of explorers and divers noted for having salvaged the Spanish ship *Mantanceros* in the Caribbean). As Thompson suspected before his untimely departure, there was much more treasure in the cenote to be salvaged. Hundreds of pieces (including gold, silver, obsidian, copper bells, carved bone, and other artifacts, plus a few more skeletons) were brought to the surface. In order to see in this well, thousands of gallons of chemicals were successfully used to temporarily clarify the water (an unusual experiment by the Purex Co.). The chemicals destroyed many of the blindfish and shrimp in the cenote.

Observatory

One of the most graceful structures at Chichén Itzá is the **Caracol,** a two-tiered observatory shaped like a snail, where advanced theories of the sun and moon were calculated by Maya astronomers. Part of the spiral stairway into the tower/observatory is closed to tourists in an effort to preserve the decaying building. The circular room is laid out with narrow window slits facing south, west, and toward the summer solstice and the equinoxes. The priests used these celestial sightings to keep (accurate) track of time in their elaborate calendrical system.

Kukulcán

The most breathtaking place to view all of

Temple of the Warriors

OZ MALLAN

Chichén Itzá is from the top of Kukulcán, also called El Castillo. At 24 meters it's the tallest and most dramatic structure on the site. This imposing pyramid, built by the Maya on top of another, smaller pyramid, was probably constructed at the end of a 52-year cycle in thanksgiving to Maya gods for allowing the world to survive the elements—maybe even Halley's comet (Halley's swept by this part of the earth in A.D. 837 and, most recently, in 1986). The construction of the second temple was in approximately A.D. 850.

Kukulcán was built according to strict astronomical guidelines. Giant serpent heads repose at the base of the stairs. Each of the four sides has 91 steps. Including the platform on top, there are a total of 365 steps—one for each day of the year. On March 21 or 22 and September 22 or 23 (equinox days) between noon and 5 P.M., the sun casts an eerie shadow darkening all but one bright zigzag strip on the outside wall of the north staircase. This gives the appearance of a serpent slithering down the steep north-facing steps of the pyramid, giving life to the giant heads at the base. It seems to begin at the bottom in the spring and at the top in the fall. This was first noticed only a few decades ago. In the days when there were only a few people on the grounds watching, you could not only observe the serpent slithering down the steps, but also watch the shadow on the ground move toward the road to the sacred well—maybe looking for a sacrifice? Today the ground is covered with people. A visit during the dates of the equinox is a good time to observe the astronomical talents of the Maya, but be prepared for thousands of fellow watchers. Note: Some scientists have serious questions as to whether this effect was deliberately created by the Mayas or just a fluke caused by recent reconstruction.

Be sure to make the climb into the inner structure of Kukulcán where you'll see a red-painted, jade-studded sculpture of a jaguar, just as it was left by the Maya builders more than a thousand years ago. Check the visiting hours since the inner chamber is not always open.

Others

The largest building on the grounds is the **Nunnery,** named by the Spaniards. From the looks of it and its many rooms, it was a palace of some sort built during the classic period.

Tzompantli, meaning "Wall of Skulls," is a platform decorated on all sides with carvings of skulls. The figures are anatomically correct but have eyes staring out of large sockets. This rather ghoulish structure also depicts an eagle eating a human heart. It is presumed that ritualistic music and dancing on this platform culminated in a sacrificial death for the victim, the head then left on display, perhaps with others already in place. It's estimated that the platform was built A.D. 1050–1200.

A much-damaged pyramid, **Tomb of the High Priest,** has been taken apart piece by piece and rebuilt. The ruin is intriguing because of its inner burial chamber. Sometimes referred to as **Osario** (Spanish for "ossuary," a depository for bones of the dead), the pyramid at one time had four stairways—one on each side (like El Castillo)—and a temple at the crest. From the top platform, a vertical passageway lined with rock leads to the base of this decayed mound. There, from a small opening, stone steps lead into a cave about three meters deep. Seven tombs were discovered containing skeletons and the usual funeral trappings of important people, in addition to copper and jade artifacts. Archaeologists are working all around this area (commonly called "Old Chichén Itzá") and have several partially exposed ruins roped off. Work is expected to continue for several years and should result in significant findings about the Maya.

TIPS AND PRACTICALITIES

The only way to see this place is by walking. Wear walking shoes as climbing around in sandals can be uncomfortable and, more importantly, unsafe. Arrive early to take advantage of the weather (it's much cooler in the early hours) and the absence of the tour-bus crowds that arrive later in the day. Or, if the weather doesn't bother you, drop in around 4 P.M., when most people have left (while official closing time is 5 P.M., guards rarely kick visitors out). Either way, it's worth coming at a time when you can have the park almost to yourself. The shadows, either morning or afternoon, make great photos.

For some, a short walk around the grounds is all it takes (enough to say they've "been there"), but most require at least a day to get a good idea of what Chichén Itzá is all about. Still, we recommend you spend two full days here. Only then will you be able to study these archaeological masterpieces at your leisure, climb at your own pace, and be present at the odd hours when the inner chambers are open (only for short periods each day).

For a ruins nut, the best advice is to spend the night either at a hotel adjacent to the ruins, where you can be up and on the grounds as soon as the ticket taker is there (usually 8 A.M.), or at the nearby town of Piste with a good shot at getting to the site as early as you wish. This also allows time to return to your hotel for a leisurely lunch (maybe a swim), a short siesta, and an afternoon return visit (free with your ticket, hang on to it).

The ruins are open daily 8 A.M.–5 P.M., though some of the structures have special hours (posted on the buildings, or ask at the entrance). Admission is US$8.50 per person. There's an additional charge of US$8.50 if you bring in a video camera, and there's a small parking fee. The visitor's center offers clean restrooms, a café, a small museum, an auditorium (where short, informative films are shown), a bookstore, a gift shop, and an information center. You'll also find restaurants in the hotels near the site; check the hours since they're usually open for lunch (12:30–3 P.M.) only. Protect yourself from the sun and bring water.

A nightly sound and-light show is presented in English at 9 P.M. and Spanish at 7 P.M. French, Italian, German, and Maya versions may also be added. The fee is about US$5.

ACCOMMODATIONS NEAR THE RUINS

Only a few hotels are close to the ruins. Other hotel options are in nearby Piste (see below).

Hotel Dolores Alba, 2.2 kilometers east of the ruins, is comfortable, small, simple, and clean, with a swimming pool, dining room, and private baths. Rooms are under US$100. Free transportation to the ruins is available. For reservations and information, write Calle 63 #464, Mérida, Yucatán 97000, Mexico, tel. 992/8-5650, fax 992/8-3163. Be sure to designate that you want a room in the *Chichén Itza* Dolores Alba, since this address also takes reservations for

its sister hotel, the Mérida Hotel Dolores Alba.

Near the ruins, **Villa Arqueológica,** owned by Club Med, is a pleasant hotel with a lighthearted ambience. "Almost" deluxe, small-though-functional rooms have private baths and air-conditioning (some rooms have noisy air-conditioners; listen to yours before you sign the register). Amenities include a *shallow* swimming pool, a delightful garden and pool area, a bar, covered patio, and the best restaurant on this side of the ruins. Don't forget to bring along your receipt, voucher, or any other communication that says you have reservations and have paid. This hotel has been known for overbooking. Prices drop slightly in the summer. Reservations are suggested; from the United States call 800/258-2633.

The **Hotel Mayaland** is in the heart of the archaeological zone surrounded by over 100 acres of tropical fruit and flowering trees filled with unique species of birds. The lovely colonial hotel has 164 comfortable rooms with private baths, as well as a restaurant, bar, swimming pool, and tropical gardens. It's been around since the early 1930s and provides visitors with an ambience of beauty and tranquility. A long, winding staircase in the lobby, ornate leaded-glass windows in the original dining room, tile floors, tall ceilings, and overhead fans lend an exotic look.

Many rooms have been renovated, and TVs and air-conditioning have been added to rooms in the main building. The hotel offers a variety of accommodations, from standard rooms to villas to suites. Prices vary with the season, but a standard double runs about US$138. Reservations are suggested. From the United States call Mayaland Resorts, tel. 800/235-4079, and ask about their package deals, including their family plan. Also, ask about the free car rental with a stay at the hotel. And if you really want to splurge, see if you can sleep in the Pavarotti Suite for just US$2,500 per night. This is where Pavarotti slept when he sang in concert at the Chichén Itzá ruins. What a magnificent sound echoed through the stone ruins that night!

Note: Many people remember how convenient it once was to walk from Mayaland to the archaeological zone; as we go to press, the gate from Mayaland to the Chichén Itzá grounds is again open for business. This keeps changing!

Lovely **Hotel Hacienda Chichén Itzá,** tel.

992/4-2150, U.S. tel. 800/223-4084, is another historic place to stay. Once a working hacienda, it was the site of archaeologists' original bungalows. Narrow-gauge railroad tracks used in the 1920s for transportation and for hauling artifacts back to the hacienda still go through the outlying hotel grounds. The old mule train is also still in its place, but not used today. Rooms (US$100, reservations suggested) have been thoroughly renovated to accommodate modern travelers and include private bathrooms. You'll also find a pool, a dining room, and the main building of the original hacienda.

PISTE TO CHICHÉN ITZÁ

The village of Piste, 2.5 kilometers west of Chichén Itzá, has for years provided the workforce for the site's archaeological digs. Originally the workers were chosen because they were the closest, but now it's a matter of tradition.

Piste is growing up. The once-quiet village is becoming a viable addendum to Chichén's services. More hotels and restaurants are available each month as the number of tourists interested in Chichén Itzá grows. Be sure to look around at the many cafés and gift shops as well.

Puebla Maya
This pseudo Maya village is set up as a tourist attraction and rest area. Once inside the entrance, visitors walk along man-made rivers and lagoons to a large *palapa*-covered restaurant, often filled with tour bus groups. The US$10 buffet lunch is a good deal, especially since Piste's restaurants are typically overpriced and serve only mediocre food. Musicians play in the restaurant while artisans give pottery and hammock-weaving demonstrations in small Maya huts. Puebla Maya is open daily 11:30 A.M.–4:30 P.M.

Accommodations
Posada Olalde is a cheap (under US$50), pleasant, and modest place that's very convenient to the ruins, about a half-mile walk or 10 minutes by bus. It's a little complicated to find, so ask in town for directions, and there is no phone. **Posada El Paso** is another low-priced (under US$50), simple, and clean inn with screened windows, fans, a locked parking area, and

(sometimes) hot water. It's right next door to a café by the same name offering good and inexpensive food.

The **Piramide Inn Hotel,** no phone, offers a swimming pool and peaceful, grassy, tree-shaded grounds. The 40 pleasant rooms (US$50–100, add 10 percent if paying by credit card) have baths and air-conditioning and the dining room is open to both hotel guests and the public. Unfortunately, there's no longer a campground on the premises, so campers are out of luck. They may allow RVs to park in the lot, without hookups. If you're there and have no place to park, ask them.

What was formerly the rundown Hotel Misión Chichén is now the renovated and entirely spiffed up **Chichén Itzá Hotel,** U.S./Canada tel. 800/235-4079, Mexico tel. 988/7-0870, email: info@mayaland.com. Located in the heart of Piste, just a mile west of the ruins on Highway 180, it's the nicest place in town. It offers 44 rooms (US$88, credit cards accepted), comfortable beds, a pool, air-conditioning, nice gardens, and a dining room. Reservations are suggested. The hotel was taken over by the Mayaland Co. (at Chichén), and they know how to treat their guests.

Camping
Some camping is allowed at **Stardust Inn.** There's a good pool here, but it can get crowded.

TRANSPORTATION

By Car
Chichén Itzá lies adjacent to Highway 180, 121 kilometers east of Mérida, 213 kilometers west of Cancún, and 43 kilometers west of Valladolid. An eight-lane *autopista* connects Cancún and Mérida; exit at Piste. Tolls from either Mérida or Cancún are about US$18. The *libre* (free) roads to Chichén Itzá are in fair condition, as long as you slow down for the *topes* (traffic bumps) found before and after every village and school. Hitchhiking at the right time of day will put you in view of many autos on the highway, but be at your destination before dark or you may spend the night on the roadside; there's little traffic on this road after sunset.

entrance to the Balankanche Caves

OZ MALLAN

By Bus

Local buses leave for Piste from Cancún and Puerto Juárez (three-hour trip), and from Mérida (less than two hours). Ask about the return schedule.

By Plane

Small planes offer commuter service to Piste from Playa del Carmen, Cozumel, and Chetumal. For information and reservations check with **AeroFerinco, Playa del Carmen Airport,** tel. 987/3-1919, email: yourwings@aeroferinco.com; **AeroSaab,** located on 20th Av. south next to the Playa del Carmen airport, tel. 987/30804, email: info@aerosaab.com,; or **Aerocaribe,** tel. 988/4-1231 in Cancún, tel. 987/2-0877 in Cozumel. Expect to pay around US$60 for one-way travel between Piste and Cancún.

Escorted Tours

Escorted tours on modern air-conditioned buses leave daily from Cancún. Check with your hotel or one of the many travel agencies in the city. A variety of tours and prices are offered; ask around before you make a decision.

Check with your travel agent either in the United States or in Cancún or Cozumel; some agencies in Mexico offer pickup services for travelers who wish to spend the night near an archaeological zone.

THE BALANKANCHE CAVES

Only six kilometers east of Chichén Itzá, take a side trip to the Balankanche Caves. Here you'll descend into the earth and see many Maya ceremonial objects that look as though they were just left behind one day, 800 years ago. Discovered in 1959 by a tour guide named Gómez, the site was studied by prominent archaeologist Dr. E. Wyllys Andrews, commissioned by the National Geographic Society. What he saw, and what you can see today, is stirring: numerous stalactites and a giant stalagmite resembling the sacred "Ceiba Tree," surrounded by ceramic and carved ceremonial artifacts. This was obviously a sacred site for the Maya—a site that perpetuates the mystery of the ancient people.

At the entrance you'll find a parking lot, a cool spot to relax, a small café, a museum, interesting photos of Maya rituals, and guides; a sound-and-light show is offered nightly. The entrance fee is about US$6.50; the sound-and-light show is under US$4. The caves are open 8 A.M.–5 P.M. Guided tours are offered in Spanish at 9 A.M. and noon; in English at 11 A.M., 1 P.M., and 3 P.M.; and in French at 10 A.M. Surrounding the site you'll find a botanical garden with a variety of plants native to the Yucatán Peninsula.

Note: Remember that all museums and archaeological sites in Mexico are free on

Sundays and holidays, and children under 12 are always free.

X'KEKEN/DZITNUP

On the highway about four kilometers west of Valladolid, you'll see a small handmade sign that says Dzitnup. Turn off at the sign and follow the road about two kilometers to a delightful underground cenote. Wear comfortable walking shoes and your swimsuit in case you decide to take a swim. After a reasonably easy descent underground (in a few places you must bend over because of a low ceiling; there's a hanging rope to help), you'll come to a beautiful, circular pond of crystal-clear water. It's really a breathtaking place, with a high dome ceiling that has one small opening at the top letting in a ray of sun and dangling green vines. Often an errant bird or fluttering butterfly can be seen swooping low over the water before heading to the sun and sky through the tiny opening.

You'll see dramatic stalactites and a large stalagmite. You also might see catfish and blind-fish swimming in the placid water. This place is typical of the many underground caverns and grottoes common around the Peninsula, and well worth the small admission. Expect to be cajoled by small and tall sales people to buy their souvenirs. There's another cenote (on private property) at the southeast corner of the intersection of Highway 180 and the Dzitnup road. It's worth a stop on your way back. For a few pesos a guide will take you down some steps to an open area and a scum-covered cenote. The sight of tree roots reaching down into the cenote far below is unusual.

UXMAL AND VICINITY

Located 80 kilometers south of Mérida (a one-hour drive) in a range of low hills covered with brush, Uxmal is still another of the "greatest" Maya cities, this one in the Puuc region. Some believe it was founded by Maya from Guatemala's Petén in the 6th century. Others contend it dates back even further, perhaps to the preclassic period.

Unlike most of northern Yucatán, the Puuc region has good soil, allowing for greater population density than other areas. The city is believed to have been the hub of a district of about 160 square kilometers encompassing many sites, including Kabah, Sayil, Labná, and Xlapak. These Maya sites all reached their apogee during the late- to terminal-classic eras (A.D. 750–925).

Uxmal was probably the largest of the Puuc sites. It emerged as the dominant city-state between A.D. 850 and 900, when the House of the Magician, the Great Pyramid, and the Nunnery were built. Uxmal's control may have encompassed Kabah, because a *sacbe* (raised causeway) extended from Uxmal to that nearby city. Few stelae have been found at the site, but we know the name of at least one ruler, Lord Chac, who could have ordered the monumental construction.

In the mid-10th century, Uxmal was abandoned, probably after being defeated by Chichén Itzá's armies. During the postclassic era, the Xiu clan, based in the nearby town of Mani, spuriously claimed to be descended from Uxmal's rulers and occupied the ruins.

Puuc Architecture
The Maya word Uxmal (oosh-MAHL) means "Thrice Built," and, in fact, refers to the number of times this ceremonial center was rebuilt (though some believe it was rebuilt five times). In many instances structures were superimposed over existing buildings; all are examples of the purely Maya "Puuc" style.

Puuc architecture is one of the major achievements of Mesoamerica; hallmarks of the style include thin squares of limestone veneer, decorated cornices, boot-shaped vault stones, rows of attached half columns, and upper facades heavily decorated with stone mosaics and sky-serpent monster masks.

Precious Water
Because of the almost total absence of surface lakes or rivers in Yucatán, the collection of water was of prime importance to the survival of the

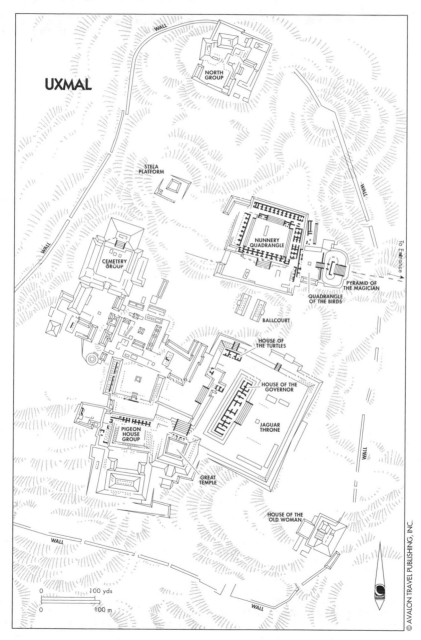

UXMAL

WALL

NORTH GROUP

STELA PLATFORM

CEMETERY GROUP

NUNNERY QUADRANGLE

To Entrance ▲

PYRAMID OF THE MAGICIAN

QUADRANGLE OF THE BIRDS

BALLCOURT

HOUSE OF THE TURTLES

HOUSE OF THE GOVERNOR

PIGEON HOUSE GROUP

JAGUAR THRONE

WALL

GREAT TEMPLE

HOUSE OF THE OLD WOMAN

WALL

WALL

0   100 yds

0   100 m

© AVALON TRAVEL PUBLISHING, INC.

Maya. Unlike most Maya centers in Yucatán, Uxmal was not built around a cenote, since there are none in this arid part of the Peninsula. Rainwater was collected in *aguadas* (natural holes in the ground) as well as in man-made *chultunes* (cisterns) built into the ground, sometimes right inside a house or under a patio.

Most of the Maya religious ceremonies and idols were devoted to the worship of Chac, the rain god. The constant threat of drought inspired the people to build great centers of worship, with hundreds of carvings and mosaics representing Chac and his prominent hooked nose.

EARLY EXPLORATIONS

Father López de Cogulludo explored the ruins in the 16th century, long after the Indians had abandoned the site. Without any facts to go on, he referred to the Nunnery Quadrangle (Las Monjas) as the dwelling of the Maya "Vestal Virgins," who kept the "Sacred Fire."

Cogulludo was followed by Jean-Fredric de Waldeck in 1836, who published a handsomely illustrated folio showing the structures of Uxmal peeking over thick brush. He compared them with the ruins of Pompeii. In 1841 the adventurous "dynamic duo" of John L. Stephens and Frederick Catherwood began their well-documented journey through the Peninsula. By that time, the Indians must have cleared plots of land around Uxmal to plant corn, since Stephens commented that "emerging from the woods we came unexpectedly on a large open field strewn with mounds of ruins and vast buildings on terraces and pyramidal structures grand and in good preservation"—shown beautifully by Catherwood's sketches.

The first real excavations, led by the noted Danish archaeologist Frans Blom, began in 1929. Blom was involved in many archaeological digs in the Maya hinterland. Since Blom's time, many other archaeologists have worked with the Mexican government at Uxmal; the result is a fine reconstructed site open for the enjoyment of the public. The small area (700 by 800 meters) of Uxmal presents some of the finest examples of Maya design, without Toltec influence.

THE TEMPLES OF UXMAL

House of the Magician/
House of the Diviner

This "pyramid," the tallest on the grounds, rises 38 meters. It's shaped in a distinctive elliptical form, rather than a true pyramid. The west staircase, facing the Nunnery Quadrangle, is extremely steep (a 60-degree angle). Before you begin your climb do some leg stretches to loosen your muscles! Under this west stairway you can see parts of the first temple built on the site; the date on one door lintel is A.D. 569. On the east fa-

House of the Magician, Uxmal

OZ MALLAN

cade, the stairway has a broader slant, and though it's still a steep incline, it isn't nearly so hard on the legs.

In the upper part of the east staircase you can enter an inner chamber, which is **Temple Two**. **Temple Three** consists of nothing more than a small shrine at the rear of Temple Two. Climbing the west stairway brings you to **Temple Four** and an elaborate Chac mask with an open mouth large enough for a human to pass through. **Temple Five** dates back to the 9th century and is reached by climbing the east stairway. From this viewpoint you'll be able to see the entire site of Uxmal and the surrounding brush-covered Puuc hills. These five temples were built one over the other!

Nunnery Quadrangle
The Nunnery, northwest of the House of the Magician, is a courtyard covering an area of 60 by 45 meters, bounded on each side by a series of buildings constructed on platforms of varying heights during different periods of time. The buildings, which contain numerous small rooms, reminded the Spaniards of the nunneries in Spain.

House of the Turtles
A path leads south from the Nunnery to the House of the Turtles. This simple structure is six by 30 meters. The lower half is very plain, but the upper part is decorated with a frieze of columns; a cornice above that has a series of turtles along its facade. The turtle played an important part in Maya mythology.

Governor's Palace
Just south of the House of the Turtles is the Governor's Palace. Its facade is even more elaborate than those found at the Nunnery, culminating in a portrait-relief over the central doorway that may represent Lord Chac, Uxmal's most powerful ruler. The palace is considered by some to be the finest example of pre-Hispanic architecture in Mesoamerica. It sits on a large platform; measures almost 100 meters long, 12 meters across, and eight meters high; and has 11 entrances. The lower facade is plain, but the upper section is a continuous series of ornate carvings and mosaics of geometrical shapes and Chac masks. Two arrow-shaped corbel

arches add to the delicate design of this extraordinary building. The double-headed jaguar in front of the palace (presumed to be a throne) was first found by John Stephens in 1841.

The Great Pyramid
Another large structure is the Great Pyramid (30 meters high), originally terraced with nine levels and a temple on the top. According to early explorers, at one time four small structures sat on each of the four sides of the top platform. The top story is decorated in typical Puuc fashion, with ornate carvings and stonework depicting flowers, masks, and geometric patterns.

Others
Walking through the grounds, you'll find many other structures and a ball court. Be sure to visit the **Dovecote, House of the Old Woman, Phallic Collection, and the Temple of the Phallus,** other small structures, and as-yet-unexcavated mounds.

TIPS AND PRACTICALITIES

Uxmal is not a city, so don't expect much in the way of services. There are a few hotels with restaurants, but nothing else. To do justice to this fascinating antiquity, plan to stay at least a full day. Because Mérida is only an hour away, it's easy to make this a day trip by bus or car. Or continue on and spend the night in Ticul, 65 kilometers (one hour) farther.

You can pick up a guide (or he'll try to pick you up) at the entrance to the ruins. If you feel a need for this service, be sure you agree on the fee before you begin your tour. Also something to remember: Every guide will give you his own version of the history of the ruins, part family legend (if you're lucky) and part fairy tale. And let's face it, no one really knows the history of this obscure culture shrouded by the centuries. Many good books are available on the archaeological ruins of the larger sites (see "Booklist").

The grounds are open 8 A.M.–5 P.M.; admission is about US$6.50, parking is about US$1.50, use of a video camera is about US$8 extra. A sound-and-light show is presented each evening (see "Entertainment," below). The restaurants and shops in the visitor's center and the artisan stands on the grounds are open until 9 P.M.

ACCOMMODATIONS

About one kilometer from the ruins is **Hotel Misión Uxmal,** 78 Campeche Rd., www.travelhero .com. Transportation to the ruins is available. This hotel has all the modern amenities, including a pool, a bar, and a dining room. Its nice rooms (US$88) include private baths and air-conditioning. Credit cards are accepted.

Hotel Villa Arqueológica, U.S. tel. 800/258-2633, is the newest of Uxmal's hotels and is owned by a branch of Club Med. A clone of its sister hotels in Cobá and Chichén Itzá, the hotel has small, attractive, and functional rooms (US$71 per person, double occupancy), with twin beds on built-in cement platforms, air-conditioning (a few readers have complained that the air-conditioning can be noisy), and private bathrooms with showers. Both floors look out onto a tropical courtyard.

The flower-covered patio has a sparkling (shallow) pool, outside bar and table service, a covered cabaña area, and a complete library on the history and culture of the Maya. You'll find some French dishes along with local specialties in the large dining room. Room rates (US$41 per person) include breakfast. Dinner is an additional US$30 per person. Á la carte lunches and dinners average about US$25 per person, breakfast is about US$12. Credit cards are accepted.

An older colonial-style favorite, **Hotel Hacienda Uxmal,** U.S./Canada tel. 800/235-4079, Mérida tel. 99/25-2122 or 25-2133, fax 99/25-7022, has undergone some renovations in the past few years. Air-conditioning and cable television have been added to some rooms, and a spacious wooden deck has been built around the pool. Other features include tile walkways and floors, large old-fashioned rooms with heavy carved furniture, pathways through tropical gardens, and a gift shop and bar. Rates range from US$98–114. Credit cards are accepted.

A spacious dining room serves typical Yucatecan food and some continental dishes in fixed-price meals. There are usually four entrée selections at dinner (nothing too exciting), plus a fruit salad or soup and dessert for about US$18. Snacks and lower-priced meals are available at the café Nicte-Ha, next to the hotel's second pool, just across from the road to the ruins (open 1–8:30 P.M.).

The Lodge at Uxmal, U.S./Canada tel. 800/235-4079, Mexico tel. 988/7-0870, email: uxmal@mayaland.com is the newest of the hotels at Uxmal. More luxurious than the others, it's surrounded by lovely gardens and includes a nice restaurant and a swimming pool. Bungalow rooms (US$174–188) have comfy beds, private bathrooms, air-conditioning, and fans. There's also free access to sister hotel Hacienda Uxmal's tennis court and pool. This is a lovely spot, just a short distance from the Uxmal ruins site.

FOOD

The hotel dining rooms welcome visitors. Expect to pay about US$12–16 for a complete three-course lunch (or ask what light meals are available). The hotels used to allow those who paid for a meal to swim in their pools, but that practice seems to have ceased. Ask before you dive in.

At the Uxmal Visitor's Center at the entrance to the ruins, a small restaurant serves cold drinks and light meals and a kiosk just outside offers cold drinks. If you're driving, another alternative is to take the road back toward Mérida (Highway 261) 18 kilometers north to Muna where there are small cafés in the villages and a few on the road.

ENTERTAINMENT

Every evening a **sound-and-light show** is presented in Spanish (7 P.M.) and English (9 P.M.) at the ruins overlooking the Nunnery Quadrangle. Escorted tours to the shows are available from Mérida. If you've never seen one of these shows, check it out. It's a wonderful experience. Sometimes Mother Nature adds her own drama: the rumble of thunder from a distant storm, or jagged streaks of luminous light in a black sky. The already eerie temples reflect a supernatural glow evoking the memory of the Maya, their mysterious beginnings, and their still unsolved disappearance. Small admission.

SHOPPING

The visitor's center at the entrance to the Uxmal site is modern and beautiful. It offers clean restrooms, gift shops, a small museum, an auditorium showing a short film about the Yucatán Peninsula, a bookstore with a good supply of English-language books about the various ruins on the Peninsula, an ice-cream shop, and a small cafeteria.

Outside the entrance are kiosks where local women sell the *huipil* (Yucatecan dress). Their prices are often much better than those you'll find in gift shops frequently the garments are made by the saleswoman or someone in her family. Some dresses are machine-embroidered or made of polyester, though many are still handmade from white cotton with bright embroidery thread. Be sure you get what you want. The *huipiles* worn by Maya women always look snow white with brilliant colors. Don't forget to bargain.

The only other shopping at Uxmal is at the small gift shops adjoining the hotels near the ruins. Most of them sell the usual curios, clothing, tobacco, postage stamps, and postcards.

Note: If you're driving or on a tour bus (not a local bus), you'll have the opportunity to stop at the little shops selling *huipiles* and crafts along the highway close to the ruins.

GETTING THERE

Local **Autotransportes del Sureste** buses leave Mérida's main bus station (Calle 69 #544) daily, with departures at 6 A.M., 9 A.M., noon, and 3 P.M.; the last return bus to Mérida departs Uxmal at 7:30 P.M. Check at the bus station in advance, since schedules are apt to change. Allow at least one hour for the trip (79 kilometers), and be sure to check the return time to Mérida. Buses to Uxmal leave Campeche from the ADO station (Gobernadores 289).

Buses do not go onto the ruins road, but stop on the side of the highway at the turnoff to the ruins. Highway 261 from Mérida to Campeche passes close to the Uxmal ruins and is a good road. From Mérida the drive to Uxmal takes about one hour; from Campeche allow two hours (175 kilometers). Travel agencies in Mérida offer tours of the ruins at Uxmal. Check with the government tourist office at Teatro Peón Contreras on Calle 61 in downtown Mérida for more information.

PUUC RUINS

An entire day could be spent making a loop from Uxmal to the smaller Puuc sites of Kabah, Sayil, Xlapak, and Labná, lying in the jungle-covered hills southeast of Uxmal. For the most part these are small sites and easy to see or photograph quickly, and the ornate Puuc design is well worth the time and effort. The government has reopened the ruins to anthropologists and archaeologists, and some excavation and renovation is underway. The countryside for some 15 kilometers around Uxmal and the Puuc sites is now a national preserve, and

ladies sell colorful huipiles *at Uxmal*

OZ MALLAN

arch at Labná

some of the indigenous animals and birds are beginning to multiply.

The politics of the smaller Puuc sites were certainly dominated by their larger neighbor. Kabah was settled as far back as the late preclassic (300 B.C.–A.D. 250), but the ruins we now see at all four sites date from the late and terminal classic. Although the buildings are generally smaller than those found at Uxmal, they are all fine examples of the Puuc style, and some, like the temple at Xlapak, have a gemlike beauty. Sayil, the only one to be fully mapped, covered 1.7 square miles at its late-classic height and had a population of over 10,000. These sites were abandoned in the 10th century at the same time as Uxmal. Admission to each of the sites is about US$3.50; all sites are open daily 8 A.M.–5 P.M.

Kabah

Kabah was constructed between A.D. 850 and 900. Nineteen kilometers south of Uxmal, structures are found on both sides of Highway 261. The most ornate building is the **Codz-Pop,** dedicated to the rain god, Chac. This temple is 45 meters long and six meters high. Part of the original rooftop comb (at one time three meters high), with its uneven rectangular openings, can still be seen. The entire west facade is a series of 250 masks with the typical elongated, curved nose, some almost a complete circle. The Puuc architecture is colored beige, rust, brown, and gray from the oxides in the earth that engulfed the building for so many years. Small pits on

each mask are said to have been used to burn incense or oil; Codz-Pop must have shone like a Chinese lantern from great distances throughout the rolling countryside. Inside the building are two parallel series of five rooms each. Archaeologists are currently doing intensive reconstruction work at Kabah; when finished, it will be a truly impressive site.

The Arch

West of the road is the impressive Arch of Kabah. It is presumed that this arch marks the end of a ceremonial Maya *sacbe* extending from Uxmal to Kabah. A few more structures have been partially restored—look for the **Great Temple** and the **Temple of the Columns.**

Sayil

A short distance brings you to a side road to Oxkutzcab (Highway 184); follow this road first to Sayil (in Maya this word means "anthill"). This is probably the most imposing site on the loop. Several hundred known structures at Sayil illustrate a technical progression from the earliest, simplest building to the more recent, most ornate **Chultun Palace,** constructed in A.D. 730. The palace is a large, impressive building, over 60 meters long, with three levels creating two terraces, again showing the outstanding architectural talents of the Classic period. The second level is decorated with Greek-style columns and a multitude of rich carvings, including the ever-present rain god and one distinctive portrayal of a descending god (an upside-down figure referred to as the bee god). By A.D. 800 this site was abandoned.

Because of the lack of rainfall in this area, *chultunes* are found everywhere, including the sites of the ceremonial centers. One example of a *chultun* that holds up to 7,000 gallons of water can be seen at the northwest corner of the palace. The fast-decaying **Temple Mirador** (on a path going south from the palace) and the monument of a human phallic figure lie beyond.

Xlapak

Six kilometers farther on the same road (east of Sayil) is the Xlapak turnoff. Though this Puuc site is small, do stop to see the restored building with its curious carvings: tiers of masks, curled Chac noses, and geometric stepped frets. It's easy to pick out the light-colored areas of restoration compared to the darker weathered stones that were covered with bushes and soil oxides for so many years. The word Xlapak in Maya means "Old Walls."

Labná

Another Maya arch (really a portal vault) of great beauty is at Labná, located three kilometers beyond Xlapak. Be sure to examine the northeast side of this structure to see two outstanding representations of thatched Maya huts, one on each side of the portal. This arch is one of the largest and most ornate built by the Maya; the passageway measures three by six meters.

The Palace

This Puuc-style structure was built at the end of the classic period, about A.D. 850. The elaborate multiroom pyramid sits on an immense platform 165 meters long, and the structure is 135 meters long by 20 meters high. A *chultun* is built into the second story of the palace and, according to archaeologist George Andrews, at least 60 *chultunes* have been located in the Labná area, indicating a population of about 3,000 residents within the city.

El Mirador

This stark, square building stands on a tall mound with a roof comb gracing the top. The comb on the small temple was originally decorated with a carved seated figure and a series of death heads. The carvings were still in place in the 1840s when John Stephens traveled through the Peninsula. The elements and time continue to wreak their destruction on the ancient structures of the Maya.

MANI

This small town east of Ticul was the scene of early surrender by the Xius (prominent Maya rulers with descendants still living in the state of Yucatán). Montejo the Elder quickly took over, and by the mid-1500s a huge church/monastery complex had been built; 6,000 slaves working under the direction of Fray Juan de Mérida completed the structure in only seven months. This old building, still with a priest in residence, is huge and in its day must have been beautiful, with graceful lines and pocket patios. Fray de Mérida also designed and built similar structures at Izamal and Valladolid.

Historians believe it was in Mani that Friar Diego de Landa confiscated and burned the books held in reverence by the Maya. These codices, the first books produced in North America, were hand-lettered on fig bark carefully worked until it was thin and pliable, then coated with a thin white plaster sizing and screen folded. According to Landa they were filled with "vile superstitions and lies of the devil." Since that time, only four more codices have been found. The most recent (1977), though its authenticity was doubted at first, is gaining more and more credibility among archaeologists. The remaining three books are in museums in Dresden, Paris, and Madrid. Replicas can be seen at the Anthropological Museum in Mexico City. The destruction of the codices was a monumental tragedy not only for the Maya—the loss to the world is incalculable. Only a little progress toward learning the mysterious glyphs has been made; who knows, the destroyed books may have been the lost key to their language, their history, and their mystery. It is hoped that other codices exist and will some day turn up—perhaps in an unexcavated tomb still buried in the jungle. Many villages still practice the ancient rituals of their ancestors and appoint keepers of the sacred records. However, these people have learned from the experiences of their ancestors and tell no outsiders of their task.

WEST OF CHETUMAL

KOHUNLICH

Sixty-seven kilometers west of Chetumal on Highway 186, turn left and drive eight kilometers on a good side road to this unique Maya site. The construction lasted from the late preclassic (about A.D. 100–200) through the classic (A.D. 600–900) periods. Though not totally restored nor nearly as grand as Chichén Itzá or Uxmal, Kohunlich is worth the trip if only to visit the exotic **Temple of the Masks,** dedicated to the Maya sun god. The stone pyramid is under an unlikely thatch roof (to prevent further deterioration from the weather), and unique gigantic stucco masks stand two to three meters tall. Wander through the jungle site and you can find 200 structures or uncovered mounds from the same era as Palenque. Many carved stelae are scattered throughout the surrounding forest.

Walking through luxuriant foliage, you'll note orchids in the tops of trees, plus small colorful wildflowers, lacy ferns, and lizards that share cracks and crevices in moldy stone walls covered with velvety moss. The relatively unknown site attracts few tourists. The absence of trinket sellers and soft-drink stands leaves the visitor feeling that he or she is the first to stumble on the haunting masks with their star-incised eyes, moustaches (or are they serpents?), and nose plugs—features extremely different from carvings found at other Maya sites. The site is well cleared, and when we last visited, archaeologists from INAH were excavating a burial mound. Like most archaeological zones, Kohunlich is fenced and open 8 A.M.–5 P.M.; admission is US$3.50.

Accommodations: While you're here, check out the lovely new **Explorean Kohunlich Hotel,** tel. 877/346-6116. Almost at the entrance to the ruins, we haven't seen it, but we hear it's quite lovely. Rates are US$660 per person, double occupancy, for a three-night all-inclusive vacation—all meals, beverages, diving, tours, and tax. Many jungle trips are offered. Rooms include many touches of luxury. Ask about van transfer from the airport in Cancún.

If you're driving, Kohunlich is an easy day trip from Chetumal or Bacalar; in Chetumal check with local buses or travel agencies or your hotel for information about organized tours to Kohunlich and the nearby ruins at Xpujil, Becán, and Chicanná in the state of Campeche.

RÍO BEC SITES

Driving west on Highway 186 will ultimately bring you to Xpujil (also written Xpuhil), Becán, and Chicanná, the most accessible sites of south-central Yucatán's Río Bec culture. They share the distinctive Río Bec architectural style, whose hallmarks are "palaces" with flanking towers that appear on first glance to be classic pyramids with temples on top. When you look closer, you realize that the "pyramid's" steps are actually reliefs and the temple is just a solid box with a phony door. It is as if they wanted the look of a Tikal-style temple without going through the trouble of building one. The towers are usually capped with roof combs, and sky-serpent masks are frequent decorations on all ceremonial buildings.

The earliest occupation of the Río Bec area occurred between 1000 and 300 B.C. The great earthworks at Becán, which were probably defensive, were built around A.D. 150. Shortly afterward, the distant city of Teotihuacán's influence appears at the site in the form of ceramics and other evidence. Researchers believe that during the early-classic period, Becán was ruled by trader/warriors from that great culture. Most of the existing structures in the Río Bec region were constructed between A.D. 550 and 830. Then the population gradually dwindled away and by the time of the Spanish conquest the sites were completely abandoned. The Río Bec sites were rediscovered early in the 20th century by chicle tappers.

The sites of Chicanná, Becán, and Xpujil are well worth the visit and are easy to get to from the main highway 186/that crosses from Escarcega to Chetumal. In order to further develop the Mundo Maya project (also called La Ruta Maya), the Mexican government has recently agreed to spend big bucks in this area of Campeche, where some of the most interesting archaeological sites have been fairly well ignored until now. Water has always been a stumbling block for tourist development, but rumor has it there will soon be plenty of water and electricity with which to begin upgrading the area. INAH (the archaeological arm of the Mexican government—National Institute of Anthropology and History) has begun work on some of the main structures, and many more structures and caves in the jungle continue to be "found." Because of the proximity to Calakmul, one of the largest Maya sites found thus far, and the concentration of sites (though presently not fully developed), there will be many tourists coming through this part of Campeche.

The adventurous may also want to explore the sites of Río Bec itself and El Hormiguero, which lie south of the road. They're most easily reached during the dry season along poor packed dirt and gravel roads, but they are accessible during the rainy season by four-wheel-drive vehicle.

Xpujil

Past the nearby small village of Xpujil is this classic example of Río Bec architecture: the remains of three false towers overlooking miles of jungle. On the back side of the central tower, check out what's left of two huge inlaid masks. Xpujil is one of the best-preserved Río Bec–style structures, unique for having a taller central tower in addition to the flanking twin towers. If you're in a vehicle that can handle a primitive jeep road, you can reach Río Bec by taking the road south of the gas station near Xpujil.

Just before you get into the small town of Xpujil, you'll see a large, circular *palapa* restaurant called **Maya Mirador.** This is an okay lunch stop, serving simple Mexican fare (with killer salsa!) and cold drinks (no wild game sold here). It serves an uninspired but healthy plate of steamed vegetables with bean soup and tortillas, as well as *bistec ranchero,* so-so enchiladas, or garlic shrimp. Behind the café, a few small clean, wooden cabins are available, with screened windows, mosquito nets, fans, and clean sheets. Best are rooms with a private bath (US$15 double), as you have to walk through the restaurant to get to the communal baths. Rooms with shared bath are US$15. The restaurant also changes dollars at reasonable rates. Ask about a van that takes passengers from

giant masks of Kohunlich

Chetumal to Tikal. Public restrooms are available.

This is also an ideal place for bird-watching in thick jungle with little or no tourist traffic. Don't forget your binoculars and bug repellent! If you're traveling by bus to Chetumal, check with the tourist office or a travel agency for bus trips to these sites. Not fully restored, the ruins will give you an indication of what the archaeologists find when they first stumble upon an isolated site. You will have renewed wonder at how they manage to clear away hundreds of years of jungle growth, figure out a puzzle of thousands of stones, and end up with such impressive structures.

Note: Don't be surprised to see lots of soldiers in Xpujil. This has become a major checkpoint for the army looking for drug smugglers. It hasn't improved the look of the town. Just cooperate with their questions; in most cases tourists aren't bothered.

Note: Although you should be careful of those few strangers who look to rob and steal, the majority of the people in the Yucatán Peninsula are friendly, kind folks. On a recent visit to Belize, we took a day trip into Mexico to the ruins of Xpujil, and our car gave up without warning. There we were, stranded; it was almost dark, there were no phones, nor was there much of anything else. We eventually flagged down a pickup truck and a kind-hearted farmer agreed to drive us to the Mexico/Belize border (as long as we didn't mind riding in the back with various and sundry animals). We were grateful, animals and all, for the friendly helping hand.

Becán

Another six kilometers along Highway 186 (275 kilometers south of Campeche city) is the turnoff to Becán. Dating back to 500 B.C., Becán offers archaeology buffs some of the largest ancient buildings in the state of Campeche. **Structure VIII,** just off the southeast plaza, offers a labyrinth of underground rooms, passageways, and artifacts, indicating this to be an important religious ceremonial center. You'll see an unusual waterless moat—15 meters wide, four meters deep, and 2.3 kilometers in diameter—surrounding the entire site and indicating that warring factions occupied this part of the Peninsula during the 2nd century. Historians claim that the residents were constantly at war with Mayapán, in what is now the state of Yucatán.

Chicanná

Five kilometers west, the Maya site of Chicanná is about a half kilometer off Highway 186. The small city included five structures encircling a main center. An elaborate serpent mask frames the entry of the main palace, **House of the Serpent Mouth**—it's in comparatively good repair. Across the plaza lies **Structure I,** a typical Río Bec–style building complex with twin false-temple towers. Several hundred meters south are two more temple groups. If you want to compare the subtle differences of design and architecture of the ancient Maya throughout the Peninsula, the group is worth a day's visit.

Accommodations: Near Chicanná note the sign that says, "hotel." Turn off onto a deserted limestone road and in the middle of nowhere you'll find a white oasis/hotel, the **Chicanná Ecovillage** (there's no phone here; make reservations at the Ramada Hotel in Campeche city:

tel. 981/6-2233). Here one- and two-story solar-powered stucco villas (US$90) are tastefully decorated and well landscaped. The lodge offers a small, solar-heated pool, and good food in a small dining room. Nearby ruins include Calakmul. This place has a special ambience—no city sounds, just the song of the birds and the rhythmic swish of a broom sweeping the stone walkways. The hotel's entire operation functions according to stringent ecological rules.

Zoh Laguna

Zoh Laguna village is 10 kilometers north of Xpujil. In the midst of the forest, it was created in the 1930s as a mill town to house Maya workers, 35 years before Xpujil was founded. The mahogany veneer mill is no longer in full operation.

The small, tree-shaded town is laid back and slow moving, and unlike the typical Maya village, the houses are all built of whitewashed wood planking. This makes a comfortable hub to explore the Río Bec and Calakmul archaeological regions.

The village houses the **Calakmul Model Forest,** part of an international network of Model Forests helping the locals diversify their economy and adjust to the extreme changes taking place in their lives—in this case the increasing numbers of tourists eager to visit the ruins close by. In 1994 Becán—the best known archaeological site in the area—welcomed about 30–40 visitors per month. In 1997 the numbers had risen to 300 per month.

For now there's very little choice of hotels in the area, but that may change in the future. Right now, visitors will find the fine little **Hotel Bosque,** which offers just six simple rooms, each with washbasin, towels, a large window, tiled floors, and a mirror, desk, and small dresser. Bathrooms (toilet and shower) are shared between two rooms (no hot water); hammocks are available to rent. The hotel has a nice breezy common room at the entrance. All proceeds go to sustainable forestry work in the region.

CALAKMUL RESERVE

Located in the Petén region in the southern area of Campeche, 35 kilometers from the border with Guatemala, Calakmul has given its name to

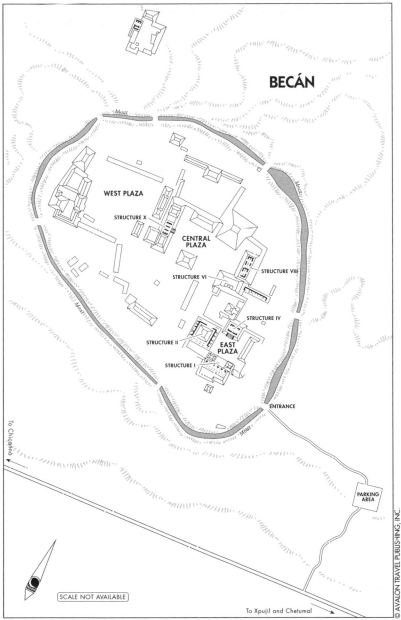

BECÁN

Moat

WEST PLAZA

STRUCTURE X

CENTRAL PLAZA

STRUCTURE VI

STRUCTURE VIII

STRUCTURE IV

STRUCTURE II

EAST PLAZA

STRUCTURE I

ENTRANCE

Moat

To Chicanná

PARKING AREA

To Xpujil and Chetumal

SCALE NOT AVAILABLE

© AVALON TRAVEL PUBLISHING, INC.

one of the newest, largest biosphere reserves in Mexico. This site was once home to more than 60,000 Maya. What may turn out to be the largest of all the structures built by the Maya, a massive pyramid, looms 53 meters (175 feet) over a base that covers two hectares (five acres).

An archaeological team from the Universidad Autónoma del Sudeste in Campeche has mapped 6,750 structures; uncovered two tombs holding magnificent jade masks, beads, and two flowerlike earcaps; excavated parts of three ceremonial sites; and found more stelae than at any other Maya site. From the top of pyramid two, it's possible to see the Danta pyramid at Calakmul's sister site, El Mirador, also part of the Calakmul reserve on the Guatemala side of the border. Both of these sites predate Christ by 100 years.

Heading the archaeological team at Calakmul, William Folan has made startling discoveries, but even more important, he has been instrumental in pushing through the concept of the biosphere reserve. Today it has become a reality. Calakmul is not yet on the usual itinerary because of the difficulty reaching it.

Expect 60 kilometers of a paved, though very narrow, one-lane winding road off the highway. The jungle grows to the edge of the road, making it impossible to see another vehicle coming around a curve. Drive carefully and be ready to pull over. Fortunately there is very little traffic. If that doesn't scare you off, you'll be glad to know that there are now toilet facilities along with water, and a reliable one-kilometer trail from the parking lot to the ruins through the brush. Climbers will discover exquisite views from the top of the structures. Wildlife is rampant—in the morning you'll see toucans, monkeys, and parrots (and if you don't see them, you'll hear the howler monkeys roaring). You might feel like the only person in the universe at this still-undiscovered site.

If you'd like more information, contact the tourist office in Campeche city. Also see the October 1989 issue of *National Geographic* magazine for color photos of the Calakmul archaeological site.

BOOKLIST

The following titles provide insight into the Yucatán Peninsula and the Maya people. A few of these books are easier obtained in Mexico, but all of them will cost less in the United States. Most are nonfiction, though several are fiction and great to pop into your carry-on for a good read on the plane, or for any time you want to get into the Yucatecan mood. Happy reading.

Coe, Andrew. *Archaeological Mexico: A Traveler's Guide to Ancient Cities and Sacred Sites.* Emeryville, CA: Avalon Travel Publishing, 2001.

Coe, Michael D. *The Maya.* New York: Thames and Hudson, 1980. A well-illustrated, easy-to-read volume on the Maya people.

Cortés, Hernán. *Five Letters.* Gordon Press, 1977. Cortés wrote long letters to the king of Spain telling of his accomplishments and trying to justify his actions in the New World.

Davies, Nigel. *The Ancient Kingdoms of Mexico.* New York: Penguin Books. Excellent study of pre-conquest (1519) indigenous peoples of Mexico.

De Landa, Bishop Diego. *Yucatán Before and After the Conquest.* New York: Dover Publications, 1978. This book, translated by William Gates from the original 1566 volume, has served as the base for all research that has taken place since. De Landa (though the man destroyed countless books of the Maya people) has given the world insight into their culture before the conquest.

Díaz del Castillo, Bernal. *The Conquest of New Spain.* New York: Penguin Books, 1963. History straight from the adventurer's reminiscences, translated by J.M. Cohen.

Fehrenbach, T.R. *Fire and Blood: A History of Mexico.* New York: Collier Books, 1973. Mexico's history over 3,500 years, told in a way to keep you reading.

Ferguson, William M. *Maya Ruins of Mexico in Color.* Norman: University of Oklahoma Press, 1977. Good reading before you go, but too bulky to carry along. Oversized with excellent drawings and illustrations of the archaeological structures of the Maya Indians.

Franz, Carl. *The People's Guide to Mexico.* New Mexico: John Muir Publications, 1998. A humorous guide filled with witty anecdotes and helpful general information for visitors to Mexico. Don't expect any specific city information, just nuts-and-bolts hints for traveling south of the border.

Greene, Graham. *The Power and the Glory.* New York: Penguin Books, 1977. A novel that takes place in the '20s about a priest and the anti-church movement that gripped the country.

Heffern, Richard. *Secrets of the Mind-Altering Plants of Mexico.* New York: Pyramid Books. A fascinating study of many subtances, from ancient ritual hallucinogens to today's medicines.

Laughlin, Robert M. *The People of the Bat.* Smithsonian Institution Press, 1988. Maya tales and dreams as told by the Zinacantán Indians in Chiapas.

Lewbel, George S. *Diving and Snorkeling Guide to Cozumel.* New York: Pisces Books, 1984. A well-illustrated volume for divers and snorkelers going to Cozumel. The small, easily carried volume is packed with hints about different dive sites, reefs, and marinelife of Cozumel.

Mallan, Chicki and Oz Mallan. *Colonial Mexico: A Traveler's Guide to Historic Districts and Towns.* Emeryville, CA: Avalon Travel Publishing, 2001.

Meyer, Michael, and William Sherman. *The Course of Mexican History.* Oxford University Press. A concise, one-volume history of Mexico.

Nelson, Ralph. *Popul Vuh: The Great Mythological Book of the Ancient Maya.* Boston: Houghton Mifflin, 1974. An easy-to-read translation of myths handed down orally by the Quiche Maya, family to family, until written down after the Spanish conquest.

Riding, Alan. *Distant Neighbors.* Vintage Books. A modern look at today's Mexico.

Sodi, Demetrio M. (in collaboration with Adela Fernandez). *The Mayas.* Mexico: Panama Editorial S.A. This small pocketbook presents a fictionalized account of life among the Maya before the conquest. Easy reading for anyone who enjoys fantasizing about what life *might* have been like before recorded history in the Yucatán. This book is available in the Yucatecan states of Mexico.

Stephens, John L. *Incidents of Travel in Central America, Chiapas, and Yucatán.* 2 vols. New York: Dover Publications, 1969. Good companions to refer to when traveling in the area. Stephens and illustrator Frederick Catherwood rediscovered many of the Maya ruins on their treks that took place in 1841. Easy reading.

Thompson, J. Eric. *Maya Archaeologist.* Norman: University of Oklahoma, 1963. Thompson, a noted Maya scholar, traveled and worked at most of the Maya ruins in the 1930s.

Thompson, J. Eric. *The Rise and Fall of the Maya Civilization.* Norman: University of Oklahoma Press, 1954. One man's story of the Maya Indian. Excellent reading.

Werner, David. *Where There is No Doctor.* California: The Hesperian Foundation. This is an invaluable medical aid to anyone traveling not only to isolated parts of Mexico, but also to any place in the world where there's not a doctor.

Wolf, Eric. *Sons of the Shaking Earth.* University of Chicago Press. An anthropological study of Indian and mestizo people of Mexico and Guatemala.

Wright, Ronald. *Time Among the Maya.* New York: Weidenfeld & Nicolson, 1989. A narrative that takes the reader through Maya country of today with historical comments that help put the puzzle together.

MAYAN GLOSSARY

MAYA GODS AND CEREMONIES

Acanum—protective deity of hunters
Ahau Can—serpent lord and highest priest
Ahau Chamehes—deity of medicine
Ah Cantzicnal—aquatic deity
Ah Chhuy Kak—god of violent death and sacrifice
Ahcit Dzamalcum—protective god of fishermen
Ah Cup Cacap—god of the underworld who denies air
Ah Itzám—the water witch
Ah kines—priests, lords who consult the oracles, celebrate ceremonies, and preside over sacrifices
Ahpua—god of fishing
Ah Puch—god of death
Ak'Al—sacred marsh where water abounds
Bacaboob—the poureres, supporters of the sky and guardians of the cardinal points, who form a single god, Ah Cantzicnal Becabs
Bolontiku—the nine lords of the night
Chac—god of rain and agriculture
Chac Bolay Can—the butcher serpent living in the underworld
Chaces—priest's assistants in agricultural and other ceremonies
Cihuateteo—women who become goddesses through death in childbirth (Nahuatl word)
Cit Chac Coh—god of war
Hetxmek—ceremony when the child is first carried astride the hip
Hobnil Bacab—the bee god, protector of beekeepers
Holcanes—the brave warriors charged with obtaining slaves for sacrifice. (This word was unknown until the postclassic era.)
Hunab Ku—giver of life, builder of the universe, and father of Itzámna
Ik—god of the wind
Itzámna—lord of the skies, creator of the beginning, god of time
Ix Chel—goddess of birth, fertility, medicine; credited with inventing spinning
Ixtab—goddess of the cord and of suicide by hanging

Kinich—face of the sun
Kukulcán—quetzal serpent, plumed serpent
Metnal—the underworld, place of the dead
Nacom—warrior chief
Noh Ek—Venus
Pakat—god of violent death
Zec—spirit lords of beehives

FOOD AND DRINK

alche—inebriating drink, sweetened with honey and used for ceremonies and offerings
ic—chile
itz—sweet potato
kabaxbuul—the heaviest meal of the day, eaten at dusk and containing cooked black beans
kah—pinole flour
kayem—ground maize
macal—a type of root
muxubbak—tamale
on—avocado
op—plum
p'ac—tomatoes
put—papaya
tzamna—black bean
uah—tortillas
za—maize drink

ANIMALS

acehpek—dog used for deer hunting
ah maax cal—the prattling monkey
ah maycuy—the chestnut deer
ah sac dziu—the white thrush
ah xixteel ul—the rugged land conch
bil—hairless dog reared for food
cutz—wild turkey
cutzha—duck
hoh—crow
icim—owl
jaleb—hairless dog
keh—deer
kitam—wild boar
muan—evil bird related to death
que—parrot

thul—rabbit
tzo—domestic turkey
utiu—coyote
yac—mountain cat
yaxum—mythical green bird

kuche—red cedar tree
k'uxub—annatto tree
piim—fiber of the cotton tree
taman—cotton plant
tauch—black zapote tree
tazon te—moss

MUSIC AND FESTIVALS

ah paxboob—musicians
bexelac—turtle shell used as percussion instrument
chohom—dance performed in ceremonies during the month of Zip, related to fishing
chul—flute
hom—trumpet
kayab—percussion instrument fashioned from turtle shell
Oc na—festival of the month of Yax; old idols of the temple are broken and replaced with new
okot uil—dance performed during the Pocan ceremony
Pacum chac—festival in honor of the war gods
tunkul—drum
zacatan—a drum made from a hollowed tree trunk, with one opening covered with hide

MISCELLANEOUS WORDS

ah kay kin bak—meat seller
chaltun—water cistern
cha te—black vegetable dye
chi te—eugenia, plant for dyeing
ch'oh—indigo
ek—dye
hadzab—wooden swords
halach uinic—leader
mayacimil—smallpox epidemic, "easy death"
pic—underskirt
ploms—rich people
suyen—square blanket
xanab—sandals
xicul—sleeveless jacket decorated with feathers
xul—stake with a pointed, fire-hardened tip
yuntun—slings

ELEMENTS OF TIME

chumuc akab—midnight
chumuc kin—midday
chunkin—midday
emelkin—sunset
haab—solar calendar of 360 days made up with five extra days of misfortune, which complete the final month
kaz akab—dusk
kin—the sun, the day, the unity of time
potakab—time before dawn
yalhalcab—dawn

PLANTS AND TREES

ha—cacao seed
kan ak—plant that produces a yellow dye
ki—sisal
kiixpaxhkum—chayote
kikche—tree the trunk of which is used to make canoes

NUMBERS

hun—one
ca—two
ox—three
can—four
ho—five
uac—six
uuc—seven
uacax—eight
bolon—nine
iahun—ten
buluc—eleven
iahca—twelve
oxlahum—thirteen
canlahum—fourteen
holahun—fifteen
uaclahun—sixteen
uuclahun—seventeen
uacaclahun—eighteen
bolontahun—nineteen
hunkal—twenty

SPANISH PHRASEBOOK

PRONUNCIATION GUIDE

Consonants

c as **c** in **cat**, before **a**, **o**, or **u**; like **s** before **e** or **i**
d as **d** in **dog**, except between vowels, then like **th** in **that**
g before **e** or **i**, like the **ch** in Scottish **loch**; elsewhere like **g** in **get**
h always silent
j like the English **h** in **hotel**, but stronger
ll like the **y** in **yellow**
ñ like the **ni** in **onion**
r always pronounced as strong **r**
rr trilled **r**
v similar to the **b** in **boy** (not as English **v**)
y similar to English, but with a slight **j** sound. When **y** stands alone it is pronounced like the **e** in **me**.
z like **s** in **same**
b, f, k, l, m, n, p, q, s, t, w, x as in English

Vowels

a as in **father**, but shorter
e as in **hen**
i as in **machine**
o as in **phone**
u usually as in **rule**; when it follows a **q** the **u** is silent; when it follows an **h** or **g** its pronounced like **w**, except when it comes between **g** and **e** or **i**, when it's also silent

NUMBERS

0 . . . . . *cero*	11 . . . . . *once*	40 . . . . . *cuarenta*
1 . . . . . *uno* (masculine)	12 . . . . . *doce*	50 . . . . . *cincuenta*
1 . . . . . *una* (feminine)	13 . . . . . *trece*	60 . . . . . *sesenta*
2 . . . . . *dos*	14 . . . . . *catorce*	70 . . . . . *setenta*
3 . . . . . *tres*	15 . . . . . *quince*	80 . . . . . *ochenta*
4 . . . . . *cuatro*	16 . . . . . *diez y seis*	90 . . . . . *noventa*
5 . . . . . *cinco*	17 . . . . . *diez y siete*	100 . . . . . *cien*
6 . . . . . *seis*	18 . . . . . *diez y ocho*	101 . . . . . *ciento y uno*
7 . . . . . *siete*	19 . . . . . *diez y nueve*	200 . . . . . *doscientos*
8 . . . . . *ocho*	20 . . . . . *veinte*	1,000 . . . *mil*
9 . . . . . *nueve*	21 . . . . . *viente y uno*	10,000 . . *diez mil*
10 . . . . . *diez*	30 . . . . . *treinta*	

DAYS OF THE WEEK

Sunday — *domingo*
Monday — *lunes*
Tuesday — *martes*
Wednesday — *miércoles*

Thursday — *jueves*
Friday — *viernes*
Saturday — *sábado*

TIME

What time is it? — *¿Qué hora es?*
one o'clock — *la una*
two o'clock — *las dos*
at two o'clock — *a las dos*
ten past three — *las tres y diez*
six a.m. — *las seis de mañana*
six p.m. — *las seis de tarde*
today — *hoy*

tomorrow, morning
  — *mañana, la mañana*
yesterday — *ayer*
day — *día*
week — *semana*
month — *mes*
year — *año*
last night — *anoche*

USEFUL WORDS AND PHRASES

Hello. — *Hola.*
Good morning. — *Buenos días.*
Good afternoon. — *Buenas tardes.*
Good evening. — *Buenas noches.*
How are you? — *¿Cómo está?*
Fine. — *Muy bien.*
And you? — *¿Y usted?*
So-so. — *Más ó menos.*
Thank you. — *Gracias.*
Thank you very much. — *Muchas gracias.*
You're very kind. — *Muy amable.*
You're welcome; literally, "It's nothing."
  — *De nada.*
yes — *sí*
no — *no*
I don't know. — *Yo no sé.*
it's fine; okay — *está bien*
good; okay — *bueno*
please — *por favor*
Pleased to meet you. — *Mucho gusto.*
excuse me (physical) — *perdóneme*
excuse me (speech) — *discúlpeme*
I'm sorry. — *Lo siento.*
goodbye — *adiós*

see you later; literally, "until later"
  — *hasta luego*
more — *más*
less — *menos*
better — *mejor*
much — *mucho*
a little — *un poco*
large — *grande*
small — *pequeño*
quick — *rápido*
slowly — *despacio*
bad — *malo*
difficult — *difícil*
easy — *fácil*
He/She/It is gone; as in "She left," "He's
  gone" — *Ya se fue.*
I don't speak Spanish well.
  — *No hablo bien español.*
I don't understand. — *No entiendo.*
How do you say . . . in Spanish?
  — *¿Cómo se dice . . . en español?*
Do you understand English?
  — *¿Entiende el inglés?*
Is English spoken here? (Does anyone
  here speak English?)
  — *¿Se habla inglés aquí?*

TERMS OF ADDRESS

I — *yo*
you (formal) — *usted*
you (familiar) — *tú*
he/him — *él*
she/her — *ella*
we/us — *nosotros*
you (plural) — *vos*
they/them (all males or mixed gender)
  — *ellos*
they/them (all females) — *ellas*

Mr., sir — *señor*
Mrs., madam — *señora*
Miss, young lady — *señorita*
wife — *esposa*
husband — *marido* or *esposo*
friend — *amigo* (male), *amiga* (female)
sweetheart — *novio* (male), *novia* (female)
son, daughter — *hijo, hija*
brother, sister — *hermano, hermana*
father, mother — *padre, madre*

GETTING AROUND

Where is . . . ? — *¿Dónde está . . . ?*
How far is it to . . .?
  — *¿A cuánto queda . . . ?*
from . . . to . . . — *de . . . a . . .*
highway — *la carretera*
road — *el camino*
street — *la calle*
block — *la cuadra*
kilometer — *kilómetro*

mile (commonly used near the
  U.S. border) — *milla*
north — *el norte*
south — *el sur*
west — *el oeste*
east — *el este*
straight ahead — *al derecho* or *adelante*
to the right — *a la derecha*
to the left — *a la izquierda*

ACCOMMODATIONS

Can I (we) see a room?
  — *¿Puedo (podemos) ver un cuarto?*
What is the rate? — *¿Cuál es el precio?*
a single room — *un cuarto sencillo*
a double room — *un cuarto doble*
key — *llave*
bathroom — *lavabo* or *baño*
hot water — *agua caliente*

cold water — *agua fría*
towel — *toalla*
soap — *jabón*
toilet paper — *papel higiénico*
air conditioning — *aire acondicionado*
fan — *ventilador*
blanket — *frazada* or *manta*

PUBLIC TRANSPORT

bus stop — *la parada del autobús*
main bus terminal
  — *terminal de buses*
railway station
  — *la estación de ferrocarril*
airport — *el aeropuerto*
ferry terminal
  — *la terminal del transbordador*

I want a ticket to . . .
  — *Quiero un boleto a . . .*
I want to get off at . . .
  — *Quiero bajar en . . .*
Here, please. — *Aquí, por favor.*
Where is this bus going?
  — *¿Adónde va este autobús?*
roundtrip — *ida y vuelta*
What do I owe? — *¿Cuánto le debo?*

DRIVING

Full, please (at gasoline station).
— *Lleno, por favor.*
My car is broken down.
— *Se me ha descompuesto el carro.*
I need a tow. — *Necesito un remolque.*
Is there a garage nearby?
— *¿Hay un garage cerca?*
Is the road passable with this car (truck)?
— *¿Puedo pasar con este carro*
(esta troca)?

With four-wheel drive?
— *¿Con doble tracción?*
It's not passable — *No hay paso.*
traffic light — *el semáfora*
traffic sign — *el señal*
gasoline (petrol) — *gasolina*
gasoline station — *gasolinera*
oil — *aceite*
water — *agua*
flat tire — *llanta desinflada*
tire repair shop — *llantera*

AUTO PARTS

fan belt — *banda de ventilador*
battery — *batería*
fuel (water) pump —
bomba de gasolina (agua)
spark plug — *bujía*
carburetor — *carburador*
distributor — *distribuidor*
axle — *eje*
clutch — *embrague*

gasket — *empaque, junta*
filter — *filtro*
brakes — *frenos*
tire — *llanta*
hose — *manguera*
starter — *marcha, arranque*
radiator — *radiador*
voltage regulator — *regulado de voltaje*

MAKING PURCHASES

I need . . . — *Necesito . . .*
I want . . . — *Deseo . . .* or *Quiero . . .*
I would like . . . (more polite)
— *Quisiera . . .*
How much does it cost? — *¿Cuánto cuesta?*
What's the exchange rate?
— *¿Cuál es el tipo de cambio?*

Can I see . . . ? — *¿Puedo ver . . . ?*
this one — *ésta/ésto*
expensive — *caro*
cheap — *barato*
cheaper — *más barato*
too much — *demasiado*

HEALTH

Help me please. — *Ayúdeme por favor.*
I am ill. — *Estoy enfermo.*
pain — *dolor*
fever — *fiebre*
stomache ache — *dolor de estómago*
vomiting — *vomitar*
diarrhea — *diarrea*

drugstore — *farmacia*
medicine — *medicina, remedio*
pill, tablet — *pastilla*
birth control pills — *pastillas*
anticonceptivas
condoms — *preservativos*

FOOD

menu — *lista, menú*
glass — *vaso*
fork — *tenedor*
knife — *cuchillo*
spoon — *cuchara, cucharita*
napkin — *servilleta*
soft drink — *refresco*
coffee, cream — *café, crema*
tea — *té*
sugar — *azúcar*
purified water — *agua purificado*
bottled carbonated water — *agua mineral*
bottled uncarbonated water — *agua sin gas*
beer — *cerveza*
wine — *vino*
milk — *leche*
juice — *jugo*
eggs — *huevos*
bread — *pan*

watermelon — *sandía*
banana — *plátano*
apple — *manzana*
orange — *naranja*
meat — *carne*
without meat — *sin carne*
beef — *carne de res*
chicken — *pollo*
fish — *pescado*
shellfish — *mariscos*
fried — *a la plancha*
roasted — *asado*
barbecue, barbecued — *al carbón*
breakfast — *desayuno*
lunch — *almuerzo*
dinner (often eaten in late afternoon)
    — *comida*
dinner, or a late night snack — *cena*
the check — *la cuenta*

ACCOMMODATIONS INDEX

RESTAURANT INDEX

INDEX

ARCHAEOLOGICAL SITES

SNORKELING

SHOPPING

thor of *Moon Handbooks: Yucatán Peninsula, Moon Handbooks: Cancún, Moon Handbooks: Belize,* and *Colonial Mexico,* and as co-author of *Moon Handbooks: Mexico.* She also wrote *Guide to Catalina Island* (Pine Press).

In 1987, Chicki was presented the Pluma de Plata writing award from the Mexican Government Ministry of Tourism for an article she wrote on the Mexican Caribbean which was published in the *Los Angeles Times.* Chicki is a member of the Society of American Travel Writers.

ABOUT THE PHOTOGRAPHER

Oz Mallan has been a professional photographer his entire working career. Much of that time was spent as chief cameraman for the Chico *Enterprise Record.* Oz graduated from the Brooks Institute of Photography, Santa Barbara. His work has often appeared in newspapers and magazines across the country via UPI and AP. He travels the world with his wife, Chicki, handling the photo end of their literary efforts, which include travel books, newspaper and magazine articles, and lectures and slide presentations. Oz's photos are also featured in *Moon Handbooks: Yucatán Peninsula, Moon Handbooks: Mexico, Colonial Mexico,* and *Moon Handbooks: Belize,* as well as in Pine Press's *Guide to Catalina Island.*

ABOUT THE AUTHOR

Chicki Mallan discovered the joy of traveling with her parents at an early age. The family would leave their Catalina Island home yearly, hit the road, and explore the small towns and big cities of the United States. Traveling was still an important part of Chicki's life after having a bunch of her own kids to introduce to the world. At various times Chicki and kids have lived in the Orient and Europe. When not traveling, lecturing, or giving slide presentations, Chicki and photographer husband Oz live in Paradise, California, a small community in the foothills of the Sierra Nevada. She does what she enjoys most when between books, writing newspaper and magazine articles. She has been associated with Moon Publications, now a part of Avalon Travel Publishing, since 1983, as au-

ABOUT THE BANNER ILLUSTRATOR

The banner art at the start of each chapter was done by Kathy Escovedo Sanders. She is an expert both in watercolor and this stipple style that lends itself to excellent black-and-white reproduction. Kathy is a 1982 California State University Long Beach graduate with a B.A. in Art History. She exhibits drawings, etched intaglio prints, and woodcut prints, as well as her outstanding watercolor paintings. Her stipple art can be seen in all of Chicki Mallan's Moon Handbooks.

U.S.~METRIC CONVERSION

1 inch = 2.54 centimeters (cm)
1 foot = .304 meters (m)
1 yard = 0.914 meters
1 mile = 1.6093 kilometers (km)
1 km = .6214 miles
1 fathom = 1.8288 m
1 chain = 20.1168 m
1 furlong = 201.168 m
1 acre = .4047 hectares
1 sq km = 100 hectares
1 sq mile = 2.59 square km
1 ounce = 28.35 grams
1 pound = .4536 kilograms
1 short ton = .90718 metric ton
1 short ton = 2000 pounds
1 long ton = 1.016 metric tons
1 long ton = 2240 pounds
1 metric ton = 1000 kilograms
1 quart = .94635 liters
1 US gallon = 3.7854 liters
1 Imperial gallon = 4.5459 liters
1 nautical mile = 1.852 km

To compute celsius temperatures, subtract 32 from Fahrenheit and divide by 1.8. To go the other way, multiply celsius by 1.8 and add 32.

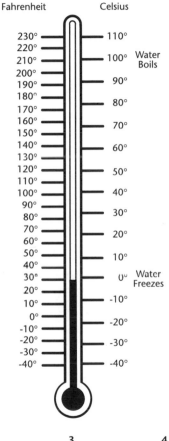

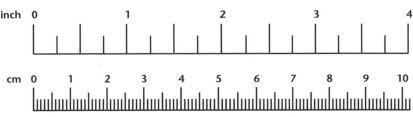

AVALON
TRAVEL
p u b l i s h i n g

How far will our travel guides take you? As far as you want.

Discover a rhumba-fueled nightspot in Old Havana, explore prehistoric tombs in Ireland, hike beneath California's centuries-old redwoods, or embark on a classic road trip along Route 66. Our guidebooks deliver solidly researched, trip-tested information—minus any generic froth—to help globetrotters or weekend warriors create an adventure uniquely their own.

And we're not just about the printed page. Public television viewers are tuning in to Rick Steves' new travel series, Rick Steves' Europe. On the Web, readers can cruise the virtual black top with Road Trip USA author Jamie Jensen and learn travel industry secrets from Edward Hasbrouck of The Practical Nomad. With Foghorn AnyWare eBooks, users of handheld devices can place themselves "inside" the content of the guidebooks.

In print. On TV. On the Internet. In the palm of your hand.
We supply the information. The rest is up to you.

Avalon Travel Publishing
Something for everyone

www.travelmatters.com

Avalon Travel Publishing guides are available at your favorite book or travel store.

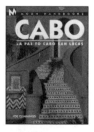

MOON HANDBOOKS
provide comprehensive coverage of a region's arts, history, land, people, and social issues in addition to detailed practical listings for accommodations, food, outdoor recreation, and entertainment. Moon Handbooks allow complete immersion in a region's culture—ideal for travelers who want to combine sightseeing with insight for an extraordinary travel experience in destinations throughout North America, Hawaii, Latin America, the Caribbean, Asia, and the Pacific.

WWW.MOON.COM

Rick Steves shows you where to travel and how to travel—all while getting the most value for your dollar. His Back Door travel philosophy is about making friends, having fun, and avoiding tourist rip-offs.

Rick's been traveling to Europe for more than 25 years and is the author of 22 guidebooks, which have sold more than a million copies. He also hosts the award-winning public television series *Rick Steves' Europe*.

WWW.RICKSTEVES.COM

ROAD TRIP USA

Getting there is half the fun, and Road Trip USA guides are your ticket to driving adventure. Taking you off the interstates and onto less-traveled, two-lane highways, each guide is filled with fascinating trivia, historical information, photographs, facts about regional writers, and details on where to sleep and eat—all contributing to your exploration of the American road.

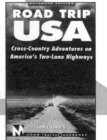

"[Books] so full of the pleasures of the American road, you can smell the upholstery."
~BBC radio

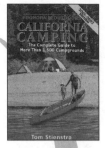

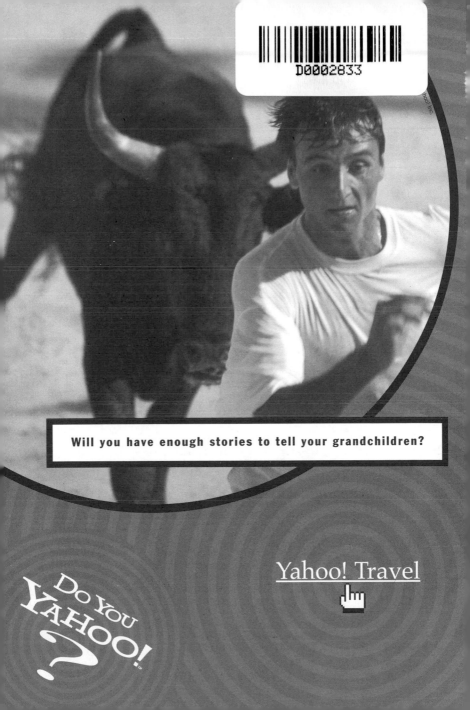